THE NEW ROMANIAN CINEMA

Traditions in World Cinema

General Editors
Linda Badley (Middle Tennessee State University)
R. Barton Palmer (Clemson University)

Founding Editor
Steven Jay Schneider (New York University)

Titles in the series include:

Traditions in World Cinema
Linda Badley, R. Barton Palmer and Steven Jay Schneider (eds)

Japanese Horror Cinema
Jay McRoy (ed.)

New Punk Cinema
Nicholas Rombes (ed.)

African Filmmaking
Roy Armes

Palestinian Cinema
Nurith Gertz and George Khleifi

Czech and Slovak Cinema
Peter Hames

The New Neapolitan Cinema
Alex Marlow-Mann

American Smart Cinema
Claire Perkins

The International Film Musical
Corey Creekmur and Linda Mokdad (eds)

Italian Neorealist Cinema
Torunn Haaland

Magic Realist Cinema in East Central Europe
Aga Skrodzka

Italian Post-Neorealist Cinema
Luca Barattoni

Spanish Horror Film
Antonio Lázaro-Reboll

Post-beur Cinema
Will Higbee

New Taiwanese Cinema in Focus
Flannery Wilson

International Noir
Homer B. Pettey and R. Barton Palmer (eds)

Films on Ice
Scott MacKenzie and Anna Westerståhl Stenport (eds)

Nordic Genre Film
Tommy Gustafsson and Pietari Kääpä (eds)

Contemporary Japanese Cinema Since Hana-Bi
Adam Bingham

Chinese Martial Arts Cinema (2nd edition)
Stephen Teo

Slow Cinema
Tiago de Luca and Nuno Barradas Jorge

Expressionism in Cinema
Olaf Brill and Gary D. Rhodes (eds)

French Language Road Cinema
Michael Gott

Transnational Film Remakes
Iain Robert Smith and Constantine Verevis

Coming-of-age Cinema in New Zealand
Alistair Fox

New Transnationalisms in Contemporary Latin American Cinemas
Dolores Tierney

Celluloid Singapore
Edna Lim

Short Films from a Small Nation
C. Claire Thomson

B-Movie Gothic
Justin D. Edwards and Johan Höglund (eds)

Francophone Belgian Cinema
Jamie Steele

The New Romanian Cinema
Christina Stojanova (ed.) with the participation of Dana Duma

edinburghuniversitypress.com/series/tiwc

THE NEW ROMANIAN CINEMA

Edited by Christina Stojanova
with the participation of Dana Duma

EDINBURGH
University Press

Edinburgh University Press is one of the leading university presses in the UK. We publish academic books and journals in our selected subject areas across the humanities and social sciences, combining cutting-edge scholarship with high editorial and production values to produce academic works of lasting importance. For more information visit our website: edinburghuniversitypress.com

© editorial matter and organisation Christina Stojanova and Dana Duma, 2019
© the chapters their several authors, 2019

Edinburgh University Press Ltd
The Tun – Holyrood Road
12 (2f) Jackson's Entry
Edinburgh EH8 8PJ

Typeset in 10/12.5 pt Sabon by
Servis Filmsetting Ltd, Stockport, Cheshire
and printed and bound in Great Britain

A CIP record for this book is available from the British Library

ISBN 978 0 7486 4264 9 (hardback)
ISBN 978 0 7486 9644 4 (webready PDF)
ISBN 978 1 4744 0361 0 (epub)

The right of the contributors to be identified as authors of this work has been asserted in accordance with the Copyright, Designs and Patents Act 1988 and the Copyright and Related Rights Regulations 2003 (SI No. 2498).

CONTENTS

List of Figures viii
Notes on the Contributors x
Acknowledgements xiv
Traditions in World Cinema xvi

Introduction 1
Christina Stojanova

PART I. MODERNISM/MINIMALISM

1. Beyond Modernity: The Stylistic Divide and the New Romanian Cinema 23
   Dominique Nasta

2. Minimalism in the New Romanian Cinema: Absent, Omnipresent or Misjudged? 36
   Irina Trocan

3. No Melo: Minimalism and Melodrama in the New Romanian Cinema 50
   Ioana Uricaru

PART II. INTERMEDIALITY/INTERTEXTUALITY

4. 'Exhibited Space' and Intermediality in the Films of Corneliu Porumboiu
   Ágnes Pethő — 65

5. Filming the Camera: Reflexivity and Reenactment in *Reconstruction* and *Niki and Flo*
   Katalin Sándor — 80

6. Ephemeral History and Enduring Celluloid: Cinematic Reality and Theatricality in Nae Caranfil's Films
   Melinda Blos-Jáni — 93

7. Remediation and Minimalism in New Romanian Cinema: The Example of Cristi Puiu
   Liviu Lutas — 107

PART III. ETHICS/NEW AESTHETICS

8. Authenticity in New Romanian Cinema: 'Ethics and Aesthetics Are One'
   Christina Stojanova — 123

9. The Square and the Screen: The Ethical Dimension of the New Romanian Cinema
   Ioana Uricaru — 137

10. *Beyond the Hills* and Austerity Politics
    Kalling Heck — 151

PART IV. GENDER/GENRE

11. Woman Films: Body and Will
    Dana Duma — 167

12. Traces of Genre in New Romanian Cinema: A Narrow Path for a Small Entity?
    Andrea Virginás — 180

PART V. NATIONAL/PLACE AND TRANSNATIONAL/SPACE

13. Kitchen Encounters: Scenes of Face-to-face Dialogue in Films of the New Romanian Cinema
    Mircea Deaca — 197

14. New Romanian Cinema: Geography and Identity 211
    Marian Țuțui and Raluca Iacob

15. The 'Transnational Turn': New Urban Identities and the
    Transformation of Contemporary Romanian Cinema 225
    Doru Pop

PART VI. HISTORICAL OVERVIEW

16. Historical Overview of Romanian Cinema 243
    Christina Stojanova

Combined Bibliography 283
Filmography of the New Romanian Cinema 297
General Filmography 303
Index of Authors and Film Titles 312
Index of Terms and Concepts 316

FIGURES

1.1	Pierre Bonnard, *The Box* and *4 Months, 3 Weeks and 2 Days*	31
1.2	Pierre Bonnard, *Dining Room in the Country* and *Aurora*	32
2.1	Donald Judd exhibition at the Chinati Foundation, Marfa, Texas	39
2.2	*The Death of Mr Lăzărescu*	41
3.1	*Police, Adjective*	56
3.2	*Police, Adjective*	57
4.1	*12:08 East of Bucharest*: the irony of 'décadrage'	70
4.2	*Police, Adjective:* the world as *tableau*, and reality as dictionary entries	73
4.3	*When Evening Falls on Bucharest, or Metabolism*: permutations of a *tableau* shot of protagonists at a table	75
6.1	*Philanthropy*: Puiuţ's window on the Romanian reality	98
6.2	*The Rest is Silence*: scene with theatricality enhanced by red curtains and recurring planimetric composition, featuring Caranfil	101
7.1	*Stuff and Dough*	112
7.2	*The Death of Mr Lăzărescu* and Hans Holbein's *Dead Christ*	115
8.1	*Everyday God Kisses Us on the Mouth*	129
8.2	*The Last Day*	133
9.1	*The Paper Will Be Blue*	146
9.2	*The Paper Will Be Blue*	147
10.1	*Beyond the Hills*	158

10.2	*Beyond the Hills*	162
11.1	Doroteea Petre in *Ryna*	170
11.2	Monica Bârlădeanu in *Francesca*	173
12.1	*Pulp Fiction* and *Killing Time*: gangsters side by side	184
12.2	*In the Mood for Love* and *When Evening Falls on Bucharest, or Metabolism:* lovers at a table	186
12.3	*Written on the Wind* and *Tuesday, After Christmas:* yellow patch in the mirror	187
13.1	*Tuesday, After Christmas*	198
13.2	*The Apartment*	200
14.1	*Stuff and Dough*: on the way to Bucharest	215
14.2	*California Dreamin'*: Captain Jones meets station master Doiaru	221
15.1	*Closer to the Moon*: the first post-1989 international film, starring Mark Strong and Vera Farmiga	228
15.2	*Child's Pose*: Luminiţa Gheorghiu as mother from Romanian new social elites	235
16.1	*A Stormy Night*	248
16.2	*The Forest of the Hanged*	259
16.3	*The Oak*	273

NOTES ON THE CONTRIBUTORS

Melinda Blos-Jáni is lecturer at the Department of Film, Photography and Media at Sapientia University (Cluj-Napoca, Romania). She has written articles related to contemporary silent films, documentaries, amateur films and archival images. She published a book entitled *The Genealogy of Home Movies: Transylvanian Amateur Media Practices from Photography to New Media* (2015, in Hungarian). She is currently researching East European found footage films with a special emphasis on their mediality (photographs within films, medium specific noises, montage) as a member of a research project entitled 'Rethinking Intermediality in Contemporary Cinema' led by Ágnes Pethő.

Mircea Deaca completed his PhD studies at the Paris III – Sorbonne Nouvelle with a thesis on the carnival tradition and Federico Fellini's films. He currently teaches at the Doctoral School of the Faculty of Letters at the University of Bucharest. His books include: *The Carnival and Federico Fellini's Films* (2009), *Postfilmic Cinema* (2013), *The Anatomy of Film* (2013) and *Investigations in Cognitive Film Analysis* (2015). He edited the 2014 issue of *Images, Cesi*, dedicated to Cristian Mungiu, and is now working on a study on cognitive grammar of film analysis.

Dana Duma is Professor in Film Studies at the Bucharest National University of Theatre and Film. A member of FIPRESCI, she is a regular contributor to the film press in Romania and abroad, and a frequent member of international festival juries. She published the books *Self-Portraits of Cinema* (1983); *Gopo* (1996); *Woody Allen: A Buffoon and a Philosopher* (2003); *Benjamin Fondane: Cineaste* (2010); and co-edited the anthologies *Cinema 2000* (2000); *Tendencies in European Cinema* (2003); and *The Personality of Latin-American Cinema* (2006). She is the director of *Film* magazine and the editor of film and media studies journal *Close Up*.

Kalling Heck is Lossett Visiting Assistant Professor of Media & Visual Culture Studies at the University of Redlands. His work uses theoretical approaches to media in order to examine global art cinema, in particular focusing on films made in the wake of transitions from authoritarianism or totalitarianism to democracy.

Raluca Iacob is an independent researcher, working as a film curator. She graduated in 2015 with a PhD in Film Studies from the University of St Andrews, with a thesis on postcommunist Romanian cinema. Her research engaged with understanding the development of postcommunist identities by analysing Romanian films through the perspective of marginality. Her research interests include world cinema, documentary film, communist and postcommunist cinemas and critical theory.

Liviu Lutas is Assistant Professor in French Literature at Linnaeus University, Sweden. His research interests include metalepsis in different media, narrative questions in film and literature, intermedial theory and French literature from the Caribbean. He has published articles such as 'Storyworlds and Paradoxical Narration' (2015), 'Sur la syllepse narrative – Un concept théorique négligé' (2012) and 'Narrative Metalepsis in Detective Fiction' (2011). He is currently a member of Linnaeus University Centre for Intermedial and Multimodal Studies.

Dominique Nasta is Full Professor at the Université Libre de Bruxelles and series editor for the *Rethinking Cinema* Collection (Peter Lang). She is the author of *Contemporary Romanian Cinema: The History of an Unexpected Miracle* (2013) and of *Meaning in Film* (1992) and co-editor of *New Perspectives in Sound Studies* (2004), *Revisiting Film Melodrama* (2014) and more recently for *La Chanson dans les cinémas contemporains: 1960–2010* (2018). She has published widely on East European Cinemas, the aesthetics of silent melodramas, and emotions and music in films.

Ágnes Pethő is Professor and head of the Department of Film, Photography, and Media (Sapientia Hungarian University in Cluj-Napoca, Romania). She is the executive editor of the English-language international peer-reviewed journal,

Acta Universitatis Sapientiae: Film and Media Studies. Her most important works include the monograph, *Cinema and Intermediality: The Passion for the In-Between* (2011) and the edited volumes: *Film in the Post-Media Age* (2012), *The Cinema of Sensations* (2015) and *Intermediality in Contemporary Eastern European and Russian Cinema*, forthcoming at Edinburgh University Press.

Doru Pop is Associate Professor at the Faculty of Theatre and Television, Babeş-Bolyai University in Cluj in Romania, where he researches visual culture, film and media studies. Among his publications is *Ochiul si corpul: Modern si postmodern in cultura vizuala* (*The Eye and the Body: Modern and Postmodern in the Philosophy of the Visual Culture*, Cluj: Dacia Publishing House, 2005). His most recent book is *Romanian New Wave Cinema: An Introduction* (2014).

Katalin Sándor is Assistant Professor at Babeş-Bolyai University (Cluj-Napoca, Romania). Her research interests include intermediality in literature and film, contemporary Hungarian and Romanian cinema. Her volume, *Nyugtalanító írás/képek: A vizuális költészet intermedialitásáról* [*Unsettling Image/Texts: The Intermediality of Visual Poetry*] appeared in 2011. She has published articles in both Hungarian and English in scientific journals and volumes of studies, for example *The Cinema of Sensations*, 2015 edited by Ágnes Pethő; *Discourses of Space*, 2013, edited by Zsuzsanna Ajtony and Judit Pieldner; and *Media Borders, Multimodality and Intermediality*, 2010, edited by Lars Elleström.

Christina Stojanova is a media historian, specialising in philosophical, ideological and analytical-psychological aspects of narrative modes and fictional representation in the cinemas of Quebec, interwar Germany, and Eastern and Central Europe. An Associate Professor at the Department of Film, University of Regina, since 2005 she has contributed twenty chapters to internationally acclaimed publications, two of which – *Wittgenstein at the Movies* (2011) and *The Legacies of Jean-Luc Godard* (2014) – she has co-edited. She is currently working on a monograph about Canadian animator Caroline Leaf.

Irina Trocan is a PhD graduate and teaching assistant at the National University of Theatre and Cinema in Bucharest, whose doctoral thesis traces the roots of contemporary video essays in the tradition of essay cinema. Her writing was published in journals and film magazines such as *Close Up*, *Sight & Sound*, *IndieWire*, *Dilema Veche*, *Istoria Filmului*. She coordinates the online film magazine *Acoperişul de Sticlă*, and has recently co-edited – together with Andra Petrescu – a Romanian-language anthology of documentary film theory.

NOTES ON THE CONTRIBUTORS

Marian Țuțui is a leading film researcher in the field of early cinema in the Balkans. Between 1993 and 2013 he was the curator of the Romanian Cinematheque. Currently he is a researcher at the 'G. Oprescu' Institute of Art History and Professor of Film History at Hyperion University. He is a member of FIPRESCI (2008) and author of several books on cinema, including *A Short History of Romanian Cinema* (2005), *Manakia Bros, or the Image of the Balkans* (2005) and *Orient Express: Romanian and Balkan Cinema* (2008).

Ioana Uricaru is a Romanian filmmaker and film scholar. She holds a Master of Science in Molecular Biology and a PhD, with a dissertation about the relationship between film theory and the neuroscience of emotion. She directed the short films *The Sun and the Moon* (AFI Fest Official Selection) and *Stopover* (Sundance Official Selection) and co-directed the omnibus *Tales from the Golden Age* (Cannes Official Selection). She is currently Assistant Professor of Film and Media Culture at Middlebury College, Vermont.

Andrea Virginás is Associate Professor in the Department of Film, Photography and Media at Sapientia University (Cluj-Napoca, Romania), with an MA in Gender Studies (Central European University, Hungary, 2002) and a PhD in Literary and Cultural Studies (Debrecen University, Hungary, 2008). She is member of the board of Cambridge Scholars Publishing (film studies, 2018–) and *TNTeF e-journal of Gender Studies*, University of Szeged, Hungary (2010–). Her research concerns film cultures in mainstream and peripheral contexts, feminist film theory, cultural trauma theory, and analogue and digital media theory.

ACKNOWLEDGEMENTS

This book has been in the making for almost ten years now. First planned as a co-authored monograph by Dana Duma and myself, it morphed into a single-edited anthology in order to reflect better the evolution of New Romanian cinema.

My appreciation therefore first goes to Dana, who proferred invaluable help and advice at the early stages of this project, and whose commitment to our co-edited Special Issue on the emerging phenomenon of New Romanian cinema (*Kinokultura*, 2007) was instrumental in laying the foundations of its English-language scholarship.

I am indebted to Ágnes Pethő, Dominique Nasta and Doru Pop, who – over a few unforgettable days in March 2015, during the Society for Cinema and Media Studies conference in Montreal – helped adjust the concept of the project to the swiftly-changing scholarly *paysage* of New Romanian cinema, and have been extending their both friendly and learned support ever since.

I am particularly grateful to Linda Badley and R. Barton Palmer, the editors of the *Traditions in World Cinema* series – as well as to Gillian Leslie and Richard Strachan from Edinburgh University Press – without whose encouragement, informed advice and considerate patience this book would not have been possible.

Raluca Iacob, my assistant and Romanian-language consultant, deserves a special appreciation for her hard and prompt work, for her construction of the filmographies and for affably bearing with my sometimes tyrannical perfectionism and last-minute revisions.

ACKNOWLEDGEMENTS

Finally, I would like to thank my home Department of Film at the University of Regina, particularly my former Dean Sheila Petty and my current Dean Rae Staseson, for their continuous encouragement and support of this project, both moral and financial. And last but not least, my heartfelt gratitude goes to my dear family – Ivan, Theo, Laura, Benny and Paul, for their unwavering inspiration!

Christina Stojanova
Montreal, June 2018

TRADITIONS IN WORLD CINEMA

General editors: **Linda Badley and R. Barton Palmer**
Founding editor: **Steven Jay Schneider**

Traditions in World Cinema is a series of textbooks and monographs devoted to the analysis of currently popular and previously underexamined or undervalued film movements from around the globe. Also intended for general interest readers, the textbooks in this series offer undergraduate- and graduate-level film students accessible and comprehensive introductions to diverse traditions in world cinema. The monographs open up for advanced academic study more specialised groups of films, including those that require theoretically oriented approaches. Both textbooks and monographs provide thorough examinations of the industrial, cultural and socio-historical conditions of production and reception.

The flagship textbook for the series includes chapters by noted scholars on traditions of acknowledged importance (the French New Wave, German Expressionism), recent and emergent traditions (New Iranian, post-Cinema Novo), and those whose rightful claim to recognition has yet to be established (the Israeli persecution film, global found footage cinema). Other volumes concentrate on individual national, regional or global cinema traditions. As the introductory chapter to each volume makes clear, the films under discussion form a coherent group on the basis of substantive and relatively transparent, if not always obvious, commonalities. These commonalities may be formal, stylistic or thematic, and the groupings may, although they need not, be popularly identified as genres, cycles or movements (Japanese horror, Chinese martial arts cinema, Italian Neorealism). Indeed, in cases in which a group of films is not already commonly identified as a tradition, one purpose of the volume is to establish its claim to importance and make it visible (East Central European Magical Realist cinema, Palestinian cinema).

Textbooks and monographs include:

- An introduction that clarifies the rationale for the grouping of films under examination
- A concise history of the regional, national or transnational cinema in question
- A summary of previous published work on the tradition
- Contextual analysis of industrial, cultural and socio-historical conditions of production and reception
- Textual analysis of specific and notable films, with clear and judicious application of relevant film theoretical approaches
- Bibliograph(ies)/filmograph(ies)

Monographs may additionally include:

- Discussion of the dynamics of cross-cultural exchange in light of current research and thinking about cultural imperialism and globalisation, as well as issues of regional/national cinema or political/aesthetic movements (such as new waves, postmodernism or identity politics)
- Interview(s) with key filmmakers working within the tradition.

INTRODUCTION

Christina Stojanova

The New Romanian cinema exploded onto the international film festival scene in the mid-2000s, catching audiences and critics completely by surprise. And if the 'Un Certain Regard' Best Film at the 2005 Cannes Film Festival for *The Death of Mr Lăzărescu* could be ignored as a happenstance, the numerous awards that followed in quick succession for *The Paper Will Be Blue*, *Ryna* and *How I Spent the End of the World* suggested a tendency. The Camera d'Or at the 2006 Cannes for *12:08 East of Bucharest* and especially the dual success at Cannes 2007 – Un Certain Regard Award for Cristian Nemescu's *California Dreamin'* and especially the Palme d'Or for Cristian Mungiu's *4 Months, 3 Weeks and 2 Days* – sealed the rise to prominence of this hitherto obscure national cinema. It took however another couple of years for critics to finally agree that a 'new wave has finally arrived at the Black Sea' (Scott 2008), and to admit that 'Romanian filmmaking is now perceived as the hotbed of a fresh, expressive, and pertinent cinematic renewal' (Kaceanov 2008). A few years later, such sentiments would become a common media occurrence, corroborated by a respected film programmer, who wrote on his blog that Romanian cinema 'never ceases to surprise and impress with the rigour of its execution, its intelligence and moral dimensions' (Père: 2012). Almost fifteen years later, with more than two hundred prestigious awards for forty or so notable films by world-renowned directors like Cristi Puiu, Cristian Mungiu, Corneliu Porumboiu, Cristian Nemescu, Radu Jude, Radu Muntean, Tudor Giurgiu, Călin Peter Netzer, Cătălin Mitulescu, Nae Caranfil and others, Romanian cinema remains securely in the limelight of the international film festival circuit.

In the mid-2000s, however, there was no serious indication that New Romanian cinema would last much longer than the Czech cinema of the 'Velvet Generation' from the 1990s, whose crown achievement was the Oscar for Jan Sverák's *Kolya* (1996). All the more so, as this 'New Czech Miracle' was built on the 'old miracle' of its internationally celebrated predecessor, the 1960s Czechoslovak New Wave, while the New Romanian Cinema sprang from a literal *terra incognita*. To be sure, prior to the fall of the Berlin Wall in 1989, East European[1] (or communist)[2] cinema had been associated mostly with the cinemas of Poland, Hungary, Czechoslovakia and Yugoslavia. In the immediate post-1989 aftermath, Albania, Bulgaria, Romania and post-Yugoslavia were lumped together under the geopolitical term 'the Balkans', whose negative connotations have been examined by Maria Todorova in her seminal 1997 book *Imagining the Balkans*. Yet in the heavily politicised cultural context of the Yugoslav wars, the term 'Balkan cinema' gained quick currency among film historians and critics.[3] This was surprising, bearing in mind that the substitution of Eastern European with Balkan cinema had already proven its impracticality with the publication of Michael Jon Stoil's *Balkan Cinema: Evolution after the Revolution* (1982).[4] By conceptualising these four cinemas as a post-Second World War Eastern European transnational entity, modelled after Soviet cinema both structurally and ideologically, Stoil makes a rather unconvincing case for the Balkan-ness of his corpus. Therefore his laudable, though inconsistent – and at times paradoxical – attempt at a comparative approach to 'Balkan' cinema, has unfortunately remained on the margins of a scholarly field dominated by Daniel J. Goulding and Ronald Holloway, who were primarily interested in the Yugoslav, much less in Bulgarian, and not at all in Romanian or Albanian cinemas.

Mira and Antonin Liehm's 1977 thorough English-language history of East European cinema, *The Most Important Art: Soviet and Eastern European Film After 1945*, whose three chapters remain the backbone of any serious study of Romanian film history – was followed almost three decades later by Dina Iordanova's 2006 anthology *The Cinema of the Balkans*, featuring four essays on major Romanian films from the communist period. After yet another ten years, briefly interrupted by a few Special Issues on the emergent New Romanian cinema[5] and several chapters in anthologies,[6] a cluster of books appeared, obviously inspired by the growing international prestige of New Romanian cinema. Published in English by authors of Romanian origin, these works were helmed by Dominique Nasta's 2013 *Contemporary Romanian Cinema: The History of Unexpected Miracle*, followed by Doru Pop's *Romanian New Wave Cinema: An Introduction* (2014), and most recently, by Monica Filimon's monograph on Cristi Puiu and László Strausz's *Hesitant Histories on the Romanian Screen*.

A MOVEMENT, A SCHOOL, A WAVE …?

It is well known that naming a phenomenon conceptualises it to a large extent, therefore throughout this volume the moniker New Romanian Cinema (or NRC) is used, following the original suggestion by the late Romanian film critic Alex Leo Şerban and further popularised by the 2007 *Kinokultura* Special Issue on Romanian cinema (edited by C. Stojanova and D. Duma), and by Andrei Gorzo in 2012. A concurrent term, 'Romanian New Wave', was initially proposed by Mihai Fulger in 2006,[7] and posited by Doru Pop, while some authors, like Dominique Nasta, eschew the issue altogether. All the more that American film critic Bert Cardullo calls it just a 'film surge', brought about by a 'capricious occurrence of talent' and 'good luck in distribution', which in his view is the *raison d'être* of all recent 'waves' including the Iranian, the Chinese, and the South Korean (2012: 327). Conversely, Puiu's joke that the NRC consists of 'a bunch of desperate directors' captures the stubborn resistance of NRC directors to being fitted upon the procrustean bed of a school, a movement or a wave. Scriptwriter and filmmaker Ioana Uricaru underscores the main traits that bring these directors together: a preoccupation with 'complete creative freedom' and 'control of the product' (2012: 429).

To be sure, most significant artistic movements have been theorised post factum, and even then with mixed results, as the 'fragile notion of [German] Expressionism demonstrates' if the list of its alleged common traits is applied to more than two films from the historic movement (Marie 2003: 28). Yet 'expressionism' – like the concept of New Romanian Cinema– 'continues to return through the windows of critical discourse' (ibid.), as Filimon's and Strausz's recent books[8] and the current anthology demonstrate.[9] Whatever the case may be, at the time of writing of this introduction the movement has dominated the Romanian film scene since its accepted early beginnings, marked by Puiu's 2001 film *Stuff and Dough*.

The taxonomy of a film school characterisations, proposed by Michel Marie on the basis of the French New Wave experience, features six parameters, out of which New Romanian Cinema meets barely half upfront. The filmmakers have clearly coalesced on all levels of the creative process as an 'ensemble of artists' and 'collaborators', who define themselves against their predecessors and adversaries and, despite the absence of 'a basic critical doctrine, artistic program, [or] manifesto', have been producing a 'group of works' whose common aesthetic criteria have been identified independently by a number of critics and theorists (2003: 28).[10]

The place of a leader –whom Marie calls the 'pope' or 'mentor' of the group, and who could do for the New Romanian Cinema what producer Erich Pommer did for German Expressionism, film critic and theorist André Bazin for the French New Wave, or film critics Antonin and Mira Liehm and writer Milan Kundera for the Czechoslovak New Wave – has never been claimed. Yet it could be said that Puiu has amply fulfilled that role, a fact recognised by Alex Leo Şerban back in 2009 when he anecdotally divided the history of Romanian cinema into BC and AC: 'before and after Cristi [Puiu]' (qtd in Filimon 2017: 58). As Pop rightfully notes, by virtue of his 'prolific activity as director, writer and producer, and even actor in his own movies', Puiu 'reinvented the entire Romanian cinema', thus becoming 'a true Master, a leader of his generation' (2014: 43). In his numerous and generous interviews – including the one he gave in March 2017 for this introduction – Puiu appears also as an eloquent spokesperson of the movement. Indeed, *The Death of Mr Lăzărescu* – whose eponymous hero dies after a nightmarish journey through the crowded Bucharest hospitals – has been acknowledged time and again as paradigmatic film of the movement and Puiu – as its aesthetic and philosophical trend-setter (Stojanova and Duma 2012).

The extant popular and specialised academic publications in Romania have been demonstrating a benevolent engagement with the movement since the early 2000s, thus meeting the need, identified by Marie, of 'vehicles for diffusing ... namely press and broadcast media' (ibid.). And although it is difficult to discern any specific 'promotional strategy' comparable to that practised by *Cahiers du Cinéma* in the 1950s and early 1960s, the sheer volume of articles and in-depth interviews published in both Romanian and English by the three foremost Romanian English-language academic journals – *Close Up*,[11] *Ekphrasis*[12] and *Film and Media Studies*[13] – speaks for itself. Through its nineteen branches worldwide, the Romanian Cultural Institute (Institutul Cultural Român) – modelled after UniFrance[14] and directly subordinate to the President of Romania – has been playing an indispensable role in the NRC's promotion and distribution. Moreover, the Transylvanian International Film Festival (Cluj-Napoca) with its famous Romanian Days, is part of the long line of prestigious international film festivals which, helmed by Cannes, have bestowed worldwide recognition on New Romanian Cinema.

The New Romanian Cinema as Ensemble of Artists

The violent rupture with the communist past has made the experience of New Romanian Cinema directors comparable to that of Soviet Montage filmmakers, or that of German Expressionists and Italian Neorealists, as they have all 'emerged from societies that have undergone drastic socio-cultural trauma', and have consequently contributed to a 'major aesthetic break with existing tradition' (Tudor qtd in Hames 2005: 4). As Peter Hames suggests, the '1960s movements such as the Czechoslovak, French and British new waves, were more limited in their significance and cannot be related to social disorders of such magnitude', which apropos speaks in favour of considering the New Romanian Cinema as a movement rather than an aesthetic style, all the more so as NRC directors, like the Italian neorealists, have remained deliberately vague with regard to a 'basic critical doctrine' understood in both aesthetic and broader ideological terms (Hames 2005: 4).

The fifteen or so NRC directors, born between 1967 and mid-1980s,[15] belong to the 'decree generation', bookended by the strict ban on abortions introduced by Nicolae Ceaușescu's government in 1966, and its consequent repeal after the fall of the regime in 1989. Paradoxically, as reflected in Florin Iepan's documentary *Children of the Decree* (2005), the generation, which experienced the 1989 revolution in their teens or early twenties, were, so to speak, a side effect of the abortion ban. Yet along with producing most of the ardent participants in Ceaușescu's deposition as well as its numerous victims, this unique generation, as Pop has it, was also destined to become the 'demographic engine' of Romania's post-1989 transformation (2014: 25). Indeed, the biographies of the NRC filmmakers are marked by their urban[16] middle-class upbringing,[17] and by the drastic changes triggered by the revolution, but mainly by the opportunities for unhindered personal expression offered by this time.[18] Among the reasons Nasta nominates Mungiu's Palme d'Or winner *4 Months, 3 Weeks and 2 Days* as the movement's second major achievement after *Mr Lăzărescu*, is the way the film recreates 'the atmosphere reigning among family and friends in relation to the abortion ban . . . silenced for years by the terror of the regime' (2013: 189).

THE NEW ROMANIAN CINEMA AND THE GENERATIONAL DIVIDE

Summarising the history of post-Second World War European cinema, both in the capitalist West and the communist East, Kristin Thompson and David Bordwell emphasise *auteurship* as its major feature (2002: 357). Due to the peculiarities of the historical evolution of Eastern European intelligentsia over the previous two centuries, the best known pre-1989 Romanian directors have seen themselves overwhelmingly as auteurs, and therefore equally resentful of commercial and propagandist 'cinema for the masses'.[19]

The prestigious auteur status of their predecessors however elicited little respect from the NRC directors despite their shared disdain for commercial and propagandist cinema. Even Lucian Pintilie, one of the few dissident and internationally recognised Romanian directors prior to 1989, whose influence on New Romanian Cinema is undeniable, has not remained unscathed. Mihai Chirilov, one of Romania's foremost critics, in his criticism of Pintilie's 'obsessive reassessment of the past', points out that *The Oak* (1992) – the highly awarded film he made upon his return to Romania after two decades of forced exile – should have been 'enough to exorcize [the director's] ghosts of the past', yet with *The Afternoon of a Torturer* (2001) and *Niki and Flo* (2003), Pintilie 'went back to where he had started' (2007). Clearly, for the NRC generation, the veterans were too weary to precipitate the radical changes, needed to bring Romanian cinema into the twenty-first century.

Uricaru takes a similar stand with regard to the squabbles over the constrained state funding, lumping renowned pre-1989 auteurs like Dan Pița and Mircea Daneliuc together with the 'ubiquitous' Sergiu Nicolaescu,[20] declaring them as 'obsolete dinosaurs' after 2001 (2012: 433–5). The most unceremonious expression of this generational stand-off belongs to Puiu, who said in a 2004 interview that '[historically] good [Romanian] movies … are nothing but accidents. In Romania there isn't really a film school or a cinema, but only a forced effort' (qtd in Pop 2014: 120).[21]

In their turn, veteran directors – with the notable exception of Pintilie, who in addition to helming the Ministry of Culture-funded Film Studio, was instrumental in 'financing a few landmark works from the 1990s' (Uricaru 2012: 436)[22] and also collaborated with Puiu and Răzvan Rădulescu on the script of *Niki and Flo* – did little to remedy this generational discord. More shocking than Nicolaescu's post-1989 demarches – reproached by both Uricaru and Filimon,[23] but understandable within the context of his decades-long ideological and commercial opportunism – was the brash commercialisation and speculative cinematic exhibitionism (also known as miserabilism),[24] exemplified by the 'surprisingly low quality, didactic message and unconvincing scripts' of Pița's works from the late 1990s and early 2000s (Nasta 2013: 56) and by the failure of Daneliuc's films to 'measure up to the outstanding quality of his earlier productions' (71). As Puiu has sarcastically put it, the miserabilist tendencies in postcommunist cinema, with their uncensored language, graphic violence, misogynistic sexuality, and scenes of abject poverty, are but 'survival tactics', or 'special effects', meant for the Western gaze, and a cheap surrogate for 'Hollywood CGIs' (Puiu interview, 2017).

Then again, this generational rift has been unjustifiably exacerbated by the wholesale rejection of the communist legacy, resulting in aesthetic and historic decontextualisation of the pre-1989 cinema. Thus the metaphoric-allegorical trend from the 1980s and its Aesopian language, associated with peak achievements of Eastern European art cinema[25] and based on the great interwar Romanian literature, tend to be seen in abstract isolation rather than as oblique criticism of the regime. True, due to heavy censorship, from today's vantage point, these films yield a 'codespeak' (Uricaru 2012: 430) that is burdened with connotations that are increasingly difficult to decipher (Chirilov 2007). Yet this hardly justifies disparaging them as suffering from 'symbolitis', or from the 'sickness of the metaphor' (Popescu qtd in Pop 2014: 95), and accusing them of reinforcing the communist ideology.

The complex rapport of the New Romanian directors with their *papas kino*[26] and its perceived 'certain' tendencies[27] thus make the rupture look like a fundamentally existential one, more akin to the fateful confrontation between Cronos and Zeus than to the conventional Freudian stand-off between fathers and sons, whose phenomenology on and off camera Pop scrutinises in detail.[28] Still, we are reminded that, along with Pintilie, 'among the most quoted as favourites by then teen-age Puiu, Mungiu and Muntean' are Daneliuc and Pița, members of the short-lived first, or 'old', Romanian New Wave from the 1970s and early 1980s (Filimon 2017: 16). In our interview, Puiu reconfirmed the importance of that daring 'old' wave by citing four of its prominent works – Daneliuc's *The Cruise* 1981), *Sequences* (1982) by Alexandru Tatos, Stere Gulea's *The Moromete Family* (1987), and *A Girl's Tear* (1980) by Iosif Demian – 'an undeservingly ignored masterpiece' – considering them as 'important for Romanian cinema' as Pintilie's *Reconstruction* (1970).[29]

AUTEURSHIP OF AUSTERITY AND PERSONAL RESPONSIBILITY

New Romanian directors have secured their artistic freedom by moving towards a type of film that would ensure maximum artistic control within constrained budgets, since, 'from a business point of view', it is easier to 'assemble the funds by using financing mechanisms, designed to encourage auteur rather than commercial initiatives' (Uricaru 2012: 429).

The NRC funding is doled out in three major ways: through the National Film Fund (via the Romanian Film Centre: Centrul Național al Cinematografiei, or CNC);[30] through 'small private sponsorships'; and through 'European grants[31] as well as co-production funds'.[32] While the tradition of state funding is often associated with what Stephen Croft calls '*maximal, centrally controlled economy*' of communism[33] (original emphasis, 1998: 389), it actually dates back to the first half of the twentieth century, when it was designed in tune with pervasively protectionist European policies in the sphere of arts and culture.[34] Similarly, thanks to the traditionally close cultural and linguistic relations with France, the post-1989 reform of the Romanian film industry was fashioned after the model of French Cultural Exception – that is, the exclusive right to treat culture and cultural products differently from other commercial products, reconfirmed by the General Agreement on Tariffs and Trade (GATT) negotiations in 1993 (Martel 2001: 8). Therefore CNC, the current hub of Romanian national cinema – created by virtue of Decree 80 on 8 February 1990, which also put an end to pre-1989 Romanian centralised cinema industry – is a replica of its French counterpart, including its identical acronym. Moreover, by introducing a number of young NRC filmmakers to the world, the Cannes film festival also played a decisive part in the continuous French support for the New Romanian cinema.

The NRC directors, as Pop argues, share a common view regarding 'the role of cinema and preferred filmmaking practices', comparable to the French New Wave's *politique des copains* by 'not only supporting each other conceptually', but also being 'involved directly in each other's projects' (2014: 26).³⁵ This *politique* includes the group of versatile cinematographers and actors, whose creative vision is inextricable from the success of the movement and is yet so often ignored.³⁶ And although thus far it may appear that the NRC is funded by a steady flow of state funding and foreign grants, it actually owes its success to the ingenuity of the directors themselves, who have become 'prominent voices of European and global cinema' (Uricaru 2012: 435). With the creation of their own production companies, they secured creative independence and found additional 'merit as entrepreneurs as well as artists': Mungiu with Mobra Films, Puiu – and Bobby Păunescu – with Mandragora, Porumboiu with Km 42 Film; Mitulescu with Strada Film, and Giurgiu with Libra Film (Uricaru 2012: 438).

Towards a Definition of the Existentialist Realism of New Romanian Cinema

The major disruption of Romanian cinema in the aftermath of 1989 put an end to the official production of propaganda, but also to the prestige of literary adaptations, especially from the metaphoric-allegorical trend, and their 'deeply political narratives' about 'the effects of history on the individual' (Elsaesser qtd in Pop 2014: 16). This preoccupation with the pre-eminence of history³⁷ over the individual – typical of the doctrinal intertext of Eastern European communist cinema – was in fact deeply entrenched in the *engagé* slant of pre-Second World War Eastern European artistic and intellectual output.³⁸

The New Romanian Cinema categorically rejected this politicised legacy and its strong predilection for construing characters as victims of socio-historical circumstance, thus securing their immunity from personal moral responsibility and yet denying them moral agency. By focusing on the crucial importance of personal choices, the NRC has circumvented the traditional role of Eastern European cinema as a form of potentially propagandistic public service and education – and 'high' and intricate form of artistic expression – but also placed itself in direct opposition to the role of cinema as pure entertainment. Thus the qualitatively new approach of New Romanian directors, predicated on the existentialist necessity of integrity and individualism, has resulted in a veraciously consistent 'group of works' that encodes the existential metaphysics of the ethical experience into the ironic ambiguity of its aesthetic representation.

This new kind of *auteurship* displays formative – stylistic and ethical – features that amount to what could be called the existentialist realism of New Romanian cinema, a notion which grasps its specificity, yet is flexible enough to accommodate further evolution. Predicated on Puiu's influence, this Existentialist Realism – as pointed out in his interview – was groomed under Eastern as well as Western influence. While studying abroad,[39] he found inspiration in directors like John Casavettes, whereas at the Bucharest Film School UNATC,[40] the NRC *alma mater*, his colleagues developed 'under the influence of Andrey Tarkovsky or Czech New Wave master Milos Forman', which '*Occident* or *Furia* [the first films by Mungiu and Muntean, made in 2002] clearly demonstrate' (Puiu interview, 2017). For his own debut *Stuff and Dough*, premiered almost concurrently, Puiu came up with a radically different style which – after *Mr Lăzărescu* – would 'profoundly affect' the aesthetics of NRC, bringing it abreast with current tendencies of world cinema. 'You could tell', Puiu says, 'that maybe because of the prize it won [*Prix un Certain Regard*] at Cannes, Mungiu's and Muntean's second films [*4 Months, 3 Weeks and 2 Days*, 2007 and *The Paper Will Be Blue*, 2006], as well as other films from that time, were made in the stylistics of *Mr Lăzărescu*' (Puiu interview, 2017).[41]

Puiu describes his films as 'testimonies' or 'witnesses', perhaps not of the 'loud whistleblower kind, shouting from the rooftops as the kid from Andersen's story', but rather as 'happening naturally, and by their very existence exposing the truth that the emperor has no clothes' (Puiu interview, 2017). Building on the ethical–aesthetic congruity of his works, he insists that '"realism" is an overrated term', and tends to agree with solipsist philosophers that there is no such thing as a physical reality beyond one's own self, and that therefore 'all artists are realists, although some focus on the reality within their minds, while others on the reality without' (ibid.). It is then hardly surprising that a sense of personal responsibility has become the most salient feature of New Romanian Cinema. With its insistence on subjectivity and authenticity, on choice and commitment and on the inevitably ensuing anxiety in the face of nothingness (as Jean Paul Sartre had it) – the existentialist realism of New Romanian cinema is presented as a way of life best captured in the words of Søren Kierkegaard, as 'a truth that is true for me . . . the idea for which I can live or die' (qtd in Kosciejew 2014: 143). Moreover, Puiu's contention chimes with Bordwell's description of Western European modernist cinema, born under the post-war influence of existentialism. In his view, while the 'objective' and 'subjective' verisimilitude of modernist cinema are of equal standing, their inevitable frictions are resolved through expressionist 'authorial commentary' through 'the device of ambiguity', since, 'ideally, the film hesitates,[42] suggesting character's [sic] subjectivity, life's [objective] untidiness and author's vision' (Bordwell 1985: 721). In New Romanian cinema, the frictions between the subjective and the objective are resolved through the ambiguity of irony and ironic modes – tragic or comic – as preferred forms of authorial commentary. According to the celebrated Canadian critic Northrop

Frye, ironic narratives are populated by characters, whose knowledge of their situation and their 'ability to change it' are either 'inferior' or 'equal to ours' (1990: 34).[43] Moreover, our 'sense of looking down on a scene of bondage, frustration, or absurdity' is enhanced by the author's propensity for 'detached objectivity and suppression of all explicit moral judgements', suggesting little in a direct way, but 'meaning as much as possible' (1990: 40). Such an author is the quintessential Aristotelian *eiron*, the 'ironic artist ... [who] deprecates himself and, like Socrates, pretends to know nothing, even that he is ironic' (ibid.). Therefore Puiu's reference to his own films as 'testimonies' or 'witnesses', and even 'natural occurrences', reminds one of the Kierkegaardian ironist who, by self-effacing, prevents 'the addressee from merely emulating the speaker without attempting self-knowledge' (Mulaem 2017: 222).

The testimonial ethos of New Romanian Cinema is enhanced by the terse narrative formats that follow an Aristotelian, tripartite dramatic structure of a single plot-line, supporting the complete action of one main character, and is 'confined within one revolution of the sun' (Aristotle 1961: 40). Intended to stimulate the aesthetic as well as the ethical experience in the perceptive viewer, this narrative format – known as the 24-hour story – can be found in about one-third of the movement's features,[44] as well as in most of its numerous shorts.[45] These curt stories thus 'begin in realism and dispassionate observation ... and move steadily towards myth', or the archetypal dimensions of human existence (Frye 1990: 42). That is, they move towards 'conventionalized or stylized' biblical, classical or local anecdotal motifs, which – being 'not fully adapted to plausibility of "realism"' – are used to facilitate the perception of film as a 'testimony' (366). And they serve as what Ludwig Wittgenstein calls 'outward criteria' for the inexpressible, of 'things' that could only '"show themselves"', like 'ethics, religion, the meaning of life, logic and philosophy' and certainly love and death (Wittgenstein qtd in Monk 2005: 17–21).

Thus the tragic-ironic mode, favoured by Puiu, Mungiu and Muntean among others, 'merely' objectifies the 'human, all too human' facts of life as 'outward criteria' for the inexpressible depths of human existence. The mythical intertext of the Christ-like plight of Mr Lăzărescu, Costi (*The Paper Will Be Blue*), Ryna (*Ryna*), Silviu (*If I Want to Whistle, I Whistle*), and Alina (*Beyond the Hills*) construes them as *pharmakoi* (victims or scapegoats), whose ability to cope with exclusion from an uncaring society is much lower than ours.[46] This type of ironic austerity is consistent with the NRC audio-visual minimalism, complemented by carefully designed camera positions and movements,[47] reminiscent of the observational style of direct cinema.[48] What these aesthetics accomplish is to '"draw your attention to a thing, to place things side by side", and to make another person "see what you see"' (Wittgenstein qtd in Szabados and Stojanova 2011: 112).

A different kind of irony is championed by Porumboiu, whose films Puiu describes as standing apart from the NRC *œuvre* for they 'belong to a tradition, which cultivates a macabre smile, a destructive lucidity, a tragic absurdity and a refined misanthropy' (Riding 2007: AR8). Yet again, while Puiu refers to the 'dryness and minimalism' of Jarmusch's *Stranger than Paradise* (1984)[49] as a major influence, Porumboiu admits to drawing inspiration for *12:08* from *Down by Law* (1986).[50] Indeed, if the first part of *12:08* is stylistically closer to the objectified ironic mode, the second discloses Porumboiu's authorial presence from the subjective point of view of the amateur cameraman, and makes us literally 'see what he sees' and does behind the scenes. Actually, Porumboiu has claimed to have 'aligned himself with the much-derided cameraman of the show' not only because of his 'faulty camerawork', but also because of his 'failure to find the truth in all the different versions of the story he is given' (qtd in Bardan 2012: 141).

The comic-ironic mode in the works of Nemescu, Jude, Gabriel Achim, Netzer and Giurgiu could broadly be defined as subjective realism in the sense of externalising characters' mental states with ironic authorial commentary, marked by 'heightened affective charges of irony' (Hutcheon 1994: 47). It ranges from simple estrangement to aggressive forms of ludic, contentious, bellicose satire that justifies the affinity for avant-garde stylistics augmented by absurd incongruities and intermedial layering of meanings.

In these films, the comic-ironic points to personal and collective delusions of individuals who, like Don Quixote, are victims of the excessive idealisation of their own role, or that of the society they manically strive to integrate into, or of both, and therefore could be defined as *alazons* (or imposters). The three TV interlocutors (*12:08*) and the hapless workplace safety instructor (*Adalbert's Dream*) come to mind, since their intelligence (which is 'lower than ours') exposes not only self-delusion but also the duplicitous nature of film and TV as social institutions (Frye 1990: 39–42). Furthermore, the humiliation suffered by the protagonists of *Medal of Honor*, *Of Snails and Men* and *Everybody in Our Family* is also a 'testimony' to the hypocrisy of a conservative environment that likes to see itself as progressive. Unsavoury revelations about incompatibilities between humanism and the law are brought to bear in *Aferim!*, which is designed as a folkloric picaresque about the adventures of a shrewd policeman and his sickly apprentice of a son throughout southeastern Europe in the early nineteenth century. By exposing an array of contradictory, mostly bigoted attitudes to a fugitive Gypsy slave they are hunting for, the film becomes a satirical fable about the perennial state of affairs in that part of the world. Conversely, the seemingly naïve present-day rendition of the Robin Hood legend in *The Treasure*, whose idealistic protagonist turns out to be much smarter and nobler than his environment, is actually a sardonic comment on Romanian consumer society.

In the final analysis, the austere aesthetics of New Romanian Cinema, reinforced by its archetypal narrative structures, bring together content, form and ethics into a compact philosophical entity, not unlike Wittgenstein's propositions, which he considered to be a "picture of reality" (Proposition 4.01, Wittgenstein 2015: 32). As A. O. Scott has famously suggested, the inspiration for the New Romanian cinematic realism 'seems to be as much ethical as aesthetic, and less a matter of verisimilitude than of honesty' (2008). Not surprisingly, then, Puiu strongly agrees that Wittgenstein's proposition that 'ethics and aesthetics are one' captures the fundamental essence of the movement (Puiu interview, 2017).[51]

Book Overview: Issues, Formal Devices and Critical Approaches

The current anthology brings together fifteen prominent specialists whose chapters foreground the aesthetic, philosophical and ethical aspects of what has been defined as the existentialist realism of New Romanian cinema. Primarily, the authors explore the way in which filmmakers – as well as their characters– act as moral and rational agents under their immediate circumstances, which Sartre has famously summed up as the 'hand one has been dealt'. Therefore the focus of **the first two parts** is on (self-)reflexivity, minimalism and irony, seen in their (post-)modernist, intermedial and intertextual context since, as argued above, these aesthetics devices underwrite the extraordinary success of New Romanian Cinema. **Part III** examines the ethical–aesthetic congruity of New Romanian cinema, which is defined as its fundamental feature. By exploring the idiosyncratic handling of time as a diegetic, personal, historical and philosophical category, this part elucidates ethical issues in the light of discourses ranging from Freudian, Lacanian and Jungian psychoanalysis to existentialism and neo-liberalism. **Part IV** tackles authenticity within the discursive confines of gender and genre, foregrounding the cosmopolitan and transnational nature of New Romanian Cinema. By the same token, the conclusive **Part V** scrutinises ways of grafting individual and national space onto the private and public places, deployed in New Romanian films; and, after positioning them within the discursive context of the marginal and the peripheral, puts the most recent developments of New Romanian Cinema on the transnational cinematic map.

* * *

Part I, *Modernism/Minimalism*, comprises three chapters, which contextualise the reflexivity and minimalism of New Romanian Cinema within European and global cinema. In Chapter 1, Dominique Nasta – author of *Contemporary Romanian Cinema: The History of an Unexpected Miracle*, a frequently quoted source in this anthology – places the movement firmly within European modernism of the 1960s and 1970s. In her view, '[t]he achievements of the New Romanian cinema are the result of a subtractive principle that has its roots in

Modern cinema's attempt to shift from goal-oriented narratives to classical filmmaking alternatives'. Nasta then turns to the specificities of sound design (and soundscape), whose complexity, she argues, is often more powerful than the visuals in supporting the most salient (post-)modernist features of New Romanian films – their minimalism, their handling of time, and certainly the deployment of irony, whose crucial role in the NRC *œuvre*, discussed above, is recognised by most contributors to the volume.

Whereas Nasta operates within the contextual framework of European modernism in Bálint Kovács' understanding, the other two authors discuss various aspects of minimalism both as modernist aesthetic trope and theoretical concept. Thus Irina Trocan – as implied by the title of her chapter 'Minimalism in the New Romanian Cinema: Absent, Omnipresent or Misjudged?' – focuses first on the modernist etymology of the term. She then moves to describing its potential as a means of eliciting critical awareness, and a tool for analysing reception and perception. '[T]he art-house ambitions of recent Romanian productions', she writes, 'their aim to perturb the habits of entrenched spectators, can be proven by association with, and in comparison to, established minimalist works of art since the 1960s, whether pertaining to cinema, sculpture or music'.

In Chapter 3, Ioana Uricaru argues that minimalism – manifested as exclusion of non-essential elements like diegetic music, which, along with Nasta, she also identifies as an 'exemplary trait' of NRC– actually results from a 'worldview that rejects the myth of melodrama'. Moreover, building on Pop's term 'purposeful minimalism', she argues that the aesthetics of New Romanian Cinema is the end product of 'risky decisions and sophisticated strategies'. And, as the only practising filmmaker among the contributors to this volume, she illuminates the complexities of 'industrial, extradiegetic and intradiegetic employment of music' from an economic, historical, traditional and ideological perspective.

Part II, *Intermediality/Intertextuality*, features four chapters, which scrutinise New Romanian cinema in light of theoretical investigations in this fairly new academic field. Fittingly, the cluster is helmed by '"Exhibited Space" and Intermediality in the films of Corneliu Porumboiu' by Ágnes Pethő, the author of *Cinema and Intermediality: The Passion for the In-Between* (2011). Focusing on the *tableau* shots in the first four feature films by Corneliu Porumboiu and their intermedial associations to other art forms – painting, theatre and installation art – Pethő succinctly concludes that 'in each of these films, the *tableau* appears not only as a liminal space conceived in-between the visible and the invisible, the grand theatre of politics and the private world of everyday people, it also reveals in different ways the shifting demarcation between the "public" and the "domestic"'.

Then again, through the prism of intermediality and remediation, the other three authors also focus on reflexivity, irony and minimalism. In Chapter 5

Katalin Sándor sees Pintilie's works as 'aesthetic and conceptual antecedent[s]' of the 'perception of the real as a medially layered, heterogeneous experience', which she argues is characteristic of New Romanian Cinema. In Chapter 6, Melinda Blos-Jáni focuses on the works of a versatile director, Nae Caranfil, whose passion for remediation and intermedial devices, borrowed from theatre, sets him apart from the NRC cohort. Yet, she writes, Caranfil's intermedial 'self-reflexive aesthetics and his ironic, narcissistic narratives' constitute a specific 'notion of cinema(tic realism), considered to be the "other" of the minimalist realism of the New Romanian cinema'. This nearly axiomatic status of minimalism in New Romanian Cinema is however contested by Liviu Lutas in Chapter 7, where he points to a number of moments in Puiu's films, whose 'suggestive power' – rooted in other forms of media such as posters, paintings and music, and enhanced by 'the complex transference of remediation and stylisation' – call into question the very notion of minimalism.

The chapters of **Part III**, *Ethics/New Aesthetics*, are brought together by ethical issues, reflected in their representation of time in its various hypostases. In Chapter 8, Christina Stojanova, following Wittgenstein and Heidegger, sees the handling of time as a manifestation of existentialist authenticity that identifies temporal confusion with moral confusion both socially and personally. In her discussion of the representability of good and evil in terms of analytical psychology, existentialism and philosophy of religion, she emphasises – following Wittgenstein – the particular sensitivity of NRC directors to values 'whereof one cannot speak' that could only be found in the works of 'great artists, musicians, and novelists', who, Wittgenstein believed, 'could teach people a lot more than scientists'.

Ioana Uricaru's Chapter 9 examines the cinematic representation of the turbulent period between the 1989 Romanian revolution and its 1990 aftermath as an ethical corrective to their representation by the media. In light of Lacanian concepts of the Real and the Symbolic, she demonstrates how the 'discursive tools' of the NRC films 're-create and reassert the authenticity of experience', since 'the only basis for ethics can be found in individual solidarity, in truly empathising with another even if this empathy comes at an extraordinary price'.

In Chapter 10, Kalling Heck foregrounds the ethical tensions between the political economy of liberalism proper and current neo-liberal practices. In his view, the drama of the two female leads is the result of the 'cruelty of austerity', which – being imposed by the EU – affects Romanian society at all levels, including New Romanian Cinema. Therefore the author believes that the tragic outcome in Mungiu's film would generate – not unlike Italian neorealism and the films of the Dardenne brothers – an ethical impulse in affluent EU nations, which have the power to alleviate the austerity that they have imposed on postcommunist countries.

The first chapter of **Part IV**, *Gender/Genre* constitutes an attempt to rectify the overall impression that women in New Romanian Cinema are underrepresented, especially behind the camera. Yet the successes of Ruxandra Zenide and Melissa de Raaf, crowned by the triumph of Adina Pintile's *Touch Me Not* at the 2018 Berlinale – let alone that of versatile producers like Ada Solomon, Anca Puiu and Oana Giurgiu, responsible for producing more than half of the NRC films – call this argument into question. Dana Duma's Chapter 11 is bookmarked by a brief discussions of works by two female Romanian directors, Zenide's *Ryna* and Ana Lungu's *The Self Portrait of a Dutiful Daughter*. Through the prism of European feminist theory, Duma demonstrates that 'female issues and gender inequality' remain endemic in a society which she calls 'neo'-patriarchal. In her view, screen representations of women fall into three major periods. The first is associated with propagandist 'images of "women in leadership roles"', propounded during communism 'to justify the ascent of Elena Ceaușescu' to absolute power. The second – synonymous with the rampant 'commercialisation of sex and the media' in the 1990s – points to the plight of women 'as losers in the transition to capitalism'. The current moment is associated with the 'decisive [female] role in the narrative structures' of New Romanian Cinema, which – judging by the 'sheer number of female names and pronouns in its titles' – unequivocally supports 'female characters and issues'.

In Chapter 12, Andrea Virginás discusses the potential of the 'objectively descriptive notion of small (national) cinemas' like those of Hungary and Romania, to successfully supplant the loaded 'geopolitical angle of the term "postcommunist Eastern European cinema"'. She argues that although in a heated global market, 'small cinema' auteurs from New Romanian Cinema tend to 'integrate certain genre elements' borrowed from mainstream Hollywood films, they nonetheless remain firmly 'within the confines of the arthouse discourse'.

The conclusive **Part V**, *National/Place and Transnational/Space*, opens with Mircea Deaca's chapter 13, which looks into representations of 'gatherings around the kitchen table', where 'members of the family show their "true" face and abandon [the usual] role playing'. The author argues that the kitchen transcends its diegetic role and, thanks to the NRC affinity for *huis clos* shots and long alienating takes, becomes an instrument for converting the topographical into psychological, the physical into metaphysical, and – not unlike the previously mentioned 'traces of genre' – the national into transnational.

Chapter 14, by Marian Țuțui and Raluca Iacob, links the perceived marginality of New Romanian Cinema within the European context to the centre–periphery tensions between the capital Bucharest and the Romanian provinces as filming locations and featured diegetic spaces. As the authors argue, although the NRC films 'offer multiple examples' of either 'ascribed or internalized' geographical, cultural and psychological marginality, they also bring into high relief the universality of such micro and macro identity issues, invariably predicated on one's space and place within society.

In Chapter 15, Doru Pop – the author of *Romanian New Wave Cinema: An Introduction*, another frequently referenced source in this anthology – forcefully argues that 'contemporary Romanian cinema is changing from a national to a transnational film industry'. Building on recent domestic admission figures, Pop contends that – while the international success of New Romanian Cinema remains largely unrecognised domestically – commercial genre films, both Romanian and American, account for the lion's share of box office revenues in Romania. As a result of this continuing trend, 'aesthetically accomplished' NRC works like Muntean's *Tuesday, After Christmas*, Netzer's *Child's Pose* and Porumboiu's *When Evening Falls on Bucharest, or Metabolism* move increasingly towards the '"transnationalisation" of New Romanian cinema'.

Indeed, if the latest successes of Romanian cinema with Constantin Popescu's *Pororoca* (2017), Adina Pintilie's *Touch Me Not* (2018), and Radu Jude's *I Do Not Care If We Go Down in History as Barbarians* (2018) – made within and outside the confines of New Romanian Cinema aesthetics – are a good indicator, Pop's claim that 'directors are increasingly agglutinated into a cosmopolitan identity . . . transnational lifestyle' could indeed be considered prophetic for the future of Romanian cinema.

The **Historical Overview**, included as **Part VI** at the end of the volume, offers a comprehensive look at the political and ideological, as well as the cultural, industrial and artistic aspects of Romanian national cinema from its beginnings in the early 1900s to the arrival of New Romanian Cinema in the 2000s. Part and parcel of the idiosyncratic evolution of Eastern European culture and society over the last couple of centuries, Stojanova sees Romanian cinema as a form of displaced negotiation between the state and the intelligentsia, resulting in the latter's crisis of self-knowledge about its place in society. The 'sustained and diverse tradition' of Romanian interwar cinema is therefore discussed in light of its fluctuating loyalties of public service, propaganda and high art – but rarely entertainment – while the post-war period is seen as negotiating aesthetic and ideological templates, enforced ubiquitously throughout the region after the communist takeover. The author emphasises the importance of the *totalitarian genre paradigm*, and highlights its peak moments during the subsequent four decades, focusing on its challenges. Among those, she singles out the mythopoetic and metaphoric-allegorical trends, along with the 'old' wave, and pays particular attention to auteurs like Pintilie, Daneliuc and Pița, who have been valued highly by the NRC directors.

In Stojanova's view, the 'abdication of the state' in the immediate post-communist aftermath 'exacerbated the filmmakers' crisis of self-knowledge, and – under the pressure of reinforced delusions about 'salvation from the omnipotent West' – they reverted to the traditionally auteurist slant of what she calls 'realistic-descriptive' and 'naturalistic-nihilistic' trends.

The New Romanian Cinema, as Stojanova claims – while clearly breaking away from the legacy of interwar, communist and early postcommunist Romanian national cinema – is also an inspired successor of their best traditions: the penchant for visual and psychological verism, and for existentialism, which is rooted in nativist literary and philosophical sources. As Stojanova concludes, citing Karl Mannheim and Václav Havel in their capacity of 'free-floating (*freischwiebende*) intelligentsia', the NRC directors have emerged as 'moral and rational agents', courageous enough to contrast 'ideas and free minds to ideological mentalities' and capable of advancing 'a higher, more real, more objective kind of (self) knowledge', thus bestowing 'a unique voice to the frustrated denizens of our postmodern times'.

Notes

1. On the basis of a profound academic research (Stojanova 1999), it is assumed that over the last two-and-a-half centuries the similarities in the economic, political and social structures of Albania, Bulgaria, Czechoslovakia (now the Czech Republic and Slovakia), Poland, Romania, Hungary and Yugoslavia (now Bosnia-Herzegovina, Croatia, Kosovo, Macedonia, Montenegro) – including most recent social and cultural processes and products – justify the usage of the term Eastern Europe.
2. The term 'communist' and 'communism' fits the needs of this introduction as it connotes both the regime and its ideology, and works semantically well with 'postcommunism'.
3. *Inventing Ruritania: The Imperialism of the Imagination* (1998), *Cinema of Flames: Balkan Film, Culture, and the Media* (2001), *Once Upon a Time There Was a Country – National and Cynicism in the Post-1990s Balkan Cinema* (2008).
4. The second part of *Cinema beyond the Danube: The Camera and Politics* (Stoil 1974).
5. Special Double Issue on New Romanian Cinema in *Film Criticism* (2010), 2: 3, Winter/Spring; Special Issue on Romanian New Wave in *Film International* (2012), 10: 1, pp. 7–50, and Special Issue on Cristian Mungiu, coordinated by Mircea Deaca (*Images, Imagini, Images: Journal of Visual and Cultural Studies*), University of Bucharest (2014), Issue 4). Most recently, Special Issue on New Romanian Cinema in *Film Criticism*, 41: 2, October 2017, edited by Alina Haliliuc and Jesse Schlotterbeck.
6. Most notably, *The Eastern European Cinemas* (2005) and *A Companion to Eastern European Cinemas* (2012), both edited by Anikó Imre.
7. *Noul val în cinematografia românească/New Wave In Romanian Cinema* (2006), București: Grupul Editorial Art.
8. Strausz privileges New Romanian Cinema or contemporary Romanian cinema over 'the historically weighted label "new wave"' (2017: 9).
9. The current volume retains its title from an earlier project by Stojanova and Duma, unrelated to the historical legacy of *New Cinema* (Noul Cinema) magazine (see Pop 2014: 19).

10. A school:

    > requires a body of [shared] basic critical doctrine; an aesthetic program; publication of a manifesto, announcing the doctrine; a group of works, responding to these criteria; an ensemble of artists (directors, but also collaborators in creation, including writers, technicians, and actors); a promotional strategy and hence vehicles for diffusing that strategy, namely press and broadcast media; a leader (such as the strongest personality or spokesperson of the group and/or theoretician (the so-called 'pope' of the group), to represent the movement; finally, adversaries are needed, since every school defines itself at least partially in opposition to those who precede it. (Marie 2003: 28)

11. Published by the Universitatea Națională de Artă Teatrală și Cinematografică (National University for Theatre and Film) 'I. L. Caragiale', Bucharest, Romania, ISSN 2286-4466.
12. Published by Babes-Bolyai University, Cluj-Napoca, Romania, ISSN 2067-631X.
13. Published by Sapientia Hungarian University of Transylvania, Cluj-Napoca, Romania ISSN 2066-7779 (online version); ISSN 2065-5924 (printed version).
14. The promotional arm of CNC (Centre national du cinéma et de l'image animée), founded in 1949.
15. The NRC directors arrived at the scene in clusters of three to five. First were the pioneers Cristi Puiu (b. 1967), Mungiu (b. 1968), Rădulescu (b. 1969), Muntean (b. 1971), Netzer (b. 1975), and Ruxandra Zenide (b. 1975), who made their breakthrough films between 2001 and 2003. Then, in 2006 and 2007, came Giurgiu (b. 1972), Mitulescu (b. 1972), Porumboiu (b. 1975), and Nemescu (b. 1979–d. 2006), followed between 2009 and 2011 by Adrian Sitaru (b 1971), Bogdan Apetri (b. 1978), Constantin Popescu (b. 1973), Marian Crișan (b. 1976), and Jude (b. 1977). Bogdan Mirică (b. 1978), Iulia Rugină (b. 1982) and the youngest so far, Tudor Cristian Jurgiu (b. 1984) came to the fore between 2013 and 2015. Andrei Gruzsniczki (b. 1962) is an isolated latecomer.
16. Puiu, Muntean, Mitulescu, Nemescu and Jude all grew up in Bucharest; Mungiu and Porumboiu come from small Moldovan towns; and Crișan, Florin Șerban, Giurgiu, Sitaru, Jurgiu and Netzer were all born in Transylvanian towns (Iacob 2015).
17. Puiu's father was a hospital administrator in Bucharest, and Mungiu's was a pharmacy studies professor, while their mothers worked in education. Porumboiu's father was an internationally certified soccer referee who, after his retirement in the mid-1990s, went into business. Muntean's father worked for the national television station in Bucharest and Constantin Popescu's father was a film production manager and head of the production company Filmex after 1990 (Iacob 2015).
18. A number of NRC directors came to filmmaking in their thirties, after trying different professions. Thus, being barely twenty years old, Mitulescu immigrated to Italy, where he worked in restaurants, before returning to Romania three years later to pursue his studies. Prior to enrolling in UNTAC, Porumboiu studied management, Mungiu pursued literary studies and worked as a teacher, journalist, radio and TV entertainer, and Crișan studied international relations. Puiu wanted to be a painter, but failed the High Art School admission exam and was then drafted into the military, where the Revolution found him (Iacob 2015).
19. For discussion of the role of Romanian intelligentsia, see the Historical Overview in this volume.
20. As Uricaru writes, 'all [Nicolaescu] needs to do is enter a project … and … funding is guaranteed' (2012: 433).

21. Puiu, as Pop has it, was simply rephrasing Șerban's 1993 contention that 'Romanian filmmaking after 1989 was "non-existent"' (2014: 28).
22. In addition to his own films from the 1990s, Pintilie helped produce such landmark films as the documentary *University Square* (1991), *Sundays on Leave* (1993), *The Snails' Senator* (1995), and – prior to *Stuff and Dough* (2001) – the medium-length *The Firemen's Choir* (2000).
23. According to Filimon, in one of the 'most infamous' of the 'televised public debates regarding the new law for cinematography' with the participation of 'the future NRC directors' in the early 2000, Nicolaescu, 'MP for the Social Democrat party in power, confronted Puiu and Mungiu with the condescension of a father bothered by two children's insubordination' (2017: 51).
24. Eddie Cockrell sanctioned the term officially by defining György Pálfy's *Taxidermia* as an 'exercise in Central European ultra-miserabilism'. See <https://variety.com/2006/film/markets-festivals/taxidermia-1200518771/> (last accessed March 2017).
25. For discussion of the metaphoric-allegorical trend, see the Historical Overview in this volume.
26. Famous quote from Oberhausen Manifesto (1962), the foundational text of New German Cinema.
27. Francois Truffaut's 'Une certaine tendance du cinéma français/A certain tendency of the French cinema' is the French New Wave cinema quasi-manifesto, published in *Cahiers du Cinéma*, 31, 1954.
28. See Pop, 'Killing of Old Romanian Cinema' (2014: 119–20).
29. For discussion of the 'old' wave, see the Historical Overview in this volume.
30. Uricaru cites Romanian National Television as a third source of funding that – although 'functioning as a for-profit commercial enterprise' – is 'state/public property', and has (co-)produced most post-1989 Romanian films (2012: 448).
31. The most significant European grants are provided by MEDIA (Measures to Encourage the Development of the Audio Visual Industries) and *Eurimages* funds (a European Council programme for supporting audiovisual industries).
32. While the largest share of international investment, public and private, comes from France (Uricaru 2012: 442), contributions from European agencies and other national companies have resulted in 57 co-productions out of total 174 Romanian films, produced between 2006 and 2015 (Raluca Iacob, personal correspondence, 2017).
33. Croft introduces 'four modes of production' on the basis of state participation – *minimal* (market economy), *mixed economy*, *maximal* (centrally planned, totalitarian economy), and *other* (outside state provision) (1998: 389).
34. Postcommunist cinemas owe their survival to France, as 'in 1990 the French government stepped up to help the rapidly disappearing film industries of Eastern and Central Europe with the setting up of a special co-production Fund ... known as Fonds ECO' (Jäckel qtd in Uricaru 2012: 441).
35. Mitulescu scripted for Șerban, Rădulescu for Puiu, and Muntean and Puiu – for Păunescu. Also part of NRC strategy is producing each other's films and encouraging newcomers: Libra Film produced T. C. Jurgiu's *The Japanese Dog* (2013), Mandragora produced Păunescu's *Francesca* (2009), Crișan's *Morgen* (2010) and *Horizon* (2015), while Km 42 Film produced the promising debut of another NRC newcomer – Mirică's *Dogs* (2016). Păunescu is the producer of nine NRC films!
36. It is enough to mention internationally well-known DOPs like Oleg Mutu (who works with Mungiu, Puiu and Crișan), Andrei Butică (with Puiu, Jude, Netzer), Marius Panduru (Jude, Porumboiu, Giurgiu, Caranfil, Mitulescu), Tudor Lucaciu (Muntean's preferred DOP), and newcomers like Achim's cameraman George

Chiper. Equally important are the NRC fetish actors like Luminița Gheorghiu and Victor Rebengiuc, Vlad Ivanov, Dragoș Bucur, Anamaria Marinca, Șerban Pavlu, Mihaela Sîrbu, Teodor Corban, Doru Ana, Bogdan Dumitrache – to name indeed but a few.

37. Significantly, Graham Petrie's 1981 history of Hungarian cinema is called *History Must Answer to Man*.
38. For discussion of Romanian national cinema, see the Historical Overview in this volume.
39. At the école Supérieure d'Arts Visuels in Geneva.
40. Universitatea Națională de Artă Teatrală și Cinematografică (National University for Theatre and Film) 'I. L.Caragiale', Bucharest.
41. The impact of *Mr Lăzărescu* on both Mungiu's and Muntean's second features has been acknowledged by both Șerban and Gorzo (Filimon 2017: 58).
42. While Strausz builds his main theoretical argument on hesitation, he acknowledges the NRC's 'hesitant, ambiguous, representational mode', but also sees it as a 'specific mode of production of history and social reality' that is prompted by a general 'uncertainty about the status of the profilmic', and is typical of works from 'the state socialist era and the media event of the December 1989 television broadcasts' (2017: 1–2).
43. In myth and romance, this power is higher than that of other men in both kind and degree; in high mimetic mode, it is superior to other men but not to nature; in low mimesis it is similar to that of other men and not superior to environment; and in irony, is inferior to both that of ordinary men and to environment (Frye 1990: 33–4).
44. *Stuff and Dough, The Death of Mr Lăzărescu, 12:08 East of Bucharest, The Paper Will Be Blue, 4 Months, 3 Weeks and 2 Days, Hooked, The Happiest Girl in the World, First of All, Felicia, Aurora, Principles of Life, Adalbert's Dream, Everybody in Our Family, Sieranevada*.
45. Among others, Puiu's *Coffee and Cigarettes* (2004), Mitulescu's *Traffic* (2004), Jude's *The Tube with a Hat* (2006) and *It Can Pass through the Wall* (2014).
46. According to Frye, the relationship of the protagonist to society could be either tragic – he dies, fails, and is isolated – or comic, when he is integrated into society. If he is rejected (in comedy), the result is tragic-comic (1990: 33).
47. Strausz describes those as entailing 'lengthy takes, verisimilar mise-en-scène, and complex in-depth staging', whose 'central component [is] the constantly hovering mobile frame' (2017: 1–2).
48. For discussion of the antecedents of NRC realism see Pop (2014: 42–73).
49. With his short *Coffee and Cigarettes* (2004), Puiu pays tribute to Jarmusch's series of four vignettes, *Cigarettes and Coffee* (Filimon 2017: 129).
50. Interestingly enough, other postcommunist 'new cinemas' – the Czech 'Velvet Generation' whose Petr Zelenka also claims Jarmusch as an influence, along with Gogol, Beckett and Ionesco; the Polish 'black series', the Slovenian New Wave and the Hungarian 'succession of young talents' from the 2000s (Hames 2008) – have all demonstrated an emphatic predilection for the incongruous, the absurd and the surreal, which, in the words of Jan Švankmajer, are 'not just an artistic style, but a means of investigating and exploring reality' (Hames 2001: 28).
51. 'It is clear that ethics cannot be expressed. Ethics are transcendental. (Ethics and aesthetics are one)' (Proposition 6.421, Wittgenstein 1922: 108).

PART I
MODERNISM/MINIMALISM

1. BEYOND MODERNITY: THE STYLISTIC DIVIDE AND THE NEW ROMANIAN CINEMA

Dominique Nasta

Over the last decade, the 'New Romanian Cinema' has fuelled an unprecedented amount of exegesis worldwide. Piecemeal analyses and specific case studies have most naturally focused on seminal films and auteurs. Though mainstream audiences have not reacted to the filmic output at home and abroad in the same enthusiastic manner as theorists, critics and film buffs have, in the long run everybody has agreed that this Romanian 'wave' of directors has undisputedly helped bring in some fresh, intellectually and emotionally rewarding air into the global film sphere. The generational, thematic and aesthetic common genome, shared by most Romanian contemporary auteurs, has naturally triggered comparisons with similar film waves from the post-Second World War era, like the essential milestone represented by Italian neorealism from the late 1940s and early 1950s, with its extension into abstract modernism during the following decade; the mythical French *Nouvelle Vague* and its *ciné-vérité* subcategories at work from the early 1960s, as well as their Eastern European naturalistic and 'ornamental' counterpart, the Young Czech cinema, which had its wings brutally broken during the politically charged summer of 1968. The New Romanian film phenomenon has consistently changed the dynamics of filmmaking in the same way the French *jeunes turcs* or the Young Czech cinema did in the early 1960s, bringing forth highly innovative solutions in terms of storytelling, dialogue, editing and staging, the use of soundtrack and last but not least, new and challenging audience interactions with characters and situations.

Reputed domestic critics and theorists have argued that the trendsetting origins of the New Romanian Cinema pioneering aesthetic revolution are to be found in Cristi Puiu's first two features, *Stuff and Dough* (2001) and *The Death of Mr Lăzărescu* (2005) (Gorzo 2013; Șerban 2010; Pop 2014). Though I find Puiu's films groundbreaking, such a generalisation may prove misleading and restrictive. The achievements of the New Romanian Cinema are the result of a subtractive principle that has its roots in modern cinema's attempt to shift from goal-oriented narratives to classical filmmaking alternatives. Some common features are to be found in Romanian arthouse films from the late 1960s and early 1970s but also from the early 1980s, as well as in some mainstream genre films (heritage adaptations, comedies, Romanian-style Westerns, films for children, melodramas). Those were isolated cases that could barely be seen as innovative outside the domestic sphere; therefore few of these titles or their directors are familiar to international scholars and audiences. However, on closer scrutiny, some modernist elements that were developed in these works are to be found in the current wave, which emerged three or four decades later. Ignoring the thin red line that unites them is like deciding to approach Picasso's abstraction without taking into account his *Blue* or *Rose* periods, which proved essential to his subsequent figurative revolution.

Intimations of Romanian Modernity

In his essential *Screening Modernism: European Art Cinema, 1950–1980*, András Bálint Kovács distinguishes between those who consider modern cinema to be the result of an aesthetic, stylistic, or intellectual evolution and those who see it as a specific combination of aesthetic choices (2007: 8). Kovács resorts to two basic principles to define modernism. One is homogeneity of style; the other is a fundamentally ontological approach to reality, in other words, a sense of objective reality. Both are closely related to the central role attributed to the 'auteur', who is considered a *Demiurge*. The innovations often imply abstract, subjective, self-conscious and self-reflective behavioural patterns. Throughout the second half of the twentieth century, the principles and styles of Western and Eastern European modernism are present according to Kovács, within four distinctive stylistic trends: ornamentalism, naturalism, minimalism and the theatrical style. Folkloric and mythological ornamentalism was most often associated with works from Eastern and Central Europe, incorporating traditional motifs into the modernist form (Kovács 2007: 121, 182, 384).

There isn't the slightest mention in Kovács's book of any Romanian film, while most important Western and Eastern European auteurs receive extensive coverage, in as much as their films feature modernist elements. However, though not resulting from a structured movement as is the case with other

Eastern European New Waves, Romanian modernism, from the arthouse circuit, is palpable in films by Lucian Pintilie, Liviu Ciulei, Mircea Săucan or Dan Pița, made in the late 1960s and early 1970s. Undisputedly closer to the deconstructive and reflexive directors of the 1980s, such as Mircea Daneliuc (still active nowadays) or Alexandru Tatos, twenty-first-century Romanian filmmakers such as Cristi Puiu, Cristian Mungiu, Corneliu Porumboiu, Adrian Sitaru, Radu Jude or Radu Muntean have innovated content and style-wise, while sticking to principles set by their modernist predecessors.

Lucian Pintilie's first feature film *Sunday at Six* (1965) is a 'politically' connoted love story where the filmmaker decides to highlight the experimental aspect of the cinematic language with editing techniques close to those applied by Alain Resnais' *Hiroshima mon amour* (1959), where mental flashes are brilliantly translated on screen through daring cinematography and a challenging sound score. Of interest to Pintilie is not only the way characters and situations relate to objects, which stand for their inner states, but also the innovative sound design and atonal music in the vein of Giovanni Fusco's compositions for Michelangelo Antonioni (Nasta 2013: 90). In Liviu Ciulei's eponymous adaptation of the novel *The Forest of the Hanged* (1965) by Liviu Rebreanu, the first-person singular of the novel disappears and is changed into subjective audio-visual flashes. In a self-reflexive twist, the director himself plays one of the main characters. Modernist editing favours discontinuity: the film's overall syntax is complex, with frequent movement between time periods and recurring subjective visions. Mircea Săucan's film about missed meetings, *Meanders* (1966), is an audio-visual elegy with discontinuous editing via jump-cuts and lyrical interludes backed by an atonal score. In his second, highly controversial film, *One Hundred Lei* (1973) a Cain/Abel relationship between brothers from diverging social spheres features the same concern with an elaborate and experimental audio-visual discourse: images contain a whole range of freeze frames and jump-cuts. Authentic, unusually true-to-life dialogue alternates with voice-over poems, songs and TV broadcasts. Avant-garde composers produce an ensemble containing musicalised noises, atonal clusters, recycled music from classical composers and ethnic music.

Stone Wedding (1972) by Mircea Veroiu and Dan Pița is an adaptation of two short stories by Romanian classic Ion Agârbiceanu. The ornamental *tableaux*, the pictorial, silent-cinema-like black and white quality of interior but mostly exterior locations, serves the depiction of highly evocative chronotopes. Long shots and staged, in-depth compositions stress the importance of Fefeleaga, a truly tragic heroine in the classical Greek sense, who is resigned to accept her destiny. The soundtrack sustains this symbolic undercurrent: natural noises are foregrounded and different vocal occurrences, mostly a capella songs by Dorin Liviu Zaharia (Romania's prematurely departed iconic psychedelic singer/composer from the 1970s), are conceived as ballads inspired by Romanian folklore, summarising her tragic fate with simple, repetitive rhymes.

Mircea Daneliuc's *Jacob* (1988) recounts in a predominantly naturalist key the tragic destiny of a middle-aged miner from Transylvania, who eventually falls off a cable car at night and dies. The film's opening sequence features a strange, almost Tarkovskian, apocalyptic universe backed by a totally modernist, non-harmonic score. Its visually breath-taking twenty-minute coda echoes the fundamental Romanian myth of the prophetic lamb *Mioritza*, as Iacob's foretold death occurs in the midst of a wintry natural environment.

For Kovács, the basic trends of the post-1967 period are shaped by a reconstruction of the concept of reality on film as a means of political action and as a form of direct auteurial and conceptual discourse, in which the author creates a self-contained ideological and mythological universe (2007: 356). A 'naturalist' film style reminds the viewer of real-life experiences, whether by the characters' natural way of acting and talking, or the visual style of a documentary or newsreel (for example: shaky hand-held camera movements, wide-angle lenses, random panning around and characters communicating directly with the camera). Pintilie's seminal *Reconstruction/The Re-enactment* (1970) eventually debunks an episode of juvenile delinquency, which is supposed to be reenacted for propaganda purposes but ends in tragedy. The film's action unfolds simultaneously on different spatial planes, brought together within a stage-like structure. Planned as a one-day event, the reconstruction is constantly delayed and becomes a huge metaphor for a deranged and malfunctioning authority. The film's outstanding naturalist modernity in terms of screenwriting, acting, editing and sound design, made it, as evoked on various occasions by different directors, a harbinger for the New Romanian Cinema with long-term effects (Nasta 2013: 94).

Systemic self-reflexivity is at stake in Mircea Daneliuc's *Microphone Test* (1980): played by the director himself, the cameraman Nelu and his crew are filming people who transgress socialist standards. In line with French or Czech New Wave predecessors, the film features much brilliantly edited semi-documentary footage, innovative camera work, direct sound, ironic or rough everyday language and even a few sexually explicit scenes. In his subsequent *The Cruise* (1981), young workers who are offered a cruise as a reward eventually wreak havoc, creating a cynical, *désabusé* atmosphere that pervades the film. Yet another variation on the paradigm of 'revealing while filming' is *Sequences* (1982) by Alexandru Tatos, a portmanteau film with three episodes that is fragmented, reflective and packed with propagandistic footage and untold stories about life during communism. Both Daneliuc and Tatos have exerted essential influence on Puiu, Jude and Sitaru.

According to Kovács, theatre is another main inspiration of late modern cinema. There are two general characteristics of what he defines as the 'theatrical' style: one is the excessively unnatural way of acting, emphasising artificiality rather than psychological realism. The other is the artificial look of the sets as well as the artificial, expressionist lighting (Kovács 2007: 243). In cases where ironical dialogue is at stake, the viewer brings to the dialogue a level of knowledge and interpretation superior to that of the characters. Pintilie's adaptation of a Romanian repertoire classic, Ion Luca Caragiale's *Carnival Scenes* (1981), encapsulates in a highly effective manner the 'theatrical' and the 'ornamental'. The film's opening quote from Caragiale sets the general tone: 'I feel enormously and see monstrously'. It forms an ensemble of reflexively embedded genre scenes (Pintilie and his crew appear in the film), in which fits of hysteria and outbursts of passion constantly reflect a gigantic masquerade. Still governed by modernist cinematic principles, Pintilie's postexilic *The Oak* (1992) also unfolds by means of constant *mise en abymes*: home movies, Polaroid photos and reconstructed events from the past, culminating with the apocalyptic finale, featuring a film variant of the biblical 'Massacre of the Innocents'. In his equally eclectic *Next Stop Paradise* (1998), the overt biblical references are meant to transform the naturalistic approach to the everyday misery of an agonising postcommunist Romania into an allegorical message.

Minimalism for Kovács is a systematic reduction of expressive elements in a given form: in films by Bresson, Bergman or Dreyer, it achieves semantic richness by introducing the rule of systematic variation of motives instead of enhancing the expressive power of the motives by multiplying emotional effects of a similar kind. It involves a reduction of redundancy as well as eliminating random diversity (Kovács 2007: 142). Pintilie's *The Afternoon of a Torturer* (2001) is clearly one of the forerunners of the Romanian minimalist trend. The film's audience almost simultaneously watches the ongoing action and mental images from the hero's macabre past. A chamber piece close to the spirit of Kammerspiel, conceived as a series of vignettes with visions across time, the scenes are meant to highlight the terrifying confession of a communist ex-torturer. The low-key acting, static shots, absence of a musical score and unobtrusive editing are to be found again in *Niki and Flo* (2003), narrated in a diary mode with no pre-existing score, and based on an idea by Cristi Puiu and screenwriter Răzvan Rădulescu. A confined space perfectly serves the complex narrative purposes by means of a highly sophisticated double-bind dialogue. The film's reflexive pattern foregrounds two symptomatic moments of the postcommunist social disruption – a wedding and a funeral.

Crystals of Time, Subtractive Narratives

The highly original mixture of naturalism, theatricality and minimalism, obviously related to the European modernist heritage may partly explain the worldwide intellectual and emotional appeal of the New Romanian Cinema. Its auteurs seem to have assimilated almost three decades later, quite a few modernist approaches from their predecessors, essentially those related to audio-visual deconstructive and reflexive devices at large, as well as the diversified uses of the actors' performances, capable of both over- and under-playing. Content-wise, the favoured topics of the New Romanian Cinema directors, with the exception of the 1989 revolutionary moment and its extensions, have been deeply rooted in what Guido Kirsten (2015) has labelled as 'fictions of everydayness'. In a way, the modernist heritage accounts for Cristi Puiu's attachment to the spirit of Éric Rohmer's modern 'Moral Tales', or for Cristian Mungiu's obvious proximity to the 'being thereness' of the tenuous characters from the films of the Dardenne brothers. It may also act as a corollary for the parallels one is tempted to draw between the consistently 'physical' films of Radu Jude, Radu Muntean, Adrian Sitaru or Peter Netzer, and the turn to the essentially 'behaviourist immediacy' introduced by the films of John Cassavetes in the post-studio Hollywood era, which the Scandinavian Dogme manifesto further radicalised.

Recurrent ordinary, immediate topics and features are actually the result of a very complex phenomenon. In an attempt to conceptualise the phenomenon, it might be argued that the limits of the Heideggerian 'Dasein' are literally exploded. Mungiu, Puiu and Porumboiu do refute flashbacks, modes of traditional editing, framing and staging, and any form of non-diegetic musical scoring. Nonetheless, they categorically *do not* aim, verbally or musically, to stick to the 'here-and-now' hyperrealist, documentary, post-neorealist agenda. The Second World War, dictatorship and the alienating effects of immigration are featured through often ironic subtexts like the ones lurking inside *The Death of Mr Lăzărescu*'s intricate dialogical set-up. Or in referencing the devastating human consequences of orphanages from Ceaușescu's despotic era and its aftermath, frequently alluded to in Mungiu's *Beyond the Hills* (2012). Or, when depicting the complexities of unresolved aspects of the Romanian revolution, which arise at different moments in *12:08 East of Bucharest* (Corneliu Porumboiu, 2006). Conversely, there are palpable forms of 'Ostalgia' to be found in *The Paper Will Be Blue* (2006) by Radu Muntean or in Porumboiu's *Police, Adjective* (2009), suggested by means of incidentally diegetic musical quotes.

Many films unflinchingly address terminal situations by resorting to subtractive strategies, opting for reduced time frames, simple set-ups and repetitive visual patterns: imminent death ensuing deficient medical assistance (*The Death of Mr Lăzărescu*), explicit abortion (*4 Months, 3 Weeks and 2 Days*), murder (*Niki and Flo, Aurora*), excruciating domestic violence (*Everybody in our Family*, Radu Jude, 2012), the accidental killing of an innocent victim (*Child's Pose*, Peter Călin Netzer, 2013), death by primitive exorcist practices

(*Beyond the Hills*), unbridled violence in penitentiaries (*If I Want to Whistle, I Whistle*, Florin Șerban, 2010), and so on. Concomitantly, the same situations provide highly ironic, powerfully lyrical and ultimately cathartic moments, frequently leading to the conclusion that we are witnessing new beginnings as part of new spiral social structures.

Gilles Deleuze's *crystalline structure*, a synchronous blending effect between actual and past images, is clearly at work inside the aforementioned films. Deleuze establishes a complex relation between the open whole of *durée* and the cinematic elements of the frame, of the shot and montage. *Movement images* are mobile cuts of durée, while *time images* are change images, durée images, relation images, images beyond movement itself. Deleuze finds implicit in Bergson's account three specialised images: the *perception image*, whereby the living image senses the outside world; the *action image*, which structures the space surrounding the living image; the *affection image*, which connects the living images outside perceptions, inner feelings and responses to other images. The tripartite division is regulated by the *sensori-motor schema*, which provides the common sense temporal and spatial coordinates of our everyday world. In modern cinema, the *sensori-motor schema* might break down and with the collapse of that schema, new images appear in *opsigns* and *sonsigns*, pure visual and sonic images that defy common sense understanding (Bogue 2003: 4–6; 25–7).

Among the New Romanian auteurs Corneliu Porumboiu, while clearly acknowledging his admiration for the modernist lessons derived from Antonioni's body of work, has undoubtedly managed to address in new ways all three types of image theorised by Bergson and Deleuze, while also elaborating crystalline structures inside apparently straightforward *sensori-motor schema*. In *12:08 East of Bucharest*, for example, the *action image* is constantly delayed and recollections related to the 1989 moment render past actions almost impossible to objectively acknowledge in the present. In Porumboiu's replica to Fellini's *Otto e Mezzo* (1963), *Metabolism or When Evening Falls on Bucharest* (2013), the *perception image*, namely the medical X-ray of the film director's entrails, is part of a series of *opsigns* and becomes the reflection of the whole shooting process, as it turns out that the director, who is the main character, is sick and will probably be unable to shoot the film as planned. Last but not least, Porumboiu's latest film *The Treasure* (2015) brilliantly combines the Robin Hood fairy-tale intertext with the search for a treasure 'from the past' that needs to be excavated so as to secure a better financial status in the present life of a family. Although the outcome is not as positive as expected, the fairy-tale mode prevails, as the protagonist symbolically offers his son the most wonderful (fake) jewel box he has ever dreamed of: the *affection image* thus provides a highly satisfactory pay off, while remaining confined to the inner, imaginary world of the characters.

Tableaux Vivants and Wandering Cameras: New Romanian Cinema and the 'World Viewed'

The visual set-up of prominent New Romanian auteurs most often favours minimalist *mise en scène* and/or editing devices, while at the same time maintaining principles derived from modernist fragmentation and deconstruction, both when handling the narratives in a highly naturalist manner (jump-cuts, tracking shots, multiple pans and zooms, a hand-held camera, long shots in outdoor locations), and when resorting to purely static, theatrical, albeit ornamental representational strategies. In his seminal contribution *The World Viewed*, Stanley Cavell argues that, contrary to Bazin's theory which claims that cinema and photography have freed the plastic arts from their obsession with 'likeness':

> cinema's presentness, its *Dasein*, does not only reflect reality but holds a projection... it screens that world from me (...) The screen *is* a frame; the frame *is* a whole field of a screen... Drawing the camera back and panning it are two ways of extending the frame. (...) Early in its history the cinema discovered the possibility of calling attention to persons and parts of persons and objects; but it is equally a possibility not to call attention but rather to let the world happen. (1971: 69–71, original emphasis)

New Romanian auteurs brilliantly combine both possibilities, as if wanting to catch up and fill in the gap of decades during which national cinema, though diversified and professionalised, could not give free rein to its entire expressive range.

A challenging cross-cultural parallel could be drawn between the Romanian New Wave auteurs and the figurative breakthrough accomplished by French painter Pierre Bonnard. The latter produced a highly original body of work, at the intersection between the nineteenth-century Impressionist movement and the more radical, deconstructive, modernist revolution provoked by early twentieth-century Cubism. In both *The Box* (1908), and his famous *Dining Room in the Country* (1913), Bonnard's unorthodox spatial organisation and unusual 'tricks' of perspective anticipate framing devices and camera angles used by filmmakers one century later for diverse, though not utterly different narrative purposes.

In *The Box*, a self-reflexive work commissioned by his art dealers, Bonnard uses the Paris opera box pretext for experimenting in form, perspective and expressivity. The face of one of the dealers is deliberately cut by the top edge of the painting and though united, characters seem distant, isolated and somehow weary. In *4 Months, 3 Weeks and 2 Days*, Mungiu and cinematographer Oleg

BEYOND MODERNITY: THE STYLISTIC DIVIDE

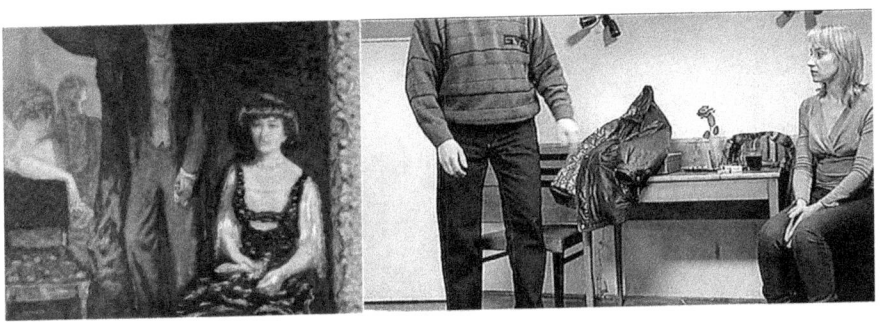

Figure 1.1   Pierre Bonnard, *The Box* and *4 Months, 3 Weeks and 2 Days*

Mutu turn the hotel room into a powerful symbol of secrecy and despair. True to their minimalist principles, Mungiu and Mutu do not reframe or cut to another set-up, but deliberately introduce framing errors, such as Mr Bebe's beheaded silhouette, which also point to the subjective, powerfully emotional point of views of the two heroines.

Dining Room in the Country enables Bonnard to capture both the interior and exterior space in one scene, integrating the human being within the natural world, but privileging an external, neutral point of view, the woman's perspective being quite recessive. The extended field of vision resembles a wide angle, thus questioning the limits between vision and reality. *Aurora* (2010) has Cristi Puiu directing himself as Viorel, a recently divorced father with a deliberately expressionless demeanour, carefully preparing the murderous acts he will eventually perpetrate. We see him repeatedly wandering and driving around the city, but also getting from one apartment to another, alone or with his daughter. Teaming with cinematographer Viorel Sergovici, Puiu frames and embeds actions and dialogues, by family members or neighbours he interacts with, in a detached, cynical, ultimately ironic way, recalling Pintilie's figurative strategies from *Niki and Flo*. Inside the set-up from Figure 1.2 there are at least three distinct points of view inside three distinct spaces, not to mention the ubiquitous TV set and the space reflected by the mirror image. In Vivian Sobchack's terms, what the viewer gets here is 'a synthesis of the *refractive* (several sub-spaces), *reflexive* (the director as character) and *reflective* (the mirror in the background)' (1991: 17).

Intricate staging and fixed horizontal shots, converging towards a pictorial climax – and related by David Bordwell not only to a refusal to cut, but also to a non-Western tradition of the shot as symbolic whole (2005: 222) – have found their perfect illustration in Cristian Mungiu's literally 'iconic' compositions from *Beyond the Hills*. The film proves a perfect heir to the modernist transcendental lineage of Dreyer, Bresson or Kawalerowicz, yet it is still innovative sound-wise, by means of ironic subtexts about harsh post-totalitarian realities.

Figure 1.2 Pierre Bonnard, *Dining Room in the Country* and *Aurora*

What Bordwell has defined as a 'come-and-go pattern' often leads New Romanian directors to build their shots so as to privilege psychology over action and allows them to 'structure their scenes around a visual arc' that may or may not be synchronised with the conventional dramatic one (2005: 178). This pattern applies to films opting for long shots that contain a considerable amount of lateral panning or zooming inside confined sets, as featured in Puiu's widely discussed *Death of Mr Lăzărescu*, but also in films that opt for more classical editing strategies. Obviously inspired by Puiu's film in terms of style and theme, Adrian Sitaru's *Best Intentions* (2011) is an autobiographical tale about an immature son who is unable to cope with his parents' mortality. The film alternates tracking shots, which clearly side with the main protagonist's kinetic wanderings, with more static though highly meaningful *tableau* setups. Jude's *Everybody in our Family* or Netzer's *Child's Pose* feature wandering, restless characters, pursued by hand-held cameras in an attempt to 'scan' their respective psychological confusion: the action is filmed within the scene and not from outside.

Deleuze writes that film produces a *nooshock* – actually a new kind of thinking through images – which provokes a *sensory* shock. As developed by Daniel Frampton in *Filmosophy*, characters in motion, such as the ones inhabiting the filmic universes of the Dardenne brothers, are accompanied by another consciousness, a *filmind*. An omniscient, free mode of thinking, film produces a shock effect forcing a heightened presence of the mind (Frampton 2006: 96–7; 177). Such is the case for instance of *Rosetta*'s Romanian 'counterpart', Otilia, who is ostensibly tracked by an empathetic camera in extreme situations in Mungiu's *4 Months, 3 Weeks and 2 Days*. Similarly, in Porumboiu's *Police, Adjective*, most actions are rendered objectively in long takes viewed from a distance, while the hero's stakeout also contains POV shots. In the long run, Cristi's frequent comings and goings, as well as his perceptive and ironic dialogue lines, perfectly voice his sophisticated mind and his refusal to apply absurd police constraints (Naremore 2010: 18).

'I Hear You with My Eyes': Empathetic Aural Universes

In her survey on the impact of Deleuze on film theory, Patricia Pisters takes up Deleuze and Guattari's theory from *A Thousand Plateaus*: for them, sound has a much stronger capacity to de-territorialise than sight (Pisters 2003: 188–9). In Slavoj Žižek's terms:

Voice does not simply persist at a different level with regard of what we see, it rather points towards a gap in the field of the visible, towards the dimension of what eludes our gaze. In other words, their relationship is mediated by an impossibility: ultimately we hear things because we cannot see everything. (1996: 93)

While some films favour static shots and 'slow cinema' compositions in depth, often refuting traditional editing patterns, most Romanian auteurs opt for what Phil Brophy has coined a 'spatialisation of atmosphere', sound not being consistently in service to the visuals (2007: 148). The canonical Godardian approach favouring dislocation and overload of sound layers is somehow complemented by a cinesonic experience that is not only intellectually but also emotionally challenging for the audience.

Sticking to the principles set by Romanian modernist predecessors, the sound design of most contemporary auteur films assigns an equal importance to the use of dialogue, noises, surround sound, silence and, in some cases, incidental and mostly pre-existing music. Pintilie's groundbreaking soundscape from *The Re-enactment* (thanks to his 'aural alter ego', sound engineer Andrei Papp) – with its foregrounded sounds acting as sensory motor shocks and incidental source music or a capella songs eliciting any possible pre-composed score – has had long-term effects. Various authors have tackled the New Romanian Cinema 'sound sphere' as a highly original entity, essentially focusing on the importance of the extremely well crafted, often tragi-comic or absurdist dialogues, whether spontaneous and authentic or derived from a long-standing theatrical tradition, with multiple national and regional subtexts. We find these at work in Porumboiu's uniquely crafted debates and phone-ins from the improvised television studio sequence in *12:08 East of Bucharest*, in the numerous paradoxical exchanges between Mr Lăzărescu and the hospital staff surrounding him, during the seminal 'supper scene' from *4 Months, 3 Weeks and 2 Days*, and during the strained though hilarious generational exchanges in *Everybody in our Family*, and so on.

Sound engineers and editors almost deserve an auteurial status. During the scenes surrounding the exorcism sessions, the almost unbearable and continuously foregrounded bell tolling from *Beyond the Hills* establishes a diegetic tension that outdoes the purely mimetic, albeit pictorial and iconic potential of the visuals. In Netzer's *Child's Pose* an isolated sound, which appears as totally motivated and contextual – the mother's mobile phone ring (incidentally from a Bach partita) – covers just a few seconds of a domestic scene, but tells a considerable number of things about the main heroine's complex personal profile.[1] In a totally different vein, the soundscape of Puiu's *Aurora*, which has benefited from developments in West European sound design, is so dense in terms of surround sound and composite layers of noise, zeitgeist source music and bits of off-screen radio material that one begins to almost wish that the non-domestic audience could be provided with some additional subtitling: aurally, Viorel's paranoid journey is much more cynical and judgemental than it appears visually.

The pragmatics-based theory of *natural* versus *non-natural meaning*, posited by linguist H. P. Grice in the late 1950s, which I have applied to cinematic narrative and music case studies on several occasions, could help better understand the kind of message that New Romanian Cinema auteurs aim at delivering. For Grice, *natural meaning* does not need a pre-established convention (that is 'clouds mean rain'), while *non-natural meaning* does, because it presupposes an intention to produce belief and a recognition of this intention. *Natural meaning* applied to the auditive sphere equals decoding of what is heard in accordance with what is shown, while *non-natural meaning* equals interpretation through inference (Nasta 1991: 19, 49). Though used parsimoniously in New Romanian films, music stresses the overt *non-natural* intention to establish bipolarity in terms of recognition of intention by audiences. Directors might choose to directly let the audience know what the musical quote means or they mighty covertly get the audience to think that something is implicitly meant by the music. A relevant theoretical explanation for the use of such a set of musical occurrences can be found in Jeff Smith's 'Movie Music as Moving Music': 'Film music', Smith argues, 'directs our attention to patterns of activity that correspond with the shared affective meanings of music, and visuals direct attention to formal features, which in turn reinforce and engender the affective meaning of a scene' (1999: 163).

Quite a few New Romanian films use pre-existing musical quotes with explicit diegetic purposes. And when they do, their treatment is almost systematically ambi-diegetic, ironical, fragmented or meta-textual. A perfect illustration is to be found in some of Porumboiu's films where music occurrences are judged either transgressive (the joyous local band that is scolded by their boss for playing Latino tunes instead of Christmas carols in *12:08 East of Bucharest*) or completely nonsensical (the linguistically hypersensitive young policeman from *Police, Adjective* arguing with his wife about her obsessional listening to an insipid Romanian hit from the 1990s).

Nonetheless, the most intriguing and original use of musical quotes most often occurs during opening and/or closing credits. And when their decoding strategies are transparent, *natural meaning* brings satisfaction to audiences worldwide. At the beginning of *Child's Pose*, for example, Cornelia, the main heroine, played by Romanian cinema's shining star Luminița Gheorghiu, dances on-screen during her birthday party to Gianna Nanini's hit 'Meravigliosa Creatura'. The same *symmetrical song* is heard during the closing credits, confirming her unique status inside an otherwise controversial, albeit tragic, set of Oedipal constraints. Conversely, if *non-natural meaning* is at stake, inferential strategies challenge the audience in diverse ways, both on an intellectual and on a purely emotional level. In *Aurora*, Cristi Puiu justifies the oxymoronic title of a narrative about a self-acknowledged series of murders, filled with despair and cynicism with an extremely fresh and dynamic, powerfully rhythmic piece of contrastive instrumental music (based on a dance: Louis Moreau Gottschalk's 'Manchega Concert Piece', 1855), which is heard during the opening and closing credits.

Finally, in *Beyond the Hills*, Cristian Mungiu remains visually true to minimalist principles in the film's highly synthetic closing *mise en abyme*, as figured by the police van's confined space. In terms of musical quotes, the audience's interpretive challenge proves even more complex. Thus mid-way through the film, in a rare moment of bedtime intimacy, Alina asks her friend and beloved Voichita to sing: Cosmina Stratan almost whispers a capella a lullaby in Romanian about an angel who promises to watch over the sleeper forever. The closing credits subsequently provide the instrumental counterpart of the melody, a very famous piece by Bernhard Flies reworked by W. A. Mozart, 'Wiegenlied: Schlafe mein Prinzchen, schlaf ein' (K530, 1803), which also contains some chorus lines. What may sound like a simple postmodern twist ultimately serves as a cathartic revival of eternally soothing principles: beyond the crude realities of medieval practices that are still to be eradicated, there are powerful feelings of universal love. We, the audience, should be ready to receive this musical message and work it out in the best possible ways.

No doubt, New Romanian Cinema's complex auteurist audio-visual aesthetics have so far provided a fertile ground for approaching the new paradigms at work in the context of an ever-changing world cinema.

Acknowledgement

I would like to thank Christine Stojanova for her editorial guidance and for her insightful comments on evolving versions of this chapter.

Note

1. Such is the case of editor Dana Bunescu who teamed up with Mungiu, Porumboiu, Netzer and Jude, and had an essential part to play in the extraordinary soundscape of Andrei Ujica's *The Autobiography of Nicolae Ceaușescu* (2010).

2. MINIMALISM IN THE NEW ROMANIAN CINEMA: ABSENT, OMNIPRESENT OR MISJUDGED?

Irina Trocan

The term 'minimalism', when applied to the art of cinema, is used often and arbitrarily. Sometimes connoting no more than the fact that a certain film is stylistically sparse, has a restrained or unemotional narration, or even that it is merely low-budget and thus constrained to show drama in contemporary settings, the label 'minimalism' in cinema could apply to most contemporary arthouse productions. The term is certainly found often enough in film reviews of Romanian productions made in the last fifteen years, and their connotation is alternately positive (in cinephile reviews, praising a film for being aesthetically daring) and negative (in popular reviews, a warning to readers to steer clear from an emotionally ungratifying production). As I will explain in more depth below, this is suggestive of the polarised relationship of the Romanian-language film criticism in what concerns New Romanian Cinema films, their success on the international festival circuit and their non-classical structure.

The purpose of this chapter is primarily to clarify and contextualise the term 'minimalism', as it has been used throughout art history and, particularly film history, in order to discuss its relevance to the New Romanian Cinema. The arthouse ambitions of recent Romanian productions, their aim to perturb the habits of entrenched spectators, can be proven by association with, and comparison to, established minimalist works of art since the 1960s, whether pertaining to cinema, sculpture or music. Since minimalism is defined as a challenge to institutional norms specific to a certain art form, there are obvious parallels to be drawn between these artefacts, regardless of the art form in which they are employed. It is thus useful to draw upon anthological texts of art theory, which could also apply to the films of New Romanian Cinema.

In order to fully understand the term 'minimalism' it is essential to view it as part of a bigger picture, namely the institutional structures within the art industry, as it can only be relevant within a historical-theoretical framework. Thus the frequent journalistic application of the 'minimalist' label to Romanian films stands as the motivation behind this chapter, rather than being its direct subject matter. The sources and contexts of applications of the term to contemporary Romanian films are too varied and numerous to address individually, or evaluate their pertinence on a case-by-case basis, although this text uses a few illustrative examples throughout to reinforce the argument. For instance, Romanian film critic Alex Leo Șerban introduced the term in association with the New Romanian Cinema, giving it a positive connotation[1] to the extent that it tells stories from reality with an economy of means, but he also expressed dissatisfaction[2] with the uncritical worship of cinematic simplicity.

Is Minimalism Exceptional in Arthouse Films?

Minimalism is an omnipresent and often misconstrued concept. With the proliferation of online film criticism, it is probable that every major arthouse director has been called a minimalist. Despite Todd Solondz's satiric humour and intricate plots, he has been described as a minimalist filmmaker,[3] and so was Lisandro Alonso, despite the quasi-touristic picturesque cinematography of recluse places that serve as backdrops to his narratives.[4] Pedro Costa, whose films have been praised for their authenticity to the point of being awarded festival prizes as documentaries, has also been described by the same term (Kotlyarenko 2010). Of course, it is difficult to trace the stylistic influences that validate the term, and harder still to explain them strictly within the limits of 'minimalist cinema', as opposed to minimalist art in the wider sense. Costa, to give a single example, has acknowledged his artistic debt to the legacy of Andy Warhol, although one has to slowly immerse oneself in Costa's cinema in order to note the similarities between the inhabitants of Fontainhas and the bohemian crowd at Warhol's Factory.[5]

However, for minimalism to be an employable critical concept, we must look for narrower definitions of the term. To use a broad analogy, dedicating one or a few rooms in the Tate Gallery to minimalist sculpture encourages a dialogue between the art pieces, and it does so by challenging the viewer to think of them in reference to each other. Their reduction in means of expression would then not be played off against the craftsmanship of traditional art, but against other works using similar economy of means used to catch the viewer's attention: Donald Judd's oversized metal cubes, which invite the visitor to step towards and away from them to contemplate them; Gerhard

Richter's plain grey painting; or Kim Lim's wooden sculptures 'Intervals I' and 'Intervals II', which take their form, vaguely reminiscent of a vertical ladder, far into geometrically regular abstraction. Conversely, hypothetically declaring the entire art display at Tate Modern as minimalist would mean blurring the line between minimalism and modernism and erasing the peculiarity of the artists' purpose. It would not serve to make the artworks more easily comprehensible. Certainly, definitions of minimalist cinema are more useful when they are specific.

What is Cinematic Minimalism?

In his well-received book on Robert Bresson, Tony Pipolo defines the French director's style as minimalist (2010: 166), a classification generally accepted by critics. Consider, for example, the way in which Bresson directs his 'models', with the actors' movement being integrated in the *mise en scène*, rather than as an expression of their autonomous bodies. András Bálint Kovács, investigating cinematic modernism throughout the history of the medium, enlists the following filmmakers as minimalist (2007: 140–1): Carl Theodor Dreyer, Yasujiro Ozu, Michelangelo Antonioni, for the first generation of modernist directors, working in the 1950s; and Jim Jarmusch, Béla Tarr, Aki Kaurismäki, Abbas Kiarostami and (at times) Takeshi Kitano, as those who adopted reductionism as their method at a time when the features of cinematic modernism were displayed across arthouse films.

Kovács crystallises a definition of cinematic minimalism in accordance with the use of the term in the art world:

> Minimalism is a systematic reduction of expressive elements in a given form. Minimalism achieves semantic richness by introducing the rule of systematic variation of motives instead of enhancing the expressive power of the motives by multiplying emotional effects of a similar kind. It involves reduction of redundancy as well as eliminating random diversity. (2007: 140)

Minimalists working in fine arts employ industrial materials and large-scale geometric shapes and colour patterns in structuring their sculptures in order to alert visitors to the strangeness and the physicality of their viewing experience, and to encourage them to be aware of the surrounding space and the rapport between their bodies and the art objects they contemplate, rather than focusing their attention directly on the isolated works of art. Similarly, minimalists working in cinema find cinematic means to alienate spectators from their cinematic expectations – mainly immersive narrative coherence – in order to make them fully conscious of the circumstances of the screening and their film-

Figure 2.1 Donald Judd exhibition at the Chinati Foundation, Marfa, Texas

viewing awareness. The same artistic purpose – a post-classical reluctance to make meaningful artworks that draw attention to themselves and disguise the processes of production and contemplation – calls for similar work methods in two different art spheres.

THE PAIN AND PURPOSE OF MINIMALIST SPECTATORSHIP

An uninitiated observer approaching one of Robert Morris' large-scale cubes (Figure 2.1) in an art gallery would become more aware of their own presence and vantage point instead of merely observing the art piece for its craftsmanship, as evidenced by an amateur photo of Morris' exhibition (Fisher 2013). Obviously, an artistic current such as minimalism, which favours duration, can find fertile ground in the realm of cinema where duration is inherent in the spectators' participation in the unfolding work of art. A visit to the Tate Gallery could be a more or less confounding experience, depending on the involvement and tenacity of the visitor, but being inside a cinema is an efficient form of temporary, consensual captivity. (This can occasionally become overwhelming, which explains the number of walkouts from Warhol's five- or eight-hour long films throughout their screenings, organised mainly in art venues.) A minimalist approach to cinema is also bound to redefine the physicality of the actor (who is no longer a stand-in for the character type he plays).

In her study of Chantal Akerman's filmic *œuvre*, Ivone Margulies cites the example of *I, You, He, She* (1976), where the actress (the director herself) 'exhausts a conjugation of positions for herself and her prop, a mattress. She adheres to Yvonne Rainer's move toward a more concrete everydayness in performance' (1996: 49–50). Akerman also moves away from the fiction-as-depiction-of-human-truth, since – in Margulies' words – in this real-time 'task-oriented performance', 'the object, rather than being the butt of an action called for by character or plot, is a prop to objectify and banalize gesture and movement' (1996: 50). The spectators' physiological response, their fatigue with these protracted representations, is also a necessary part of the reception process. Hopefully, it can enable spectators to recognise the marks of fiction in future films that are made to look authentic, yet employ referentiality and avoidance of *temps morts*; in other words, they are tailor-made for the spectators' casual involvement, designed to keep them engaged for a predetermined portion of their spare time and then send them off well-rested back into the production process.[6]

New Romanian Cinema as a Minimalist Filmography

Minimalism, like modernism – though without any reverence to medium specificity – warrants a shift of focus from representing reality to exposing the process of representation. This should be also taken into account in the analysis of any film pertaining to this tendency. It is generally agreed that the criteria of evaluation for classical and post-classical works of art are different in other art spheres and this precaution in aesthetic judgement should also be adopted in the domain of cinema. Regarding minimalist films, whether realities are depicted accurately should not be the focus of discussion. After all, the films themselves draw attention to the fact that there is no simple truth.

Could *Beyond the Hills* (Cristian Mungiu, 2012) be considered an accurate small-scale model of Romania? Maybe, maybe not. The film is, however, a slow-burning reenactment of a real-life case of exorcism and the sprawling circumstances that led to it. The metaphorical meaning of *Beyond the Hills* is a small part of its artistic worth. The texture of the film, the slow pace of the long shots, the immersive depth of field favoured in its cinematography and the opaque acting style of its three leads keep us simultaneously engaged with the diegetic world while at the same time contemplating it from a distance. Whether or not we expect any irrelevant details to slip away and reveal the underlying meaning, they do not; the diegetic world is of a piece. Is the depic-

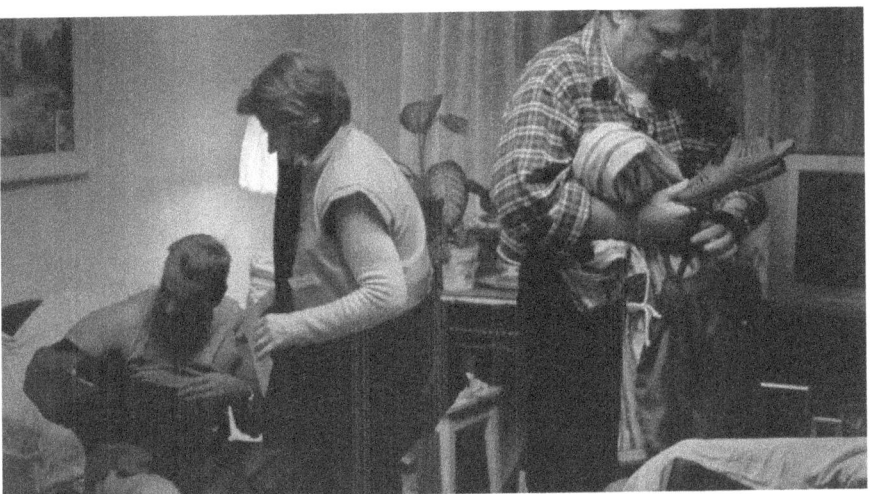

Figure 2.2 *The Death of Mr Lăzărescu*

tion of the Romanian medical system in *The Death of Mr Lăzărescu* (Cristi Puiu, 2005) a faithful one? Is this depiction a negative one? Maybe, maybe not. The point is that the pre-existing system (with a complex mode of operation and many inherent flaws) undertakes to treat the ailing protagonist of the film and no superior humanistic concern can bypass the pragmatic obstacles inherent in the system. Mr Lăzărescu is sick and in need of medical care, but so is everyone entering any hospital. The underlying provocation of *The Death of Mr Lăzărescu* is not the grimness in its depiction of an institution, but rather the overturning of comforting protagonist-centred narratives where the ordinary man, the film's protagonist, somehow manages to get extraordinary treatment. (Spectators trained by mainstream films would keep rooting for somebody to appear and give Mr Lăzărescu the attention he deserves.) The institution under observation here is not (primarily) the healthcare system, but the cinematic institution, which makes a rule of showing fortunate exceptions.

It must be added that this unwillingness to place the film's hero at the centre of their world also passes into *mise en scène* decisions, in films by Puiu and (to a lesser extent) Mungiu. The camera pans rapidly left and right to keep up with the action, voices are heard from outside the frame, Mr Lăzărescu travels to the far end of a long-shot *tableau* and is swallowed by the crowd in the hospital – the spectators' feeling that they have everything dramatically relevant under observation is constantly thwarted.

Bazinian Realism *versus* Minimalist Aesthetic

The reluctance to pour the narrative into a classical narrative shape has been explained by critics through the influence of André Bazin and his seminal theorising of the immanent realism of cinema, of which Puiu is a declared disciple (Gorzo 2012). Bazinian realism is, historically, linked to cinema's big break from its classical form, so there should be no surprise that it represents opposition to the same conventions as minimalism. However, especially in *Aurora* (2010), Puiu's chosen cinematography surpasses the striving for realism (long shots, depth of field) and goes a long way to perturb conventions of narrative cinema, the invisible editing of reality being generally performed by the author through an elliptical use of space and time. Such a disintegration of spectacle can very well be explained through the stated intentions of minimalist artists.[7]

In *Aurora* we follow the protagonist, Viorel (played by Puiu with scintillating opaqueness), for thirty hours of his life. This is condensed to three hours of diegesis, but even so the film meticulously captures the fluidity of time, as reflected in the changing luminosity of the sky. It still depicts the often confounding interaction between individuals crossing paths and clenching their teeth for long stretches of time in front of one another, throwing threats and insults at each other (resulting from their highly particular, slowly crystallised views of each other), which often force us to keep up with an indigestible amount of information, and yet, until the end of the film, there are characters and relationships that we can only speculate about. Moreover, despite the closeness of his observation of Viorel, the director refuses to offer clues about the morality of his protagonist, who, during the film, becomes a murderer, and provides no closure, except for Viorel's convoluted statement that his motivations surpass the rudimentary intelligibility imposed by the legal system. Also explainable through minimalist art principles (and strongly reminiscent of Akerman's films) is the inevitable bodily presence of Viorel, whose physical appearance and rhetoric seem to poison the atmosphere, irrespective of where he goes or with whom he comes in contact. The rifle he carries along is an accessory, a prop, for the overall menace of his alienated fictional character (one who no longer 'follows the plot', so to say, in living his life), set on his unpredictable and dangerous path. *Aurora* is a deconstruction of mainstream crime-of-passion narratives, suggesting how much incidental detail we would have to sift through – if mainstream films didn't eliminate it from the beginning for sake of dynamism – in order to understand (or think we understand) the killer. While glimpses of his murderous passion are intermittently visible, while watching the film we are invited to distance ourselves – to step backward and forward and change angle, as it were, rather than immerse ourselves more deeply in the story. Any attempt to view this film from one angle – of emotional amplification and aggravation, for example – would be as frustrating and partial as standing next to one of Judd's or Morris's cubes. Instead, one can view the observation of Viorel in *Aurora* as a full sensory experience, in accordance with what Margulies notes of minimalism: instead of an 'abstract spectatordom' [a characteristic of modernism], minimalism proposes an experience exercised by a subject whose 'corporeal density both guaranteed and was made possible by the interconnectedness of all its sensory fields so that an abstracted visuality could make no more sense than an abstracted tactility' (1996: 49–50).

The interpretation of *Aurora* as a minimalist *œuvre* is complicated by the question of authorship – the director is also the screenwriter and plays the main role – as well as by discourses that the film generates with regard to power and compromise, which can cue us to analyse it as a cine-poetic of sorts. While modernism is often self-reflexive, minimalism is believed most often not to be; however, it is hardly exceptional for a minimalist work to refer to its own making.[8]

Playful Iconoclasm

Corneliu Porumboiu's most discernible minimalist film is *Police, Adjective* (2009), in which Cristi, a policeman, is given a mission he doesn't believe in: to charge a teenager with marijuana use, which he considers an inconsequential misdemeanour. The slow tempo of the film is guaranteed to prevent any type of build-up – rather, it takes the meaning out of formal duties, such as following the suspect, and leads to the final confrontation over definitions of words between the hesitant protagonist and his no-nonsense boss, where, as is to be expected from a Porumboiu film, scepticism fails to prevail in the face of law and order.

One particular scene in the film, where the Cristi eats soup and is shown doing so for as long as it takes him to finish it, has become a sort of humorous landmark among casual spectators in discussing New Romanian Cinema – it is a metonymy for the tendency to represent reality full-bore instead of keeping the focus on the plot and eliminating irrelevant moments. Showing us this domestic scene tends to estrange the viewer from the 'man on a mission' conventional plot. Furthermore, it represents domesticity in a neutral, ambiguous way, rather than in contrast with the thrills of his professional life, as is often the norm of police procedurals. On the other hand, this approach simultaneously reinforces and denies the concreteness of the fictional protagonist, since it challenges us, as spectators, to acknowledge the police procedural conventions that we have unconsciously adopted.

Porumboiu's later film, *The Treasure* (2015), also successfully manages to problematise genre shortcuts – this time, in adventure films or perhaps in *rags-to-riches* narratives. Anyone who has seen *The Thief of Bagdad* (Raoul Walsh, 1924) could easily conclude that the lure of miraculous earnings is much more enthralling when shrouded in exoticism. By contrast, films about Wall Street employees (*Boiler Room*, Ben Younger, 2000; or *Margin Call*, J. C. Chandor, 2011) or other real-life money-makers are comparatively boring, even if their scripts are far more accurate than those of adventure films in depicting how fortunes are being made nowadays. Costi – a decent, ordinary man – looks for a buried treasure and finds it against all odds, but instead of diamonds and golden jewellery, it turns out to be stock shares of Mercedes-Benz. The scene where Costi, having sold the shares, tries to put together an actual, palpable treasure so that his son and his friends might literally grasp the importance of his discovery is a veritable comedic gem, and the humour derives wholly from depleting this surprising happy ending of any such triumphal note, as usually concludes an adventure film. *The Treasure* is also a minimalist film through what Kovács (2007) calls 'the rule of systematic variation of motives': whenever the story takes us one step closer to finding the long-awaited treasure, it changes direction.

Types of Minimalism and their Terms of Use

András Bálint Kovács recognises the variety of minimalist styles. He divides them into three main categories: metonymic minimalism (as evidenced by the work of Bresson and, we could deduce, the more recent Dardenne brothers films); analytical minimalism (Antonioni's films made between 1957 and 1966, as well as certain works by Chantal Akerman and Wim Wenders); and expressive minimalism, as typified by Ingmar Bergman, who would not shy away from expressive close-ups and dramatic light effects – the latter style being the hardest to reproduce, since it depends so much on the collaboration of Bergman's actors (Kovács 2007: 141). Kovács often focuses on the *mise en scène* – indeed, writing about Antonioni and Bresson gives him plenty to analyse in this respect – but when necessary he discusses the minimalism of missing backstory (Carlos Saura's 1966 film *The Hunt* teases the spectators with talk of past events that are never fully disclosed), the minimalist continuity in Akerman's *temps morts*-abundant *Anna's Meetings* (1978) or the network of symbolic motifs that are grounded in the films of Ingmar Bergman. As Kovács suggests, minimalism can operate with either element of film language and structure as long as it aims towards avoidance of – and estrangement from – widely used artistic effects.

In short, a large variety of breaches with classicism, drawing attention to the established (but not immanent) characteristics of an art form, can be sheltered under the umbrella term of 'minimalism'. *First of All, Felicia* (Răzvan Rădulescu and Melissa de Raaf) is a temporally and spatially restrained film about a divorced woman, visiting her parents in Bucharest, who is eager to go back to her son in the Netherlands. The action takes place during one morning against two backdrops (the conservatively decorated apartment and the flashy, noisy airport) and centres on Felicia's interaction with her mother and father as well as the people she calls in order to solve her problem of being stuck in Bucharest for another day. The amount of exposition in this film, while carefully structured to be revealed in bite-sized portions, is truly outstanding. While this is technically a short break in her busy schedule and the part of her life that she has 'moved on' from, with her immigration to the Netherlands, Felicia sees that her ties with her home and her parents' radically different way of living keep expanding. (It is enough for Felicia to miss her flight to make her dad jump to her help with his 'connections'.) It can be noted that, as in Antonioni in *La notte* (1961), Rădulescu and de Raaf's use of the airport as backdrop 'creates a feeling of loneliness within an agitated environment' (Kovács 2007: 151), hinting that 'human alienation is fundamentally a problem of adaptation' (Kovács 2007: 152). Felicia is more alert in this space and looks for a way to go back home, but during these scenes her mother is completely disconnected.

In what concerns the screenplay, at least, the domestic drama *Tuesday, After Christmas* (Radu Muntean, 2010) is also a minimalist film, a take on a love triangle. Paul, a middle-class married man, is in a relationship with a younger woman, Raluca, the dentist of his ten-year-old daughter. While the affair has established into some sort of routine and uncomfortable dependency, it is clearly sexually charged and energising and is consistently depicted as such. Paul's rapport with his wife Adriana, while fully functional and mutually respectful, is placed mainly in the realm of estimable, family-oriented consumerism. (Since the film takes place close to Christmas Eve, everybody is passing judgements on others based on what presents they buy.) While the film is structured on the – regressive, I would argue – schema of a man who must choose between two women, both women have autonomy and are dependent on him strictly from an unconscious, or deeper than conscious, emotional necessity. Thus without taking sides among the characters or being (especially) pious to bourgeois social norms, the film constructs our understanding of what he would gain and lose with choosing either of the women. (Finally, by leaving his wife, Paul is forced to move into Raluca's studio, which is large enough for a post-adolescent woman's needs but suddenly too small for a couple to live in. He is also likely to lose the custody of his daughter.) I have focused my analysis on the story structure because the *mise en scène* brings a far less liberal interpretation of the subject matter. From her first appearance in the film, the mistress is objectified by the camera, the actress' lean naked body in full view. The wife, though she herself has an attractive and neat look, is granted only a close-up of her naked foot while Paul gives her a foot massage. Secondary characters are brought to clarify the protagonists' standpoint on moral issues – they make short interventions and manage to characterise themselves in a few sentences – and the camera reinforces their peripheral importance by never shifting attention from the primary characters. In conclusion, while *Tuesday, After Christmas* can be seen to represent Romanian minimalism (narratively, it has the critical distance; as *mise en scène*, it resorts to long shots and *temps morts*), it can also be used to prove how stylistic austerity can still allow sexist or socially conformist traits to survive in these films.

The Morality of Minimalism

Minimalist musician John Cage famously said 'I have nothing to say and I am saying it', thus enforcing the association between minimalist art and amorality. Surely, minimalist art is not the vehicle of choice for artists' reflections on contemporary society. However, it can be argued that denying art any social or spiritual meaning is still saying something about the artists' perspective – at the very least, it betrays their scepticism about social change and moral transcendence and their view of art appreciation as an immediate, or, to borrow a term from Michael Fried, 'theatrical' experience. Furthermore, in drawing a sustainable parallel between John Cage's attitude towards his art and his implied attitude towards power, Joseph understandably names Cage an anarchist (2007: 62). Cinematic minimalism is even more frequently prone to analysis from a moral or spiritual perspective than Fine Arts or music. It would be easy to argue that Robert Bresson's films are religious art, Pedro Costa is a socially engaged filmmaker, Todd Solondz is an American satirist with leftist views, and so on, and that the minimalist construction of their subjects is intrinsic, not incidental, to their morality.

A potential gain from discussing films of the New Romanian Cinema through the framework of minimal art theory is a more articulate debate about the form of fiction films and how it relates to ideology. As this chapter has argued, minimalism disrupts the power play between artist and audience, which is as strong – if not stronger – in popular art than in gallery art. Many questions about structure go unasked. Why are we made to think, while watching mainstream films, that we could identify with a killer? Even more so, why are his motivations made understandable to rational, law-abiding spectators? Why do we indulge in our fantasy of easy wealth while we watch adventure films, especially in a way that associates easy wealth with moral validation? This refusal to submit to institutional conventions is motivated by the artists' wish to urge audiences to examine the act of reception. It is evidenced by the interviews given by Romanian directors, as well as through statements from first-generation minimalist artists.

Minimalism in the Romanian Context

There is one complicating circumstance in equating the NRC with the subversive tendencies of minimalism in the arts, in that the latter had a more established venue. Placing a pile of bricks[9] in the Tate Gallery in the 1970s was sure to stir spirits, but Romanian films of the past decade have had such a small audience that it would be almost self-delusionl to talk about social impact. It is estimated that only 88,000 cinema-goers bought a ticket to a Romanian film in 2011 (Stanca 2014), and the figures are usually better, but not by much. It is hard even for well-promoted films, which bring home awards from prestigious festivals, to go past the small core of cinephiles and attract at least 150,000 spectators. In 2015, Radu Jude's *Aferim!* sold 76,000 tickets after multiple weeks in cinemas and with screenings organised across the country, which is still much lower than that year's box office hit (*Fast and Furious 7* sold an amazing 650,000 tickets), and even significantly lower than George Miller's *Mad Max: Fury Road* (which sold around 165,000 tickets). Moreover, it is widely assumed and repeatedly stated that, at international festivals, the formally ambitious Romanian films fare better than those that are classically constructed. While this should not lead to the conclusion that directors would do better to 'go quaint', it is a sufficient appeal for more caution in the critical approach of their films. Financial risks do not represent a pragmatic issue when making arthouse films and the audience is self-selecting. While this is largely the fault of the Romanian film distribution system, it is challenging to present films that shake mainstream film viewing reflexes as successful when in actuality they never come in contact with mainstream viewers. Formal audacity is not the sole and most precious characteristic for praising the films, and it shouldn't be a justification for defending them from ideologically motivated critiques.

Dominique Nasta includes a chapter in her study of recent Romanian films called 'Less is More: Puiu, Porumboiu, Muntean and the Impact of Romanian Film Minimalism' (2013: 155–79). As the phrasing of the title suggests, it praises New Romanian Cinema films that equate formal audacity with artistic success through rather large leaps of logic.[10] Although it is standard practice in cinephile journalism to commend filmmakers for every proof of particular style, I have tried to argue that an accurate evaluation of these films calls for a more complex contextualisation and a certain dose of scepticism.

Minimalist artist Donald Judd famously opposed the idea of (then) new forms of sculpture being reductive, claiming they are unfairly held up against traditional forms: 'If changes in art are compared backwards, there always seems to be a reduction, since only old attributes are counted and these are always fewer. But obviously new things are more' (1965). The critics' role should be to identify and articulate these 'new things', simultaneously challenging those viewers who look to the artworks to find traditional forms of making meaning and those who are uniformly enthusiastic when facing novelty.

NOTES

1. A fairly in-depth discussion is to be found in Şerban's interview with Alexandru Budac on the topic of minimalism (Şerban 2008).
2. For instance in the short article titled *Iran prêt-à-porter*, where he criticises the overpraise of post-Kiarostami Iranian films (Şerban 2006: 57–9).
3. As demonstrated by an independent film critic Richard Propes of Solondz's film *Palindromes* (2004) (n.d.), found at: <http://theindependentcritic.com/palindromes> (accessed 14 August 2015).
4. Brent Lang, in an article announcing that Alonso has been chosen as filmmaker in residence for the Lincoln Center, identifies him as 'minimalist' (2014).
5. To consider Warhol a minimalist artist, we should primarily view him as a filmmaker rather than a patron of the arts and a pop artist. It was usual for him to employ steady-camera long shots that would capture a reposing subject for several hours. If this doesn't suggest reductionism, nothing does. However, an assessment of his individual works of art is hard to accomplish, as this would mean separating them from the notorious persona of Andy Warhol. In a more detailed analysis of Warhol's work, which I have published elsewhere, what started as an investigation of Warhol's *Screen Tests* (an epitome of minimalist cinema) led me back to his mechanical reproduction of celebrity portraits, which is to say, to a documented piece of pop art with a documented aim, often quoted in pop art theory. Warhol's celebrity portraits were interpreted as dissipating the aura of fame, the assumed uniqueness of star image. His *Screen Tests* could thus well be read as having a related purpose, since the subjects of these recordings (most of them well-known figures in New York City circles) would sit in front of their camera so long that their persona, the superficial impression they make, was brushed aside, leaving what might be considered their 'true personalities' to be revealed. Following this train of thought, Costa's portraits of ordinary villagers would be radically different in intent, although similar in means of representation (see Trocan 2011: 49–52).
6. Not to leave the impression that it was strictly a phenomenon of the 1960s and 1970s, time-dependant extreme minimalist cinema is alive and well. At the 2015 Rotterdam Film Festival, the premiere of *Park Lanes* by US director Kevin Jerome Everson offered an eight-hour exercise of endurance, taking the audacity of Akerman's *Jeanne Dielman, 23, Quai de Commerce, 1080 Brussels* (1975) to a new extreme. The routine of this film is even harsher and more provocative to the willingly captive audience. Reproduced from the press materials: 'With a screening time equivalent to a full day's work, Everson turns the cinema into a factory floor. Workers are observed while performing specific tasks, as well as while taking breaks.' Even more interestingly, the festival scheduled a screening of the film every other day, so if spectators would want to submit themselves again to the workday experience, they were given a chance to do so.
7. Branden W. Joseph's account of John Cage's orchestra arrangements testify to his

break with art as audience manipulation. After writing his scores to avoid any pre-established sound relations with practically institutionalised effects, Cage moved his attention to the mechanics of the orchestra performance:

> Going beyond a priori connections between sounds, Cage sought to disarticulate determinate a posteriori connections as well. Quickly realising that, once fixed, a chance score like *Music of Changes* (which was indeterminate with regard to *composition*) was still determinate upon *performance,* Cage made indeterminate the relation between composer and performer, as well as that between performer and listener – for instance, by arranging musicians around the audience so that no two listeners would hear the same 'mix' of sounds. [. . .] Cage's goal, in all such endeavors, was to eliminate from the acoustical experience – as much as possible – creation of any form that could be received as existing on a level above what Deleuze and Guattari, discussing what Cage among others, would term 'a plane of immanence'. (Joseph 2007: 77–8)

8. The minimalists' interests expand to accommodate reflexivity, as evidenced by Robert Morris' *Box with the Sound of Its Own Making*, which according to Joseph, 'problematized process and object, temporality and form, art and music, and, not least, performance and score' (2007: 64–5).
9. I am referring to Carl Andre's *Equivalent VIII*, discussed here: <http://www2.tate.org.uk/archivejourneys/historyhtml/people_public.htm> (accessed 15 August 2015).
10. Nasta does little to contextualise what she perceives as cinematic minimalism in any historical, cinematic or artistic account of minimalism. Her methods of approaching the films varies conspicuously (either way, being rather an *auteur*-ist account or old-school hermeneutic), and it is certainly debatable whether many films she chooses to discuss in this chapter are minimalist: *Liviu's Dream* (Corneliu Porumboiu, 2004) has a wealth of satiric and surrealist touches. Radu Muntean's *The Rage* (2002) was at least by comparison to his later work an attempt at an audience flick – and the commercial coolness of it cannot have been lost on Nasta, since she compares the filmic couple with *Bonnie and Clyde* (Arthur Penn, 1967). Likewise, Muntean's *The Paper Will Be Blue* (2006), a historical film in a Revolution setting, needs to be discussed separately in terms of representation, since the re-enactment of past events can hardly be compared to 'observational' cinema. Although, as I have argued, 'minimalism' makes for an encompassing label, this sort of use is bound to further muddle the analysis and evaluation of the films.

3. NO MELO: MINIMALISM AND MELODRAMA IN THE NEW ROMANIAN CINEMA

Ioana Uricaru

Recent Romanian films have been acclaimed internationally under various labels that attempt to name their specificity: Romanian New Wave, Romanian Minimalism, the New Romanian Cinema. Several common features have been identified by critics, scholars and reviewers, such as: a preference for raw realism, long takes, real time (or at least the illusion of it), naturalist performances, uncanny attention to detail.

One characteristic that has invariably been noticed is the absence of non-diegetic music (scoring), which Dominique Nasta repeatedly identifies as an exemplary trait of minimalism (Nasta 2013: 157, 168, 171, 187). On the other hand, Nasta also points out the strong emotional effect generated when music is exceptionally used – as source music, or during the credits – (Nasta 2013: 177, 196), which raises the question of the relationship between music, melodrama and realism, of their conjugation in the minimalist paradigm, and eventually of the definition of this paradigm. In his recent book *Romanian New Wave: An Introduction*, Doru Pop attempts to describe the nature of cinematic minimalism as best exemplified by the films of Cristi Puiu, proposing the term 'purposeful minimalism'. According to Pop, purposeful minimalism is an approach that is not determined simply by the 'reduction of the comic or melodramatic excess' or by 'limited resources'; it is a 'technical abstinence' in search of 'pure and simple realities' (Pop 2014: 66). While I agree with the phenomenological analysis of the resulting product (and of the accompanying experience), and I have written elsewhere about the historical context of Romanian cinematic self-restraint (Uricaru 2008: 398), I will, in the following pages, expand – or perhaps narrow down – the use of the term 'minimalism', arguing that its opposition to melodrama comes not just from the stripping down of the generically understood elements of excess, but from a worldview that rejects the myth of melodrama. In looking at the practical realities in the process of reaching this abstinent purity, I predictably chose to focus on the use of musical score in New Romanian Cinema, as music belongs by definition to melodrama, and its lack represents a statement as strong as the use of long takes and real time.

Examining the deep levels of textual productions reveals the paradox of how complicated a process lies behind the apparent austerity of some recent Romanian films, and therefore of the intensity of minimalist purposefulness. From the perspective of the practitioner, achieving the threadbare impression of what we perceive as a basic, essential, stripped-down version of cinema is actually a bold challenge that requires high technical expertise and the confidence of a very experienced filmmaker who is willing to take great creative risks.

Intuitively, the process of minimalism is usually understood as reduction to the essentials – the way in painting the picture can be reduced to shape, line or colour. An analogous approach was, for example, the Dogme 95 manifesto, imposing a series of interdictions in the filmmakers' pledge: we will not use artificial light, we will not use scoring, we will not use tripods, and so on. Called *The Vow of Chastity* (1995), the manifesto's intention was to steer cinema towards a condition of purity, where technological intervention and anything that intervenes between camera and reality are seen as contaminants. Preserving purity requires, in reality, risky decisions and sophisticated strategies. Behind every long take in a film by Cristi Puiu or Cristian Mungiu lie hours of rehearsals, precise choreographing of camera and actors, impeccable technique from performers and sometimes extremely challenging lighting set-ups. Any shot from *4 Months, 3 Weeks and 2 Days* (Cristian Mungiu, 2007) or from *Beyond the Hills* (Cristian Mungiu, 2012) took between half a day and two days to complete, and it was not always obvious what elements would increase the production time. One of the most elaborate shots in *4 Months 2 Weeks and 2 Days*, which required over two days of shooting, was the dinner scene in which the character of Otilia is seated, stationary, and speaks only a few words in the whole eight minutes, while most of the dialogue and action happens off-screen. What increased the difficulty of the shot was the continued search for the best framing, the best lens, the right texture and the right energy that would maintain the tension for the whole eight minutes. It becomes obvious that there is not enough physical time to shoot more than one shot per scene; therefore the action cannot be covered from different angles, there will be no alternative options in editing, and the directorial decisions made during production involve an unusual degree of risk-taking.

One of the chief elements seen as a potential contaminant of minimalist purity is the musical score (non-diegetic music), perhaps the most obvious convention of cinema. The audience's acceptance of a soundtrack that has no logical connection with the story, and its pretence that there is, in fact, a good reason for the music, are surpassed by only the fundamental convention of characters never looking at the camera. Theorist-practitioners such as Michel Chion and Stephen Deutsch have catalogued the various functions that can be fulfilled by musical score: a signifier of emotion, it 'tells the audience things that the director wishes them to know' (Deutsch 2003: 31), it construes irony (when the music and the emotional tone of the scene are at odds), it proposes a metaphorical meaning or interpretation of the images (such as the soundtrack at the beginning of *2001: A Space Odyssey*, Stanley Kubrick, 1968), and from a more practical perspective it helps with issues such as calibrating the pace of the scene (an added score will make it feel faster and more alert) and with easing transitions or making cuts feel smoother (Chion 1994: 8; Deutsch 2003: 31). In all these cases, music functions in what I will call an additive logic: the music is used to add emphasis, emotion, commentary, rhythm or continuity to the diegesis.

The purity imperative in recent Romanian cinema leads to the mystique of the diegetic world, whose integrity must be preserved above all – a principle illustrated by the reluctance to shoot and edit coverage, the attachment to continuous duration and to narrative time approximating real time and the rejection of unmotivated camera movements. We could conceive of the purpose of the 'purposeful minimalism' as residing in the protection of diegetic integrity – which, I argue, could find its roots in the radical reaction of post-2005 filmmakers against the permanent intrusion of ideology into the pre-1989 diegeses, as well as against the intrusion of vehement authorial perspectives into the majority of cinematic texts produced in Romania between 1990 and 2005 (such as Lucian Pintilie's *The Oak*, 1992; *Too Late*, 1996; *Next Stop Paradise*, 1998; or Mircea Daneliuc's *The Conjugal Bed*, 1993; *The Snails' Senator*, 1995; and *Fed Up*, 1994). Otherwise put, the integrity of the text requires protection against 'the tyranny of music as a superficial and manipulative tissue', in the words of sound designer Amie Siegel (2003: 148).

To understand the significance – and purposefulness – of protecting the diegesis from the contamination of musical score, I will examine three instances of the employment of music in recent Romanian cinema: an industrial, an extradiegetic and an intradiegetic context. This investigation of the aesthetic specificity of Romanian films as gleaned through the perspective of the use of music gives important clues about the position of recent Romanian filmmakers towards melodrama. I am particularly interested in understanding the logic of this aesthetic as expressed in the practice of production.

In the industrial context of Romanian cinema, musical score has a particular status that invites a default mode of using a musical score. The first step of financing a Romanian film is submitting it as a project for one of the biannual competitions organised by the Romanian Film Centre (CNC), which awards interest-free loans to production companies according to a point system that weighs the quality of the script at 50 per cent, the production company's performance at 25 per cent and the director's past accomplishments at 25 per cent. The competition is fierce – about five or six feature film projects receive financing in any session, and only those ranked in the first and perhaps second top spots receive amounts that will realistically constitute financing seed money.[1] The submission file requires a complete budget for development, preproduction, production and postproduction. In the template offered as a guideline, the music department is present and, additionally, the composer's work is highlighted with a fee set at no more than 4 per cent of the total budget (the same as the screenwriter and just 1 per cent lower than the director's fee). The composer is one of the three contributors that retain the creative/intellectual rights of their work, together with the director and the screenwriter (the composer is understood, legally, to mean the author of music especially created for the film). From the get-go the musical score is understood, by default, to be an essential presence in the production and post-production processes. When submitting a budget for the financing competition, a blank space in the 'music' column might raise unwanted questions – and would forfeit the possibility of including a monetary amount to justify the total budget.

As the awarded amounts cannot surpass 50 per cent of the requested budget, the production companies routinely inflate the numbers in order to obtain the largest amount possible. For example, for a film with a budget of one million USD, the amount of financing would be capped at 500,000, but if the submitted project can justify a 1,200,000-USD budget, the cap increases to 600,000. As a result, producers hesitate to eliminate the original music and composer from the budget at this stage, and these items end up being allocated funds regardless of directorial intention. The budget necessary for contemporary Romanian films varies between a few hundred thousand and a couple of million USD (probably the most expensive Romanian film in the last twenty-five years, Nae Caranfil's *The Rest is Silence*, cost almost 3 million USD but a 1 million budget is now considered average), and the CNC financing usually covers 20–40 per cent of the budget. The next step is looking for coproducing partners abroad, almost exclusively in Europe. This is when the original music budget line comes into play even more forcefully. European funding comes primarily from government programmes similar to the Romanian one, and in most if not all European countries, awarding funding for co-production is restricted by the requirement to have anything from 80 to 120 per cent of these funds spent on resources from that respective country, with a mandatory inclusion of some essential creative contribution.

As the language barrier usually precludes the use of foreign actors or screenwriters, and it doesn't make economic sense to bring crew from abroad for a Romanian shoot (with the notable exception of the sound department), the post-production process becomes a prime target for allocating budgetary resources that can be covered through foreign co-production funds. From this perspective, it is clear why the music score and especially the composer's honorarium constitute the go-to budget lines for this purpose, as the composer is considered a key creative position and therefore can satisfy the substantial artistic contribution requirement in order to access funds. At the latest European co-production market that I have attended with my project *Lemonade*, the Sarajevo Cinelink market, I met with representatives from about forty production companies and eventually found a co-producer from Germany. German companies have the distinct advantage of being able to access relatively rich regional funds, but this is counterbalanced by the disadvantage of requiring that those funds be spent entirely in that region. The budget for *Lemonade* is about 1 million dollars, and the German co-producer hopes to obtain up to a quarter of that amount from their regional fund for post-production expenses. Spending that money in their homeland of Saxony-Anhalt increases the chances of obtaining the funds, but what will help increase our chances is the fact that I offered two key creative positions – sound designer and composer – to be filled by residents of Saxony-Anhalt.

I am not necessarily planning to have a musical score in *Lemonade*. However, for now, and until we reach the end of post-production, in principle *Lemonade* is projected to have a composer and an original music score. Deciding against the use of scoring is becoming less of a forgone conclusion and more of an active position that I will have to defend and justify, as the planned scoring budget will have to be repurposed and the decision becomes a forceful one – to eliminate an element that is already assumed to be present. The decision to forfeit the musical score is an explicit one, an interventionist one, of removal and not simply of non-inclusion, which goes directly to the argument of purposefulness.

In the most significant films of Romanian New Cinema – from Puiu's *The Death of Mr Lăzărescu* (2005) to Mungiu's *4 Months, 3 Weeks and 2 Days* (2007) to Radu Muntean's *The Paper Will Be Blue* (2006) and *Tuesday, After Christmas* (2010), the only non-diegetic music is featured during the credits sequence (generally at the end, at both the beginning and the end in *The Death of Mr Lăzărescu*). The credits music, a mainstream convention widely used in Hollywood blockbusters, is seemingly the only concession made to the codes of impure cinema (cinema not abiding by the unwritten vow of integrity of New Romanian Cinema). These musical pieces fulfil some of the traditional functions already mentioned in the additive logic, such as establishing an emotional mood (the dynamic party-and-drinking music that starts and ends

The Death of Mr Lăzărescu might be in part responsible for the film's publicity campaign in the US, which marketed it as a dark comedy). The 1980s pop song at the end of *4 Months, 3 Weeks and 2 Days* and Nana Mouskouri's rendering of the famous Hebrew Slaves' Choir from Verdi's opera *Nabucco*, featured at the closing of Radu Muntean's *The Paper Will Be Blue*, put a time stamp on the films' narratives and, as Dominique Nasta has pointed out, they recover for Romanian audiences a specific zeitgeist in a very precise and condensed way, with the advantage of conjuring both the nostalgia for a past time and a comforting feeling of shared recognition (2013: 177).

Because during the 1980s, TV programming, reduced to two hours a day, was still the main medium of mass entertainment, musical pieces such as the choir from *Nabucco* – periodically broadcast by the national television – or the hit Italian song *Ci Sara* by Al Bano and Romina Power (used in the omnibus film *Tales from the Golden Age*, 2009) had the ability to gain emotional attachment over large swathes of the population, cutting across age, generation, gender, class and urban/rural distinctions. For Romanians who remember the 1980s, these tunes could simultaneously mean family dinners, staying home from school on snowy days, holiday celebrations, romantic interludes, vacations and first dates.

However, the choice of music still stays generally faithful to a certain notion of integrity: it usually comprises full, pre-existing songs rather than score composed specifically for the film. They are attached to the diegesis: they are part of the zeitgeist, present a counterpoint to the emotional tone of the film, or emerge directly from it. *Tuesday, After Christmas* ends with a piano piece played presumably by the character of the little girl in the film – her performance is endearingly bad, her chair squeaks, we hear the noise of the pedals when they are being pressed and the voice of the very patient teacher counting along. Already charged with associations and significance, the musical pieces are designed to maintain textual integrity as much as possible as a spillover of the text into the titles sequence, again a refusal of the additive logic. Their forceful and diegetically charged presence is emphasised by the fact that this is the first time we have heard any music, which in itself causes a strong emotional impact. Phenomenologically, the arrival of the credits song is equivalent both to a realisation – we have been following a text without musical score – and with a reinsertion into our world, which positions the diegesis as more-real-than-reality (the text is unadulterated, raw, direct, absolutely present, while the real world we regain allows for detachment, artificiality and strategies of deception).

Of the directors that can be grouped under the banner of the NRC, Corneliu Porumboiu is most interesting in his use of diegetic music – music that is justified by the story, when the characters listen to the radio, are in an environment where music belongs naturally such as a club or concert hall, or where they sing themselves (such as in *Beyond the Hills*, where one of the main characters sings a lullaby to the other) or play records, etc. In the few examples of this nature in New Romanian films, whenever present, the music has to fit into the story and contribute to it, or else remain so far in the background that it essentially blends in with the ambiance.

Porumboiu gives a superb example of integrating music within the diegesis in *Police, Adjective* (2009). The film is an exploration of meaning, both literal and figurative. The main character Cristi (Dragos Bucur) is a young policeman in a small provincial town, charged with investigating and making a case against a kid who smokes pot. Through long, uneventful scenes that observe Cristi while he watches the kid's house in a painstaking surveillance operation, and then through conversations with colleagues and superiors in the police station, we come to question and dissect the meaning of all the words used in the film as well as in our real lives. To 'investigate' means to passively watch, to 'do police work' means to fill out paperwork and make a narrative of everyday events or rather the lack thereof (Cristi's superior specifically asks him to create a dramatic narrative of crime, punishment and justice out of insignificant trespassing), to watch a 'police film' means to stare at non-action for a good portion of the two hours. The spoken and written words – and the signifier/signified dialectic – are examined relentlessly. Towards the end of the film, Cristi and his policeman colleague are called into the police chief's office (Figure 3.1). Before going in, the secretary tells them to 'wait a few minutes'. They sit down and we watch them doing nothing for a very long time – they are doing exactly that, waiting a few minutes, which makes us very aware of

Figure 3.1 *Police, Adjective*

the difference between reality and cinema, of how reluctant we are to accept real durations on screen and how our use of words – and images – conceals their meaning.

About halfway through the film, we see Cristi coming home after work, to his wife, Anca, who is a teacher of Romanian language and therefore attentive to semantics and semiotics. The scene makes use of music in a very bold way. Anca is listening to an Internet streaming of a pop song, performed by Romanian star Mirabela Dauer. The song is playing while an exhausted Cristi dines alone in the kitchen – his wife cannot step away from the computer, enraptured by the song – then joins Anca and they have a conversation that could be reproduced in a dictionary to exemplify the word 'subtext'. The song's lyrics speak about the kind of romantic love that gives meaning to existence and makes life worth living, and Cristi performs an ad-hoc analysis calling into question the logic and meaning of the lyrics.

The characters' commentary on the words of the song is of course a way to reveal questions and doubts about their relationship and their marriage, about their different outlooks on life and romance, on meaningfulness and priorities, on happiness and love. Anca doesn't 'pay attention' to the words until Cristi points them out – he works on a literal, denotative level, while she is receptive to connotation and performs a hermeneutics of the text (Figure 3.2). Beyond the rich, layered and yet naturalistic dialogue, what surprises most is the director's courage in playing the song three times in a row and of recording the whole scene in one very long shot.

In what I have called additive logic, which constitutes the functioning

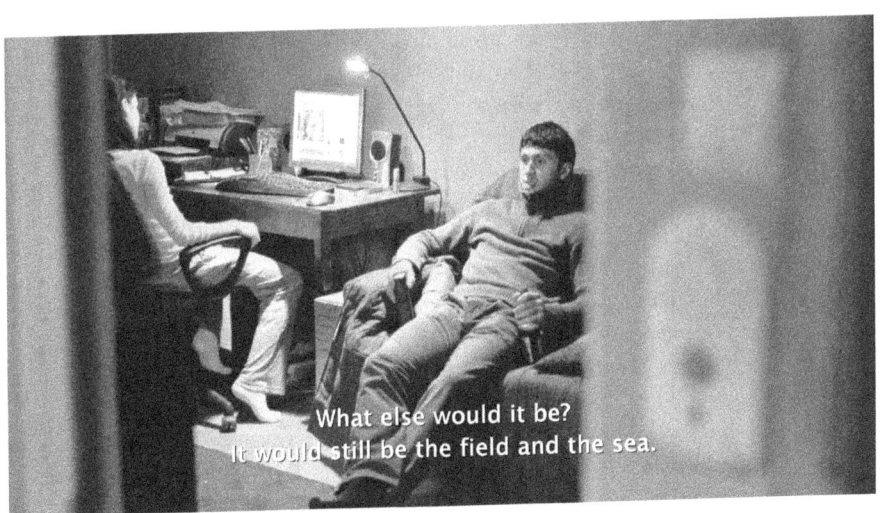

Figure 3.2 *Police, Adjective*

framework of mainstream – and indeed of most – cinema, redundancies are to be eliminated and the meaning (narrative, emotional, symbolic) has to be as concentrated as possible by intervening with added cuts, added sounds, added signifiers such as words and gestures, added music. In the non-additive logic of Romanian minimalism, the content of the text should have the same organic integrity as the real world. This doesn't mean that the text should attempt to reproduce reality one to one (although this is often the result), but that the text should have a metabolism and a physiology that approximate the behaviour of the real world: just as much dramatic substance, just as much symbolic content, just as much uninterrupted presence. From this perspective, we can glimpse the opposing positions of New Romanian Cinema minimalism and the approach of melodrama, which rests on precipitating the most intense and emotionally expressive bits from the thick fluid of reality.

The thrice-repeated song becomes a determinant of the scene that supersedes the usual primary determinants (image and performance) in order to maintain the integrity of the text. The scene has its own physiology, controlled by the repeated song and not by the convenience of the camera or the necessity of line delivery or the requirements of mainstream narrative economy. By using the music not only as a diegetic element (for example as one more component that is talked about or that conveniently plays into the characters' intentions), by using the song not just as an added device but as an internal generator and controller of the diegesis, Porumboiu achieves an integration of music with the text that finally supersedes the additive logic. The success of this scene in terms of opening a completely different vision of music in cinema confirms that the analysis of music in New Romanian Cinema is a productive point of entry into the 'purposeful minimalist' aesthetic and it could elucidate, at least partially, the nature of this purposefulness, revealing its intriguing opposition to melodrama.

In her recent book *On the Wire*, devoted to the famous American TV series *The Wire* (2002–8), Linda Williams crystallises the definition of melodrama as a genre that expresses an a priori acceptance of the (moral) good/bad dichotomy. In melodrama, according to Williams, the genre conventions are shaped not by the imperative of an overt, sometimes overwhelming display – for display's sake – of exaggerated sentiment, convoluted conflicts, extreme character traits and the whole battery of emotion-inducing techniques (what is commonly known as melodramatic excess). This excess is nothing but a means to an end: a proven and effective methodology for involving the audience, psychologically and even physically (when tears, anxiety and adrenaline secretion are involved), in the story of good and evil that fight and attempt to vanquish each other. The protagonist(s) fight(s) the antagonist characters and a host of other obstacles (from societal forces to historical circumstances to personal or family prejudice to unbelievably bad luck) in an attempt to help the good side win. Sometimes they win, sometimes they lose – the relevant aspect here is the premise: the hero/protagonist identifies and embraces the good and fights for it until he or she wins or dies trying. The conventions of the genre are the tools employed to ease the audience's empathy with this good cause, in the most effective way possible, which often means the most embodied, emotional, visceral way.

The foundational myth of melodrama could be defined therefore as the belief in the existence of a good that is opposed to evil, complemented by the protagonist's ability to choose this good and act in its support. As Williams writes:

> melodrama is the dramatic convention in which timely social problems and controversies are addressed. It is not opposed to what we recognize as realism. Rather, it enlists realism to generate outrage against realities that could and, to its creators should, be changed. Melodrama feeds upon the problem of these realities – the very injustice of them. To this extent, much melodrama is allied with dreams of revolution or at least the kind of change that might be able to rectify the social injuries they diagnose. (2014: 104)

Within these parameters, Williams makes the argument that the genre is defined not by its conventions but by its foundational myth – there is a way to make melodrama without excess and without music when the narrative embraces the foundational belief in the good–evil–fight triangle.

In recent Romanian cinema, we consistently encounter the same two characteristics that raise questions about *The Wire*'s melodramatic quality: a commitment to realism and a rejection of musical scoring. But while *The Wire* manages to stay within the mythical territory of melodrama (although it brilliantly questions and redefines it), the essential texts of New Romanian Cinema reveal a fundamental, existential distrust in the very premise of melodrama – the existence, comprehensibility, accessibility and dynamic opposition of good and evil. In other words, in recent Romanian cinema the idea that people can count on the existence of an order of good and evil, and have the agency to enter this order at their point of choice, is being exploded and then recalibrated at a much more modest scale.

Elucidating the cultural roots of this attitude goes beyond the scope of this chapter, but just to give a loose context let us recapitulate some facts about Romanian tradition and culture. Most Romanians identify as Christian Orthodox even if they are not practising – and one of the characteristics that sets aside Orthodoxy from Catholicism and Protestantism is a component of mystical arbitrariness in man's relationship with God: grace is given, not earned. The Marxist–Leninist ideology that was enforced on the country from 1948 to 1989 had a decidedly melodramatic narrative: we were all soldiers enlisted in the fight on the side of the good (building the perfect communist society) and against the bad (bourgeois ideology, capitalism, imperialism and so on). It is no wonder that after decades of intoxication and outrage erosion, there was a reaction against modes of proclaiming righteousness, drawing clear lines and proposing any model solution. Finally, it is perhaps not accidental that among Romania's most important and enduring contributions to world culture we count the founders of Dada (Tristan Tzara) and of the theatre of the absurd (Eugen Ionescu), two artistic stances that preclude the melodramatic imagination. For complex reasons that include historical, geopolitical and anthropological circumstances, Romanian culture has a tradition of openness to the complications of shifting ambiguity and of distrust of the melodramatic promise of moral decantation.

In a way, melodrama does what every narrativisation does: makes sense of the 'excess of reality', to use Baudrillard's concept, in order to make it palatable and manageable. The position of the New Romanian Cinema is that melodramatic excess (of plot intricacies, of character transformation, of revelations, of dilemmatic enhancements and sharp moral conflicts, of emotional dynamism and display) can obfuscate actual conflicts and dilemmas that might not fit the conventions of melodrama but correspond to real circumstances. Minimalism – the excision and avoidance of excess in aesthetic form as in narrative modality and in character development – becomes a way of recovering the complexity of social systems and human behaviour that cannot be encapsulated in a good/evil dynamic (although we would very much like that to be the comfortable case). An example that can put in sharp relief the difference between treating roughly the same themes in the key of melodrama *versus* the key of minimalism is the comparison between *4 Months, 3 Weeks and 2 Days* and Florian Henckel von Donnersmarck's *The Lives of Others* (2006). Dealing with the same period (mid-1980s) in two countries from the Eastern Bloc (Romania and East Germany respectively), the films broach similar subjects and themes including surveillance, underground/illegal activity, the repressive apparatus, the necessity of a female character to sacrifice her body and surrender it sexually in order to help somebody else (a friend needing an illegal abortion in the Romanian film, a lover whose career and freedom are endangered in the German one). The stories are even set in similar environments: the middle-class intellectual milieu from the capital city. Where the Romanian film famously sticks to an austere aesthetic of long-take, no-music, real-time, naturalist performance, painstaking attention to detail and extreme restraint in the use of obvious tropes (the word 'communism' isn't uttered once), the German text opts for a heavily plotted narrative complete with spectacular betrayals and conversions, excursions into West Berlin, sex triangles, suicide and phone spying that calls to mind scenes from *The Wire*. While the German film responds very satisfyingly to the demands and expectations of an audience trained to understand moral issues through melodrama (consequently winning an Academy Award for Best Foreign Language Film), Mungiu's work prefers to strive for an authenticity that actually proves much more effective in representing that historical period and the true nature of moral dilemmas in totalitarianism. It is significant that in *The Lives of Others* the moral transformation of the antagonist, a STASI agent, happens in a spectacular fashion, under our very eyes, as he is listening to classical music through the wiretap that he has set up to spy on the protagonist – a fine piece of melodramatic construct that makes full use of the emotional effect of music. However, in the real context of a regime enforced by a bureaucratic apparatus of repression, this plot point becomes preposterous, erasing the ruthlessly mundane experience of totalitarianism. The conceit of a STASI agent having a moral conversion because he listened to Bach exposes the extent to which *The Lives of Others* is less a work rooted in the specificity of totalitarian East Germany and more a generic Hollywood melodrama that happens to be set in 1980s Berlin. The crucial plot point of the protagonist – a playwright whose work is successfully produced on the East Berlin stage – discovering, with surprise and horror, that his phone is being tapped by STASI, is an equally preposterous revelation tailored for the already-set melodramatic reading of the targeted audience. My personal memory of having lived in the same milieu of writers, poets and playwrights in communist Romania tells a different story: any intellectual with access to an audience (be it print publishing, radio broadcast, filmmaking or stage performance) was not only very aware of being permanently under close surveillance, but even knew personally the Securitate officer who was responsible for that surveillance, as they were routinely called in for friendly talks. Sometimes, the officer would hint in conversation at details (such as the placement of objects in the house), which made it clear that somebody – perhaps a close friend who was visiting regularly – was an informant. This sounds already like fodder for a life-changing revelation heightened by moral indignation in a Von Donnersmarck film, but in fact things were a lot more complicated – the friend reporting to the Securitate might have been doing you a favour, informing about relatively harmless things such as the presence of a Solzhenitzin novel on your bookshelf and not relaying the much more dangerous things that were said in conversation. While *The Lives of Others* uses melodramatic conventions to offer an already-familiar narrative rooted in the good-evil-fight triangle, complete with outrage and dreams of change, *4 Months, 3 Weeks and 2 Days* stays true to the detailed specificity of historical circumstances and human behaviour and prefers an 'excess of reality'.

Williams is right to point out that the mere absence of music does not suffice to make a text realist (as opposed to making it a melodrama). However, I will argue – following Pop – that in the case of New Romanian Cinema the treatment of music reveals the purposefulness of finding an alternative to melodrama, preserving the focus on personal experiences but rejecting the instinct to inflate their emotional impact so as to better make a moral point. The implicit critique that this cinema performs of melodrama is that it uses excessive conventions to get across a simplified morality myth. Instead, New Romanian Cinema proposes simplified, minimised conventions to reveal the complicated, messy texture of reality.

Just as the essence of melodrama rests not in its conventions of excess but in its myth of moral outrage and the possibility of revolt against it, the essence of this particular realism rests not in its apparent reproduction of reality on a one-to-one scale but in its laying bare of a complicated, absurd reality that precludes revolution in the melodramatic key and requires a different set of tools for negotiating one's survival. In the case of the exemplary texts of New Romanian Cinema, the minimalist attitude is about honestly confronting the messiness, ambiguity and complexity of the 'excess of reality', complete with lack of closure, of clarity or of bounded, knowable moral territories. The moral legibility of melodrama (a Brooksian concept usefully recovered by Williams) is inauthentic for filmmakers such as Puiu, Mungiu, Muntean and Porumboiu – a point brilliantly made in the latter's *Police, Adjective*. In the second-to-last scene of the film, a high-ranking police officer (played by Vlad Ivanov) uses dictionary definitions to beat his subordinate into submission and prove that his interpretation of the concept of conscience does not exist in the language – it is not written (and therefore not legible) in the dictionary. We can therefore articulate a major opposition: melodrama expresses a belief in the power of narrativisation, while recent Romanian minimalism explores the limits of narrativisation, the territory where the tormentor is also your only ally, where the daily grind precludes heroic gestures and transformations, where morality is not legible but has to be fished out from murky waters that inevitably soil you. If the spectators of melodrama are meant to gain comfort and pleasure from empathising with characters that respond to outrage with a matching amplitude of gesture and emotion, the spectators of New Romanian minimalism are perhaps meant to experience the baffling, shocking sensation of the void that follows exposure to unacceptable, well-hidden truths – to the excess of reality. In a way, the spectators themselves are put in the situation of a melodrama character, confronted with a cold-hearted, stunning revelation. How they will react to this spectatorial experience might reveal who they are as characters in their own life stories.

Note

1. At the 2014 session of the CNC financing competition, thirty projects were submitted in the fiction feature film category and only five received financing in amounts between 600 and 280,000 USD (Centrul Național al Cinematografiei Results 2014).

PART II

INTERMEDIALITY/INTERTEXTUALITY

4. 'EXHIBITED SPACE' AND INTERMEDIALITY IN THE FILMS OF CORNELIU PORUMBOIU

Ágnes Pethő

(Re)framing the *Tableau* Shot

'Realism' and 'minimalism' have been perhaps the most frequent labels attached to the style of the New Romanian cinema. Critical analyses have highlighted the connection between the austerity of cinematic language, the hand-held camera, the long tracking shots and the heritage of neorealism, as well as documentary, *cinéma vérité* practices of the middle of the twentieth century.[1] However, some of the features of these films, as I will show through the example of Corneliu Porumboiu's works, should also be considered in relation to the aesthetic of so-called 'contemplative, slow cinema', which has etched out its own niche on the international film festival circuit in the last decades and should be interpreted not only in comparison with any earlier New Wave in European cinema (and defined accordingly, as a belated New Wave in the region), but also within the contemporary context of the so-called post-media age.[2] This double perspective is in fact closely connected, as slow cinema is quite often practised as a kind of post-media cinema, making use of the possibilities of convergent, digital media, blurring the boundaries between fiction films and documentaries, feature films and motion picture installations.[3] This chapter will cover a very narrow slice of a possible larger research area determined by this premise: I will merely focus on one particular type of image, the prolonged *tableau* shot, and the way it is repeatedly used and inflected in Corneliu Porumboiu's first four full-length films. Although the *tableau* shot is not an exclusive stylistic device of so-called slow movies, it is undoubtedly a prominent and versatile figure, providing these films with a pronounced permeability towards painting, theatre and installation art.

Defined as a frontal long take, filmed with a more or less static camera, the *tableau* offers the impression of viewing a painting, a photograph in motion, or gives the viewer access to what seems like the interior of a box, thus harking back to the theatrical *tableaux* of early cinema. What is common in the different manifestations of the *tableau* is that it sustains both a particular type of spectatorship (based on the distance maintained between the viewer and the screen), and a particular relationship between the characters, objects and the natural or architectural space visible on the screen, which all appear to be sealed off and closely interconnected within the frame of the *tableau*. In comparison we may remember how in classical narrative films the spectator is continually drawn into the illusory world of the screen. The mobile camera eliminates our position of fixed distance, and, in the words of Béla Balázs, it puts us spectators 'in the very heart of the image'. He writes: 'The camera takes my eye along with it. . . . I have no standpoint of my own. I travel with the crowd, I fly up, I dive down, I join in the ride' (2010: 99). In classical cinema, this identification with the camera together with seamless editing enables a fluid orientation in space, where the spectator sees the cinematic world oblivious of its frame. Conversely, in modernist films of authors like Michelangelo Antonioni or Jean-Luc Godard, for example, we are constantly reminded of watching a world through a frame with a deliberate composition of elements, sometimes with an abstract fragmentation of space achieved through images modelled on the characteristic de-framings of individual photographs. These images are then employed as the basic units of a kind of photo-graphic 'writing' (cf. Stewart 1999), resulting in a high degree of abstraction and conceptualisation of the cinematic discourse.

The specificity of the *tableau*, in the most general sense, is that it appears (in the words of Balázs 2010: 99) as an 'insulated space, manifesting itself as a microcosm', to which there is no fluid access such as a mobile camera would allow; instead it is something we are not in the middle of, but are always watching from outside. So while such a shot preserves the voyeuristic distance of spectator and screen, inasmuch as we view the scene from the same fixed position for a considerable length of time, this is a construction in which we are more in the position of the 'pensive spectator' described by Raymond Bellour (2007) and Laura Mulvey (2006). In Bellour's words, the relative stillness of the images 'tempers the "hysteria" of the film [. . .]. Though drawn more deeply into the flow of the film, the spectator is simultaneously able to reflect on it with a maximum of intensity' (2007: 122). At the same time, observing characters absorbed in their action and interacting with each other in a static shot, as if arranged on a canvas, a stage or in a photographic light box, may paradoxically heighten *both* the sensation of reality and that of artificiality, producing the effect of an 'artification' or 'exhibition' of an everyday experience. In this way, the more 'vernacular' *tableau* shot appears to take shape according to a similar, yet somewhat reverse principle to the *tableau vivant* proper (that is, the explicit reproduction of a painting), in which, according to Brigitte Peucker (2007: 31), the flesh of human presence introduces the 'real' into the 'image', merging reality with representation. Whereas the *tableau vivant* proper creates the illusion of pictures coming alive, the *tableau* shot reframes a 'slice of life' within the aesthetic constructedness of a picture. Accordingly, both the *tableau vivant* and the *tableau* shot can be seen as highly transgressive and performative structures that build on tensions ensuing from the duality of the illusion of immediate access to the real and the perceivable mediation of the 'image'.

Although *tableau* shots are frequently used in the works of other contemporary Romanian directors such as Cristian Mungiu[4] or Cristi Puiu, and can be seen in the films of other Eastern European directors,[5] Corneliu Porumboiu's films seem remarkable for the way in which they systematically and self-reflexively reframe this type of image, excavating its multiple affordances (drawing on a combination of realism and artificiality) to offer different conceptualisations of the same structure.[6]

12:08 East of Bucharest (2006): The Irony of Framing and De-framing

Analysing Carl Theodor Dreyer's early films, David Bordwell explains:

> as image and structural principle the *tableau* is firmly tied to a tradition of what we might call *chamber art*. Historically, the stylistic premises of this tradition are the perspective discoveries of quattrocento panting and theatre, whereby space is conceived as a cube to be filled by human figures. With the increasing secularization of subject matter, in northern baroque painting, chambers housing the Virgin or various saints were replaced by everyday interiors, the bedrooms, parlors, and kitchens of bourgeois homes. (1981: 41–2)

Here, we see people engaged in quiet, everyday activities in situations where space is often divided by doors and windows. Thus Bordwell traces back the origins of an important type of the early cinematic *tableaux* in film to this tradition in painting whose masters can be seen in Johannes Vermeer, Samuel Dirksz van Hoogstraten or Pieter de Hooch.

Porumboiu's *12:08 East of Bucharest*, a deadpan satire of postcommunist Romania, is a film that rests its whole argument on reframing and de-framing, both visually and conceptually, this traditional *tableau* construction. The story of the film is simple: sixteen years after the revolution, in a small provincial town East of Bucharest, two days before Christmas, on the anniversary of Ceaușescu's infamous last speech just before he was ousted, the owner and talk show host of a shabby local TV studio, for lack of better eye witnesses, invites a cranky old pensioner and an alcoholic schoolteacher to discuss whether or not there was a revolution in the town.[7] The crucial question to be answered is this: did people come out to protest against Ceaușescu's regime before the dictator fled Bucharest in his helicopter, at exactly 12.08 on 22 December 1989, or did they react only to the news of the events in the capital city? So was there or wasn't there a revolution on a local scale in this provincial town? The film begins with the introduction of the main characters and reaches its climax with the talk show itself, with a last scene at the TV studio. In the first part we see a series of *tableaux* depicting domestic interiors presenting each of the talk show participants in their natural 'habitat' in the manner close to what Bordwell described as 'chamber art'. As we pass from one drab interior to another, the poorly lit spaces stuffed with heavy furniture are further narrowed down by massive doorways acting as interior frames, which, in contrast to Dutch paintings, appears not as a means to extend the space but serves (sometimes quite frustratingly) to partially block our field of vision. The medium-length shots do not allow us very close to these characters, who are also often partly masked by walls or furniture. In such shots, as the camera does not move closer to the human figures or follow them around,[8] people become no more important than the objects filling up the space. Bordwell's remarks on Dreyer's technique are valid in this case as well: 'our attention swerves to objects and furnishings; details of these chambers become as clearly articulated as figures' (1981: 48). Paradoxically, such compositions constructed around the characters thus manage to de-centre their subjects even though they are physically placed in the centre, by pushing them into the background and by diverting our attention towards other items in the rooms, pictures on the wall, TV sets turned on, and so on.

Moreover, we may observe that a *tableau* shot is usually remarkable not only for what it boxes in but also for what it boxes out. As opposed to the notion of 'off-screen', which denotes, according to Pascal Bonitzer (2000), an imaginary/fictional dimension, 'off-frame' can be conceived as an actual, material space, outside the cutting edge of the frame encompassing both the extension of the diegetic world, and the space of the spectator facing the screen. In Porumboiu's film, beside the allusion of the doorways, the duality of off-screen and off-frame is also continually present through the repeated action of characters speaking on the phone or communicating with someone beyond the visible space. At the same time, due to the frontality of the shots, the *tableau* offers a reflexive vantage point from which the spectator's gaze may behold the image as a container, and from which on-screen space becomes not merely staged in a theatrical *mise en scène*, but can be conceived as a display, an 'exhibited' space. We can see a condensed form of this in the scenes in which the characters are shown through the windscreen, boxed inside a car. The TV studio with its aquarium-like glass box in the end appears as an explicit, self-reflexive manifestation of this type of space, where the perception of the cinematic image as a transparent window to the world is effectively replaced by the impression of watching an arrangement in a showcase, a shop window, making the passage in the film from 'domestic chamber' to public diorama. In the TV studio the disembodied voices of the people who phone in paradoxically personify the external vantage point of the spectators' gaze.

Bordwell notes that the pictorial stasis of *tableau* compositions is usually balanced either by 'situating intense narrative action in the human face' (in the case of Dreyer, 1981: 41) in close-ups, or by the play on the movement of the figures within the fixed frame judiciously used to mask or reveal areas of space (in the case of Feullade's theatrical staging technique, 2005: 50). Although there are a few expressive close-ups (like that of the old man having a meal alone, sitting opposite the kitchen window, with a blank stare),[9] these are not really offered as counterpoints. Instead Porumboiu insists on the dull, repetitive actions in the frame (eating, speaking on the phone, passing the time around TVs that nobody is actually watching). What really counterpoint the rigidity of these pictures are the dialogues with their colourful language (the ironic puns, allusions, and so on) and the visual gags based on the repetition and incongruence of elements within the given frame (for example, the exterior long shot of the typical East European run-down block of flats with the glitzy new Western car parked outside, the old man dressed as Santa Claus playing a naughty practical joke on some kids by lighting a firecracker in the hallway and running away). A leitmotif of incongruity and displacement is perceivable in the characters and situations running through the film: the TV show host is an engineer-turned-amateur philosopher and media entrepreneur, a Chinese shop owner in the Romanian provincial town is acting as a local, and references to the French revolution vis-à-vis the alleged provincial 'revolution' of the small town are both connected to the figure of the alcoholic teacher.

These displacements culminate in the scene at the TV studio, where the motley crew of talk show panellists arrive to find that instead of the traditional Christmas programme, a Latino band is bringing down the house. When the panellists take their place in front of the camera a young cameraman begins to film them in a shaky, amateur video style. The scene can be interpreted also as an ironic, self-reflexive reference to this being the new, fashionable way to do video recordings, and, as such, in contrast with the 'old' static cinematography made with cameras on tripods that is implicit in the *tableau* aesthetic employed throughout the film. Here, through this clumsy camera work we witness a hilarious disintegration of the *tableau* (and of the neat arrangement of the three figures, the white haired pensioner and the morose, alcoholic teacher sitting on each side of the pompous talk show host, as an ironic 'holy trinity'). The images become de-framed and askew and the panellists move around and fidget uncontrollably while the telephone interventions of viewers make the scene more and more cringeworthy. In his seminal article on 'décadrage' Bonitzer speaks about 'the sadistic irony of off-centre framing' (2000: 201), and Porumboiu uses the visual gag of characters trying to stay in the frame or being pushed out of it in a sophisticated interplay between framing and de-framing, between the still photograph of the town hall in the background and the chaotic movement in front of it, which ultimately calls attention to the principle of *decenteredness*, of *being off-centre*, *out of frame* as the main metaphor for the whole film. All the characters are derailed from their original course, as mentioned before, and ultimately the film presents a failed attempt to reframe the everyday idleness in a provincial town, far from the centre of action in Bucharest, as 'revolution'.

POLICE, ADJECTIVE (2009): BOXING IN A 'THEATRE OF THE ABSTRACT'

In *12:08 East of Bucharest* we move from one box to another and the *tableau* compositions create the feeling of observing specimens encapsulated in their naturalistic environment (the blocks of flats appearing as piles of concrete boxes housing the smaller rooms that the protagonists inhabit) or, in the penultimate scene before we return to the image of the grey buildings, show-

Figure 4.1 *12:08 East of Bucharest*: the irony of 'décadrage'

cased in a glass box. In Porumboiu's next film, *Police, Adjective*, we don't just observe the characters from a distance, in the figure of the policeman who is surveilling three high-school students (two boys and a girl) suspected of using drugs; we observe, almost in real time, a character who is himself observing other characters from a distance, and moving continuously on a meandering trajectory around the same typically dreary postcommunist blocks of flats, garages and sports grounds, in and out of spaces presented as boxes, again in a string of *tableaux* (alternated with travelling shots tracking his movement). At one point the protagonist is seen going around the labyrinthine offices of the police headquarters, entering from one small, cubic room into another, while this vertigo of boxes within boxes is emphasised through the recurring in-depth compositions of hallways.

The teenagers smoke hash cigarettes, and Cristi, the young policeman, is supposed to arrest one of the boys after the other one informs on him.[10] Because smoking a few cigarettes of hashish does not really seem such a big deal (with no evidence about who provides the kids with the drugs), and considering that probably even the law will be changed soon to tolerate such an offence, Cristi is torn by a crisis of conscience, and does not want to ruin the kid's life. He keeps procrastinating, looking for ways to avoid the arrest. Like the previous film, *Police, Adjective* also culminates in a *tableau* staging of an improvised panel of three people arranged symmetrically in a room. In this absurd, anti-climactic final scene, Cristi's commander puts him in his place by making him look up the meaning of the words 'conscience', 'moral', 'law', and 'police' in a dictionary, and finally we see detailed field tactics to apprehend the kid being chalked up on a blackboard. Thus the letter of the law imposed with the authority of the hierarchic institution of the police prevails over the qualms tormenting the young detective. Instead of the act of 'de-framing' that emerged as the ultimate metaphor in the previous movie, here we have a film which is built on the structural principle of 'en-framing': *containment, entrapment, the definition of the indefinite* (that is, putting things into a box, underscored by the image of the grid, of various inner frames, of things neatly organised in bookcases, and so on). The character's movement in and out of boxes is echoed many times over in this way, on a more conceptual level.

In his highly influential works on art history Michael Fried (1980) introduced the notions of 'absorption' and 'theatricality' for describing the passage from realist painting to modern art. While the realist tradition presents figures that are absorbed in their daily activities and seem totally 'oblivious' of the viewer (resulting in a *tableau* that is 'hermetically' sealed off from the world surrounding it), modern art relies on the presence of the viewer in front of the artwork; its constructedness is obvious and the awareness of the spectator's gaze (the quality he names, 'theatricality', 'to be seen-ness') is encoded within the picture.[11] However, Fried also observes, following the ideas of Chevrier

(2003), that the emergence of large-scale photographs, made accessible not in print form but on the walls of a gallery, has effectively reopened the field of debate between 'absorption' and 'theatricality' with photo exhibits like Jeff Wall's lightboxes, for example, that manifest both of these qualities. I suggest that the recent revival of the *tableau* form in films of the slow cinema canon has produced further challenges to these concepts through many different ways of foregrounding (or even thematising, as we see here) the inherent duality of theatricality (constructedness) and absorption underlying the *tableau* aesthetic. Porumboiu's *Police, Adjective* seems not only to exploit this duality, but to expose the clash between the absorptive features of the scene and awareness of the image as a construction, to confront direct access to the flow of life with different forms of mediation, to brutally overwrite presentation with representation. We see the policeman completely absorbed in his daily activities, in a true-to-life environment, deeply embedded in his world (as the series of inner frames suggest), and there is no scene in the film that would show us his subjective viewpoint; we always behold everything from the 'outside', watching it all perceptibly from somewhere off-frame.[12] The *tableau* shot appears here not as a vehicle for satire, but as a minimalistic container for reality presented as a fragment torn from a larger whole, a 'found object', framed by the viewfinder of the camera.

Moreover, by reframing modernist practices of reflexivity in conceiving the image as a collage of media,[13] Porumboiu introduces into the film a subtle interplay of image and language. Self-consciousness about language runs as a leitmotif in the film: people in this film don't just engage in conversation, they pedantically dissect the meaning of words, the relationship between signifier and signified, both in their domestic lives (see the scenes between Cristi, the policeman and his young, schoolteacher wife, arguing about the lyrics of a pop song), and in situations involving official hierarchy (the policeman and his boss), as we see in the last scene. In addition to this, if *12:08 East of Bucharest* infuses the rigidity of static compositions with the expressivity of verbal language, in *Police, Adjective* we see an increased emphasis on different forms of writing. This ranges from the colourful, exclamatory statement of the graffiti inscribed in an open space that we see behind Cristi at his place of stakeout, to the handwritten police report (an iconic imprint of the conflict between what is personal and what is official), and the printed page in the dictionary, which lays down the conceptual meaning of words. The final face-off about semantics appears as a cynical literalisation driving to the extreme the mechanisms of distanciation, abstraction (or 'theatricality') that are already manifest in the visual construction of the film. The scene also happens to be the most rigid and meticulously composed visual *tableau*, arranged around another secularised 'trinity'. The decorative bowl of fruit brought in and placed in the middle of the table even brings back a touch of the deadpan humour based on incongrui-

Figure 4.2   *Police, Adjective*: the world as *tableau*, and reality as dictionary entries

ties that dominated the previous film, not only because it is out of place in a police station, but also because it reminds us of the conventional symbolism of the holy trinity in orthodox icons (as we see it, for example, in *Andrei Rublev*'s Troitsa).

This last scene stages a kind of 'theatre of the absurd', conceived as a 'theatre of the abstract', by playing off the objectification of written language[14] against the 'absorptive' realism of the images unfolding the situation in which Cristi is caught up. 'Police' (used as an 'adjective' in the title) thus becomes the attribute of the procedure in which subjective conscience is stifled by bureaucracy, and the complexity of reality is traded in for entries in a dictionary.

From 'Black Box' to 'White Cube' (*When Evening Falls on Bucharest, or Metabolism*; *The Second Game*)

Porumboiu's next two films, *When Evening Falls on Bucharest, or Metabolism* (2013), and *The Second Game* (2014), both make tentative moves towards the format of expanded cinema within cinema, interrogating through the extension of *tableau* issues of cinematic mediality, representation, and reflexivity. As a consequence, both are much easier to describe as experiments bordering on installation art than as traditional movies.[15] *When Evening Falls on Bucharest* is about a film director named Paul who is supposedly in the process of making a film; however, throughout the movie we see him on the outside of any film set, in the off-space of the actual process of shooting a film. This external vantage point was richly exploited in his previous works. (The whole town of Vaslui was in the 'off-space', compared to the revolutionary events of Bucharest in the first film; Cristi was also an outside observer of the drug-consuming kids in *Police, Adjective*, whose position as an outsider was absurdly sealed by the letter of the law and the definitions of the dictionary.)

Here, however, observing something from a distance is replaced with reflexivity: the filmmaker is contemplating the film he is making, and films in general, viewing the world from the emotional and intellectual standpoint of a cinematic author. The very first shot of the film visibly introduces this change in the character's position by showing the man and the woman from behind in the interior of a car, looking at the street ahead of them as if sitting in front of a movie screen (as a reversal of scenes in earlier films in which we were looking in at people sitting in a car). However, the viewer's position remains the same: it is still a composition boxing in the human figures, a visual structure Porumboiu uses even more consistently throughout this film than in any of his previous works. There is no impression of urban *flânerie*;[16] the sights of Bucharest revealed through the window remain in the background and mostly off-focus, and the protagonists appear as if locked inside a shell.

Paul explains to his actress and mistress the difference between analogue and digital film, how one cannot shoot for more than eleven minutes using traditional film stock, and how digital technology enables the extension of the shot almost indefinitely, adding that he prefers the structure resulting from restrictions imposed by analogue technology. Accordingly, the film itself is constructed of a series of just seventeen long takes (all around seven minutes), each of them presenting nothing more than a dialogue between the two protagonists (and occasionally a third person). The effect is paradoxical: while it makes visible the structural limitations of its own analogue medium (the film was shot on traditional film stock), it actually seems to demonstrate the real-time effect enabled by digital technology as we watch these scenes run much longer than we are used to in a conventional fiction film. And in this fragmentation into autonomous one-take sequences we have an even more pronounced emphasis on the inherent qualities of the *tableau* shot, as each element of composition becomes magnified. As we watch the man and woman talking in these fixed-frame, medium-length shots, we see spaces fluctuating between haptical and optical (between an actual room allowing the protagonists to move around, and a mere frame with the figures appearing as in a stretch of a frieze, pushed against the more or less ornate walls of restaurants and bars, emphasising the painterly qualities of the image).

We can observe the furnishing, the colours, the physical bodies of the actors, the gestures they use to make these spaces their own, to 'consume' them as the dialogue progresses. We can savour each of the audio-visual ingredients, and experience it in 'a slow mode', just as we would do in a video installation that runs in a loop (and has no necessity to include elements of theatrical drama). In

Figure 4.3   *When Evening Falls on Bucharest, or Metabolism*: permutations of a *tableau* shot of protagonists at a table

fact, one could well imagine the film transformed into such a project. Moreover, what we see is a series of permutations: the shot in the car is repeated twice (once at night, once during daytime), there are two scenes in Paul's apartment, both times with a love scene taking place off-space (with the spectator being left to stare at closed doors), followed by three scenes at the restaurant and the bar, concluding with two scenes in the trailer used for the purposes of the film shoot. The trailer appears as a really claustrophobic box in which, quite adequately, we are shown on a video monitor (in another box), the visceral images of the director's endoscopy taking us further, into an enclosed, biological 'space').[17] Because we see no progress being made, no real dramatic conflict arising or being solved, despite intellectual debates and fluctuating emotions in the dialogues, the scenes are only loosely linked; we could even view them in a different order. So, we may observe how the format of the image defines our perception of its content (just like the parable of eating with chopsticks suggests in the dialogue), and we may wonder whether analogue film is being framed in these prolonged *tableau* shots by a digital medium, or vice versa. Is nostalgia for the limitations of analogue film poured into a form tailored by digital cinema? Furthermore, does the film self-reflexively enact the passage of moving images from the traditional 'black box' of the movie theatre to the 'white cube' of the art gallery (cf. Uroskie 2014), or their 'reflux' (the content of a gallery movie poured into a fiction film), as the 'metabolism' of slow cinema?

The clash between traditional and new media forms, the position of looking at the screen as if watching a box, appears in an even more challenging way in Porumboiu's next film, *The Second Game*, which reframes a peculiar 'found', or 'ready-made' media object (literally an image within a box) as a relic from the communist past. The filmmaker and his father sit down to watch an old VHS tape of a football match (a showdown between the teams of the military and secret police) that the father refereed in 1988, one year before the downfall of the Ceaușescu regime. Father and son remain off-frame for the entire length of the match; we stare with them at the fuzzy image of the snowy game in 'real time' and listen to their spontaneous commentaries. In contrast to the poetic intensity of Douglas Gordon's and Philippe Parreno's *Zidane: A 21st Century Portrait* (2006), which also incorporates an entire football match, Porumboiu pushes the boundaries of slow cinema[18] towards an austere docu-installation form combining the mere 'objecthood' of the TV broadcast and the unscripted, untheatrical, not too revealing or verbose commentary. While the film about Zidane foregrounds the affordances of the latest digital technology in film, Porumboiu makes a statement through the palpable, unassuming realism of the 'poor image' (cf. Steyerl 2009), and also through what remains unsaid and unseen.

Accordingly, both of these two films also draw attention to features that defined the earlier works. In each of these films there is dramatic action going on, only somewhere else, in the mental dimension of the off-screen. The revolution took place in Bucharest, not in Vaslui as we learn from *12:08 East of Bucharest*, the police raid on the drug users is planned but not shown in *Police, Adjective*; a film is being made but we cannot see it in *When Evening Falls on Bucharest*, and around the time of the football match shown in *The Second Game* Ceaușescu's regime is in its death throes. Through an emphasis on moments of stasis, on *temps morts*, on counterpointing action with non-action, these films reveal the small-scale dynamic, the 'texture' of a private reality, the stillness of the everyday that underlies colloquial interactions, ordinary events, as well as the large-scale mobility of history. In all its different variations presented here, Porumboiu constructs the cinematic *tableau* as a container for the interaction between frame and out-of-frame, cultivating in it a tension between the 'commonplace' and the conceptual, the ironic perspectives offered by different media – television, language, painting, digital and analogue film, video – in the context of the ubiquity of moving pictures,[19] and a genuine yearning for immediacy and authenticity in the cinematic image.

Moreover, in each of these films, the *tableau* appears not only as a liminal space conceived between the visible and the invisible, the grand theatre of politics and the private world of everyday people, it also reveals in different ways the shifting demarcation between the 'public' and the 'domestic'. In *12:08 East of Bucharest* the low-key cinematic parody of the *tableau* mode originating in genre painting can be interpreted as a satirical commentary on the post-communist spaces of life where the new petty entrepreneurs set up their businesses in the old housing projects by repurposing private apartments.[20] The makeshift TV studio and the places where the protagonists live not only look similar, they are in fact the same specimens of rooms in typical Eastern European blocks of flats built during the time of communism. *Police,*

Adjective pushes the irony further by emphasising the similarities between the building of the school, the police station and the policeman's home. The protagonist of *When Evening Falls on Bucharest* discusses his film project in his own apartment presented in the same way as Dutch interiors opening up through inner frames, yet the empty walls and basic furniture make it look more like a film stage waiting to be properly furnished than a home. Equipped with a brand new Apple computer the apartment speaks of a new way of life mimicking Western models, and appears as a clinical and impersonal 'any space whatever' in the middle of the nation's capital. *The Second Game* not only folds the off-screen space onto the TV screen through the commentary, but also welds intimacy, family, politics and public broadcast, past and present into a dissoluble unity through the single image exhibited in front of the viewer.

Short Epilogue: Dreams in a Box

After these experiments, Porumboiu's last film to date, *The Treasure* (2015), seems to leave the allure of the 'white box' of contemporary art, and to return to the magic of the 'black box', to more conventional narrative structures in the form of a contemporary fable more in line with the trend of magical realism but with the minimalism associated with New Romanian Cinema. We have the archetypal story of a quest reduced to a search for buried treasure in someone's backyard, igniting the imagination of the characters, and a symbolic journey into the layers of the past through the attempt to dig it up. We have the already familiar frontal shots of offices, with rooms filmed as boxes, and we have a laborious search for an actual box that appears as a symbolic container for the characters' dreams of wealth. But as the rigorous *tableau* arrangements become scarcer and the screen is filled with the airy, atmospheric shots of the garden, the story also dissolves into a fairy tale. Despite the manifold irony of the situations, the austere realism is diluted with the light-hearted and unlikely ending, where the prosaic content of the box, the real, palpable treasure, is exchanged for a fantasy shared by father and son. Thus the search for the hidden treasure box unearths some old myths and a childlike longing for everyday miracles, but blazes no untrodden trails regarding the *tableau* composition. It remains to be seen whether this means a depletion of Porumboiu's aesthetic of the 'boxes', or whether the *tableau* form can still act as a relevant, performative space in his future films.

Acknowledgements

This work was supported by two consecutive grants of the Romanian Ministry of National Education, CNCS – UEFISCDI, PN-II-ID-PCE-2012-4-0573 and PN-III-ID-PCE-2016-0418.

Notes

1. Cf. Nasta (2013), Pop (2014), Gorzo (2012), Gorzo and State (2014), and so on.
2. On the general changes brought about by the so-called post media age in cinema see: Kim (2009), Casetti (2011), Pethő (2012), and so on.
3. See some of the films of Alexander Sokurov, Pedro Costa, Carlos Reygadas, Tsai Ming-Liang, Lav Diaz, Apichatpong Weerasethakul, and so on, which resist categorisations into conventional film genres and are conceived as a series of slowly unfolding motion picture *tableaux*. Parts of some of these films have also been presented as video installations in art galleries.
4. For example, Cristian Mungiu's *4 Months, 3 Weeks and 2 Days* (2007) used a series of variations on frontally framed *tableau* shots in which people were placed into box-like small spaces (in many ways similar to the parametric technique of Yasujiro Ozu) in order to confront the viewers with the harsh realities of the Ceauşescu era in a blunt, matter-of-fact style.
5. Other major Eastern European authors who have also created some memorable *tableau* shots in their films include, among others, Béla Tarr, Szabolcs Hajdu, Sharunas Bartas, Lech Majewski, or more recently Pawel Pawlikowski. See an analysis of Lech Majewski's, Sharunas Bartas's and Ihor Podolchak's painterly images in Pethő (2015a).
6. His works can therefore be placed also alongside European authors like Joanna Hogg or Roy Andersson who have both elaborated highly original film styles based predominantly on the rigorous aesthetic of the *tableau*. See a comparative analysis of their films in my article (which contains the first draft of the ideas presented here), 'Between Absorption, Abstraction and Exhibition: Inflections of the Cinematic *Tableau* in the Films of Corneliu Porumboiu, Roy Andersson, and Joanna Hogg', in *Acta Universitatis Sapientiae: Film and Media Studies*, 2015, Volume 10 (Pethő 2015b).
7. It is Porumboiu's home town, Vaslui, but in the film it remains unnamed.
8. This is quite similar to the technique of silent cinema also described by Noël Burch as the Primitive Mode of Representation (see Burch 1990).
9. This can be seen in contrast to Mungiu's *4 Months, 3 Weeks and 2 Days*, which also employs a series of *tableau* compositions, and balances them with highly expressive close-ups of faces, or medium close-ups (even if one of the most intensive images shows only the back of the protagonist's head).
10. He does this most likely because he hopes to win the girl for himself.
11. Although Fried's notions have been widely debated, and he himself later revisited his original ideas, the two concepts may prove productive in describing the dynamic of the cinematic *tableau* in these films.
12. Thus our presence as spectators is inscribed in the film's techniques devised to produce images 'to be seen', to be comprehended at one glance as a *tableau*. This feature is emphasised also by Gorzo (2012: 277) relying on Porumboiu's own words about the film.
13. We can also note here strong similarities with Robert Bresson's use of actors as 'models' along with parallels with Jean-Luc Godard's emphasis on words and images within the cinematic frame.
14. The strictest sense of the written word is found in the 'letter of the law', as the film well demonstrates.
15. Both have also been heavily criticised for this and considered as more or less failed experiments (partly because they were met with expectations regarding traditional genres of fiction or documentary films, and partly because viewed as experimental works they were not considered radical enough).

16. Strangely enough, the tracking shots of *Police, Adjective* offer much more of a *flâneuristic* presentation of a postcommunist urban landscape (although, not without a sense of irony: emphasising uniformity and monotony).
17. Although there is indication that this endoscopy is fake, and is used by the director merely to delay the shooting, it is nevertheless an authentic projection of the director's anxiety (and ironic, self-reflexive introspection).
18. Porumboiu even inserts a joke about it in the film, remarking in a dull moment that nothing really happens on screen like what we see in his films.
19. All of his characters 'cohabitate' with traditional pictures or new media, and most of them are even directly engaged in some capacity or another in the industry of making pictures (the talk show host is also the owner of the local TV studio, *When Evening Falls on Bucharest* is about making a film, Porumboiu's father appears as a protagonist in an important televised event).
20. We see this situation presented in Cristi Puiu's *Stuff and Dough* (2001) as well.

5. FILMING THE CAMERA: REFLEXIVITY AND REENACTMENT IN *RECONSTRUCTION* AND *NIKI AND FLO*

Katalin Sándor

Lucian Pintilie's cinematic *œuvre*, dating back to 1965, has become a most significant reference point in the discussion of contemporary Romanian cinema. His films, made during the period of communism,[1] were equally sensitive to modernist aesthetics and their socio-political context. After 1989, Pintilie was among the few directors who continued their work by raising similarly valid and artistically challenging questions about cinematic representation and the socio-political situation in postcommunist Romania.[2] Therefore a historical approach to media reflexivity in his films might be particularly revelatory: spanning communism and postcommunism, Pintilie's work reveals a different facet of reflexivity in each historical context.

Cinematic reflexivity (by exposing the presence of the camera, the process of filming and the mediality of the moving image) can be conceptualised as a modality that disrupts the transparency of the film and discloses the event of representation as an intervention. The disruptive effect of reflexivity is described in some theoretical approaches through the metaphor of the break, gap or hole. According to Paech, the mediality of the filmic image is exposed by the 'breaks, gaps, and intervals of the form processes' that 'refer to the media conditions of their construction' (2000). These are observable in various instances of montage, superimposition or framing techniques, as well as in 'appearances or traces of materiality and dispositive construction that "figure" in the film' (Paech 2000). András Bálint Kovács, who identifies abstraction, subjectivity and reflexivity as the main principles of modernist (European) art cinema, considers that reflexivity 'creates a *hole*, so to speak, in the texture of the fiction through which the viewer is directly connected to the aesthetic apparatus of the fiction' (2007: 225). Reflexivity (especially in late modernism) 'means not simple self-referentiality but also a fundamental *critical approach vis-à-vis the medium* within which it is realized' (Kovács 2007: 225).

In Pintilie's films, reflexivity as a critical approach to the medium and its socio-cultural and institutional contexts has a historically changing function, where the act of mediation, in terms of technical means (camera, voice recorder, photo camera), is exposed not merely as recording some intact reality, but as a way of intervening and constructing what counts as 'real', provoking a critical reflection on the ideology of representation. Before 1989, cinematic reflexivity could function as a critical act disclosing the crisis of representation and the mechanisms of maintaining the illusion of transparent, 'realistic' images in state-sanctioned films and propaganda.[3] After 1989, by foregrounding the private use of the camera and the home movie in *Niki and Flo* (2003), Pintilie offers a reflection on a domesticated medium, located at the intersection of older, local cultural practices and new ones and representing the altered post-communist mediascape and social context.

Below I will examine media reflexivity as critical practice in *Reconstruction* (1970), and will argue that the film has become an aesthetic and conceptual antecedent of contemporary Romanian cinema. Furthermore, I will discuss the function of reflexivity within the historically changed context of *Niki and Flo*, pointing out that Pintilie's cinematic *œuvre* is not only one of the precursors of contemporary Romanian films, but in this particular film – besides maintaining allegorising tendencies – it also displays characteristics that anticipate the stylistic and conceptual paradigm of New Romanian Cinema.

Reflexivity in *Reconstruction*

Pintilie's *Reconstruction* (1970) – banned by censorship[4] and therefore almost a novelty on its re-release in 1990 – is based on Horia Pătraşcu's short story,[5] and inspired by real-life events. The film has been apostrophised as the 'tragedy of violated reality' (Mihăilescu 2010: 10), and as a metafilm about cinematography, reflecting on the ethics of representation. Given its historical context, *Reconstruction* is referred to as a dissident film (Nasta 2014: 88), as it is one of the first films 'produced during communism in Romania to explicitly criticise authority and indirectly the abusive power of the regime' (Pop 2014: 164).

Reconstruction stages the absurd, farcical reenactment of a drunken fight between two young students and a bartender at a small bar for the purpose of making a propagandistic-educational film about the effects of alcohol. An amateur camera operator, a prosecutor, a policeman and a professor take part in the reenactment, whose purpose however is undermined from the beginning by the disinterested, tired and occasionally jovial prosecutor (what happened is in his view a 'stupid thing', an 'accident'). During the continually interrupted filming, the two youngsters are being encouraged with promises they would not have to face trial and imprisonment for injuring the bartender and destroying some property if they cooperate. In the end, one of the students, Vuică dies due to an unintended head injury. The film seems to expose the process of reenactment in a quasi-documentary style, yet any stylistic homogeneity is deconstructed by Vuică's elusive, harlequin-like acting; by the farcical scenes and the allegorical character construction; by the insertion of clips from music videos and TV cartoons; by the surrealistic imagery of woods and flying geese, and by the heterogeneous 'architecture of sounds' (Mihăilescu 2010: 12).

Pintilie's film ironically foregrounds the workings of a quasi-institutionalised yet amateurish camera, directed by a representative of the authorities, thus grasping the dynamics of power as reflected in the act of propagandistic image-making. Nonetheless, in *Reconstruction* the criticism of authority and the abuse of power is not unequivocal or predictable: the film validates multiple viewpoints about the reenacted past event, and avoids construing power relations according to a reductive, binary logic. The social and interpersonal relations continually shift from hierarchical, power-abusive and paternalising acts to humanising gestures; from humiliating orders to cooperation, even to resistance and subversion, identifiable in Vuică's behaviour.

In the film, the unprofessional camera recording becomes a parodic extension of state authority: its quasi-institutionalised gaze penetrates the private sphere, which, in its turn, is disrupted by the participants' subjectivity and the vulnerability of their bodies. The process of reenactment affects the participants' bodies, producing the unruly excess of wounds and death. This reenactment, described by Vanessa Agnew as a 'body-based discourse in which the past is reanimated through physical and psychological experience' (2004: 330), is however unable to transcend its own limits. Indeed, as Agnew writes about the ethics and politics of historical reenactment, its 'central epistemological claim that experience furthers historical understanding, is clearly problematic: body-based testimony tells us more about the present self than the collective past' (2004: 335). In Pintilie's film reenactment is thus not about the collective, but the personal past, and yet the reenacted event is both familiar and grotesquely foreign. It is the act of transposing the past occurrence on to film that becomes the event itself, in which reality and (its) representation cannot be separated.

At the beginning of *Reconstruction* (in a flash-forward), the violent scene of the reenacted fight is extricated from the chronological narrative flow and thus evokes the past event through a self-iterating act. The repeated scenes, the intrusion of the clapperboard, accompanied by off-screen directorial instructions, enhance spectatorial detachment and foreground artificiality by exposing reenactment as mere role playing. But its very process slowly takes over the body. The images touch the viewer in a visceral way: mud, blood and saliva, the fluids of the setting (located on the shore of a lake) and those of the bodies on screen intermingle, folding the role playing into the real. The instructions for the two youngsters, given by the policeman sound like a parody of (normative) realism: 'It should be exactly as it was. (...) Don't imitate, don't pretend! (...) Break the soda bottle with all your heart! (...) Do as we tell you to do!' The unreflected insistence on 'realism' is undermined by the resistance of the participants, or rather by the vulnerability of their bodies.

If we juxtapose Pintilie's *Reconstruction* with Virgil Calotescu's 1960 eponymous film, a state-commissioned propaganda reenactment, the critical, subversive reflexivity of the former becomes even more pronounced. Calotescu's documentary recasts a real-life event, the 1959 robbery of the National Bank of the Romanian People's Republic, as communist propaganda material. The six perpetrators (former Jewish members of the communist nomenclature) are caught, sentenced to death and executed (except for the only woman in the group), but not before playing themselves in the filmic reconstruction of the robbery commissioned by the secret police. This reenactment also foregrounds the camera with a paradoxical claim at unequivocal transparency and objectivity of the propagandistic documentary. The voice-over narration describes the camera in tune with the official ideology of representation: it is an 'eye', an 'automatic scribe' recording history in 'live images identical to reality' that 'cannot be questioned by anyone'.

Pintilie's *Reconstruction* reflects on the mediality of film through displaying the diegetic camera and the image-making process that – despite its grotesque and farcical character – is nonetheless a fatal act of power. Moreover, the diegetic camera is subjected to close scrutiny – it is opened up and its entrails exposed – which reveals on a narrative level what Paech (2000) calls the 'media conditions' of image making. While the prosecutor handles the diegetic camera, the actual shooting camera replaces it and 'allows' the viewer to look through its lens. This sequence of images displays a 'gap' (Paech 2000) in the transparency of the film by showing acts of framing and de-framing, zooming in and out in blurred and sharpened images, folding the diegetic into the non-diegetic and disclosing the mediated accessibility of the real. The act of substitution between the two cameras foregrounds the mediality of the image and exposes both the gaze of the diegetic camera and the gaze of the actual one, exposing the former. Moreover, the film folds the on-screen and the off-screen into one another, exposing the perception of the real as a medially layered, heterogeneous experience: the ambulance we see on the screen of the small bar TV set during the live broadcast of the football match drives off-screen and enters the diegetic world.

Wounds and Scars in *Reconstruction*

Reconstruction confronts the viewer with images of scars and wounds. The first scar is shown in a de-framed close-up as an almost palpable, conceptually elusive, still image: we see an injured head (the bartender's, as we eventually find out), where a scar, the trace of a past wound, is 'archived' by the skin, thus pointing to a ripple in time, to the evasive, folded multiple temporalities of the reenactment event. The other wounded party is Ripu, whose hand accidentally catches a nail when he and Vuică are compelled to destroy a wooden stand during the reenactment. Vuică's fatal wound is not shown, but only the stream of blood gushing from it.

Thus the film displays reenactment as corporeal (and psychological) trauma through the image of wounds and scars, and also by exposing its mediality through self-reflexive interruptions and ruptures. The corporeal wound is an excess that implodes meaning and representation, and opens up the gap of a twofold failure: 'a failure to speak about the body, [and] a failure to keep silent about it' (Nancy 2008: 57).

The traumatic rupture of the wound in *Reconstruction* reveals the fundamental vulnerability of the body and its exposure to the other – a body that is not simply represented but is also disrupted by representation. The event of reenactment, therefore, becomes an unpredictable corporeal experience: the vulnerable yet resistant and foreign body becomes the medium of the past-in-the-present, making it impossible to separate the past occurrence from the perspective of the present, or the 'real' from (its) representation.

Like the way in which the modernist aesthetics of the film leave the wounds unsutured, the viewer is left to deal with a disruptive excess of representation, where 'the body is always other' and the image is 'an othering of the real' (Morrey 2008: 29). Within the appropriating educational film, Ripu's wound (and his exposure to the crowd leaving the football stadium), and ultimately Vuică's wound and death are an uncontainable, erratic excess. Thus Pintilie – with his subversive irony – exposes the absurdity of the politics of representation in the context of communism through the appropriation of the body and its past by a grotesque moralising discourse.

Reconstruction and Contemporary Romanian Cinema

Due to its metafilmic inquiry, critical potential[6] and modernist poetics, *Reconstruction* has become a point of reference for Romanian cinema and film criticism, yet its influence is far from being forthright. Nasta, for example, considers the film a 'harbinger for the younger post-Communist generation of filmmakers' (2014: 94), and, according to Pop, it left a 'distinctive mark' on post-2000 Romanian cinema with its dark humour, minimalist treatment of time and space, its documentary look and its non-judgemental mode of raising questions (2014: 165).

The status of the film as aesthetic precursor of the 'new Romanian realism' is contested by Andrei Gorzo, who questions Marina Roman's claim that *Reconstruction*, *Microphone Test* (1980) by Mircea Daneliuc, and *The Death of Mr Lăzărescu* (2005) by Cristi Puiu are '*sui generis* investigative quasi-reportages', '[e]ach with a perfectly justified contiguity of space and time' and 'classical structures in which ellipsis is declared *non grata*' (Roman 2010: 174). Gorzo points out differences between *Reconstruction* and *The Death of Mr Lăzărescu*, with regard to character construction, narration and editing. More important for this study, however, is Gorzo's observation that Pintilie's film is closer to a 'certain allegorical stylization' (2013: 6),[7] and does not build up a narrative 'restricted by the physical possibilities of an observer' like Puiu's *The Death of Mr Lăzărescu* (2013: 7).

With regard to post-2000 Romanian cinema, Mónika Dánél (2015) considers *Reconstruction* a precursor to contemporary (and not only cinematic) reenactments of the 1989 Romanian events (the so-called 'televised revolution'), due to the reflective way in which Pintilie connects a technical means of mediation (the camera) to the reenactment, as well as the 'reality' of a past event. Thus *Reconstruction* can be linked – among others – to Corneliu Porumboiu's *12:08 East of Bucharest* (2006), Radu Gabrea's *Three Days before Christmas* (2011), or to Irina Botea's reenactment-performance, *Auditions for a Revolution* (2006) – as Dánél suggests.

The question of the mediated 'reality' of the historical and personal past, the 'televised revolution', is at the core of Porumboiu's *12:08 East of Bucharest*. The film stages a talk show in a provincial Romanian town (Vaslui), hosted by the owner of the local television station. The topic, discussed by the host and his two guests – a history teacher and a retired man – is whether there was or not a revolution in their town, or, more specifically, whether people went out to protest before 12:08 – the time when Ceaușescu fled the capital on 22 December 1989 – or after. The theme of the impossibility of reassembling the past event, as well as the unruly, albeit prearranged process of filming the talk show within the amateurish studio environment, resulting in black humour and self-ironic cinematic reflexivity[8] – all of these point back to Pintilie's metafilmic inquiry in *Reconstruction* as a possible conceptual-thematic (rather than stylistic) antecedent. Moreover, in Porumboiu's film the remaking of the past does not only emerge as a discursive question and as a live media event, reminding of the 'televised' revolution, but it also evolves unpredictably in a non-discursive, corporeal way (as it does in *Reconstruction* despite the controlling efforts of the authorities). The effort of the participants in the talk show to force their bodies into the TV frame evokes the first chaotic television broadcasts during the December 1989 events, in which revolutionaries were struggling to fit within the camera frame at a moment when the making of a televised media event and the making of history could not be separated.

Despite the obvious generic and stylistic differences, the theme of Pintilie's film – mainly the way its reflexivity exposes the theatricality and absurdity of the 1960 communist propaganda reenactment – could be considered possible antecedents to Nae Caranfil's *Closer to the Moon* (2013), inspired by Calotescu's *Reconstruction*.[9] Caranfil's self-reflexive, English-speaking fiction targets an international audience (casting Vera Farmiga and Mark Strong) and recreates the historical reconstruction of the bank robbery within the conventions of classical Hollywood narrative film, but with a self-consciously pronounced theatricality.[10]

Gabriel Achim's 2011 satirical comedy, *Adalbert's Dream*, evokes Pintilie's *Reconstruction* in an explicitly reflexive, pastiche-like way. Set in 1986 and featuring Iulica Ploscaru, a sub-engineer with filmmaking ambitions, as protagonist, the film stages the celebration of the sixty-fifth anniversary of the Romanian Communist Party in a factory. The festivities provide an opportunity for the screening of two amateur films made by Ploscaru – sarcastically labelled as 'the Pintilie of my dick' by one of his superiors – a short 'artistic' film entitled *Adalbert's Dream*, and an 'artistic' documentary about workplace safety, telling the story of a recent accident at the factory. The 'artistic' short, *Adalbert's Dream*, casts a woman in a man's role, and turns into a farcical, albeit unintended subversion of communist propaganda about young workers, the ethics of work. The insertion of this short within the principal narrative functions as a self-reflexive interruption, or 'break' as Paech has it. It discloses the mediality of the film through a variety of means: the hastily put together *mise en scène*, costumes and the amateur camera work, culminating in the burlesque, theatrical scene; the allusions to Buñuel's *Un chien andalou* (1929) and Tarkovsky's *Stalker* (1979); the intrusion of the off-screen cameraman into the on-screen space; the references to the medial experience of silent films – since the film has no sound, the director provides commentaries and reenacts the dialogues.

The screening of the 'artistic' documentary about a real-life victim of a real accident is interrupted by a concurrent workplace accident, in which a worker loses his hand. The consequent reenactment of this accident openly quotes Pintilie's *Reconstruction*, especially the grotesque scene, where the accidentally dislocated camera literally turns 'reality' upside down, exposing not only the mediation and the inaccessibility of the past event but also the absurdity of 'processing' it into a safety-at-work piece of propaganda. Thus in Achim's 2011 film Pintilie's name becomes the epitome of filmmaking – acknowledged, paradoxically, even by the sarcastic remark of Ploscaru's superior – whereas *Reconstruction* is reflexively evoked as a momentous part of Romanian film history. As an act of cinematic anamnesis – along with the other less explicit movie connections discussed above – *Adalbert's Dream* relates to (and reinforces) the canonical status of Pintilie's film in a self-reflexive way.

Filming the Private: The Camera in *Niki and Flo*

Among Pintilie's post-1989 films, *Niki and Flo* (2003) – written by Cristi Puiu and Răzvan Rădulescu, two prominent filmmakers of the new generation – comes closest to what is commonly referred to as New Romanian Cinema, known mostly for its (quasi)documentary style and 'low-key realism' pointing back to Italian neorealism, direct cinema or *cinéma vérité*. The thorough inquiries into social actualities in Pintilie's work, the preference for intense verbal scenes and for a low-key setting, paired with irony and a reflexive awareness of the film medium, also anticipate the stylistic-conceptual paradigm of New Romanian Cinema.

In *Niki and Flo*, home movies and amateur filmmaking are staged in the altered mediascape and socio-cultural context of postcommunism. The predominant setting is an apartment in a block of flats, a recurrent – both enclosed and transient – space in the topography of contemporary Romanian cinema. In these films, as Hajnal Király argues, '[t]he typical scene of interpersonal conflict is intensely verbal and dramatic and is often framed by the claustrophobic space of a blockhouse apartment' (2015: 172). Király considers that:

> [t]he directness of these scenes of great tension' (which are mostly responsible for the critical label of "realism" used for this cinema) goes hand in hand, however, with alienating shots, camera movements and silences depicting an isolated, lonely subjectivity, reminiscent of both the neorealist and modernist tradition. (2015: 172)

In *Niki and Flo* the suffocating, yet intimate space of the apartment with reproductions of paintings, a poster with the Twin Towers[11] and several religious icons, both houses and displaces the life of the Ardelean family, consisting of Niki, a retired colonel, his wife, Poucha, their daughter, Angela and her husband. The apartment building as an inhibiting, yet personalised/inhabited space seems to validate Svetlana Boym's words (n.d.) grasping the generic ambivalence of the 'the anonymous buildings of our common modernity, a part of the other International Style' in a chiasmic figure: 'The inhabitants of these buildings dream of elsewhere, homesick and sick of home.'

Niki, who finds it difficult to adapt to the new conditions of postcommunism, loses his son to a banal electrocution accident, his daughter to emigration to America, and eventually his wife to Alzheimer's. Ultimately he seems to lose his own self, falling under the control of his in-law, Florian or Flo, a free-lance entrepreneur and an arrogant, loud, self-assertive character. When Flo tries to force on Niki his opinion about Romanian participation in the Second World War, the latter – in a desperate, last-resort attempt at self-assertion – murders him with a hammer. The last scenes of the film leave the viewer with the disturbing image of Flo's gushing head wound, that is, with the image of the comprehensible (social) body turned into uncontainable flesh. The film – through its allegorising character construction – exposes the socio-cultural context of events as a clash of realigning, competing mentalities and cultural codes, epitomised respectively by *Niki and Flo*. The nostalgic reenactment of the past that keeps returning as 'other' is embodied by Niki, while the hasty, uncritical adoption of Western(ised) mentalities, consumerist-capitalist logic and conspiracy theories is exemplified by Flo as a member of the younger generation.

The codes of Niki's identity gradually lose or change their meaning: his grotesque image, adorned with Mickey Mouse ears next to a religious icon and a cross, points to a broader ongoing realignment of collective and personal identities situated at the volatile intersection of globalized, local, Western and Eastern European cultural practices. The collapse of identity is also revealed in the final scene where the military uniform Niki wears only on important occasions is mismatched with slippers and a cheap shopping bag. This incongruity disrupts not only his act of self-assertion, the murder of Flo, but also his past, as the murder takes place on Romanian National Army Day, an important date under communism. Yet Niki's disintegration is revealed not only through the failure of meaningful codes, but also through corporeality: his body – crushed by an unrepresentable trauma and turned into an imperceptible wound – collapses at his daughter's departure for the airport.

Niki and Flo relates not only thematically to contemporary Romanian films that reflect on the social actualities of postcommunism, but also conceptually, through the way it constructs figures of authority. Here, as in Călin Peter Netzer's *Medal of Honour*, (2009) or Răzvan Rădulescu's and Melissa de Raaf's *First of All, Felicia* (2009), the marginalised father figures – along with other 'defective authority figures' in institutional contexts – 'appear in circumstances that void them of relevance and representativeness' (Pop 2010: 29). The sceptical attitude towards authority – both familial and social – in these films reflects processes within the broader context of socio-cultural, institutional shifts and realigments of power relations after the collapse of the Ceaușescu regime.In *Medal of Honor* the discordant cultural codes and mentalities are embodied respectively by the Romanian father and his son, living in Canada. In *First of All, Felicia*, on the other hand, while the difference of socio-cultural codes affects the mother–daughter relationship, it is also internalised by the title character, Felicia, who is stuck between Romania and the Netherlands, the East and the West of Europe, unable either to leave home or ever return to it.

In *Niki and Flo*, the question of the private practice of filmmaking and of fictitious home movies is addressed within the family institution. The diegetic camera is operated by Flo, the 'director' of the amateur videos about the son's funeral and the daughter's wedding. The mediality of the home movie and the fictional enactment of its practice create a reflexive context for displaying a domesticated medium-usage with all its ambiguities. Thus home movie making, as a way of narrativisation and archiving of familial and private memory, becomes an act that objectifies the private, but also a modality for memory and identity construction of the filmmaker and his subjects.

The film displays an elusive, both controlling and uncontrollable camera gaze, defined by an ambivalent intimacy between the filming and the filmed subjects, as well as by specific, self-conscious acting (cf. Czach 2012). When Flo films the funeral, not only is his camera too intrusive, but he also directs the participants, asking them at one point to reenact the closing of the coffin for the sake of taking a better shot. Thus the moment as a traditional part of religious funeral customs is turned here into a gag-like, absurdist episode of a filmed spectacle, folding the tragic into the grotesque. In this context, the private use of the camera and the intrusive act of image-making do not favour intimacy between filmmaker and subjects, but disrupt the familiar (and the familial).

Flo's second home video, artily entitled *Pași în doi*,[12] records the wedding of his son and Niki's daughter. The amateurishly operated camera recycles cinematic clichés and home movie techniques, and records a fluid, carnivalesque flow of images. Niki and his wife watch the home video after their son's death and their daughter's departure, in the confined space of the apartment marked by their absence. The small TV set is inserted between two photographs of their dead son. From an anthropological perspective, this can be seen as an intimate memorial space, a triptych for private remembrance that domesticates public TV images (the broadcast of 9/11, for instance) by placing them within the private 'archive' of memory, which in its turn is displaced by the televisual. Viewed from the perspective of cinematic mediality, the mixed-media triptych 'breaks' the transparency of the film and foregrounds its (inter)mediality (Paech 2000) by juxtaposing still photography and moving images. Thus the triptych is refigured into a site for intermedial and cultural folds, where the still photograph overlaps with the moving image; the mediality of television with the mediality of home video; the secular with the religious; the public with the private; the globalised and local images of the world with the intimacy of the personal archive. The photographic index – according to Laura Mulvey – 'reaches out towards the uncanny as an effect of confusion between living and dead' (2006: 31), between presence and absence, past and present. In the triptych, the photographic and the filmic produce an uncanny, yet farcical effect: between the still photographs of the already dead son, the moving image of his musical performance (from Flo's wedding video) seems to be animated, alive, amplifying his absence through the uncanny liveliness of his mediated image,[13] while the trauma of the loss remains irrecuperable in the medial layers of memory.

Niki and Flo does not reveal only the intrusive aspect of the camera, but also the way the diegetic, hand-held apparatus is displaced and diverted by the subject it shoots. In the long insert of the wedding home movie, the mobile camera performs an unpredictable, fluctuating choreography: apparently it does not follow a pre-established concept as when the funeral is filmed, but is distracted by the incalculable movements of the bride, as well as other subjects. The bride, Angela, flirts with the camera, undressing and revealing her early pregnancy in an elusive mixture of spontaneous corporeal intimacy and self-conscious acting. The event of mediation and the presence of the technical apparatus are revealed by a mirror reflection, as well as by the unstable camera movement and the direct looking at and posing for the camera. The filmed subjects, the bride and the groom, recycle cinematic clichés by 'acting out' a horror and erotic movie scene that subverts any impression of an unmediated, intact reality. Thus in the act of filmmaking, the camera gaze intervenes into and constructs what counts as 'real'. Moreover, the off-screen dimension folds into the on-screen one as Flo's hand, in an act of unframing, penetrates the image to help the bride unzip her dress. This border-crossing gesture exposes not only the 'media condition' of the film (Paech 2000) by revealing the presence of the camera, but also the embodiedness of the hand-held apparatus as an extension of the hand and the gaze, relocating image-making in the in-between of the technical and the corporeal, the in-between of seeing and touching.

The home movie as a whole and the use of the camera remain however ambivalent. On the one hand, the act of filming enables the identity positions of both the filming and the filmed subjects – Angela, for example, enjoys being filmed, plays her role self-consciously, interacts with the camera and intervenes into the process of shooting. Nevertheless, the identity positions remain unequal, as Flo's voice-over commentary, along with the conclusive voyeuristic, fetishising images of nudity, reinscribe the asymmetrical relations of power between the subject and the object of the gaze. This appropriation of the intimacy of private memory profoundly disturbs Niki and his wife as they watch the wedding video. Contrarily, Flo and Niki's daughter, who belong to a younger, differently socialised generation, acknowledge camera usage as a 'familiar' domesticated practice of private and social life. Thus in *Niki and Flo*, the significance of medium usage is emphatically linked to the socio-historical context of media practices shaped in this case by the heterogeneous – old and new, religious and secular, local and globalised – cultural codes of postcommunism.

Coda

Pintilie's films, alternating between a (quasi-)documentary gaze and allegorical, stylised filmmaking, display a critical sensitivity to both cinematographic and social actualities. *Reconstruction* uncovers the absurdity of a reenactment for educational propagandistic purposes and questions the ideological appropriation of the camera gaze. Through the grotesque and fatal reconstruction and through the unruly, wounded body consumed by the event of reenactment, the film discloses the mechanisms of power and representation in the context of a totalitarian regime. Thus the modernist reflexivity of *Reconstruction* has become an aesthetic and conceptual antecedent of contemporary Romanian films reflecting on the medial and socio-cultural conditions of filmmaking. *Niki and Flo* displays an altered mediascape and social context: it exposes the ambivalent use of a domesticated film medium within the realigning socio-cultural and representational practices of the postcommunist period. *Niki and Flo*, the result of a collaboration between Pintilie, Cristi Puiu and Răzvan Rădulescu, also marks a point of transition, for – even while maintaining allegorising tendencies in character construction – it anticipates the stylistic and conceptual paradigm of New Romanian Cinema.

By displaying the quasi-institutional and private use of the camera, as well as the power relations and socio-cultural conditions of the act of image making, Pintilie turns cinematic reflexivity into a critical practice with a historically changing stake – often through an absurd, subversive humour. In his films, the traumas or the corporeal wounds that implode the sphere of the meaningful point to something beyond the representable in a world ruptured by social and existential crises. The image of scars or Ripu's and Vuică's wound, as well as Flo's bleeding head and Niki's stumbling body, seem to validate Morrey's words that 'the image always contains an excess of sense while the real only gives itself to be experienced as wound or scar' (2008: 29).

Acknowledgement

This work was supported by a grant of the Romanian Ministry of National Education, CNCS – UEFISCDI, PN-II-ID-PCE-2012-4-0573.

Notes

1. *Sunday at Six* (1965), *Reconstruction* (1970), *Why Are the Bells Ringing, Mitică?* (1982).
2. See, for example, *The Oak* (1992), *Too Late* (1996), *Next Stop Paradise* (1998), *The Afternoon of a Torturer* (2001), *Niki and Flo* (2003).
3. According to Ágnes Pethő, in Pintilie's *Why Are the Bells Ringing, Mitică?*, the appearance of the film crew at both the beginning and the end of the film conceals

the referentiality of the represented world to evade censorship (2003: 133). Nevertheless, the film, a carnivalesque adaptation of I. L. Caragiale's *D'ale carnavalului* (1885, a black comedy about the outskirts of Bucharest), was banned.
4. As Doru Pop points out, the banning of *Reconstruction* ended the period of the so-called 'ideological thaw' from the early 1960s, following the denunciation of Stalin's crimes and the attempt of the Eastern bloc to move away from Moscow. In Romania, this period of a 'more permissive film culture' lasted until the 1971 July thesis, which proclaimed compellingly 'the cultural leadership (of the filmmakers) into complete social obedience' (Pop 2014: 213). Similarly, Cristian Tudor Popescu observes that there is a kind of 'safety valve' in *Reconstruction* (in the sentence: 'Who will play in league B, in 1961?'), an attempt to contextualise the narrative within Gheorghe Gheorghiu-Dej era, which preceded Ceaușescu's presidency (2011: 178). This 'valve', however, could not save the film from being banned.
5. Pătrașcu – together with Pintilie – wrote the film's screenplay.
6. Pintilie returns to the question of the (im)possibility of reassembling the past from the perspective of the present in *Afternoon of a Torturer*, staging the continually interrupted recollection of a former torturer from a communist prison.
7. The professor is 'an essence of Impotent Intellectuality', whereas Vuică's character is 'an essence of Victimized Youthful Innocence (. . .), as well as a variation of the Holy Fool figure' (Gorzo 2013: 7).
8. Through the filming techniques of the small television studio (for example, a handheld camera), Porumboiu self-ironically comments on what are considered to be the aesthetic 'trademarks' of New Romanian Cinema.
9. Alexandru Solomon's investigative documentary, *The Great Communist Bank Robbery* (2004), also deals with Calotescu's *Reconstruction*. The film creates a meta-reflexive context by interrogating archive footage, official documents, and by interviewing relatives and friends of the victims and former communist representatives of the state.
10. For a detailed discussion of the film see Chapter 6 in this volume.
11. The towers collapse in the attack of 9/11, soon after Niki's daughter and her husband arrive in America.
12. The home movie evokes the title of Dan Pița's 1985 film, *Paso Doble* (the Romanian title being *Pas în doi*), awarded the Honorable Mention at the 1986 Berlinale Film Festival. In the 1980s, when Pintilie was exiled, Pița was a hailed director in Romania.
13. In Pintilie's *The Oak*, set in the last years of communism, home video is embedded into a different socio-historical context. Nela, the young dissident heroine of the film, watches the carnivalesque video about her childhood while lying next to her dying father, a former officer of the secret police.

6. EPHEMERAL HISTORY AND ENDURING CELLULOID: CINEMATIC REALITY AND THEATRICALITY IN NAE CARANFIL'S FILMS

Melinda Blos-Jáni

The description of the films of the New Romanian Cinema/Romanian New Wave as a unified trend, with shared narrational and stylistic traits including the return to Bazinian realism (Gorzo 2013), Italian neorealism, the French New Wave and modernist minimalism (Pop 2014), has set boundaries to the discourse about contemporary Romanian cinema. One might even say that the recent Romanian reinvention of realist cinema has prompted the need for an overarching definition of the Romanian national cinema, one that tends to situate its aesthetics within this realist/minimalist paradigm, which however leaves much narrower space for works that do not fit in and are therefore automatically marginalised. Such is the case with Nae Caranfil's *œuvre*, whose directorial debut in the 1990s received critical acclaim and was welcomed by audiences, yet theoretical interest for his films gradually diminished towards the end of the 2000s, marked by the growing attention to the new aesthetics. The status of his *œuvre* remains problematic, and – because of adherence to the principles of classical narrative cinema and more popular aesthetics – he is considered either an outsider to the New Romanian Cinema paradigm or a precursor of it.

This chapter reconsiders Caranfil's works in the context of the postmodern postcommunist condition and its specific visual culture. Based on in-depth film analyses – focusing on cinematic realism, the role of the cinematic medium, as well as on representations of history – the chapter situates Caranfil's films in the contemporary Romanian cinematic landscape. Thus the concept of reflexivity becomes the most prominent theoretical tool for analysing his films as postmodernist, and as an illustration of a cinematic paradigm that hovered on the margins of the New Romanian Cinema when it emerged.

A Romanian Postcommunist/Postmodern Filmmaker?

Although the interdependence of the two major concepts of postcommunism and postmodernism is a much-debated topic, many critics remark that the fall of communism coincided with the appearance of the theories of postmodernism (Meštrović 1994). Indeed, the collapse of the totalitarian regime was followed by a transitional period, characterised by social chaos, decentralisation of power and economics, and erosion of class and gender divisions, typically defined as markers of the 'postmodern condition'. Yet coupled with a cultural landscape still bearing traces of communist traditions, the situation in postcommunist Eastern Europe has been wittingly described as the 'postcommunist condition' (Groys 2004). As Schamma Schahadat argues, '[w]hen transported into Eastern Europe, postmodernism changes – it is affected by the post-communist condition', and exemplifies the following traits: postmodernism as time-space, as a sign of crisis, a culture of simulacra, a 'radical plurality' and the end of the grand narratives (2009).

Christina Stojanova contends that, with respect to Eastern European filmmakers, post-Berlin Wall young filmmakers worked in a 'postmodern post-communist period' (2005b), and she discusses the delayed cinematic postmodernism in their works (among other characteristics of their regional and historical specificity). The idea of a postmodern, postcommunist condition has not been adopted by film critics discussing works made during the transitional period in Romania: 'in spite of having missed the postmodernist moment and in spite of having developed within the narrow confines of what the communist socio-cultural-political system allowed, the New Romanian Cinema has become a phenomenon almost overnight' (Ieta 2010: 31).

The concept of a postmodern, postcommunist Romanian cinema has resurfaced in a recent study of post-totalitarian cinema, which focuses on the restructuring of Romanian postcommunist film industry before 1997, when a set of more transparent and democratic regulations were introduced at the Romanian Film Centre (Ştefănescu and Foamete 2013: 161). The overview of this period ends with a typology of post-totalitarian film narratives and 'different strategies adopted to compensate for the insecurity of their new role in the post-totalitarian society' (Ştefănescu and Foamete 2013: 176), with an emphasis on filmmakers who remained faithful to their artistic principles. Among the seven analysed films, defined as postmodernist, are *University Square* (1991) by Stere Gulea and *Sundays on Leave* (1993) by Nae Caranfil.[1] The former is considered postmodern because it formulates a civic response and political criticism through visual detachment, treats the pathos of the protests with irony, and deconstructs the political event as a show (Ştefănescu and Foamete 2013: 183). Indeed, the role of the TV image in 1989 Romanian events became a broadly theorised phenomenon. Vilém Flusser describes it as a new development of image culture:

> it was highly aesthetic; it was l'art pour l'art. It was the purpose of theatre to provoke sympathy and fright. So that happened. [. . .] The real experience is in the image, what happened behind the image is no use to us. Political reasoning is no longer valid. There is no reality behind the image. There are realities in the image. (1990)

Jean Baudrillard even suggested that the Romanian people were 'dispossessed of the event ... deprived of the lived experience they have of it by being submerged in the media network, by being placed under house arrest in front of their television screens' (1994: 56). As TV images became the site of the Romanian revolution, the revolution became a prototypical example of how the power of images may determine our narratives of the present and of history itself, of how images overcome the 'real'.

Caranfil's debut film, on the other hand, is located at the opposite end of the postmodern spectrum because of its self-conscious narration, which depicts a fragmented subjectivity while foregrounding its constructedness. And, as Ştefănescu and Foamete write, 'Caranfil's self-reflective postmodern narrative manner was such a novelty in Romanian filmmaking that it tended to usurp its subject' (2013: 190). Scrutinising Caranfil's early comedies – *Sundays on Leave* (1993), *Asphalt Tango* (1996) and *Philanthropy* (2002) – through a postmodernist grid, one can easily identify some of its staple aspects like the crisis of identity and traces of Western postcolonialism. In these films, the identity/integrity of the main protagonist is challenged when confronted with dreams and myths about Western life or Western values. Moreover, Caranfil defines these identities by using self-conscious parody.[2] It could be even argued that the collapse of the utopian meta-narrative,[3] which dominates Caranfil's first films, takes a postmodern tone. The disillusionment with the totalising view is present in the non-linear, three-strand narration of *Sundays on Leave*, which results in a fragmented view of fragmented subjects. And in *Philanthropy* the sensitivity to simulacra becomes crucial in understanding the struggles of a writer to decipher what is 'real' from what is simulated in his postcommunist world.

Viewed in the context of 'images' taking over 'power', as Flusser has eloquently claimed, the postmodernist films of the transitional period either perform the deconstruction[4] of the spectacular event and of the image (*University Square*) – and should thus be defined as oppositional postmodernism – or indulge the viewer with the artifice of the image, as happens in Caranfil's films, which adhere to mainstream postmodernism (see Hayward 2013).

The historical context offers several possibilities for interpreting Caranfil's *œuvre* as symptomatic of the Romanian postcommunist period. The film analyses below use this postmodern, postcommunist context as an interpretive frame for the self-reflexive aesthetics and the ironic, narcissistic narratives of the works under scrutiny. Furthermore, the discussion of Caranfil's reflexive style can bring us closer to his notion of cinema(tic realism), considered to be the 'other' of the minimalist realism of the New Romanian Cinema.

Stages of Reality and Cinematic Post-reflexivity in Nae Caranfil's Films

The status of the filmic image is closely bound to the questions of the 'real'; thus media reflexivity can function as a clue in the process of understanding the relation between the nature of the image and various concepts of realism. In different paradigms, 'real' can mean the representation of authentic experiences of history or adherence to a cinematic aesthetic of realism. Realism could pertain to the usage of the cinematic medium that is considered to be more faithful to reality than the others, or, as Virginás suggests, of some Eastern European films in which the real 'becomes articulated in medial structures that use theatrical scenery, and are prone to be interpreted as allegorical' (2011: 140). Caranfil's films are not allegorical in this sense, yet their reflexive playing with theatricality does make us question what the film medium (and consequently the 'real') means in his cinema.

The postmodern affinity with reflexivity is deductible either from the postmodern condition or from the popularisation of the critical reflexivity of high modernism, as Vincze sums up (2013: 116–20). Ágnes Pethő names this popularised form 'post-reflexivity', a type of reflexivity that is incapable of initiating a pregnant discourse about the medium of film, but instead emphasises the precession of the filmic medium over reality and is usually appropriated as a more effective way to tell a generic story (2003: 170–7). The post-reflexive techniques reiterate that the film is only a film, an artificially created fictional world. As these self-conscious pieces of artifice blend not just different discourses but also different types of media, post-reflexivity could be performed through intermediality as well (Pethő 2003: 178–80).

Caranfil's films showcase such an 'appetite for artifice' (Bordwell 2006) in their narrative construction; moreover, they are examples of postmodern *trompe l'oeil*, which is perhaps the easiest way to convey the notions of theatricality, stage, spectacle and performance. References to theatre and other kinds of performativity are to be found in all of his films, mostly embedded in the diegesis, yet allowing interpretation as metareflections on their fictitious and illusory character. Thus it becomes a case of post-reflexivity, of postmodern playfulness with self-referentiality, which is achieved through the intermediality of film and theatre. Based on the idea that intermediality can be understood as a performative act (Pethő 2011: 41–2), I propose to look behind the postmodern label, and investigate what this particular intermediality really 'does' or 'performs' in Nae Caranfil's playfully ironic cinema.

In *Sundays on Leave*, the theatre is a meeting point on the level of diegesis or the story world, situated in the mid-1980s, and on the level of narration as well, since its three subplots converge at the theatre, where their main characters – the Student, the Actor and the Soldier – find themselves attending the same show, presented by a visiting theatre company. Through bits and pieces of the play, ironically entitled *The Dawns of Hope*, randomly dispersed throughout the three subplots, the show is unmistakably recognisable as communist propaganda from the 1950s. In the protagonist's role the play features the star of the company, Dumitru Staroste, who happens to be the main character of the second storyline. Staroste's worker-hero proudly joins the Communist Party, but is betrayed by an informer and gets arrested – hence the drama.

Curiously, it is this intradiegetic theatre piece about the early days of communism that takes the harshest stance against the totalitarian regime, and its serious tone is uncomfortably juxtaposed to the light-heartedness of the subplots, taking place in the 1980s. The characters' main preoccupation remains a love affair, and nothing seems to affect their good humour – not even compulsory military service. Reality on screen thus becomes twofold: there is the amusing reality of everyday life and then there is the ideologically constructed historical reality, played out on the theatre stage. Thus the play becomes an intermedial interplay, which invites the viewer to decipher how and why the staged reality manipulates the actual historical reality. Some on-stage episodes are also replicated off-stage, for example the actor, who plays the informer in the play, turns out to be a real-life informer as well.

Despite these cross-overs, the medium of the theatre does not mirror the filmic text, neither is it a *mise en abyme* of the plot, but rather functions as a tool of irony. The play offers ironic commentary of the filmic reality (as in the case of the actor-informer), yet the filmic reality subverts the message of the play in the subsequent episode. The actors constantly play practical jokes on each other during performances, which turn the propaganda spectacle into a parody – a party pamphlet prop is substituted with a pornographic image, or the signal of the Munich-based and banned Radio Free Europe is played instead of a propaganda radio show.

In addition to these ironic interactions of theatrical and filmic reality, Marin Sorescu's poem *Actors* recurs as a text that the female student is learning to recite in preparation for her acting entry exam. The lines:

> [H]ow naturally spontaneous – the actors!
> With sleeves rolled up,
> How much better they know how to live our lives for us!

deserve particular attention because of their tongue-in-cheek ambiguity. Should they be interpreted as a declaration of what Baudrillard calls 'precession of simulacra', where signs of the real substitute the real? Or are they just another prank to deconstruct the myth of the stage performer and present him/her as just another fragmented subject who cannot live up to one's on-stage, hyper-real self? The question is hard to answer, as the real and its representation seemingly interact, although the confines between 'life' and the proscenium remain, at least in this movie.

The adventure of getting lost in the labyrinth of manipulative representations becomes more elaborate in Nae Caranfil's 2002 film, *Philanthropy*. The storyline opens more possibilities for reflexivity: an unsuccessful writer, employed as a literature teacher, falls in love with a sexy girl, and in order to impress her agrees to work for Pavel Puiuț, a Machiavellian individual, who – under the auspices of a foundation called *Philanthropy* – writes stories for beggars.

Ironically, one of the beggars is a filmmaker, an artist who suffers because he is poor and ailing, but mostly because he has been denied political power in the postcommunist world.[5] As Pavel Puiuț enters the story, the love affair of the writer-teacher becomes secondary, and Romanian reality as an intricate system of deception and appearances comes to the fore. Several scenes, which appear

Figure 6.1 *Philanthropy*: Puiuț's window on the Romanian reality

as *trompe l'oeil*, later turn out to be carefully planned by the scheming mind behind *Philanthropy*. The most versatile is a restaurant scene that ends with a scandal, because a couple celebrating their tenth wedding anniversary are unable to pay the bill. During the loud argument with the waiter, their humble circumstances are revealed, and a wealthy man, overhearing the dispute, bails them out. The subsequent scene exposes the man, the woman and the waiter as a trio of actors, performing a sketch, and the restaurant patrons as naïve by-standers, duped into participating in a fictitious melodrama. The cameo appearance of the director Nae Caranfil as a karaoke performer suggests as much – his singing of Frank Sinatra's *My Way* by reading the teleprompter implies that originality and authorship are substituted by mimicry and ventriloquism.

The final image, where Pavel Puiuţ addresses the viewer by looking in the rear view mirror of his car – intimates/implies that the film's master narrative is unreliable as well. Yet we cannot take this scene as evidence of a self-reflexive cinema, for it is just another manifestation of the *trompe l'oeil* effect, designed by a philanthropist who enjoys practical jokes. Paradoxically, this case of post-reflexivity reinforces the diegetic world.

Most of the reflexive techniques are narrative: the episodes usually end with a *détournement* of the situation, with characters discovering that they have been deceived. Since it is through storytelling that the film creates and deconstructs illusion, I therefore argue that – like the technique of the *mise en abyme* or the metaphorical image of the mirror – theatricality here serves to multiply the narrative levels of reality. According to Kovács's summary of postmodern reflexive strategies:

> [i]n postmodern artistic reflection, the idea of art's moral superiority disappears. This is why if a postmodern work breaks the texture of fiction, it only discloses another fictional layer rather than relates fiction to reality. A work of art is reflected upon as a text behind which there are only other texts, to an infinite regression. (2007: 226)

Indeed, the levels of reality get so entangled by the end of *Philanthropy* that even the main participants in the restaurant hoax begin to believe in its false premise and continue to behave like a long-time married couple 'off-stage'. Similarly, the diegetic reality gradually turns into a stage, without being limited by the classic boundaries of the proscenium.

Despite what Linda Hutcheon calls 'the narcissism of the filmic text', the post-reflexivity in *Sundays on Leave* and *Philanthropy* could be interpreted as a critique of the Romanian postcommunist condition, inferring that 'Romanian reality is highly artificial and manipulated'. If so, it could then be compared to Cristi Puiu's *Stuff and Dough* (2001), which was released at about the same time and is therefore similar to other early New Wave films in its humour and slice-of-life, narrative approach. But apart from these commonalities, Caranfil's film demonstrates a diverging ethical approach to the ontology of the filmic image, described by Flusser as 'lack of reality behind the image' (Flusser 1990).

The preoccupation with images made for television and their signification in terms of the real world is present in several post-2000 Romanian films, yet most prominently in Caranfil's *Philanthropy* as well as in Corneliu Porumboiu's *12:08 East of Bucharest* (2006). While Porumboiu's approach could be summed up in the question contained in the film's subtitle, 'Was there or was there not a revolution?' – that is, was there or was there not reality behind the images of the December 1989 revolution, and to what extent could these images distort and create realities – despite its ironic tone, *Philanthropy* takes a more pessimistic stance, revealing that behind the simulacra of TV images there is only an equally artificial, manipulated world called 'reality'.

Thus if Porumboiu's film[6] reveals a modernist art cinema preoccupation with the limits of the image to mediate reality, no matter how abstract or poor that image is, Caranfil's *Philanthropy* exhibits a postmodernist approach to reality, which is deemed lost between appearances and practical jokes. In other words, while the modernist aesthetics of the new wave cinema codifies, figures the real, Caranfil's latest films radicalise reality in the form of hyperreal, meta-cinematic tales, showcasing cinema that stands but for film itself.

Re-imagining History and the Truth of Cinema

The medium of theatre plays an important, albeit different role in Caranfil's two latest films. *The Rest is Silence* (2007) and *Closer to the Moon* (2013) are more than just playful, ironic and self-referential, they could also be regarded as metafictions about two idiosyncratic moments of Romanian cinema.[7] With their emphasis on the role of film in history (and in film history), and on fiction in relation to reality, these works have significantly contributed to discussions regarding the role of the cinematic, the institution of cinema, and their interrelatedness, and have thus offered insights into different periods of Romanian history. *The Rest is Silence* tells the story of the making of the first Romanian feature-length film, *Romania's Independence* (1912), about the War of Independence in 1877 against the Ottoman Empire,[8] and *Closer to the Moon* is about a notorious bank robbery, which took place at the height of the most repressive communist period in the 1950s, and more specifically about the making of *Reconstruction* (Virgil Calotescu, 1960), the official propaganda film, commissioned by the communist authorities to record this unusual event.

Both films expose the filmmaking process and question the difference between theatre and cinema. *The Rest is Silence* presents the intermediality of

Figure 6.2 *The Rest is Silence*: scene with theatricality enhanced by red curtains and recurring planimetric composition, featuring Caranfil

theatre and cinema as inherent in the early cinema era, when film, as a new medium, was to prove vis-à-vis the old media that, despite the fragility of celluloid, it can endure as art, transcending time and space. Theatre therefore permeates various facets of the film – as part of the narrative space (many scenes take place backstage in a theatre or in the auditorium), and embedded in the form of an intradiegetical excerpt from on-stage performances, the most notable of which is the final monologue from *Hamlet*. Theatre is also present as filmed spectacle in the screening of *Hamlet* with Sarah Bernhardt in the main role. Theatre informs also highly climactic life-events like the quarrels between the film's main characters – the father, a theatre actor, and his son, who wants to become a film director – which are enacted as theatrical performances. The film also includes a trial and two funerals, presented as meticulously choreographed dramatic acts, and even *Hamlet* is recited as a funerary poem. Ultimately, Caranfil himself appears in the cameo role of a drama school teacher against a backdrop of heavy theatre curtains. The frontal staging of this highly reflexive *mise en scène* suggests that the work of a film director can also be seen as a theatrical performance.

Yet the narrative scope of *The Rest is Silence* transcends the simple deconstruction of reality in a highly theatrical manner, for the emphasis on the specificity of theatre actually aims at defining, through contrast, the specific mediality of film. Theatre demonstrates in fact the 'otherness' of cinema as a medium capable of transcending time as suggested by the scene with the greatest Romanian actress of the early 1900s, Aristizza Demetriade, who wants to be immortalised as a moving shadow, or, by the end title, informing us that *Romania's Independence* has 'survived'. The medium of film defies both national history and its representation – the end of *The Rest is Silence* has the historical film triumphant – as more efficient in creating a 'sense of the real'. It is enough to quote the introduction of the film within the film: 'and now, ladies and gentlemen, after 35 years, the War of Independence is revived before your very eyes, more real than reality itself'. Thus the reenactment of the making of *Romania's Independence* portrays a medium that is more artificial than the enacted, or theatrical reality, yet, paradoxically, more efficient in achieving immediacy. Just as the first historical Romanian film is depicted in the metafictional narrative as a product of art for art's sake type of aestheticism, so does Caranfil's film prove to be a hypermediated piece of art as well. It is indeed the most spectacular among his films in visual terms, foregrounding his preference for colourful, meticulously composed historic *tableaux*, and a mélange of stylistic devices referencing early cinema, classical and post-classical Hollywood and even contemporary digital cinema.[9]

In my view, *The Rest is Silence* is a statement about the medium of film designed as a spectacular story, and brings together the 'birth of the Romanian nation' with the birth of Romanian cinema at the time when film was establishing itself as an art form.[10] According to Caranfil's auteur vision, the myth of cinema provokes passionate feelings and is capable of creating a reality of its own, as well as of generating 'real' experiences. Cinema, just like history, becomes a hyperrealist experience.

Closer to the Moon is a continuation of sorts of the idea that cinema generates historical reality, but also questions the idea of a constantly staged, manipulated reality in *The Rest is Silence*. Here, the everyday life of six characters of Jewish origin in socialist Romania in the 1950s is presented as highly theatrical, as illustrated below:

> – Wonderland is not what it used to be, especially for us, Yids. So, we shall all become actors, there are plenty of juicy parts for us to play these days: enemies of the state, aristocrats, speculators.
> – Why not? 1959, the year we've all become movie stars! (*Closer to the Moon*)

And despite the sombre context of this exchange, the interlocutors laugh and make merry while play acting.[11] In a paranoiac diegetic reality, ridden by conspiracies and political machinations, cinema plays a decisive role as a metafictional tale.

The film is based on a true story of five young men and a young woman of Jewish origin, who were arrested and prosecuted for robbing a bank, and as penitence had to participate in the filmic reenactment of the robbery for propaganda purposes. The story of the propaganda film, entitled *Reconstruction* is investigated in Alexandru Solomon's documentary *The Great Communist Bank Robbery* (2004). Whereas the documentary ends with a series of unanswered questions with regard to the characters of the perpetrators and their motivation, Caranfil's film fills in the gaps with self-reflexive fiction. Thus a major addition to the story is the highly cinematic vision of the robbery as designed to expose the manipulations and absurdities of life under Stalinism through staging of an even greater absurdity – that of a communist bank robbery, camouflaged as a film shooting.

Thus cinematic imagination becomes a tool of resistance: the robbery is designed as a gangster film, and one of the robbers even sees his own execution as a journey into space from a science fiction movie.[12] Cinema is used by the propaganda machine as well, since the reenactment is done for the sake of an instructive-educational film, but ends up turning into an actual artefact, used literally as an escape from the staged reality. It might be even said that, within the context of Romania in the 1960s, *Closer to the Moon* re-evaluates the myth of cinema, outlined in *The Rest is Silence*, endowing it with political power. The historical setting has changed, but cinematic imagination is capable of turning an execution into a trip to the Moon. The magic of cinema has triumphed again.

While in *Sundays on Leave* and *Philanthropy* theatricality is a tool of narrative reflexivity, and a subversion of reality, films like *The Rest is Silence* and *Closer to the Moon* combine the reflexivity of historiographic metafiction with irony – that is, the latter films foreground history as a construct, a deliberately inadequate version of the past. The self-conscious strategies employed in these films do not deconstruct but rather intensify artificiality in order to incite joy and laughter. Their images make no moral or realist claims, nor do they self-consciously reveal their manipulative nature but rather try to provoke 'sympathy and fright', a tendency that increases in Caranfil's latest meta-cinematic films.

By way of conclusion: postcommunist filmmaking, in order to distance itself from the authorial, metaphorical 'old' Romanian cinema, has taken different paths in the early 2000s even when imagining the past. While the pre-1989 allegorical cinema used the concept of the 'present-presented-as-past' in order to camouflage a hidden message about the present (Pethő 2011: 397), the new directors 'tended to recount their stories in the present time, not just in terms of their contemporary stories, but in terms of narrativity that is personally lived, even if it's happening in the past' (Pop 2014: 38). Conversely, Caranfil's approach to the historical past embraces a bizarre transformation of 'preconceptions about the past' and, in a postmodernist vein, shows the past as metafiction, a meta-cinema.

A Different New Romanian Cinema?

There seems to be consensus regarding Caranfil's films: he is an outsider to the new aesthetics. The director himself acknowledges this distinction in interviews, and even used it as gag in a self-reflexive vignette, made in 2008 as the official spot of the Transylvania International Film Festival. It shows James Bond being stopped by a traffic officer to give way to a delegation of Romanian filmmakers. And while Cristian Mungiu, Cristi Puiu, Radu Muntean and Corneliu Porumboiu drive along in contemporary cars, Caranfil follows suit in a retro car, evoking *The Rest is Silence*, but also referencing the burlesque car scenes from Jacques Tati's films.

This somewhat adversarial juxtaposition was revised by Dana Duma in a recent article, where she argues for a 'mild opposition' between Caranfil's 'maximalist aesthetics' and the minimalist realism of the new paradigm (2013: 27–9). Even though she points out dissimilarities, such as narration (non-linear/linear), use of music (diegetic/non-diegetic), editing (dynamic editing/long take), common features are taken into consideration as well: the refusal of metaphoric expression, the emphasis on screenwriting, an ironic approach to the communist past. According to Duma, the destabilisation of the elitist authorial status is the most important common trait, and has contributed to the renewal of Romanian cinema by creating a cinema saturated with life, albeit through different means (2013: 29). In light of Caranfil's rehabilitation within the contemporary Romanian cine-scape, it could be said that the contours of New Romanian Cinema cannot be drawn in straight lines, as authors concerned with defining the New Wave suggest (Pop 2014). In terms of non-linear storytelling, Caranfil's films show affinities with films like Cristian Mungiu's *Occident* (2002). And in terms of their ironic and nostalgic approach to the communist past (Duma 2013: 28), they are comparable to Cătălin Mitulescu's *How I Spent the End of the World* (2006) and *Tales from the Golden Age* (2009), an omnibus film supervised by Mungiu. Other authors identify Caranfil's authorial penchant for humour and slice-of-life storytelling as a transitional phase between the 'old' and the 'new' Romanian cinema (Nasta 2007; 2013: 121–38). Or, alternatively, they see it as suspended between two eras of Romanian cinema: 'somewhere between the dinosaurs and the brats there is Nae. His solitude is splendid in this sense. It is admirable how he stays true to his artistic credo' (interview of Șerban in Voinescu 2008).

Although Titus Muntean's *Kino Caravan* (2009) shares some of Caranfil's concerns, reflexivity and tribute to the national cinema are not among the subjects explored by the new wave of directors, who are interested predominantly in representing history through cinematic realism. Notably, Radu Jude's *Aferim!* (2015) also seems to advocate a different cinematic approach to history, denying the distance between reality and fiction, and playfully deglamourising nineteenth-century Romania by self-consciously referencing classics of Romanian literature and cinema, hence constructing history through a web of intermedial relations. Thus a reflexive approach to Romanian history and culture emerges, blending fiction and reality. This approach may effectively challenge the paradigm of minimalist realism, making it possible to refine our understanding of New Romanian Cinema. Analysing Nae Caranfil's films is an attempt to nuance our view of new aesthetics by adopting an approach that does not limit its definitions to realism or minimalism, but includes in it a self-conscious treatment of issues regarding representation, the medium of film and its historical embeddedness in Romanian culture.

Acknowledgements

This work was supported by two consecutive grants of the Romanian Ministry of National Education, CNCS – UEFISCDI, PN-II-ID-PCE-2012-4-0573 and PN-III-ID-PCE-2016-0418. Special thanks to my colleague, Judit Pieldner for her support while writing this text.

Notes

1. The list also includes *The Mirror – The Beginning of Truth* (Sergiu Nicolaescu, 1994), *Luxury Hotel* (Dan Pița 1992), *Fed Up* (Mircea Daneliuc, 1994), *The Oak* (Lucian Pintilie, 1992) and *The South Pole* (Radu Nicoară, 1992).
2. According to Thomas Elsaesser, the use of parody to assert one's identity is typical of European cinema and its post-national identity (2005: 70). In *Sundays on Leave* the student, who dreams of becoming an actor, gives up her dream to leave the country, mirroring the real action taken by another character, an actor who flees for Yugoslavia by swimming across the Danube, leaving behind his 'easy' life at the theatre. The longing for the West resurfaces in *Asphalt Tango*, where different types of people are trying to become someone else: as one of the group of girls to be 'exported' to France for an erotic show, Felicia pretends to have forgotten her native Romanian and speaks only French. This Francophilia gets another ironic spin in the scene with the girls browsing through a book of clippings of French film stars like Jean Paul Belmondo, Alain Delon, Gerard Philippe, imagining that all 'real French' men look like them.
3. This may be interpreted in terms of Lyotard's theory of the postmodern condition. See: <http://www.aatseel.org/postcommunism_and_po> (accessed 15 August 2015).
4. The sensitivity to manipulation permeated everyday life during the transitional period:

    endless television transmissions gave the possibility to participate in provisional parliamentary debates, which provided full transparency of the political act. However simultaneously with the appearance of trust, suspicion is created. [. . .] Nothing is anymore what it seemed to be. The Romanian citizen becomes hermeneutic in the market, in the media, in the family; he sees hidden meanings everywhere. (Anghelescu 2005: 13)

5. In the original Romanian text the beggar filmmaker is contrasted to Sergiu Nicolaescu, a director, who was coopted by the totalitarian regime, but managed to make films and even pursue a political career after the fall of communism. This political aspect of the cardboard text is omitted in the English subtitles, which read:

'During the dictatorship I made movies. Today our cinema is dead and I'm incurably ill myself', rather than 'Today Sergiu is a senator and I'm ill'.
6. In recent theoretical writings this view encompasses all of Porumboiu's *œuvre*, which is considered an example of reflexivity within the New Romanian cinema realist paradigm. Thus his films seem to demythologise cinematic realism through narration and a preference for the *tableau* aesthetic (see Ferencz-Flatz 2015: 77; and Chapter 4 in this volume). In Pop's interpretation (2014) the crisis of realism in *Aurora* (Cristi Puiu, 2010) and in *When Evening Falls on Bucharest, or Metabolism* (Corneliu Porumboiu, 2013) signals the end of the new wave realism.
7. Although the discussion so far might imply that Caranfil's *œuvre* evolved from self-conscious narratives to a meta-cinematic level, it is important to mention that the screenplay for *The Rest is Silence* was written in the 1980s, but the filming was delayed.
8. The film was directed by Aristide Demetriade, an actor at the Romanian National Theatre. The story behind the film – held as a masterpiece of the Romanian film history – was unveiled in a book by Tudor Caranfil (1988). However film historians mostly recognise Grigore Brezeanu as the director of this film, as they consider Tudor Caranfil's thesis debatable.
9. The director of photography, Marius Panduru revealed in an interview that the camera movements followed the patterns of American cinema from the 1970s; the zoom, the style of the 1950s; and static shots imitated the tableau aesthetic of early cinema, but without becoming a self-conscious quote (Panduru in Filippi and Rus 2014).
10. Around 1912, Film D'Art – a French trend, dating back to 1908 and created to attract the bourgeoisie to cinemas by blending the new medium with the prestige of theatre and literature – was already gaining popularity in Eastern Europe.
11. In one of the scenes Alice's teenage son, Mirel, is playfully 'arrested' by his father so that he can skip school and the two can spend some quality time together.
12. One of the characters, Dumi, is an expert in astrophysics, and another one, Max, dreams about flying to the moon. The title of the film, which also alludes to the Sci-Fi genre, serves as an ironic reference to the Cold War and the fight to conquer outer space.

7. REMEDIATION AND MINIMALISM IN NEW ROMANIAN CINEMA: THE EXAMPLE OF CRISTI PUIU

Liviu Lutas

This chapter addresses the question of minimalism in New Romanian Cinema, as exemplified and epitomised by Cristi Puiu's films, in relation to cases of remediation. It mainly follows Doru Pop's definition of Puiu's minimalism as a reduction of cinematic language to its basics, or as a 'technical abstinence', with the purpose of concentrating on the essentials, on 'pure and simple realities' (2014: 66). With regard to the concept of 'remediation', the chapter follows Jay David Bolter's and Richard Grusin's definition, which refers to the 'representation of one medium in another' (1999: 45). Although this rather broad definition has been both criticised and refined, as discussed below, it will be argued that remediation can still be used as an umbrella term covering a range of interesting cases of a medium appearing in another medium.

At first glance, remediation might seem incompatible with the minimalism that is characteristic of Puiu's films. According to Pop, Puiu's minimalistic aesthetic aims at giving an illusion of 'immediate realism' (2014: 45). In other words, one of the goals of these films is to 'give the viewer "reality itself", and not just a "representation" of reality' (Pop 2014: 37). Immediate realism therefore seems to preclude remediation for the simple reason that the target medium should be as transparent as possible, whereas remediation demands two discernible media. Indeed, how could remediation occur in cases where even the use of a target medium is supposed to pass unnoticed?

A closer look at the minimalism of New Romanian Cinema films shows, however, that it allows a certain degree of stylisation, even of the kind that actually highlights the use of a medium. Therefore, it is intriguing to consider episodes in which Cristi Puiu's films introduce, sometimes just through subtle allusions, cases of remediation. Thus in an attempt to reconcile the apparent paradox of the use of remediation in minimalistic films, the chapter offers a close look at a few instances of remediation and its various functions.

Minimalism and Immediate Realism in New Romanian Cinema

Cristi Puiu's films are particularly well suited to illustrate the minimalism of New Romanian Cinema. Indeed, it was his first film, *Stuff and Dough*, from 2001, that established this cinematic aesthetic, which represented a radical break with pre-existing principles of Romanian filmmaking such as symbolism and transcendentalism. As film critic Andrei Crețulescu claims, 'after *Stuff and Dough*, Romanian films can be viewed, with a few exceptions, as derivatives of the wave created by Puiu/Rădulescu' (2011: 57, my translation). So important is Puiu's influence on this type of aesthetic that Romanian film critic Alex Leo Şerban coined the term 'Puism' to denote it (cf. Pop 2014: 43).

It should be stated from the start that this minimalist aesthetic does not apply to all Romanian films made after 2001. It is only a number of films made between 2001 and 2011, belonging to what Şerban named 'New Romanian Cinema' and Pop 'Romanian New Wave', which follow Puiu's minimalist paradigm. The best examples of directors representing this paradigm, apart from Puiu, are Corneliu Porumboiu, Radu Muntean and Cristian Mungiu.

So what is then this minimalism that characterises New Romanian Cinema? I define it on the basis of the studies of Dominique Nasta (2013) and Pop (2014) as a meaningful and conscious reduction to the basics of the cinematic language, especially composition (sight and sound) and narrative (plot, characters and narrative techniques). Minimalism opts for ordinary, everyday situations and characters, and avoids the spectacular. It is an aesthetics characterised by 'technical abstinence' (Pop 2014: 66) and by the 'excision and avoidance of excess' (see Ioana Uricaru's contribution in Chapter 3). One of its main goals is to achieve what Pop calls 'immediate realism' (2014: 45–6), that is to give the viewer the impression of watching directly a non-mediated reality. Thus, claims Pop, a direct contact is attained with the 'essences, ideas, emotions, and realities that are simple enough to reach new depths' (2014: 66).

The relationship between the aesthetics of minimalism and immediate realism is of particular interest in the framework of this chapter. For it is indeed because of its immediacy effect that minimalism appears to be incompatible with remediation, since remediation requires the existence of two discernible media: a target medium and a represented (or a source) medium. Most of the features that are usually considered minimalistic contribute to the effect of immediate realism, mainly by downplaying the conspicuousness of the target medium. So for instance do the naturalistic and documentary tendency, which seems 'to always tell stories in present tense, to present actions taking place "here and now"' (Pop 2014: 45–6). So also do the 'stylistic premises, such as long shots, through which the director attempts at presenting/observing events in real time; depth of field; and the exclusively diegetic music' (Rogozanu 2012, my translation). So does the rejection of artifices like 'metaphors and symbols', which according to Mihai Fulger are only kept 'at the most on an onomastic level' (2011: 127, my translation). So especially do most of the features enumerated by Nasta, such as 'low-key discussions, rapid camera movements between the characters', a context in which 'everything is implied, nothing is really explained' (2013: 156), 'low-key lighting' (2013: 159), no usage of extradiegetic music (except for the opening or end credits), closeness to documentary live shooting (2013: 157), 'austere cinema that favours mood over event' (2013: 163), and 'framing errors' (2013: 192).

Meanwhile, the use of the medium is not always concealed in New Romanian Cinema, and is sometimes even played up. Gorzo, who is generally critical of the minimalistic classification of the New Romanian Cinema, considers instances where directors demonstrate a high degree of medium awareness (2012: 257). This could be an unexpected side effect of some of the features, enumerated by Nasta – such as rapid camera movements and framing errors – or where the cinematic language strikes through with unexpected artificiality. The latter is exemplified in scenes that seem to imitate paintings, as Nasta observes in her description of the work done by the cameraman in *The Death of Mr Lăzărescu* (2005): 'Oleg Mutu's cinematography once again opts for single takes making sure the flow of each scene is preserved, thus creating ravishing contemplative tableaux which recall Flemish or French seventeenth century paintings' (2013: 200). Such techniques cannot easily be seen as compatible with the simplicity of style in minimalism and with its aim of immediacy, and their use foreground a complexity that demands a closer attention. For instance, as Carlos Heredero states (2008: 22–3), there is a stylised and formalised element in the realism practised by young Romanian directors. Pop notices this too, and draws the attention to the use of (self-)reflexive devices as the crossing of the 'fourth wall', theatrical elements and iconographic references (2014: 38).

In the analyses of Puiu's three feature films, I will take a closer look at instances of remediation and see how they can be reconciled with the minimalistic aesthetics. But before embarking on the analysis, I will briefly introduce the concept of remediation and its intricate relation to two similar concepts: intermediality and media representation.

Remediation, Intermediality and Media Representation

As mentioned above, Bolter and Grusin defined the concept of remediation as 'representation of one medium in another' (1999: 45). The concept has been criticised by Lars Elleström for being 'all-embracing' and for encompassing indistinctively very different phenomena, such as intermediality, adaptation, representations of other media and simple references to other media (2014: 7). I argue that it is exactly this flexibility that makes 'remediation' useful. As an umbrella concept with a simple and straightforward definition, 'remediation' is indeed suitable for denoting a whole range of media appearing in other media; from the clearest representations, through explicit and implicit references, sometimes by just a name, to the subtlest allusions, for instance by imitation of formal aspects of the source medium, etc.

However, I agree with Elleström that further refinement is necessary, as for instance on the basis of his own model of media transformation (2014), which consists of the two classes of media representation and transmediation, and on the basis of the intermedial typologies made by Werner Wolf (2002) and Irina Rajewsky (2005). These typologies can be used, I argue, as precise methodological tools for the analysis of more subtle cases of remediation, whereas Bolter and Grusin's concept can be quite blunt. For instance, as Wolf showed, a medium can represent another medium both explicitly or implicitly. The latter cases are evidently harder to detect, and risk therefore not being analysed as remediations. Similarly, cases of what Wolf and Rajewsky call intermedial allusions, intermedial imitations or intermedial references, without the help of Elleström's theoretical distinctions, risk not being considered as forms of media representation.

All these fall, I argue, under the larger class of remediation. And as such, they participate in the meaning-making process. Indeed, as Elleström argues, '[t]o say that a media product represents something is to say that it triggers a certain kind of interpretation' (2014: 12). It is therefore all the more interesting to dig further and analyse the implications of such techniques, which can seem artificial and thus incompatible with the naturalistic aim of Puiu's films.

Stuff and Dough – Intermedial and Intertextual References

Stuff and Dough is not only Puiu's first feature film, but also the starting point of New Romanian Cinema, since it sets the rules for its minimalistic, Cinéma direct, observational style (cf. Pop 2014: 43). However, in this film as in New Romanian Cinema films in general, are stylised, artificial features that seem incompatible with this minimalistic aesthetic, of which some can be related to remediation in interesting ways.

First of all, there is the genre aspect. Indeed, the film flaunts elements, belonging to the crime and thriller genres, unanticipated in a story supposed to present a slice of life of an unspectacular kind. Some of the characters, for instance, are criminals: for one, it is Marcel, the local gangster, who charges the protagonist Ovidiu with the delivery of some dubious medical supplies. Then there are the recipients of the supplies and the people in the Jeep, chasing Ovidiu's car while he and his two friends, Vali, and Betty, drive from Constanţa to Bucharest. And then there is the gangster in the final scene, who more or less admits to having executed the people in the Jeep. Weapons and physical violence are used as well, and this is even discussed in an intriguing, self-reflexive manner when Ovidiu and his two friends reflect upon mob violence and the use of guns in Romania, finding them rather typical of American thriller films. Such reflections, according to Wolf's typology, are examples of explicit references to another media artefact. The self-reflexivity of such a comment is all the more apparent when one takes into consideration building up of suspense, which is also a reference, but of the implicit kind, to American thrillers; an imitation of their 'quality or structure', as Wolf would put it (2002: 2).

Admittedly, this self-reflexivity is superficial, and probably has a comic – or parodic – effect, since the implied comparison to American gangster thrillers emphasises the ordinariness of the characters in *Stuff and Dough*. However, it is not only a meaningless game as it demonstrates the medium awareness that Gorzo finds typical of the New Romanian Cinema. The point is to exploit the viewers' genre awareness and either meet their expectations or frustrate them on various levels, which is what happens in Puiu's film where the genre suspense actually leads to an 'existentialist crisis' with 'characters [. . .] struggling with moral decisions, always at the border of responsibility and freedom' (Pop 2014: 52). This echoes the conclusion of Mihai Chirilov, who cites the building up of a difficult moral dilemma as the main merit of *Stuff and Dough* (2011: 17). It must be pointed out, however, that these examples are not cases of remediation, but of intertextuality, or rather intramediality, since they concern relations within the same medium.

There are also, however, interesting cases of remediation in this film, the first of which has been noticed by Leo Goldsmith who writes that while Marcel 'enumerates the job's few particulars, we briefly glimpse a poster for *Get Shorty*, aligning Ovidiu's bedroom wall' (2008). Similarly, the juxtaposition of *Get Shorty* poster with those of Iron Maiden (see Figure 7.1), and Pink Floyd's *The Wall* create yet another level of remediation. Arguably, this too could be considered an intertextual reference between two artefacts of the same medium (film), but since it is made by means of a visual medium artefact – a poster – it therefore constitutes an intermedial reference.

What is more important is the interpretation of the reference to *Get Shorty*. Goldsmith does not really see any deeper signification in it, explaining it away with the supposition that it 'might well be all the young transporter-to-be

Figure 7.1 *Stuff and Dough*

knows of gangsters and shifty characters' (2008). But there is more to this, I argue, since the reference to *Get Shorty* establishes an entire self-reflexive dimension. The Hollywood movie is actually a mob comedy (translated on the Romanian poster as *Un mafiot la Hollywood*). Directed by Barry Sonnenfeld in 1995, it is about gangsters who want to make a mob film, while *Stuff and Dough* is about ordinary people (Ovidiu and his friends), who are on their way to becoming gangsters. The reference to the Hollywood original functions also as a clue to Ovidiu's personality, sketching him as a young man, influenced by Western popular culture, who tries to find a shortcut to a wealthier life, closer to Western standards. This is most likely why the poster is shown at the exact moment Ovidiu makes his first appearance at three minutes and twelve seconds after the beginning of the film, before Marcel has even begun to 'enumerate the job's few particulars', as Goldsmith has it.

A similar case could be made about the discussions between Ovidiu and his friends concerning music. Their reference to the Romanian music group from the 1980s, *Star 2000*, and to its lead singer, Petre Geambaşu, who is compared to Frank Sinatra, is a form of media representation through verbal means. A reference is thus indirectly made to the Communist period, and to its contrast to capitalism, whose meaning becomes clearer if one bears in mind that as early as the 1990s, Geambaşu was publicly lamenting Ceauşescu's Romania of the 1970s and 1980s (Cosmescu 2013).

Another kind of comparable contrast can be found in another media representation: the books on the shelf in Ovidiu's room, featured during the seminal scene of Marcel instructing Ovidiu about the job, whose image is what Elleström would call a 'pure media representation' (2014: 17), since it is only their 'shell' – that is, visual referent – that is shown, and not the content. However, a viewer who has some knowledge of the Romanian book market would recognise these books as belonging to *Biblioteca pentru toți*, (a 'Library for All', my translation), a collection to be found in most intellectual homes during the 1970s and 1980s. As such, they function as vestiges of the Communist past, connoting a certain respect for culture in Ovidiu's home, and therefore emphasising his surprising metamorphosis into a mobster. Curiously, one of these books is used as a support when 'enumerating the job's particulars'. The Communist past, connoted here by a book as one of its vestiges, invites an ambiguous interpretation. It can be seen either as a ridiculous prop through the eyes of Marcel, the new capitalist, who looks with contempt at the book, or as a vanishing trace of humanity and ethics, which are about to be sacrificed.

Finally, getting back to the existentialistic dimension of the film, the metamorphosis of the naïve Ovidiu into a mobster is suggested through another intermedial reference, namely Roman poet Ovid's *Metamorphoses*. As Goldsmith notices, the character's name was probably not chosen accidentally:

> [W]hile the extent of Ovidiu's innocence occasionally strains credibility, Puiu has christened him (as he did the pitiable Dante Remus Lăzărescu) with a name that indirectly suggests a somewhat loftier slant on the film's events. Ovid, who is apparently buried near [the Romanian town of] Constanța, is our hero's namesake, and the metamorphosis that Ovidiu undergoes, while not supernatural, nonetheless nudges him from innocence to experience somewhere along the highways of Romania. (2008)

The Death of Mr Lăzărescu – Iconographic References and Myths

Goldsmith's point above allows a natural transition to the next film under scrutiny here. Indeed, not only does Dante Remus Lăzărescu's predicament resemble Ovidiu's existential drama using the implicit reference of his name, but the film *The Death of Mr Lăzărescu* itself is in many respects a continuation of the minimalistic style of *Stuff and Dough* (Pop 2014: 43). However, its minimalism here is taken a step further, since the subject and the characters are even less remarkable in this film about a dying old man who is driven around to different hospitals in Bucharest by Mioara, a nurse who also happens to care for him genuinely. Yet it could be argued that this film also flaunts instances of remediation as most conspicuous challenges to what is expected of a minimalistic film.

An intriguing case in point is the various representations of TV sets, which could otherwise pass unnoticed, functioning as simple props and enhancing the reality effect. Nasta notes that the TV sets are often used as the 'only identifiable source of bright light in Lăzărescu's home' (2013: 159). But it is also interesting to look more closely at the broadcast content, more specifically at the news about the terrible bus accident that happens the very same evening Lăzărescu falls ill, and whose consequences would contribute to the humiliation he would be exposed to later that night. To use Elleström's model, this could be defined as a case of transmediation since it is not only the empty shell of the source medium that is remediated, but also the content. Nasta emphasises the narrative function of this transmediation, since 'the images shown and commented on anticipate the future parallels between Lăzărescu's personal journey into medical hell and a bus accident that turned the trauma centre "into a slaughterhouse"' (2013: 159). This parallel can also be interpreted as criticism of the impact of the mass media, since the victims of the bus accident are given priority in emergency rooms just because the media has heightened awareness of their suffering.

Many critics have noted a number of intermedial references to Dante's *Divine Comedy*, such as Dante, the name of the main character, or Beatrice, the name of the paramedic, yet they do not amount to more than just a simile in which Mr Lăzărescu's tribulations could be compared to Dante's on a certain level. Amplifying Mr Lăzărescu's second and last names, Nasta points to more mythological and literary references, such as 'the creation of Latin Rome, or the resurrection of Lazarus from St John's Gospel', which are 'meant to set up a multi-layered discourse about "Hell on Earth"'. This discourse moves 'between the hyperrealistic depiction of pain and suffering and a sustained ironic, albeit symbolic mode'. Further she goes on to point out more allusions and associations, provoked by the names of other characters in the film, 'such as stretcher carrier Virgil, [...] Doctor Anghel, close to "angel", and the nurse's first name, Mioara, the diminutive of which, "mioritza", is the prototypical Romanian "Mystic Lamb" [who is] accompanying the dying shepherd' (2013: 158–9). Indeed, as Ágnes Pethő claims, simple references, which she defines as 'ekphrastic metaphors', can generate infinite meanings, where 'one word' could act as a 'metaphor that refers to a whole literary text'. It might not 'suggest one particular image', yet would imply 'something too complex to be captured within a single image, therefore ultimately unimaginable (we may either not know the texts referred to or we may know them and then the meanings generated are virtually infinite)' (2011: 304).

On a general level one of the aims of remediation of myths in New Romanian Cinema could be, as Pop claims, to 'enhance their meaning into a universally valid story' (2014: 59). In his view, these 'iconographic references' have a 'syntactic function', since they 'use imaginary symbolism to connect, through the links between theatrical development and the previously existing imaginary formations, the real and the metaphoric' (2014: 39). The existing imaginary formations can thus be integrated in the creation of meaning thanks to the paradigmatic nature of images, which 'belong to an "amalgamated imaginary", one influenced by several layers of cultural dynamics and which allows the coexistence of various representations (sometimes contradictory)' (Pop 2014: 144).

Goldsmith finds this claim applicable to *Stuff and Dough*, and concludes that 'it's Puiu's goal to elevate this and other such stories above their banality and into the realm of myth' (2008). A statement all the more relevant in the case of *The Death of Mr Lăzărescu*, with its array of mythological references, both direct or subtle, like the reference to Jesus, achieved through what Wolf would call 'intermedial imitation' and Rajewsky, 'intermedial reference'. A case in point is the final scene, featuring the main character being prepared for the operation, when 'the given media-product thematises, evokes, or imitates elements or structures of another, conventionally distinct medium' (Rajewsky 2005: 53). Following Nasta's description, the 'frontal medium shot', framing the body of Mr Lăzărescu as '[t]he stark-naked original man, his body covered by a white sheet' (2013: 162), combined with the motionlessness and the soundlessness of the scene, 'thematizes, evokes, and imitates elements' of another 'conventionally distinct medium' – that of painting. More specifically, the scene evokes Renaissance paintings of the dead Christ, such as Hans Holbein's painting from 1521 (see Figure 7.2).

So Dante, Jesus, Remus and Lazarus, Anghel, Virgil and Mioara, all coexist in an unexpectedly multi-layered manner for a film, generally defined as minimalistic. It could be therefore argued that through both explicit and implicit forms of remediation, these deliberate mythological references elevate the story to another, universal level of signification. As Pop has fittingly commented, 'the ordeal of the main character [. . .] is a metaphoric translation of the ordeal of the Romanian society as a whole' (2014: 106). In his view, Mr Lăzărescu is 'metonymically replacing an entire past; he is a manifestation of a moment in recent history which is slowly and painfully passing away' (2014: 106). So the death of Mr Lăzărescu could symbolise the disappearance of a more humane past, be it even the Communist one, and the transition to a dehumanised

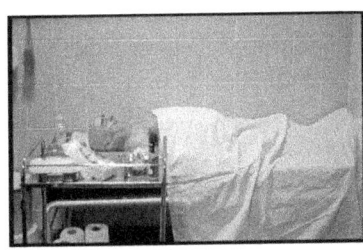 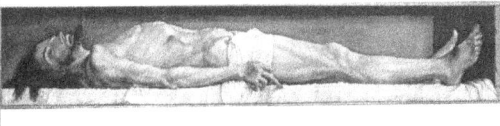

Figure 7.2 *The Death of Mr Lăzărescu*, and Hans Holbein's *Dead Christ*

form of capitalism, which harbours no place for the old, the weak and the crippled.

Aurora – Remediation, Self-reflexivity and the Meaning-making Process

Cristi Puiu's *Aurora* (2010) seems to mark a certain turning point, which heralds the presumed end of the NRC (cf. Pop 2014: 221–6). In Pop's view, *Aurora* breaks with the minimalistic rule of ordinary situations and characters, making 'an expressionistic statement, by following the twisted life of the main character, Viorel, a bizarre killer' (2014:73). Played by Puiu himself, the film covers twenty-four hours of the life of its unusual protagonist Viorel, during which he kills four people (his wife's notary, the notary's girlfriend, and his in-laws) before giving himself up to the police. Claudiu Turcuș points to the film's profound self-referential dimension, which however is not incompatible with Puiu's earlier minimalism (2014: 292), where self-reflexivity is closer to the surface – or is shell-like – as discussed above with regard to *Stuff and Dough*. Moreover, *Aurora* employs Puiu's minimalistic aesthetic alongside its expressionistic and self-referential dimensions, thus resulting in a much more effective immediate realism. As Christina Stojanova has noted, Viorel is not depicted as the glamorous serial killer, familiar from American films, but rather as 'a banal, uninteresting bore, repressed and full of complexes' (2010). And the reason for this could be unearthed in a number of intriguing cases of remediation. On the surface these might seem as simple diegetic application of broadcast TV and radio media, but their strategic placement throughout the narrative opens intricate interpretative paths, as Puiu himself claims in an interview:

> I'm the author of the film, I'm telling the story, but I'm also trying to understand this story. I have some facts only and the right way for me to understand something about what I'm doing – and about life itself – is to accept that to some extent I don't know. But it's very difficult because most people are looking for answers. (White 2010: 6)

Therefore it is worthwhile to unearth the hidden signification of some instances of remediation. Seventy-two minutes into this three-hour-long film, for example, we see Viorel eating to the sound of a sports news radio broadcast, which however cannot be dismissed as an ambient noise since the content is clearly discernible, and therefore constitutes a well-defined case of transmediation. The broadcast discusses the double standards imposed on freedom of expression in Romanian football stadia – one for fans and another for higher officials, such as Dumitru Dragomir, the president of the Romanian Professional Football League (1996–2014), who was also a member of the

Romanian Chamber of Deputies (2000–8). The newscast could thus be interpreted as a possible explanation for Viorel's lack of trust in authorities and the judiciary, which have led to his murderous vigilantism.

The remediation of music in *Aurora* is also significant since for such a pessimistic and gloomy film, it is a jarring ingredient, drawing the viewer's attention not only to its aural representation, but also to visual ones – that is, to posters of musical bands. Ninety-three minutes into the film, the camera shows three posters of the pop group Electric Light Orchestra on the walls of Viorel's room at his mother's house, thus offering – not unlike the posters in *Stuff and Dough* – clues to his personality. During communism, admiration for Western pop groups was usually synonymous with a subversive attitude, a counterweight to the official patriotic and propagandistic culture. These posters could therefore be read as yet another indication of Viorel's dissident inclinations, rooted in his communist adolescence.

In the instances of direct remediation of music (that is, without the help of another medium), it becomes evident that the tunes played bear specific connotations, which could be seen as suggestive of the irreconcilable extremes that have brought about the ever-widening rupture of Viorel's psyche. At the beginning of the film, for instance, a popular modern Romanian song is heard when Viorel is at work, and an Elton John track when he is back at his apartment, thus juxtaposing two contrasting socio-cultural conventions of work and leisure. Similarly, later on, while Viorel is at his mother's house, the radio is heard playing a Romanian choir piece from the communist era, and a church choir hymn while he's driving his car, signalling the clashing ideologies he has been subjected to during his formative years. And, most interestingly, a hundred and twenty-four minutes into the film, Viorel kills his father-in-law to the tune of a Romanian folk song, played on TV, implying yet another widening gap he is unable to transcend – that of his in-laws' village roots, and his own urban intelligentsia background.

At the end of the film, while surrendering to the police, Viorel murmurs to the policeman: 'You seem to think you understand, you seem to think you follow what I'm saying. And that scares me. I don't know if you understand.' His comment echoes the attempt of Meursault, from Albert Camus's novel *The Stranger*, to explain the murder he committed: 'I tried to explain that it was because of the sun, but I spoke too quickly and ran my words into each other. I was only too conscious that it sounded nonsensical, and, in fact, I heard people tittering' (Camus 1946: 75).

Such references can be seen as self-reflexive, referring both to our difficulty as viewers in comprehending Viorel's acts and to his own inability to do so, to which we are given a clue early in the film. His girlfriend tells him that her daughter was wondering – when 'the wolf eats granny' in *Red Riding Hood*, and 'puts on her clothes' – whether the granny would not be 'naked after the hunter cuts her out of the wolf'. Instead of appreciating the little girl's cleverness, Viorel's morosely retorts, 'I don't understand'.

Rob White interprets this episode as illustration of 'banality of evil': 'the domestic conversation is mundane', he writes, 'but violence lurks in it' (White 2010: 4). Another way of seeing this episode is as a deconstruction or rather profanation of a popular fairy tale, bringing it down to a prosaic level – a strategy, directly opposite to the elevation of an everyday story to a mythological plane in *The Death of Mr Lăzărescu*. Such an approach, applied to a thought-provoking intermedial imitation, which associates Viorel with Jesus, yields similar results. As in *The Death of Mr Lăzărescu*, the resemblance between the film character and Christ is expressed through a painting: in this case the famous icon 'non-painted by a human hand' (*archeiropoetis*).

As Pop claims, Viorel's and Christ's facial expressions are similar. Indeed, Viorel's tight upper lip (he never smiles throughout the film) and expressionless eyes could be compared to the expressionlessness of Christ's eyes, which was endorsed by the Christian icon-painting canon since its function was 'to invite the onlooker to travel through the vacant regard of the image towards the suprasensible transcendence of God' (Kearney 2003: 9). The motionlessness and the soundlessness of the scene, together with the white background, might be seen as an intermedial imitation of painting in general, as in the case of the last scene in *The Death of Mr Lăzărescu*. And as a clue to such an iconographic interpretation, Viorel appears in another long take, a hundred and eleven minutes into the film, close to two icons drawn by his daughters.

Consequently, Pop's conclusion that Viorel is 'a Christ-like figure' (2014: 146) could be accepted with the provision that he actually is, as Pop underlines, a Christ-figure in reverse – that is, an Antichrist – since all he brings is death and destruction, thus pointing to the spiritual void he symbolises. This notion is reinforced through this implicit intermedial juxtaposition between an iconic image of Christ and one of Viorel as an Antichrist figure.

As Turcuș observes, Viorel – played by the director himself as the ultimate expression of self-referentiality, additionally suggestive to Christ through the director's first name, Cristi – is often filmed while looking at himself in the rear mirror of his car, his image reflected back into the camera, thus becoming 'simultaneously subject and object of the observation'. An image, that could 'be read as a metaphor of self-referentiality, as if his glance towards the world only could send him back his own face' (2014: 293–4, my translation).

Moreover, it is not even his own face that is reflected back to Viorel, but a mediation of his face since the camera is not showing the real object, only its reflection. Yet again, self-reflexivity here subverts the tropes of immediate realism, pointing to the complexity of the meaning-making process not only for the viewer, but also for Viorel, whose world is reduced to his own reflection, staring back at him.

CONCLUSION

The above analyses demonstrate that remediations, while inconspicuous and easy to overlook or to see as parts of a filmed reality, can function as important meaning-making clusters in Cristi Puiu's three feature films. At first glance, some of them could seem incompatible with the minimalist aesthetics, characteristic of Puiu's cinema and the New Romanian Cinema in general. On one hand, they are considered incompatible with the immediate aim of minimalism, according to which the target medium should be transparent. On the other hand, these remediations bring in elements of stylisation and cultural associations that also go against the minimalist simplicity of content and style. Yet critics have noted instances, in which New Romanian Cinema films do use unexpected stylised elements and sometimes even highlight the cinematic medium devices. Although infrequent, these instances are not at odds with the realism and the minimalistic aesthetic of these films, but rather reinforce them thanks to the compression of narrative information that remediation and self-referentiality offer.

The case studies of remediation in Cristi Puiu's films, especially those precious few of the aesthetic kind, corroborate these observations. As the examples from the three films demonstrate, the prevalent functions of remediations are narrative, descriptive and self-referential. In *Stuff and Dough*, in particular, the remediations foreground the theme of the film, offering clues about the characters and the plot development, and basically contributing to a realist depiction of the socio-cultural milieu. At their best, through self-reflexive comparison to other media artefacts, they offer a self-ironic commentary.

In the *The Death of Mr Lăzărescu*, the remediations add deeper layers of meaning, opening new interpretative paths, which lift the story to universal levels through parallel discourses, based on mythological references and allusions. In *Aurora*, the mythological allusions are used in a reversed or degraded fashion, also indispensable for the multifaceted interpretations in this complex film. Thus to conclude, this chapter has argued that the instances of remediation in Puiu's films contribute to the meaning-making process by enhancing – and not hindering – their minimalistic or 'immediate realist' paradigms.

ACKNOWLEDGEMENT

I would like to express my sincere thanks, gratitude and appreciation to Christina Stojanova for her invaluable help. Without her advice, suggestions and hard editing work, this chapter would most certainly not have seen the light of day.

PART III

ETHICS/NEW AESTHETICS

8. AUTHENTICITY IN NEW ROMANIAN CINEMA: 'ETHICS AND AESTHETICS ARE ONE'[1]

Christina Stojanova

It is clear that ethics cannot be expressed. Ethics are transcendental. (Ethics and aesthetics are one.)
                      Ludwig Wittgenstein, Proposition 6.421 (2015: 108)

For Heidegger, there are two dominant modes of being human: authenticity and inauthenticity. We have a choice to make between these two modes: whether to be oneself or not to be oneself, to be author of oneself and self-authorising or not.
                      (Critchley 2009)

It is a well-known fact that, like their celebrated compatriot Eugène Ionesco, a master of the Theatre of the Absurd, the filmmakers associated with the New Romanian Cinema (NRC) avoid open engagement with direct social, political and ideological statements. Yet in the ontological game of meaning-making that New Romanian films initiate, ethics and aesthetics play an equally important role, as proposed above by Ludwig Wittgenstein. Moreover, in the existentialist realism[2] of New Romanian cinema, authenticity, or *Eigentlichkeit* – defined by Martin Heidegger as fundamental trait of existence – ensures the 'condition for being a moral agent in any meaningful sense whatsoever' (Stanford Encyclopedia of Philosophy 2014).[3]

The potential of the ethics–aesthetics congruity to bring individual, society and art together, suggested by Wittgenstein, has also been pointed out by the Russian writer Maxim Gorky, who wrote that 'Aesthetics is the Ethics of the future' (qtd in Arvon 1973: 2). The revolutionary implications of this thought are curiously regurgitated by Bruno, the main character from Jean-Luc Godard's 1963 film *Le Petit Soldat*, who – despite getting both the source and the quote wrong – finds it 'very beautiful and very moving', since he believes it reconciles political opposites.[4] If Wittgensteinian unity of ethics and aesthetics implies *sub specie aeternitatis* the accord of the world with its representation, it also unites the artist with the artefact, thus predicating the artistic integrity of New Romanian directors.

In this light, the New Romanian Cinema could be seen as an ethical 'enquiry into what is valuable, [as] enquiry into the meaning of life, into what makes life worth living, or into the right way of living' (Wittgenstein qtd in Collinson 1985: 267). And while the ethical authenticity of New Romanian Cinema is ensured by the high moral standards upheld by its directors on and off screen, its aesthetic authenticity is upheld by the self-effacing nature of the tragic or comedic-ironic modes,[5] and by mimetic faithfulness, rooted in Aristotelean antiquity when, via tragedy, it emerged as a 'basis of the human character [...] restricted by the order of nature' since 'the tragic hero cannot simply [...] summon a genie to get him out of trouble' (Frye 1990: 206).

Within the existential confines of New Romanian Cinema, the subjective time of characters acquires a particular importance as they tackle – in objective astronomical and historical time – fundamental existential problems, like the anxiety of one's loneliness; one's mortality; or one's conscience of the responsibility for choice and commitment to the rest of humanity (Heidegger 1962: 186–8).[6]

Therefore the first part of this chapter explores the distinctive handling of cinematic time as an ethical category while the second discusses representational aspects of the good *versus* evil impasse by focusing on 'cinema of process', an aesthetic trope borrowed from French existentialist cinema. The final part looks at the subjective and objective temporality of evil as manifestation of the ethic–aesthetic congruity in three NRC films.

The Ethics of Time

The significance of *The Death of Mr Lăzărescu* for New Romanian Cinema has been affirmed by the sheer number of analyses of the film, crowned most recently by Monica Filimon's extensive discussion.[7] Fittingly, *Mr Lăzărescu* is a tragedy – albeit marketed as a black comedy[8] – which establishes the fundamentals of the NRC poetics of authenticity, in the way Aristotle establishes the principles of drama on the basis of tragedy. Moreover, the film foregrounds the superb handling of time – objective and subjective, astronomical and social, and even metaphysical – as a major paradigmatic feature of New Romanian

Cinema. Indeed, as Romanian-American philosopher Costică Brădăţan points out, the loss of 'adequate temporal orientation' during communism was a result of systematic devaluation of people's 'sense of time' via 'sophisticated ideological filters' (2005: 287–9). Aimed at destroying their 'epistemic contact with the outside world', this 'tempering' seriously affected people's sense of the present, disregarded for several decades as a negligible link between the heroic past and the radiant future (2005: 287–9). The postcommunist temporal confusion, Brădăţan suggests, explains people's inability 'to come to terms with their past', their 'general mistrust in the future', but above all – their 'problematic rapport with the present' (2005: 289–90).

In this light, the masterful economy of time in *Mr Lăzărescu*, *The Paper Will Be Blue* and *4 Months, 3 Weeks and 2 Days* could be seen as an attempt at reclaiming the lost sense of temporal orientation in its somatic sense, but also as a means of recovering civic agency. By focusing on death, abortion and civil war – subjects that were considered taboo or carefully avoided – Puiu, Muntean and Mungiu catalyse the programmatic aesthetic rupture with the past of New Romanian Cinema, marked by communist and early postcommunist escapism, into the relative safety of period screen adaptations and the mythical time of metaphors and allegories. What is more, with these works they have launched NRC's philosophical platform, where the narrative patterns for handling time, designed on a formal level as conduits of narrative energy, become on an ethical level existential propositions about the human condition.

Born out of convenience, the 24-hour timeline facilitates the argument 'about the relationship between the low budgets and the thematic and stylistic choices' of New Romanian Cinema directors – and of what came to be known as hyperrealist and minimalist aesthetics, that is, 'location shooting, raw realism, the refusal of coverage and elaborate camera movements, time of action close to real time, a focused attention to detail, low-key performances' (Uricaru 2012: 429). Yet the 24-hour story transcends the exigency of financial constraints since it grafts the NRC films onto the ancient matrix of Aristotelean tragedy, which postulates that a single plot-line 'confines itself within one revolution of the sun', 'imitates' one 'complete action' of one main character, and follows the tripartite dramatic structure, based on psychosomatic Dionysian initiation rituals (Aristotle 1961: 40–4). The rigorous time frame facilitates the focus on characters whose 'ability to act'– as Canadian literary critic Northrop Frye concludes – has been progressively restricted over the last two millennia: from the omnipotent Greco-Roman gods and mythic heroes and hubris-constrained kings and nobles, through opportunistic bourgeois *alazons* (upstarts) and nihilistic *eirons* (self-effacers), to the mounting number of helpless *pharmakoi* (victims or scapegoats), populating contemporary film and media (Frye 1990: 33–4). It does not even take a 'single revolution of the sun' for Mr Lăzărescu to meet his death in the antechamber of an operation theatre after a harrowing night voyage through Bucharest hospitals. Neither innocent nor guilty, and 'no more deserving of what happens to him than anyone else would be', in his progressing infirmity Lăzărescu is reduced to an archetypal *pharmakos*, whose tragic flaw is 'living in a world where injustices are an intrinsic part of existence' (Frye 1990: 41). Within a 'single revolution of the sun', Otilia from *4 Months, 3 Weeks and 2 Days* emerges as a tragic heroine, whose *hamartia* is her selflessness, abused and misunderstood by a society that renders her 'exceptional and isolated' (Frye 1990: 38). And the young army recruit Costi from *The Paper Will Be Blue*, who – at dawn on that fateful December night of the Romanian Revolution – gets accidentally gunned down, 'inevitably and incongruously', along with his army unit (Frye 1990: 41). Both victim and scapegoat, Costi is also a veritable *pharmakos*, whose tragic guilt is living in a society where 'the gravity of what happens ... far exceeds people's frailties' (Frye 1990: 41).

The carefully designed oscillation between movement and stasis constitutes another time-handling pattern, sustained by the perennial, and often futile, motility of the NRC characters. As a metonymic expression of life and hope, it is usually contrasted by a forced stasis, which symbolises death, desperation, betrayal or moral capitulation. It is not then accidental that a significant number of NRC works deploy a quasi-road movie structure,[9] associated with Puiu's *Stuff and Dough* and *Mr Lăzărescu*, but preceded by Lucian Pintilie's *The Oak* (1992), where the characters embark on a journey, or on a shorter but fated outing, whose hectic nature denotes ubiquitous temporal confusion, enhanced after dark. It is enough to recall Lăzărescu's night-time journey through the hospital inferno, and the stasis of death at his abrupt finale. Or Otilia's anxious race against time through the pitch-dark back alleys in an attempt to dispose of the aborted foetus, which ends in the stasis, prompted by Găbița's selfishness and betrayal, masterfully captured by the final shot of the two girls at a restaurant table, staring at each other in existential desperation. And finally, Costi's senseless night meanderings in search for a Revolutionary cause worth fighting for, which is also resolved in the stasis of his equally senseless death by friendly fire.

It is however the impeccable, always right-on-cue pace of acting and editing – in the absence of extradiegetic music – that constitutes the most effective time-handling device of the NRC films. It is also the most 'imponderable' phenome of authenticity, graspable only through 'non-scientific' – subliminal and irrational – 'outward criteria' (Monk 2005: 101–2). And, like other imponderable values – 'religion, the meaning of life, logic and philosophy' (Monk 2005: 17–21) – considered by Wittgenstein to be ineffable,[10] timing is an eloquent 'outward criteria' for NRC's artistic and moral congruity. In *Loverboy*, for example, the eponymous protagonist – the seasoned pimp Luca – appears to be always ever so slightly off cue, letting others take the initiative while leaving the impression that he only 'reacts', while in fact he is a calculating predator who, in an unobtrusively silent manner, sets in motion the destructive chain of events that crush the girls he lures. In a way, his passive–aggressive stance bears a generic resemblance to Găbiţa's manipulative survival strategy, encoded in her docile demeanour. Similarly, her compulsion to misrepresent convincingly just about anything, including lying about the timing of her pregnancy, betrays a truly troubled 'epistemic contact with the outside world'.

Furthermore, for the NRC characters, the issue of timing is always already an ethical one, especially for the *pharmakoi*, whose only guilt is not so much being in the wrong place as being in the wrong time. It is enough to recall the underage drug dealer from *Police, Adjective* and the illegal Kurdish immigrant Berhan from *Morgen*, who – albeit otherwise invisible – are judged and humiliated by a flawed society whose attention they happen to attract at the wrong moment. Special attention warrants the chain of victimised females who fall prey to sex trafficking – Veli (*Loverboy*), the eponymous *The Other Irina* and *Francesca* – or to sexual assault – like Eliza in *Graduation*, and the assassinated girl in *One Floor Below* – and whose tragic fault is being 'members' of a 'flawed society' (Frye 1990: 41).

The Aesthetics of Good and Evil

Otilia, along with Nelu from *Morgen* and Voichita from *Beyond the Hills* – and for that matter Mioara Avram from *Mr Lăzărescu* – mark the higher moral ground of the NRC ethical–aesthetic congruity by cutting compelling Redeemer figures, which eloquently counterbalance the Christ-like suffering of the numerous *pharmakoi*. By featuring their acts of goodness and selfless solidarity, which put them in an exposed tragic position vis-à-vis the ubiquitous moral blindness of 'a world where injustices are an inescapable part of existence' (Frye 1990: 41), the NRC directors – in the spirit of Wittgenstein – have shown a particular sensitivity to values 'whereof one cannot speak' (2015: 108). A sensitivity which, in Wittgenstein's view, could only be found in the works of 'great artists, musicians, and novelists', who he believed could teach people a lot more than scientists (1984: 36e).

The question of evil has been amongst the most troubling for Western philosophical and psychological thought, since the correlation of God and evil has presented a largely agnostic society with a serious challenge. As Terry Eagleton rightly claims, 'evil' – like 'moral' – is a religious concept, and the belief that morality cannot exist without God, is an intrinsic part of the Western culture (Eagleton 2014, McKay and Whitehouse 2015).

Indeed, there are precious few philosophical discussions on the nature of good and evil that openly challenge the religious discourse (Nietzsche's defiant *Beyond Good and Evil* being the most famous). Moreover, the very words modern Western languages use to describe sinister entities and actions emphasise the difficulty of just replacing the religious discourse with a secular one. The (post)modern rejection of the word 'evil' prompts our failure to name 'it' outside religion, thus creating a cultural and linguistic standoff, mired in terminological confusion, and ultimately obscuring the existence of evil. Yet because we are unable or unwilling to name 'it', has 'it' really ceased to exist? The famous quote from Dostoevsky's *The Brothers Karamazov* offers a powerful take on this existential impasse: '[H]ow will man be after that? Without God and the future life? It means everything is permitted now, one can do anything?' (qtd in Lewy 2008: 1).

Carl Gustav Jung and his followers suggest yet another reason – also rooted in the Christian religion – for our inability to cope with evil not only linguistically but also psychologically. As Marie-Louise Von Frantz – a versatile feminist post-Jungian – writes, in 'most non-Judeo-Christian religions (with the exception of Buddhism), the gods (or the supreme deity) are destructive as well as good' (1993: 193). This tendency was however gradually replaced by excluding evil from the realm of Christian God, who is considered a *summum bonum* – that is, the highest good – while the evil, the dark side, was formulated by Saint Augustine as the absence of God – or *privatio boni*. Interestingly enough, according to Von Frantz' reading of the scriptures, Christ himself foresaw the implications of this dangerous bias towards the absolute good 'when speaking of the [coming of] Antichrist', which, in her view, has gradually undermined 'the Christian teachings step by step' after 'the beginning of the second millennium AD' (1993: 193–4).

Representability of Evil and 'Cinema of Process'

In this line of thought, art – and especially theatre and cinema – has made a significant contribution to the representation of evil. It would be intriguing, therefore, to see how New Romanian films construe good and evil within and outside the confines of their habitual psychological and narrative subtlety, which steers clear of genre-specific, Manichean character polarisation and open moral agenda. It particularly avoids self-nominating, melodramatic villains, albeit the genesis of these characters could be found in the poetic diabolism of Siniša Dragin's serial killer Dumitru (from *Everyday God Kisses Us on the Mouth* (2001) – one of the early New Romanian films), who 'comes to believe that he is a part of God's plans as evil incarnate', and turns into 'a spiritual werewolf, both bestial and superhuman, stuck between life and death, the demonic and the sacred' (Stojanova 2005a: 225).

Eight years later, the dashingly extrovert energy of Dragin's villain is counterbalanced – or rather sucked in – by Cristi Puiu's introverted serial killer Viorel from *Aurora* (2010). As Romanian phenomenologist Cristian Ferencz-

AUTHENTICITY IN NEW ROMANIAN CINEMA

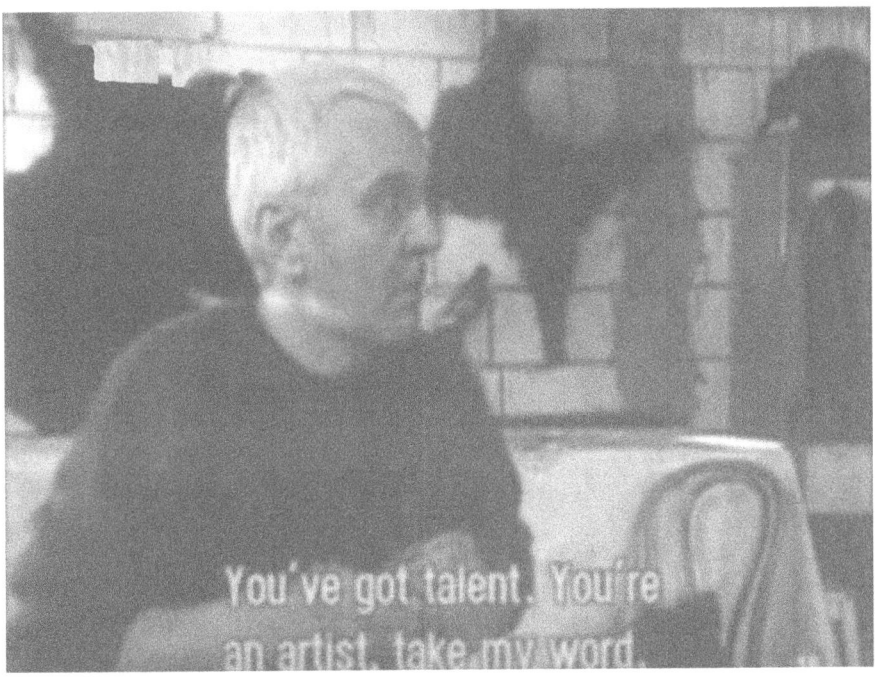

Figure 8.1 *Everyday God Kisses Us on the Mouth*

Flatz rightfully notes, the 'lack of understanding' of Viorel's 'locked-in' character evolves from a 'formal epiphenomenon of the *situation of observation* that the film constructs' – which could also be seen as a 'dysfunction', or a communicational breakdown on all levels – to a dominant 'theme of the film' (2013: 37–40). Furthermore, Ferencz-Flatz believes that 'Puiu's true ambition is, as it was with *Mr Lăzărescu*, to speak about "love"' – not unlike Sartre's on nothingness – in 'the negative, through its absence… by describing a world in which it is missing' (2013: 37–40). All the more, Puiu's films are experiments in creating a new aesthetic, capable of grasping the macabre reality by paying meticulous attention to time and the process of action. Or to what – in his analysis of Jean-Pierre Melville's 1967 film *The Samurai* (1999: 191) – Colin McArthur calls the 'cinema of process'. Shaped as an aesthetic mode under the 'brute facticity of objects in real world', brought on 'by the influence of Sartre' on French post-war literature and cinema, the 'cinema of process' is characterised by a tangible preoccupation with actions happening 'significantly closer to "real" time', and meant to disorient the viewers by seemingly showing them everything, yet telling them nothing (ibid.).[11]

Thus Puiu's preoccupation with the actions of his serial killer, enhanced by long takes and alienating frame composition, outline Viorel's psychological portrayal from the outside in, so to speak, creating a frustrating '[emotional] involvement' with the world as perceived subjectively by Viorel – that is, as infinitely bland (Ferencz-Flatz 2013: 33). This comes in stark contrast to the fact that, objectively, Viorel's life is far from bland – he has a mistress, a good job, a loving mother, two beautiful daughters, and the amount of books and CDs in his apartment suggests interests other than those of immediate survival. The point is that not even the fourfold murders and his surreal final confession before the police could disturb the flat surface of his existence. An extreme case of emotional colour-blindness, Viorel becomes synonymous with the depressing postcommunist reality, whose ugliness, long emptied of love and compassion, begs the question whether it is Viorel or his environment that is the source of evil. Indeed, Hannah Arendt's notion of the 'banality of evil' (cf. 2006) – predicated on her perception of Eichmann as indiscernible part of the formidable Nazi bureaucracy – projects him as resisting representation. Similarly inextricable from his environment, Viorel is equally resistant to representation (which most likely prompted Puiu to tackle Viorel's role himself).

Radu Muntean's *One Floor Below* (2015) offers an intriguing comment on the representability of evil in New Romanian Cinema by focusing on its consequences. Thus the protagonist Sandu, the only witness to the murder of the girl downstairs, refuses to get involved and does everything to avoid hearing out the confession of the murderer Viorel (whose name is an intertextual nod to Puiu's film). Yet Sandu becomes the conduit for the metaphysical convergence of social evil into personal suffering as is revealed by the chain of humiliations he unwittingly triggers.

A Time for Good and a Time for Evil

The lineage of the villains below – from the formidable local tyrant Samir in Bogdan Mirică's debut *Dogs* (2016), through the more sophisticated 'operations overseer' Zoli from *Horizon* (2015) by Marian Crişan, to the corrupt but intellectually refined and self-reflexive mayor (Gabriel Achim's *The Last Day*, 2016) – could be traced back to the callous drug-trafficking recruiter Marcel Ivanov from Puiu's debut *Stuff and Dough*. Like him, they belong to postcommunist kleptocratic structures, which makes them way more powerful conduits for the metaphysical convergence of social evil into personal than the hapless Sandu. True, while quintessential NRC films like Bobby Păunescu's *Francesca*, Porumboiu's *Police, Adjective* and Bogdan George Apetri's *Outbound* do touch on the criminal fringe as the epitome of social evil, terrorising the impoverished strata of postcommunist Romanian society, yet – with the notable exception of *Loverboy* – the socio-psychological mechanisms of evil are never cast into the limelight.

Dogs, *Horizon* and *The Last Day* could then be seen as a tripartite treatise on the NRC authenticity of representation of evil, with *Dogs* as its most conspicuous rendition. Quite close in spirit, if not in letter, to the legacy of nineteenth-century melodrama – which emerged in response to 'the loss of traditional values and the religious order', and whose closest heir, early cinema, portrays evil as the extreme opposite of good – *Dogs* allows us to 'locate and articulate' the postcommunist 'moral occult' in the confrontation between Samir and Roman (Brooks 1976: 5). Dragoş Bucur's Roman, cast not so much as the innocent but as the ignorant – and arrogant – victim, is completely unaware of the criminal provenance of his grandfather's wealth. As it turns out, the sprawling, fallow land masses he wants to sell are of critical importance to the local mafia of cross-border contrabandists, led by the ruthless thug Samir and played with wicked abandon by Vlad Ivanov. In order to further expose the 'domain of operative spiritual values', both 'indicated within and masked by the surface of reality' of the painfully protracted postcommunist transition, the film introduces the terminally ill and ageing cop Hogas (Gheorghe Vişu) as the unlikely hero – who, albeit late in the story, still restores justice (Brooks 1976: 5).

While in theatrical melodrama and thriller the villain – and to a great extent the victim and the hero – are more or less metaphysical constructs, epitomising occulted forces that operate beneath 'the surface of reality', here they transcend their genre limitations thanks to the powerful acting, but mostly to the film's formal ingenuity. In an elegant enantiodromic[12] reversal, the stunning visuals of Director of Photography Andrei Butica push the self-effacing minimalist aesthetic of New Romanian Cinema into its complete opposite – a refined formalism, which construes the open vistas of the southeast Romanian countryside as uncannily beautiful spaces from the edges of time. Their dusty prairie colours and deceptive tranquility exude a visceral sense of cosmic loneliness, making townspeople like Roman – a prime exemplar of New Romanian Cinema urbanised characters – feel lost and out of control.

In addition to the elliptical editing, which deliberately omits key moments and creates suspense, the camera work stands out as 'an instrument of villainy' (Rothman 1990: 29). Thus every time Samir enters the frame, hypnotising us with his arrogant self-nomination through words and deeds, the director sides with him, and the camera becomes an instrument of villainy (Rothman 1990: 30). The most commanding instance of the camera as 'an active instrument of evil' is the exquisitely shot final scene: while Hogas keeps shooting Samir at point blank, Samir – who has just murdered Roman and a few others with a blunt hammer – remains seemingly unaffected and keeps moving towards Hogas and the camera, grinning and staring unflinchingly at us, until Hogas' final shot brings him down. By capturing Samir's direct gaze, the camera lets him reveal himself as an epitome of enduring evil, which denies our innocence, and, by suggesting that the very act of viewing is villainous, turns us into accomplices.

In *Horizon*, conversely, the lines between villain and victim are blurred in favour of building psychologically – and narratively – a more complex case than expected, where the chain of events is determined not so much by the operations of occulted spiritual and moral values but is a direct result of the characters' conscious choices. Aesthetically the most conventional of the three films discussed, *Horizon* follows loosely the genre formula of what has been called elsewhere 'the Mafiosi thriller', usually featuring an honest man facing the choice either to perish, collaborate with the mafia, or kill his tormentors (Stojanova 1998: 38). Thus Lucian, a hard-working chef, rents Horizon, a small mountain hotel with a restaurant, and brings his obviously urbanised family along in the hopes that – in spite of all odds – his hard work will finally ensure the good life for his beautiful wife Andra, their son and Andra's mother, who has also tagged along. The subtle class and emotional tensions between Lucian and Andra additionally catalyse the conflict, which comes to a head when Lucian's dream is first challenged, and then shattered by Zoli and his thugs, the local mafia of extortionists. Initially Lucian complies with their racket, but when Zoli starts to openly court his wife and humiliate him repeatedly, he seeks help from the police, only to realise quickly that this would expose him to a greater danger. After killing Zoli – brutally and on camera – Lucian sets Horizon on fire, camouflaging the murder as an accident. In contrast to his quintessential New Romanian Cinema debut *Morgen* (2010), Crișan – thanks to *Horizon*'s director of photography Oleg Mutu – subtly challenges and relativises the conventions of the Mafiosi thriller from within.

According to Jung, the only way to tackle the dark side – or the individual and collective shadow – is to unflinchingly recognise its existence and power. For to identify solely with the good and project your evil side on other people, or other social and national entities, is disastrous for both the individual and the community. Jung even goes on to say that the future of the world depends on the aggregate realisations that one's psyche is a battleground of good and evil, and on the collective ability to balance out this never-ending conflict (Von Franz 1995: 205–6). As in *Morgen*, the emphasis on emotionally charged silences and eloquent glances makes up for the scarcity of verbal exchanges, thus foregrounding once again the richly nuanced acting of András Hatházi, who – after Nelu (*Morgen*) – offers yet another version of his introverted self as Lucian. Far from being innocence unprotected, Rodica Lazăr's Andra nonetheless falls victim to Zoli's wicked charm, presented with matching strength by Zsolt Bogdán as the self-nominating villain. During the two *danse macabre* scenes with Andra, his insolent gaze – highlighted by Mutu's camera – moves slowly past her pretty but unsmiling face, and lands on the camera. Through his snake-like, unblinking stare, directed right at us, Crișan not only questions the very possibility of living well and remaining honest in a postcommunist

Figure 8.2 *The Last Day*

reality, but reveals that Lucian and Zoli have moved from victim and victimiser to moral doppelgängers, that is, projections of each other's shadows.

Flanked by *Dogs* and *Horizon*, Achim's *The Last Day* emerges as the centrepiece of this triptych on good and evil, summing up both its ethical and aesthetic peculiarities, succinctly formulated in the film's promotional quote: 'The devil used to tempt people, nowadays he doesn't even bother. He just shows them the way and wishes them "safe journey!"' Unlike *Horizon* and *Dogs*, where the battle against the (d)evil's growing power is played out between two and three characters, respectively, and thus – according to Jung – creating unstable, lopsided entities, vying for resolution, here the narrative follows four protagonists, suggesting completeness. And while all three films violate the preferred 24-hour narrative regime of New Romanian Cinema, Achim does so by introducing two layers of time, epitomising what Mircea Eliade calls the profane and the sacred levels of existence (1987: 8–19). Thus the actual plot of a trip from a monastery, located high in the mountains to the flat lands – on which Adrian, a former engineer with a neck-brace and a monk-to-be, embarks somewhat reluctantly on the eve of taking his vows – covers less than twenty-four hours of astronomical, historical or profane, time. Yet the journey of the two-car convoy evolves into a mythical – or circular and sacred – experience, starting in a winter blizzard and ending up in the balmy flatlands covered in greenery. Behind the wheel of the first car is Adrian's once best friend, the autocratic small-town mayor in the forceful performance of Doru Ana. The second car is driven by the mayor's side-kick, a corrupt local cop, whose companion is the town's president of the Youth Christian League.

Jung's theory of psychological functions – his major contribution to the field of general psychology – introduces thinking and feeling as the two rational functions, and intuition and sensation as the two irrational ones. For a healthy psyche, Jung suggests, all four are to be in balance, with one superior, one inferior and two auxiliary ones, pretty much in the manner the Gnostic Holy Trinity was once equipoised by a 'fiery god, the fourth by number' (Jung: 1980/1990: Vol. 9, Part II, para. 307) – that is, by the powerful god of evil, very much present in the Egyptian and Old Testament traditions, as well as in Gnosticism, and later suppressed by Christianity.

Based on his studies in comparative anthropology, mythology and religion, Jung's approach has been since applied to the study of culture as an expression of the extant collective consciousness. In the film's quaternity, therefore, the corrupt mayor could be homologised with the superior function in contemporary society, namely thinking, as a form of overinvestment in the rational, materialistic and consumerist *weltanschauung*. The cop is easily linked to the auxiliary function of sensation since he has completely divested himself of agency for the sake of his immediate well-being. Intuition, the second underdeveloped auxiliary function, is epitomised by the church apparatchik who, despite his salaried religiosity, seems more confused than enthralled with Adrian's genuine spiritual awakening.

Adrian – in Mimi Brănescu's surprisingly self-effacing performance – endures in silence the mayor's conceited monologues and only bursts into tears at the very end, in his climactic passion scene. An obvious Christ-figure, he is however weakened and wounded (the neck-brace), epitomising the Suffering Christ rather than the Redeemer, and therefore a stand-in for the neglected and inferior feeling function, which means compassion, love, fidelity, and anything spiritual or intangible that has been dumped or repressed into the collective unconscious by our (post)modern culture. Indeed, as Jung writes, the least differentiated of the four, 'the inferior function is practically identical with the dark side of the human personality' or with our personal or collective shadow (1980/1990: Vol. 9, Part I, para. 222). Moreover, for Jung the inferior function is not just the fundamental cause of human troubles, it also poses a diabolical injunction for projecting one's evil side onto others.

It is important to recall here that – as epitomes of the least developed function of the collective consciousness – Suffering Christ-like as well as Redeemer figures in New Romanian Cinema belong to the disadvantaged social strata, whether because of their gender (Mioara and Otilia), their age (Mr Lăzărescu), their ethnicity (Nelu and Berhan), or due to a low career status (Cristi in *Police, Adjective*). Within the triptych under discussion, the cancer-ravaged Hogas from *Dogs* as a weakened Redeemer – who kills Samir more as an act of ultimate personal revenge rather than as attempt to prevent him from hurting others – is counterbalanced by Adrian, who cuts an equally frail Suffering Christ-figure, and thus, by extension, denotes a frail barrier against the influx of dark contents from the collective unconscious. A veritable illustration of this is offered in the first third of the film, when the mayor gives a lift to a poor elderly man, braving the blizzard on the way to the city hospital where, as he claims his wife is on her dead bed. Within the metaphorical-metaphysical slant of the film already obvious, the pitiful old man could easily be seen as yet another Suffering Christ-like figure, who inspires kind-hearted Adrian to bequeath generously all of his money to him, as he would not need it 'after tomorrow'. It however remains unclear whether the old man is a fraud, as the passengers in the second car energetically argue, referring to the growing number of conmen roaming the roads of the Romanian countryside with a similar or identical shtick, thus devaluing Adrian's gesture as unnecessarily sentimental, and even worse. Their reaction is a prime example of how the constellation of the feeling function as culturally inferior is bound to release from the collective unconscious the thick shadow of a doubt towards anything that is not rationally justified and explained, including love and compassion for others, and for oneself as well. Thus – in perfect tune with the apocalyptic stance of the film and its biblical allusions – Adrian, who is to be anointed on the next day, is unable to recognise 'false messiahs and false prophets', and this is to be read as a sign of the end of times, as St Matthew's Gospel warns in 24: 24.

The mayor's obsession with recording himself on video – a self-reflexive link to Achim's previous film, *Adalbert's Dream* (2011), whose protagonist is also a zealous amateur filmmaker – is used wisely by director of photography George Chiper as a convenient stylistic device that justifies diegetically the dominating frontal shots of the film. The static frontal camera allows one to follow the intriguing parallel dialogues in both cars, and also lets the mayor stare at the camera and at us for long stretches of time and seek our unconditional approval, while proudly nominating himself as the most efficient villain in the region. Moreover, upon arriving at his hunting lodge, where the Unholy Trinity subjects Adrian to another series of humiliations, Achim uses a video insert to reveal that Mica, once the love of Adrian's life, is now unhappily married to the mayor.

In another enantiodromic twist of the uncomplicated dramatic regime of New Romanian Cinema, the growing tensions within this unbalanced quaternity is resolved off camera while – in a frontal long and static shot – we are left to watch the mayor's hunting dogs devour the barbequed meats just offered to his guests. Yet just before the screen goes blank, we hear four shots from the mayor's new semi-automatic weapon.

The somewhat sudden finale offers no closure to this contemporary treatise on the weakened good and the banality of evil. One of the reasons surely lies with the fact that Adrian's abstract religious escapism is far from the self-sacrificial ethos of Otilia, Mioara, Nelu or Voichiţa, whose response to the call of conscience is immediate commitment. Another reason is that the mayor lacks the intensity and the mythological wickedness of Samir or the perverse charm of Zoli – he is rather mundane, self-consciously verbose, and – not unlike *Aurora*'s Viorel – too banal and knowable to be scary.

The abrupt ending leaves the film open to a plethora of more or less sanctimonious psychological interpretations, with existentialist, phenomenological, ethical, socio-cultural and Marxist penchants, among which Von Franz's inference to Jung's claim that 'we are the origin of all coming evil' seems most relevant (McGuire and Hull 1987: 436). 'Unconscious and undeveloped', she writes, the 'inferior feeling [function] is barbaric and absolute, and therefore [its] hidden destructive fanaticism sometimes bursts out', causing a neurosis on a large scale (1993: 82). This, as history has aptly demonstrated, usually ends up in terrible suffering or universal conflagration.

Notes

1. An earlier draft of this chapter was published in *Film: Revistă trimestrială de cinema a Uniunii Cineaștilor din România* (Stojanova 2016).
2. For discussion of existentialist realism in NRC see the Introduction to this volume.
3. Despite of his criticism of postwar existentialism, Heidegger's influence on it as a conduit for the ideas of Kierkegaard and Nietzsche is undeniable.
4. The full quote is: '[T]here is a beautiful sentence, I think it's from Lenin: Ethics are the Aesthetic of the future! I find that sentence very beautiful and very moving too. It reconciles the right and the left[.]' (Godard, *Le Petit Soldat*, 1963).
5. For more on the tragic and ironic modes in New Romanian Cinema, see the Introduction to this volume.
6. In Heideggerian terms, by 'reckoning' with the objective manifestations of 'world time' as 'clock time', 'ordinary' (or 'vulgar'), and 'elementary' (or historical time), the characters, as Beings-in-the-World, in their subjective – 'originary' – temporality (enfolding simultaneously their past, present, and future) – 'interpret' or 'express themselves' (1962: 373–5).
7. Filimon insists that, 'although stylistically many NRC films can be traced back to Puiu's 2005 feature, they embody very different approaches to cinema. What remains indisputable, however, is that *Mr Lăzărescu* was the start of a "revolution"' (2017: 59).
8. According to Puiu, he made a Monty Python-inspired poster for the film, using 'soap opera, or sitcom stereotypes', with 'all [participants standing around Mr Lăzărescu's stretcher] posing and smiling'. It was an idea that 'the distributor Tartan (UK/USA) found interesting and [so they] marketed the film as a black comedy', without consulting Puiu. And he quoted a Romanian saying 'Să faci haz de necaz', meaning 'you should laugh off your misfortune' (Puiu interview, 2017).
9. *The Paper Will Be Blue* (2006); *Angling* (2008); *The Other Irina* (2009); *First of All, Felicia* (2009); *The Happiest Girl in the World* (2009); *Morgen* (2010); *Aferim!* (2015), *The Treasure* (2015).
10. 'Whereof one cannot speak, thereof one must be silent', Proposition 7 (2015: 108).
11. Bela Tarr's *œuvre* deploys a similar aesthetic.
12. A Jungian term, borrowed from Heraclitus, enantiodromia pertains to 'the inherent compensatory tendency of all entities, pushed to the extreme, to go over to their opposites' (Stevens 1990: 140).

9. THE SQUARE AND THE SCREEN: THE ETHICAL DIMENSION OF THE NEW ROMANIAN CINEMA[1]

Ioana Uricaru

Radu Muntean's *The Paper Will Be Blue* premiered at the 2006 Locarno Film Festival. Like Corneliu Porumboiu's *12:08 East of Bucharest*, released in the same year, it dealt with the events of December 1989 – Revolution, regime change, *coup d'état* or insurrection – but unlike Porumboiu's sarcastic retrospective examination, Muntean is interested in directly revisiting the night of 22 December 1989, in all its confused emotionality and disconcerting contradictions. For Muntean – a young army recruit at the time of the events, just like the film's protagonist – this reenactment of the trauma is a necessary moral obligation, an operation of truth recovery. In *The Paper Will Be Blue* we discover one more New Romanian Cinema text striving for the experiential dimension of cinema and rejecting politicised and media discourses as a betrayal of reality. In order to understand the significance of this film – as well as of other texts belonging to the New Romanian Cinema dealing with similar subjects – it is first necessary to examine the place of media discourse(s) in the Romanian public sphere, to which Muntean's film is a direct response.

THE BATTLEFIELD OF MEDIA BROADCAST

The notion of betrayal is deeply engrained in the collective psyche of Romanians and seems to be haunting their history – certainly their recent history. Romania became a totalitarian Stalinist dictatorship in 1948 after a series of fraudulent elections and after King Michael's forced abdication. The prevalent popular explanation of what followed – not unsupported by historical facts – went like this: Churchill and Stalin had negotiated the division of Europe into geopolitical zones of influence. Initially, Romania, with its Latin heritage, strong Francophile traditions and complete allegiance to liberal democracy, was supposed to belong in the Western sphere of influence. However, Churchill wanted to protect British interest in strategically important Eastern Mediterranean, so the Allies traded Romania in exchange for Greece.

It took a number of years for the country's political class and for the people as a whole to finally accept that they had been abandoned by the Allied powers, and this deep, unforgivable betrayal became the founding trauma of post-war Romania.

In 1965, Nicolae Ceaușescu became leader of the Romanian Communist Party, and in 1974 he also became President of the republic. Ceaușescu made some political choices that endeared him to the West and to the Romanian population alike. For example, when the Soviet Union invaded Czechoslovakia in 1968, Romania was the only socialist country that refused to join in and Ceaușescu even condemned the invasion in a public speech.

In 1971, Ceaușescu visited China and North Korea and was thrilled with the spectacle of their version of communism, which he then tried to implement upon returning to Romania. The North Korean model led to several major policy decisions – from the so-called systematisation of villages, which really meant their destruction, to the national programme of scientific nutrition, which really meant the rationing of food to near-starvation levels. One important consequence was the change in the media landscape, specifically television. Up until the 1980s, the only television institution, the government-owned Romanian National Television, was broadcasting on two channels, and had between six and eight hours of broadcasting daily – more on weekends. In the 1980s, this schedule was gradually reduced, the second channel was shut down and broadcasting time shrank to two hours a day.

National Television programming became a source of frustration, boredom and bitter humour as the population tuned in only for an occasional – and heavily censored – movie or TV series. Sometimes people would also watch the live broadcasts of Ceaușescu's speeches in the hopes of seeing some sign of physical weakness or of hearing a word or turn of phrase that would signal a change in policy or in the personal mood of the dictator.

Many Romanian television sets were permanently tuned to the frequency of neighbouring socialist countries or, after 1987, became just screens attached to VCRs that allowed people to watch foreign media smuggled over the border on VHS tapes. This changed dramatically at the end of December 1989, when millions of Romanians tuned back to the National Television broadcast. The events of that memorable end of December became known to most solely through television, and entered the global consciousness as such. The

Romanian uprising that led to the toppling and eventual execution of Nicolae Ceaușescu and his wife became known as the 'Television Revolution' as most of its important moments – the dictator's last speech, his taking off in a helicopter from the Central Committee rooftop, the masses storming through various key buildings, including the TV station, the gathering of the country's new leadership, street fights and the attacks of forces apparently still loyal to the dictator, Ceaușescu's arrest, trial and execution, the proclamation of the first laws and decrees of the new regime – everything was shown live on TV, as programming abruptly went from two hours a day to round-the-clock coverage.

However, this immense live broadcast-fest was not presenting the whole picture. Its relationship with reality turned out to be tenuous at best and was apparently instrumental in supporting and propagating a certain official version of events. In fact, it helped to create and maintain the myth of the revolution as a purely popular uprising, which was later challenged by the more accurate version of a 'palace revolution' or, plainly put, a *coup d'état*.

Four decades of communist public discourse that blatantly contradicted and obfuscated the reality on the ground, in Orwellian and Kafkaesque fashions, had created an extraordinary demand for reclaiming the media access for agents perceived as authentic, truthful and real. Thus the actual use of television, and especially access to it, epitomised the political situation in Romania between December 1989 and June 1990. Furthermore, I am arguing, this demand and need for media (including cinematic) discourse to reconverge with the reality of experience is one of the fundamental engines of New Romanian Cinema's approach.

On 22 December, around noon – 12.08 to be precise – the television screens all over Romania would show what turned out to be the symbolic image of the Revolution: a bunch of disorganised civilians, wearing sweaters and waving mutilated flags, addressing the nation from the news studio that for decades had come to signify and embody the implacable order of totalitarianism.

This televisual moment divides history into 'before' and 'after'. On the day and night that preceded this dividing moment, people built barricades, stood in front of army tanks and were shot at – a few hundreds were killed in direct clashes with Army and Securitate forces. Before this momentous TV event at 12:08 on 22 December, participating in a protest was an act of true resistance, which could end in imprisonment or even death. After that, basically everyone went out into the streets, as the striking TV images gave people confidence and a feeling of security, while the fundamental site of visible authority had been undermined. The country became split between those who protested the regime before 22 December 1989, and those who did so after. It is highly significant that everything that happened before Ceaușescu's flight – the bloody clashes between government forces and protesters, the shootings, the barricades –

was not shown on television, and in a sense was, therefore, less real to most Romanians. The appearance of revolutionaries in the television studio came to be identified as the canonical representation of the events: a mish-mash of well-known faces, actors and intellectuals, and people 'from the street', unshaven, extremely emotional, agitated but victorious, saying things that had never been allowed on TV before and seeming to come up with a plan as they went along, thus creating a romantic and endearing vision of victory.

This distinction between *before* and *after* Ceaușescu's escape is at the core of Porumboiu's *12:08 East of Bucharest*. Before Porumboiu's film, the text that introduced the December events to scholarly circles was Harun Farocki's film *Videograms of a Revolution* (1992), a found footage documentary that uses both TV and amateur video camera images. I want to make the distinction between the two types of images, as their differences came to structure the political transition in 1990. As Benjamin Young notes in his essay on Farocki's work:

> While the poor quality of the hand-held camera footage attests both to the uncomposed actuality and occasional banality of the events, the general disregard for the codes and conventions of cinematography and television broadcast serves to highlight the sporadic efforts by television crews to reassert the professional norms of reportage. (2004: 246)

Later, this attempt to reassert the professional norms became an attempt at re-establishing the powers-that-be – contrasting order, discipline and 'quietness' – to the perceived (and represented) chaos, hysteria and unruliness of the street. Again, from Young's essay:

> The proliferation of hand-held cameras throughout the course of the film does work to subvert the attempts to control television through central-ized transmission. However, since the film's limited time frame does not show us the effects of the revolution, it does not assert, but rather asks if the decentralization of media technology is equal to its democratization. [...] While cameras in the studio are limited by location, and a cen-tralized transmission allows for greater programming and control, the image-gathering power of the cameras in the street is compromised by chance and bodily danger. (2004: 253)

Young is referring here strictly to *Videograms*, but if we look a few months into 1990, we discover that images from cameras in the street were eventually put in opposition to those produced by the official mass media, thus coming to signify two irreconcilable political points of view.

In January 1990, for example, the National Television – which would remain the only TV station for another five years – was still broadcasting live images of unruly politics recorded in the public square, with raw-voiced politicians addressing the crowd from atop armoured vehicles.[2] By February 1990, such images had disappeared from TV screens, as the station reined in its broadcast from non-stop live coverage to ten to twelve-hour daily structured programming. This evolution mirrored the provisional government's efforts to give an impression of calm and control, of budding legality and legitimacy, of having steered the political situation firmly onto the right track.

Let us not forget that active street presence in December only occurred in a few big cities – the majority of the population knew about the regime change only from what they saw on TV. For them, 'taking over' the TV station and making sure that the programming was under control became synonymous with a happy ending to the revolution. Any disturbance of the smooth transmission – such as interruptions in broadcasting – was synonymous with crisis and an attack on the new and hard-earned (albeit by others) democracy.

It is important to note that the legitimacy of the provisional legislative body rested on the arrogant claim that it was formed spontaneously by people who met for the first time at the television studio. Individuals as well as various civic organisations contested this legitimacy, maintaining that the provisional legislative body and government were in fact made up of second- and third-echelon Communist Party activists, who had been conspiring for years against the *ancien* regime, and who took advantage of the popular uprising to go ahead with their *coup d'état*. These voices of dissent stated that, as soon as the dictator had fled, the initial goals of the popular movement, in which over a thousand people lost their lives, were derailed and the new regime began working actively towards imposition of a long-term Gorbachev-like solution instead of initiating a radical break with the communist past. The dissenters, however, were not allowed access to mass media, and with the first democratic elections scheduled for 20 May 1990, they decided to take action to prevent a compromised electoral process.

The central point of the city of Bucharest lies at the crossroads of two major boulevards, in the shadow of the university building. Piaţa Universităţii (University Square) was drenched in blood in December 1989. In April 1990, some of the survivors came out again, to this same place, to protest 'the hijacking of the Romanian Revolution' by the new regime.

The April street demonstration quickly grew into a large-scale sit-in protest that went uninterrupted for fifty-three days, blocking the centre of Bucharest and counting anywhere from a core of one hundred devotees to crowds of hundreds of thousands, depending on the time of day. Known as 'Piaţa Universităţii' or simply 'Piaţa' ('The Square'), this phenomenon eventually spread out into Romanian society, which became split between supporters and detractors of the public protest. Its final violent repression by police forces and civilian militias turned this split into an irreconcilable rift that still haunts Romanian society today.

The protesters were essentially demanding that a collection of video recordings be broadcast on television, with an almost naïve faith that simply watching the right media content would change the nation's perspective. They put impressive amounts of energy into publicising these video recordings, and the government employed a matching effort in keeping them away from the public eye. The tape-recordings – like the ones in *Videograms* – had been made with video cameras that did not belong to the TV station and thus showed the true colours of the transitional regime, whose behind-the-scenes deals, made in person or on the phone inside the Central Committee building, were caught on camera and presented as a proof that the TV station was showing a fictitious official story.

While the 1990 protest was endorsed symbolically and sometimes in person by a great number of famous Romanians, repeated attempts at negotiating with the government failed just as the national TV station chose to represent the sit-in sporadically and extremely unfavourably, using images that evoked unruliness and disorder such as diverted ambulance traffic and agitated protesters sleeping in tents. These images and the accompanying commentary created a narrative of danger, abuse and lack of control around the sit-in – but also, because of the identity of space and the similarity in picture content, recreated the narrative of December 1989, with one major difference: the people who had courageously risked their lives on the barricades were now compared to unruly 'hooligans', as labelled by the president. In a desperate attempt to provide access to information, the protesters organised nightly showings of the tape-recordings, projecting them on the wall of the School of Architecture in the square. These very public screenings symbolically counteracted the power of 'fake' mass media with the power of 'real' media – watching the raw, unedited footage in a public space that had been physically conquered from authority was an empowering experience indeed. But these screenings also underlined the imbalance of power, since the relatively insignificant number of people who could be reached in this way constituted an ineffective political strategy. The results from the 20 May 1990 elections granted the provisional legislative body legitimacy with an immense margin. The sit-in continued until 13 June, when it was dispersed first by the police and then by militias, comprising coalminers from the Valea Jiului region. The repression, led apparently by infiltrated plainclothes government agents, was extremely brutal. When asked what prompted them to come to Bucharest, the miners replied that when the National Television suspended broadcasting for a short time on 13 June, they thought that the protesters were assaulting the TV station, and hurried to its defence, to restore order and 'quietude'.

Cinema as Restorative Justice

In the confrontation between the two spaces of change: the real – the square, with its physicality – and the virtual – the screen, with its pervasiveness and authority – the latter eventually won, prompting subsequent mobilisation of new, alternative media outlets in order to fully reclaim the lost power. In 1991, a feature-length documentary about the sit-in protest, *University Square* (Stere Gulea), was released in cinemas. Briefly, movie theatres became the site of alternative media. In the difficult search for the unattainable truth – which began with clandestine domestic video screenings from the 1980s, continued with the projection of the 'tape-recordings' on the School of Architecture's walls, and was ultimately claimed by cinema – Gulea's documentary became a very early harbinger of the New Romanian Cinema explosion.[3]

The enduring belief that '*If only the [truthful] images were shown, everything would have been different*' is, in this context of Romanian media landscape, a popular notion that insists on the responsibility of filmmakers to *show the truth* – that is, the reality of what happened. In Lacanian terms, the constructs of the Symbolic order – the treaty between Stalin and Churchill, the forty-year-long ideological subjugation, the packaging of December 1989 as a heroic, victorious revolution, the misleading media narrative, presenting the Piața Universității phenomenon as the deed of a 'bunch of thugs' – have foreclosed access to the unmediated, un-narrativisible reality of the traumatic but authentic Real. In the cultural paradigm of hope and betrayal, post-war peace was undermined by the Soviet takeover, and the long-awaited revolt against Communist Party terror was confiscated by manipulative political factions. In both cases, the repressive Symbolic order structured away the Real, attempting to banish access to it through ideological and mediatic systems of obfuscation.

The films of New Romanian Cinema emerged in this context – starting with Cristi Puiu's *The Death of Mr Lăzărescu* (2005) – as a conscious project of recovering the Real. The often-discussed minimalism of New Romanian Cinema, including a rejection of 'cinema of attractions' tools – from coverage[4] to soundtrack to editing techniques – indicates the desire to subvert the structures of the Symbolic order and search for an expression that transcends it. In a cultural landscape heavily controlled by monopolistic top-down systems – the pre-1989 repressive government, one-TV-station in the 1990s, commercially conditioned media in the 2000s – the unique, new-found status of the cinema *auteur*, who works independently relying largely on state subsidies and gets validation at prestigious foreign festivals, made possible the pursuit of an expression that was passionately committed to the unveiling of the Real.

In her book *Trauma Culture*, E. Ann Kaplan argues that the ways in which culture responds to major social trauma – such as the 9/11 terrorist attacks or colonial oppression – are similar to the individual's responses to personal trauma, the dominant one being to cope by narrativising the events in an acceptable, comforting and ultimately healing way. Thus new subjectivities are produced as a result of the traumatic shock (2005: 20). Referring to Slavoj Žižek's formulation of the 'desert of the Real' in his famous post-9/11 essay *Welcome to the Desert of the Real* (2002), Kaplan formulates trauma as an experience so raw that it feels like an unbearable nightmare, especially when compared to the relative safety of discourses that package the trauma. Catastrophes – such as the 9/11 attack – can open the door unto this desert, yet since its largely unbearable and senseless violence make for a meaningless representation, one tends to rush back to the relative comfort of the Symbolic, even if it proves to be repressive.

From this perspective, I would suggest that films such as Porumboiu's *12:08 East of Bucharest*, Puiu's *The Death of Mr Lăzărescu*, Cristian Mungiu's *4 Months, 3 Weeks and 2 Days* and Muntean's *The Paper Will Be Blue* are animated by what Žižek, paraphrasing Badiou, would call 'passion for the Real' (2002: 5). In all of these films, this passion is born from the clash between conventional discourses, and deep, inexpressible personal experiences. All these films are to a certain extent autobiographical, and therefore resist the urge of the Symbolic to narrativise at the expense of experience, thus keeping open the door unto the desert of the Real. These films bring back the power of the Real and expose the Symbolic discourse – be it historical, political, narrative, legal or formal – as either impotent or manipulative. Moreover, the films display a fundamental distrust in discursive practices, deployed in the name of the authenticity of lived experience. In each film, people are confronted with catastrophes (death, rape and abortion, December's bloody events), where moral choices can only emerge through empathic experience – nurse Mioara's kindness towards Dante Lăzărescu, Otilia's devotion to her friend Găbița, the Lieutenant's care for Costi. These films show a strong commitment to a formal discourse that is incompatible with ideological propaganda and obfuscation, and resort to discursive tools that recreate and reassert the authenticity of experience. Discourse has to be subsumed to experiential reality, otherwise it is a lie – as becomes clear in *12:08 East of Bucharest*, where after an hour of competing, pathetic attempts at acceptably narrativising historical events, it is those who have lost their lives in December 1989 who open the door unto the desert of the Real. The battle of the discourses is 'won' by an experiential reality/revelation – a fundamental strategy of New Romanian Cinema. The only role for a discourse belonging to the Symbolic order is to illuminate an experience: an approach that goes contrary to the postmodern and poststructuralist claims, yet is seen as an ethical choice by Romanian filmmakers. Thus the cinematic discourse – with its system of signs and symbols, its grammar, its tools, its powerful devices from story to images – is meant to be subsumed to the reality of individual emotional experience. As the cinematic discourse

THE SQUARE AND THE SCREEN

wanes, the door opens onto the anxiety of a revealed reality. In *12:08 East of Bucharest*, the TV studio bickering becomes a tragic paroxysm on the backdrop of the absurd December 1989 loss of life. Everybody dies irredeemably alone, reveals *The Death of Mr Lăzărescu*. The nightmare of life is neverending, and the characters in *4 Months, 3 Weeks and 2 Days* are hopelessly trapped in it. Yet the door to the Real should be left ajar so that the desert, in all its brutality, can be contemplated, because that is where the house is built.

A Film about How it Feels to Die for the Revolution

In *The Paper Will Be Blue*, the entire duration of the movie is spent wandering through the desert of the Real. It is set on the night of 22 December, after Ceaușescu's flight, when the population finally poured into the streets of every major city in Romania, but in several places, especially in Bucharest, this did not turn out to be a safe choice. The film conveys this reign of chaos – it is unclear who is now in charge of the country. Are the troops, deployed in the streets, meant to maintain order and protect the population, or could they shoot at civilians as some did the night before? Rumours are circulating: different branches of the armed forces (infantry, paratroopers, artillery, police and Securitate, the state secret police) are randomly accused and then exonerated of having remained faithful to Ceaușescu as opposed to 'stepping on the side of the people'. Hostility brews between civilians and uniformed men in the streets, while suspicion hangs heavy between those wearing different uniforms, since they do not even know whether their superiors are 'on the side of the Revolution' or not. Throughout the city, sniper shooting can be heard at close range. No one is sure who's firing at whom, but people are getting killed. And they are all engulfed in a pitch-black night that makes it impossible to recognise anyone more than three feet away.

A militia (police) patrol, led by Lieutenant Neagu (Adi Carauleanu), is surrounded by a handful of angry demonstrators and takes refuge inside their armoured vehicle, trying to get orders from their superiors and confirm the citywide safe *mot de passe* for the night. Costi (Paul Ipate), one of the recruits in the patrol, is unhappy with the officer's caution and discipline, and burns with enthusiastic desire to 'join the Revolution'. The television station, besieged by mysterious agents (rogue army units? Ceaușescu's ultra-secret faithful praetorian guard?) calls for the population to come to its defence. Costi defies his superior's orders and leaves the patrol, joining a group of rowdy civilians *en route* to the television station.

Costi is just a fresh high-school graduate fulfilling mandatory military service – a nice, well-educated teenager, he's the only son of a good family, his father being a prominent doctor. Lieutenant Neagu is mortified at the thought that Costi is now, for all practical purposes, a deserter. Feeling responsible

Figure 9.1 *The Paper Will Be Blue*

for the young man's fate, he decides to go and look for him together with his patrol. So begin their long parallel journeys through the dark, violent and deadly city, in a rescue mission that gives them some kind of purpose in the general confusion.

In his rush to defend the TV station, Costi ends up in a house where a mixture of uniformed and civilian men are holding a position against unknown attackers firing from across the street. Civilians who have hastily been given Kalashnikovs are a startling sight for Costi – but he joins them on the orders of another civilian who seems to be somewhat in charge. After shooting at the attackers for a while, he realises that their adversaries are in fact soldiers – and understands that they've been killing each other senselessly, each side assuming that the others are 'the enemy of the Revolution'. When he tells this to his new commander, he is arrested – together with a dark-skinned civilian – tied up and thrown in a basement, among jars of pickles. A young soldier watches them, convinced that they are foreign terrorists, and is ready to execute them. In a scene that calls to mind an Eugen Ionescu play – both terrifying and funny in its absurdity – the soldier asks his prisoners where they have been trained, and how come they speak Romanian so well. The dark-skinned civilian tries in vain to explain that he's a Romanian Gypsy and not a Palestinian terrorist.

In a twist of fate, Costi manages to convince his captors to verify his identity by calling the emergency room where his father is operating on the wounded. He is finally released and goes home, where he finds Lieutenant Neagu and his comrades drinking coffee, boots politely left outside in the

THE SQUARE AND THE SCREEN

Figure 9.2   *The Paper Will Be Blue*

mudroom. Costi's mother insists on feeding them – or at least on packing some pork cutlets to go – and his girlfriend manages to sneak in a kiss and a conversation about their New Year's Eve plans. The reconstituted patrol gets into the armoured car and returns to their position as dawn is breaking. And then they cross another armoured car, and are all killed because they give the wrong *mot de passe*.

This ruthless finale negates any possible hope for meaning or for the kind of narrativisation that is supposed to help in coping with the trauma. It is absurd, incomprehensible and might as well be followed by an intertitle, which could serve as motto to both Žižek's article and Muntean's film: 'Lasciate ogni speranza' ('abandon all hope') This is made all the more poignant as we finally find out that *The Paper Will Be Blue* is the (wrong) *mot de passe*. It is supposed to be safe, something certain in this chaotic night, but it gets them killed. We kept trying to figure out what the title means, only to discover that it doesn't *mean* anything. It simply kills, sordidly, anonymously, indifferently, in the grey dawn of a snowless winter day. This password stands in for the futility of language and by extension – for the Symbolic order – where the supposedly solid signified/signifier relationship (safety/password) breaks down just as arbitrarily as it was assigned, and the entire diegetic world collapses with it. What is even more remarkable, in the reality of December 1989, is that the world actually kept collapsing in this very manner, many times over, in precisely these kinds of meaningless circumstances – Radu Muntean was part of a patrol like the one in the film, and much of the story is autobiographical.

Throughout the film, it becomes clear – and viscerally understood – that any pretence of knowing who is fighting whom, and generally what is going on, is plain impossible. The very question of what would be a moral, ethical, patriotic or duty-bound action is exposed as a ludicrous conceit: under these circumstances, one can only hope that what is done in order to survive might turn out to not be morally reprehensible. As Kaplan points out, common wisdom says that trauma unites and creates community, but *The Paper Will Be Blue* insists on the *real* consequences of trauma – exposing rifts, fault lines and betrayals. Here, trauma carries a loss of innocence, in the sense of an impossibility to be narrativised and dealt with – a loss of belief in the power of discourse to heal and construct meaning. If, as Lacan theorises,[5] entering the Symbolic realm is understood as an alienation from the Real, here it is the impossibility of entering the Symbolic that is brought into high relief, and the Real emerges as a desert of non-meaning.

Overwhelmingly, the characters in New Romanian Cinema are denied the agency, causality, control, mastery and power of narrativisation that are provided by the Symbolic order. They are condemned to wander around in the desert of the real – among absurd occurrences, meaningless gestures, strong but inconsequential emotionality, moral relativism – a system of logic dominated not by the binary principle of 'tertium non datur' (or no third [possibility] is given), but by the so-called 'fallacy of the excluded middle', which always points to more unanticipated options – and to find that only fragile emotional solidarity can give them an ephemeral lifeline.

Although it does not share the technical, aesthetic and material characteristics of *Videograms*, Muntean's film shares the preoccupation of Farocki's documentary by using the camera to facilitate a brutal collision with reality, while also questioning the truth value of what we see. The representation of television – both as a discursive medium and an institution – exposes it as an irresponsible and dishonest actor in the catastrophe. The institution is, just like its post-9/11 US homologues, a conduit of 'national ideology [...] hard at work shaping how the traumatic event was to be perceived' (Kaplan 2005: 13). Costi's mother is glued to the TV set, but that doesn't give her any information; instead, her son puts in motion the catastrophe because he naïvely believes the institution needs to be defended. Many people – mostly civilians – died that night, and in the following nights and days, because they heeded the calls coming from the TV screens. A few months later, when the same TV station refused to broadcast the infamous revelatory tapes, it is no wonder that many people felt – again! – betrayed, and descended into Piața Universității. Twenty-seven years later, the question of who actually pulled the trigger killing thousands remains mysteriously and unacceptably open. With *The Paper Will*

Be Blue, Radu Muntean has made it his mission to keep the trauma alive, and the door to the desert open in our face. Any discursive working through this question – especially on behalf of the media – remains a lie as long as it fails to account fully, experientially, for the nightmarish reality experienced by the people in the streets during those nights and days.

As we wander along with the characters through the Desert of the Real during that fateful night, we get an authentic, heartbreaking experience of confusion and meaninglessness, and are forced to accept the true circumstances of reality. From this position, as in Dante Lăzărescu's journey unto death, and Otilia's running around like a mouse in a maze, we viscerally grasp the useless enormity of any prescriptive solution, of any attempt at judging or moralising, of any ideological theorisation, made from a safe distance. It is significant – and striking – that one of the bolder aesthetic choices made by Muntean and cinematographer Tudor Lucaciu is to stage the whole action in a realistic, but disconcerting darkness, which makes viewing itself difficult. This trope of wandering through darkness is quite present in many of the New Romanian Cinema works – most obviously in *4 Months, 3 Weeks and 2 Days* and in *The Death of Mr Lăzărescu*. In *The Paper Will Be Blue*, it acquires a devastatingly ironic dimension as the cold dawn finally brings visibility – and death by confusion. The light of day, which usually provides visceral comfort and respite to the cinema viewer, turns out to be nothing but a cruel taunt as the nightmare ends in annihilation. A Real, deserted of comprehensible meaning indeed.

The casualties of December 1989 – as is also suggested in *12:08 East of Bucharest* – are victims of ultimate betrayals and, as a filmmaker, Muntean's project is to not betray them once more. The subjectivity that emerges after the traumatic shock must be an unsettled one – therefore the survivor subjects (of which Muntean is one) must keep the door to the desert open.[6] In the context of the media significance in post-1989 Romania, *The Paper Will Be Blue* is a political statement, proclaiming non-submission to coping mechanisms, and a manifesto for returning to the reality of emotion and individual experience. It lays bare the desperate human condition, with the conviction that this is necessary for the subject's ethical positioning. As in other films of the New Romanian cinema, the only basis for ethics can be found in individual solidarity, in truly empathising with another even if this empathy comes at an extraordinary price.

Notes

1. Part of this chapter is based on a presentation delivered at the Society for Cinema and Media Studies conference, New Orleans, 2011.
2. One such famous live broadcast showed Ion Iliescu, the president of the new provisional government and ex-communist apparatchik, being forced by popular pressure to outlaw the Communist Party.

3. By 1995, the first private television station was founded and one of its consequences was the victory in election of the opposition forces that had been so severely crushed in 1990. The infamous tapes revealing the background dealings of the December *coup d'état* are now available on YouTube, but having lost the edge of the right historical moment they don't have the effect that they might have had in 1990.
4. The system of coverage, dominant in mainstream Western cinema, consists of 'covering' a scene by shooting several relatively standardised angles that will later be combined through editing (as opposed to decoupage, reduced to shooting only the angles and durations that will be eventually used, or to the long take which eliminates editing assembly of the scene altogether).
5. One of his most famous conceptualisations of the relationship between the Symbolic and the Real occurs in his *Seminar XI*, published separately as *The Four Fundamental Principles of Psychoanalysis* (Lacan 2004)
6. The need to keep the door to the desert open, and the concomitant refusal to resort to narrativisation as a coping tool, have an ethical dimension – that of *temoignage* (witnessing), best exemplified by Claude Lanzman's stated objective in his film *Shoah* (1985), that is, to be a witness to history, to provide evidence rather than closure and to leave the door open.

10. BEYOND THE HILLS AND AUSTERITY POLITICS

Kalling Heck

Cristian Mungiu's *Beyond the Hills* (2012) concerns two women in their early twenties, Voichiţa (Cosmina Stratan) and Alina (Cristina Flutur), who opt into but subsequently rebel against a strict convent in rural Romania. In light of the actions these characters take, and indeed the actions made available to them, I will contend here that this film renders a critique of contemporary Romanian austerity practices and furthermore directs this critique at an audience that contributes to the spread of austerity across Europe and into the postcommunist states. In order to level this argument, this chapter will discuss austerity, the broader neo-liberal practices to which austerity is closely related, and the unique position of this film in relation to the major countries of the European Union. Given the isolation that the characters here suffer and the relationship of this suffering to the contraction of government services, I contend that this film provides a glimpse of how the effects of austerity disproportionately effect those in difficult economic situations. In summary, this chapter argues that *Beyond the Hills* addresses a particular audience in an attempt to alert them to the ways that austerity functions and whom it causes to suffer, ultimately demanding that this audience *witness* the cruelty of austerity.

The film starts *in medias res*, so to speak, and most of the events that have set up the circumstances of the film are evident only through brief exchanges between the two central characters. Before the film begins, Voichiţa has joined the convent where much of the action takes place. The film starts with Alina, her long-time friend and presumed lover, arriving from Germany to bring

Voichiţa back with her. Upon Alina's arrival, however, Voichiţa is unsure about leaving, and, as a result of the delay, Alina moves in with her at the convent. Despite taking steps that include making appointments for her passport application (which Voichiţa fails to keep), Alina is unable to convince her friend to leave with her. Increasingly agitated, Alina begins to have manic episodes that result in the convent's repeatedly taking her to the local hospital. Unwilling or unable to help, the hospital continually releases Alina back to the convent. Left with no other options, Alina ultimately joins the convent in order to be with Voichiţa, but her manic episodes continue and become increasingly harmful. Finally, the members of the convent become convinced that Alina has been possessed, and in response leave her tied to a cross with little food or water for days. As a result Alina dies and Voichiţa no longer wears the dark colours that signify her dedication to the monastery, signalling her departure.

Based on a true story that took place in Tanacu, Romania, in 2005, this film paints the members of the convent and the priest who governs them as hopelessly inept and ill-equipped to deal with Alina's health, yet never fully blames them. Furthermore, the film connects the origins of Alina's mental illness to the turmoil that she suffers as a result of being placed in a position where she is unable to stay with Voichiţa without sacrificing her beliefs, identity, and ultimately mental and physical health. By articulating the situation in this way, this film shifts the emphasis from a discussion of mental illness or the post-Soviet rise of the Romanian Orthodox Church to a coherent image of the way in which the absence of social services – and the lack of any EU pressure for their formation – negatively affects and even destroys those who require these services, in essence showing how austerity politics sacrifices those in need to an economically ineffective ideology that places the possibility for market success over human safety.

In his *Austerity: The History of a Dangerous Idea*, Mark Blyth locates the lineage of austerity practices and explores their reemergence today. Blyth defines austerity as:

> a form of voluntary deflation in which the economy adjusts through the reduction of wages, prices and public spending to restore competitiveness which is (supposedly) best achieved by cutting the state's budget, debts and deficits. Doing so, its advocates believe, will inspire 'business confidence' since the government will neither be 'crowding-out' the market for investment by sucking up all the available capital through the issuance of debt, nor adding to the nation's already 'too big' debt. (2013: 2)

This is to say that austerity is a system for growing the economy by reducing spending, and it is predicated on private enterprises recognising this reduction in spending and responding by taking business initiatives. What austerity further ushers in is confidence that taxes will not rise (because the government will be spending less and will therefore be better equipped to account for its debt payments). The idea is thus twofold: debt will be reduced and growth will be promoted, all through the government's cutting spending.

But Blyth has little faith in these austerity principles. In fact, Blyth spends the majority of this book discussing how, again and again, moments where austerity has been employed have actually damaged the economy, or, at best, slowed growth. This is to say that austerity is a fundamentally flawed model. While it can perhaps yield limited gains in the occasional isolated instance, when taken up as an international solution to a global crisis, austerity slows recovery for everyone due to the simple fact that there will not be enough comfortable consumers to buy the products produced by the supposedly invigorated businesses of these austere countries.[1]

Blyth connects the principles of austerity and their ascension in the contemporary moment to the rise of another pernicious trend in modern politics: neo-liberalism. Blyth couches the rise of neo-liberalism in the problems that certain economists (including those of the Chicago school) located in the relationship between the political cycle and the economy. In order to insulate the economy from the brutal and often short-term minded vicissitudes of democratic politics, these economists argue, solutions like central banks independent of the government and an intense emphasis on fighting inflation at all costs (which so negatively affects these central banks) should be conceived (Blyth 2013: 156–7). Furthermore, much neo-liberal thought, according to Blyth, is built on Milton Friedman's notion that unemployment is an unavoidable fact, and that spending money to reduce it is useless past a certain threshold (2013: 159). In light of this neo-liberal orientation, the function of government becomes to get as far out of the way of business as possible (unless, that is, it is working to improve or create new market conditions) and to avoid any spending that might cause inflation. Neo-liberal governance, then, gradually comes to signify the reduction in spending – and subsequently public services – that is currently sweeping the world.

But, as political theorist Wendy Brown notes, neo-liberalism and its good friend austerity also carry with them disciplinary functions. Brown explains that neo-liberalism:

> is equated with a radically free market: maximized competition and free trade achieved through economic de-regulation, elimination of tariffs, and a range of monetary and social policies favorable to business and indifferent toward poverty, social deracination, cultural decimation, long term resource depletion and environmental destruction. (2003: 3)

But Brown extends this definition beyond the realm of economic policy. For Brown: 'Neo-liberalism carries a social analysis which when deployed as a form of governmentality reaches from the soul of the citizen–subject to education policy to practices of empire' (2003: 7). According to Brown, neo-liberalism serves as a set of principles that discipline subjects, demanding that they act in line with the market – in effect, as Brown explains, 'extending and disseminating market values to all institutions and social action' (2003: 7). *Beyond the Hills*, I contend, serves as an attempt to resist these neo-liberal systems of governmentality, economic policy and disciplinary demands by exploring the damage, destruction and ultimately death that they cause.

But *Beyond the Hills* launches this attack from the very heart of this conflict. For, as Blyth notes, Romania belongs to the small group of eastern European countries said to be benefiting from these very principles. Along with Estonia, Bulgaria, Latvia and Lithuania, Romania serves as the 'R' in what economists have dubbed the 'REBLL' alliance – countries where austerity has supposedly recently achieved positive results. Blyth, of course, disputes these purported successes by noting these countries' debt and fragility, and the fact that these nations rely so heavily on exports – meaning that the limited success that they have seen demands non-austerity in other countries (2013: 224). For Blyth:

> The political and economic structures of these states are neither transportable nor stable. Their policies prove nothing about expectations or the sustainability of consolidations. Their recoveries and economies are inherently fragile and are based upon sources of demand that cannot be replicated elsewhere. They are in more debt than when they started. Far from being a model, they are a reminder of the futility and costs of austerity. (2013: 225–6)

Finally, in Blyth's account, austerity in Romania is at best a meagre success, is at a worst a disaster, and regardless, is not exportable to any other countries as it relies on foreign spending in order to claim any benefits.

But what is more significant for this discussion than austerity's successes or failures is the toll that austerity practices take on the nations where they are enacted. As Blyth notes, under austerity governance:

> Those at the bottom of the income distribution lose more than those at the top for the simple reason that those at the top rely far less on government-produced services and can afford to lose more because they have more wealth to start with. (2013: 8)

It is the fact that the characters' suffering is mainly predicated on the failure of the state to provide adequate services that *Beyond the Hills* is positioned to illuminate.

Beyond the Hills is helpful in revealing the dark side of these market logics, in particular as they pertain to housing. Forced out of their orphanage, Voichiţa and Alina are left to fend for themselves, and the primary cause for their acceptance of a range of brutal conditions is their need for a living space. But their lack of access to the kinds of capital needed to prove their worth is condoned and continued by the logics that praise self-management and exclude from view those who need help. As a result, government support for non-home owners is left to erode, and these characters are labelled as failures as citizens qua consumers. This film shows how austerity politics takes hold at the level of the subject, as Voichiţa and Alina, forced to flounder in a world that they have only partial access to, are left to fend for themselves and furthermore to feel shame for having to do so.

This process is best declared by the disintegration of the two character's romantic relationship. When Voichiţa refuses Alina's wishes for the two to share a bed on the grounds of maintaining her living space by following the rules she has accepted, the film indicates the degree to which the nation's austerity practices have ushered in a set of disciplinary standards predicated on neo-liberal values. While Voichiţa's refusal of Alina has here taken the form of a moral concern (she has made the decision not to renew their previous relationship because of her newfound faith) this decision has been strongly conditioned by the need to subsist in the world where only the private sector can be relied on for housing. In their relationship the distinction between moral and economic concerns has eroded to such a degree that the wishes of this pair as they pertain to their personal romantic decisions have been overruled by a moralising force that holds their last option for a warm place to sleep, but what is particularly pernicious here is that this imperative presents itself as a personal decision. Their sharing a bed is wrong, Voichiţa has decided, and anyway expressly forbidden by the rules of the convent – a place to which they have been pushed due to the lack of social services. The characters' previous actions stand directly opposed to their current needs and there is no alternative to which they could turn to mend this opposition. Voichiţa's decision to reject her previous relationship arrives in the form of her changing her mind, but this change of mind has been conditioned by the available freedoms – and lack thereof – allowed her by the need for housing and food. Indeed, *Beyond the Hills* in this moment explores how free will itself can be positioned by governance.

For Brown, one of the primary qualities of liberal democracy – which she puts in opposition to neo-liberalism – is that it creates a 'gap' between moral and economic logics:

> The formal distinction it [liberal democracy] establishes between moral and political principles on the one hand and the economic order on the other has also served as insulation against the ghastliness of life exhaustively ordered by the market and measured by market values. (2003: 22)

Brown, however, locates the rise of neo-liberalism at the failure of liberal democracy: 'It is this gap that a neo-liberal political rationality closes as it submits every aspect of political and social life to economic calculation' (2003: 22). Voichiţa is responding to the disciplinary principles that the closure of this gap carries with it. Without government services she is left to find her own solutions to her needs, and the only solution available to her requires that she repress a range of her other concerns. Alina, however, takes a wildly different route. Moving into a foster home and then working for a brief time in Germany, Alina has managed to maintain something of her previous self, and she has returned to take Voichiţa back with her. It is Voichiţa's refusal, her comfort and familiarity with the convent (and her potential absorption of its principles) that confounds Alina and disrupts her wishes. When, in a brief sequence, Alina returns to the foster family that had until recently housed her, she learns that they have replaced her with another foster daughter capable of performing the domestic labour that had been her responsibility. The reason for this return is her need to decide if she too wants to join the convent; if she does she must bring back whatever meagre savings and possessions she has and donate them. Upon finding out about her replacement, and that Voichiţa will not be staying to discuss the decision with her, Alina gathers her belongings and asks for the savings she has left with the family for safe-keeping. She quickly learns, however, that most of her money has been either spent by her foster family or consumed by her hospital bills. Upon hearing this she gives what little money she has left to a nun who has accompanied her and returns to the convent, for good.

Alina's route to the convent, however rebellious, likewise enacts the way that moral, political and economic principals are intertwined thanks to the logics that accompany austerity politics. Regardless of her obvious and numerous concerns with the church she is ostensibly dedicating her life to, Alina is left with the decision to stay with Voichiţa, whom she loves, or to return to Germany without Voichiţa and with no guarantee of food or shelter. In *The Making of the Indebted Man*, Maurizio Lazzarato argues that it is *time* that is central in conditioning the neo-liberal subject. Lazzarato claims:

> The debt economy has deprived the immense majority of Europeans of political power, which had already been diminished through the concessions of representative democracy. It has deprived them of a growing share of the wealth that past struggles had wrested from capital accumulation. And, above all, it has deprived them of the future, that is, of time, time as decision making, choice, and possibility. (2012: 8)

In this moment from *Beyond the Hills*, and indeed throughout the film, it is the lack of time that gradually comes to destroy Alina. Her decisions are consistently reduced and rushed by a series of deadlines (the passport application being the most literal), and her need either to join the convent or immediately return to Germany is what propels her brash decision and subsequent torture. What conditions this speed and lack of consideration, of course, is the reduction of options available to her – she must make these decisions immediately or risk homelessness, starvation and loneliness.

Beyond the Hills also has a relationship with neo-liberalism and austerity practices outside of the space of the film. As Ioana Uricaru (2012) discusses, the film industry context of post-1989 Romania is rather circuitous and at times arbitrary. Maintaining a somewhat centralised public financing system has remained a national interest, functioning primarily in the hopes of preserving the creation of culture as a state responsibility. But the practices of this cultural preservation and production have become increasingly convoluted. A competition put on by the major government film financing agency, the Centrul Național al Cinematografiei, determines who will receive funding, but this funding only amounts, at most, to 50 per cent of a given production's budget and is determined in large part by previous film festival success – a system that forces filmmakers to turn elsewhere, primarily to major European powers, for the remainder of their financing (Uricaru 2012: 436). Further complicating this arrangement is the fact that this funding, provided in the form of no-interest loans, is only paid out to production companies, ostensibly forcing most filmmakers to create their own production companies complete with office staff and rented spaces (Uricaru 2012: 438). What this system produces, then, is the rewarding of a set of entrepreneurial activities centred around attempts to find outside financing, forcing those otherwise reliant on the government to develop private sector solutions even in this supposedly public film production system. This industrial context informs the oppositional stance that the film takes towards austerity politics, intensifying its argument by making claims to the very grounds of its own production.[2]

This framework of co-production financing forces *Beyond the Hills* into a set of market-minded decisions on the level of distribution as well. As of 2014 there were only seventy-eight movie theatres in the entire country, and while a quota system is in place, it demands only a meagre 5 per cent of theatre programming be Romanian (Centrul Național al Cinematografiei 2015; Uricaru 2012: 436). Accounting for the remainder of these exhibitions, and indeed the vast majority of ticket sales, is American mainstream cinema. As Uricaru notes: 'The [Romanian film] market is extremely small and almost entirely occupied by Hollywood product; and Romanian audiences explicitly shun Romanian films' (2012: 428). What remains the primary market of films like Mungiu's, then, is the international festival circuit, where – primarily EU-based – audiences continue to applaud the work of Mungiu and his contemporaries.

Given this context, it is not surprising that much of the critical reception to Mungiu's films attempts to couch his work, and the larger New Romanian

Cinema movement generally, in the European post-war arthouse tradition. In his 'Romanian Cinema: From Modernity to Neo-Realism', Alexandru Leo Șerban connects current Romanian cinema to this tradition in a number of ways. In addition to the paper's title, Șerban argues that the goal of this new generation of Romanian filmmakers is to adhere to 'the first of cinema's ten "commandments": film is truth 24 frames/second' (2010: 17). Șerban is referring, of course, to Jean-Luc Godard's famous adage, and ostensibly to the supposed goals of the French New Wave in general, and he goes on to further define the aesthetics of the New Romanian Cinema as 'small budget, hand-held camera, direct sound – and a simple, true, and powerful story which rendered all the ploys of "traditional" cinema useless'. This combination of small budgets, limited equipment, and an oppositional stance towards traditional cinema all bring to mind the approaches that accounted for (at least some of) the French New Wave (Șerban 2010: 15).

Rodica Ieta, however, is even more explicit in connecting the New Romanian Cinema to the European realist tradition. For Ieta, 'The New Romanian Cinema travels to the roots of realism after having digested various nuances of realism: kino-eye, Italian Neorealism, the French New Wave, magic realism and, perhaps most importantly, socialist realism' (2010: 23). Indeed, for Ieta the films currently coming from Romania serve as a kind of teleology of realist new waves, culminating in a style that directly builds upon previous (European) realist moments.

In *Beyond the Hills*, this tradition can be identified right away. In the first scene Voichița is coming to pick up Alina at the train station. She pushes her way through the dense human traffic that is sandwiched into a small space between two trains.

The mass of human bodies and the shaky camera speak to the film's insist-

Figure 10.1 *Beyond the Hills*

ence on location shooting and lightweight cameras. Indeed, what is called to mind in this moment is perhaps the hand-held hyper-realism of the Dardenne brothers, and, given this pedigree, it is easy to understand the praise above for the film's inter-European roots.

But what is missing from these accounts of the European tradition on display here is any discussion of the politics of this film's adopting these particular characteristics. Indeed, what is perhaps most striking about the persistence of this lineage is not merely the fact that this film seems so clearly to channel the legacy of Neorealism as filtered through recent European festival successes, but the fact that this film simultaneously takes as its audience these same nations. If the triumph of Mungiu's earlier film *4 Months, 3 Weeks and 2 Days* winning the Palme d'Or was in part due to the film's adopting the aesthetic practices of films that have succeeded in these kinds of competitions, perhaps it is also worth discussing why these films, as least those by Mungiu, seem to so deliberately address this international audience.

On the one hand, the European festival circuit is one of the few markets available to these films. But what is more valuable to this account is the fact that this particular audience is also the one that is responsible for much of the economic well-being of Romania. That is, if a film is to address the problems that austerity causes for a nation's citizens, it is perhaps best served by directing these concerns back at the major nations that in large part account for the decisions to implement austerity practices in the first place (or that at the very least normalise these practices): the major European powers – a group that also happens to celebrate films like Mungiu's.

This problem of projecting a national concern outward is also addressed in Karl Schoonover's *Brutal Vision: The Neorealist Body in Postwar Italian Cinema*, albeit in a remarkably different context. In his book, Schoonover posits that the goal of the post-Second World War Italian film movement, known as Neorealism, was to engender a particular style of seeing the world that would serve to appeal directly to the international community. Working against the common understanding of Neorealism as an Italian attempt to internally reimagine the nation, Schoonover argues that Neorealism was in fact addressed outward, with the explicit goal of generating foreign aid for post-war Italy. For Schoonover, Neorealism repeatedly presents threatened or damaged human bodies in order to make demands on its audience. In these films 'an imperilled body is offered to a bystander's gaze as an opportunity to exercise ethical judgements. These climatic viewings of the body direct attention beyond the diegesis to the position of the outside' (Schoonover 2012: vxi). By addressing the viewing public so directly, these films 'grant the foreigner's point of view a palpable textual presence' (Schoonover 2012: xvi). This is all to say that these Neorealist films interpellate a humanist spectator dedicated to alleviating the problems that they have witnessed.

There is, then, for Schoonover a clear outside perspective that is being constructed. As he puts it, 'The cinema itself becomes a means of refining that subject's agency over the world, offering him a point of view that remains outside and yet ethically engaged', and in so doing 'conjoins two modes of watching: consuming a fictional diegesis merges with eyewitnessing world events' (Schoonover 2012: xvii). What Schoonover offers, then, is a model for cinematic reception that justifies claims to realism through the presentation of events that share some relation to the (albeit fictional) events taking place in reality, and therefore asks the viewer to 'witness' and account for something like reality.

Beyond the Hills fits particularly well into this vein of the Neorealist tradition. As it is targeted outward – as evidenced by the unique situation of being designed for export and financed to a significant degree by the nations it wishes to address – *Beyond the Hills* is in the exceptional position of having a large international audience that is particularly well prepared to enact the changes it demands. Thanks to its being made by a recent Palme d'Or-winning director, *Beyond the Hills* has something like a guaranteed audience in a number of larger European nations, and it deliberately uses this advantage in the hope of producing a humanitarian response.

But, as Schoonover delineates, what constitutes a political response is drastically altered by this kind of outsider-oriented call for change. According to Schoonover,

> Neorealism's use of spectacles of suffering as a means of establishing a newly humanist spectator might then be best understood as the ultimate manifestation of a postwar cinematic politics of the image that authorizes the foreign gaze to adjudicate local politics. (2012: xvii)

Witnessing, then, becomes a kind of political positioning that engenders a humanitarian response, a project that can be as problematic as it is advantageous.

For this film to effectively make claims to both reality and a particular solution to the political circumstances it depicts, the relationship of *Beyond the Hills* with its subject matter takes on particular importance. The film is based on the book *Deadly Confession* (*Spovedanie la Tanacu*) by Tatiana Niculescu Bran, which is itself based on the aforementioned real-life incident in the town of Tanacu. The incident became a major news event in Romania, with the woman's mental illness and the priest's ineptitude being generally the focus of the coverage.[3] The downplaying of Alina's mental illness as determinative of her actions – and indeed the presentation of the hospital as profoundly ineffective, inept and uncaring, along with the emphasis on the trials experienced by Alina and Voichiţa as they pertain to the development of their romantic relationship

– reorients the film. Rather than being about the treatment of mental illness, the film is eventually about the failure of the public sector to otherwise shelter these two people. What is valuable about this adaptation process, though, is that the film maintains a relationship to recognisable real-life events.

If Neorealist standard-bearer *Rome, Open City* (Roberto Rossellini, 1945) used the identifiable spaces of war-ravaged Rome to maintain a coherent relationship to real events, while sculpting a story that presents a call for compassion and, furthermore, international aid, *Beyond the Hills* uses its relationship to a controversial and well-known event to achieve a similar goal. A fictional story is mixed with recognisable events in the hope of creating the sensation of witnessing, and the subsequent call to action that this mode of viewing demands. Speaking of *Rome, Open City*, Schoonover presents this reading:

> Its images of bodily violence serve as a venue through which the film spatializes a proposed international ethics of vision: the act of ocular witnessing becomes the exemplary moral experience that transcends subjective differences among normal individuals, and that best serves history. (2012: xxxi)

But this process, for Schoonover, has its neocolonialist undertones, and the cloak of humanitarianism has, as he notes, justified many brutal instances of economic reconfiguration around the globe (2012: xxv).

The case of contemporary Romania, however, negates much of this concern, and in effect allows this Romanian film to serve in many ways as an exemplary deployment of the system for positioning an audience that Schoonover outlines. Having already been totally reconfigured by large-scale international political movements a number of times, Romania in fact stands as a nation *already* suffering from the policies of foreign political powers. As Blyth notes, the production of German cars accounts to a large degree for the success of the Romanian economy, and Europe's relationship to consumption (and certainly not to austerity) is therefore of central importance to the Romanian recovery (2013: 224). Furthermore, what this film is asking for is not international aid so much as a large-scale rethinking of European austerity practices based on the damage these ideas do to the citizens of *every* nation, not just Romanians. This film, then, projects its argument outwards, knowing that its own politics are intimately tied to the well-being of the European Union; but what it asks for is the recognition that austerity is in fact destructive. This is to say that this film asks for a global – or at least European – rethinking of what austerity demands and, even more directly, an awareness of whom austerity asks to shoulder the burden of cuts. Ultimately, this film asks the EU to see what *they* are doing, rather than to come and save the day.

A close analysis of the film's conclusions is appropriate in delineating exactly how this film makes its call for a political alternative. After Alina has been tied to the cross for a number of days, Voichiţa is awakened by one of her fellow nuns anxious to inform her that Alina is awake and, for the first time in quite a while, fully conscious. Rushing to her side, Voichiţa is relieved to find Alina surprisingly alert. Having decided after this ordeal that she wants to leave the convent, Voichiţa asks if Alina wants to leave with her. Alina smiles and collapses. At this collapse the priest and nuns finally decide to call her an ambulance. The film cuts to the arrival of the paramedics, who question after the dark bruises on her wrists where she was tied and her lips chapped from lack of water, they then rush her to the hospital. There the frustrated doctor asks why a dead body has been brought to her. Quickly examining the girl, she locates the bruises and begins to scold the abbess who has accompanied Alina to the hospital, demanding to know what she has done to her. Defensively the abbess responds that the convent has been doing its best to help her after the hospital rejected her, but in so doing reveals that Alina was tied up. The doctor reacts by phoning the police.

An abrupt cut reveals a snowy twilight morning, a car approaching in the distance. The car arrives and drops off Voichiţa, who returns to her room and removes a tan sweater from Alina's single remaining bag of clothes. Hours later she is summoned by the other nuns. The police have arrived and Voichiţa goes to meet them, now wearing the tan sweater – its contrast against the black clothes that the convent demands serving as an obvious symbol of her coming departure. The priest and nuns quietly refuse to reveal the specifics of the event, but Voichiţa matter-of-factly explains Alina's torture, an account with which the nuns meekly agree. The priest responds by saying that they were doing their best to treat her, and that the hospital had also tied her down. The policemen respond by asking the priest, the abbess and any of the nuns who

Figure 10.2 *Beyond the Hills*

tied her to get into the police van, placing them all under arrest. Voichiţa asks if she may come as well, the police agree, they pile in the van, and the doors are shut behind them. A final shot shows a view out the windshield of the van.

The passengers look downwards as the car drives through town. In this extended take the police chat as they drive, then the car stops as the police explain that they must wait for the prosecutor. The officers chat about the weather and other notable cases in town. As they do so the camera pushes slowly forward to take a spot between them, eliminating the characters in the rear of the vehicle from the frame. In these final seconds a truck passes by, throwing mud on the parked van and dimming the already diminishing winter daylight. This mud splash serves here as a kind of reminder of the waiting Romania is asked to undertake, a waiting that is only ever punctured by the brief appearances of further depredations – here the mud, and broadly the demand for more austerity. Finally, the image abruptly cuts to black and the credits roll.

What is striking about this ending is how unexceptional it becomes. Drama is reduced here in the name of a distanced depiction that contains primarily the minutiae of this arrest. Rather than call for any set of clear actions – the punishment of those at the convent, indignation at the negligence of the police or medical services – this film ends on a note of quite literal waiting. This wait is for a figure to come and explain the course of events that might remedy this problem. Of course, the film refuses this arrival, and the camera is left to linger. Placed as it is in the back of the police van, the camera allows the viewer to occupy the same position as the perpetrators of the crime, and in fact links the viewer with those responsible for Alina's death. What this film calls for is action. It has outlined its problem and organised its events around a particular political position: the damage of austerity. The film now awaits its audience's response. Until the action it demands is taken, the images must remain locked in this position, sharing their look with the ever-growing group of perpetrators responsible for this crime. Given its relationship to the international festival circuit, this ending makes clear its call for change in the policies surrounding austerity, and indeed indicts its audience for the crimes these policies continue to perpetrate. Europe has now witnessed these events, this film seems to say, it is now their responsibility to respond.

Notes

1. Blyth points to Keynes' idea of 'the paradox of thrift' as the formative presentation of this concept (2013: 8).
2. It is worth noting that this funding system is not altogether different from many in place around Europe. I don't mean to say here that Romania's system is exceptional, but I would perhaps be willing to describe it as exemplary.
3. As is made clear by Craig S. Smith's article, 'A Casualty on Romania's Road Back from Atheism' (2005).

PART IV

GENDER/GENRE

11. WOMAN FILMS: BODY AND WILL

Dana Duma

Like their predecessors from the Nouvelle Vague and from other European 'new waves', the directors belonging to the New Romanian Cinema attempt to avoid stereotypes in depicting women. They do not limit themselves to use them as decorative props, but offer them a decisive role in the narrative structure. As their titles reveal, a number of films feature narratives focused on female characters and issues: *Ryna* (Ruxandra Zenide, 2005), *The Happiest Girl in the World* (Radu Jude, 2009), *Francesca* (Bobby Păunescu, 2009), *First of All, Felicia* (Răzvan Rădulescu and Melissa de Raaf, 2009), *The Other Irina* (Andrei Gruzsnicki, 2009) and *The Self Portrait of a Dutiful Daughter* (Ana Lungu, 2015). Atypical depictions of women can be found in other recent Romanian films. What would *The Death of Mr Lăzărescu* (Cristi Puiu, 2005), have been without the warm-hearted nurse Mioara, or *4 Months, 3 Weeks and 2 Days* (Cristian Mungiu, 2007) without strong-minded Otilia and shallow Găbița? New Romanian films often contradict mainstream cinema depiction of women, starkly described by American director Budd Boetticher:

> What counts is what the heroine provokes or rather what she represents or she is the one, or rather the love or fear she inspires in the hero, or else the concern he feels for her, who makes him act the way she does. In herself, the woman has not the slightest importance.[1]

Beyond Tradition

A comparison with Romanian films made before 1989 offers the best illustration of this focus and its novelty. As the populace at the time was under strict control, and screen representations of women had to reflect the official ideology, the only way to depict complex and humanly credible heroines, and not caricatures, was to turn to literature. Therefore the only characters that have endured the passage of time were born in the imagination of classical Romanian writers. Mara, from *Beyond the Bridge* (Mircea Veroiu, 1976), comes from the novel *Mara* by Ion Slavici, the novelist who also created Ana from *The Mill of Good Luck* (Victor Iliu, 1957), while tragic Ilona from *The Forest of the Hanged* (Liviu Ciulei, 1965) is a creation of Liviu Rebreanu, the eponymous author of the novel. And Catrina, the strong woman embodied by Luminiţa Gheorghiu in *The Moromete Family* (Stere Gulea, 1987) comes from one of the best Romanian novels about the rural world, Marin Preda's eponymous book.

Few female characters in films with contemporary subjects made before 1990 have an outstanding profile. They had to fit their image into the official rhetoric, which preached gender equality. The films that fulfilled the dogma of socialist realism were full of energetic, hardworking women, much more concerned about solving problems in industrial production and about fulfilling the 'five-year plan' than about their families. There are, though, exceptions, such as the women in Mircea Danieliuc's films about Romania in those days, in *Long Drive* (1974) or *Microphone Test* (1980).

The representation of women in the New Romanian Cinema could not ignore the changes brought by the postcommunist society, changes within trends that were common to all East and Central European countries after the fall of the Berlin Wall. Unfortunately, they only stress the gender differences, as Karen Dawisha remarks:

> The post communism transition has impacted men and women differently. Across Central and Eastern Europe, there have been more benefits for men than for women from the transition: men are richer, more men head new companies, more men own private firms ... Women have suffered more from the loss of social services, women dominate professions that remain in the resource-starved state sector, and women's issues have not been a central part of the post-communist landscape. (2007: IV–VII)

Sociologists have come up with plausible explanations for the dwindling role of women in postcommunist society. The rebirth of the patriarchal model has been in part a reaction to communist propaganda, which hypocritically placed women in the foreground of social life. In an attempt to propose a different model, small communities, especially rural ones, have returned to the image (encouraged by the Church) of the family in which the wife meekly obeys her husband. Nor does the situation change very much in poor urban surroundings, because economic restructuring has marginalised industries in which women often had an important role during the communist era. The image of women 'with leadership roles', promoted by communist propaganda to justify the ascent of Elena Ceaușescu to the highest political spheres, appropriated and compromised feminism in ways that have made it all but taboo to the current neo-patriarchal society. Increasingly, victims of domestic violence, sex trafficking, the commercialisation of sex and media-induced standards of ideal beauty, women are the losers in the transition to capitalism. A comparison between the condition of women before and after communism is offered by Jill Massino:

> In post-socialist Romania the transformation of the welfare state has altered the relationship between state and citizen, gender identity and women's everyday lives. While some feminist scholars have criticized the welfare state for reinforcing female dependency, in socialist Romania women experimented increased autonomy and, in some respects, an improved standard of living as a result of the benefits and provisions offered by the state socialism. With the shift to a market economy, however, many of these benefits have been scaled back or eliminated altogether. This in turn has affected women's ability to provide for themselves and their families, their self-identities and conception of the state, and their attitude towards the communist past. (2007: 7)

This change is acknowledged in the New Romanian Cinema, if without any obvious intention to analyse in depth the causes, forms and implications of this phenomenon, or any feminist agenda. But female issues and gender inequity are often signalled and depicted in these films, and women are shown to be confronted with various kinds of abuse.

The Patriarchal Mentality

One of the few women directors of the New Romanian Cinema to focus directly on the neo-traditionalist view of gender equality is Ruxandra Zenide. Her debut film, *Ryna* portrays a young woman (Dorothea Petre) as a victim of male abuse. The heroine, a sixteen-year-old girl, lives in the Danube Delta, far from the modern world. The owner of a filling station and repair garage, her dominating father (Valentin Popescu), exerts his authority on all family members. He is tough, rude and arbitrary and turns Ryna into a car mechanic whom he orders around. He treats her like a boy and forbids any perceptible

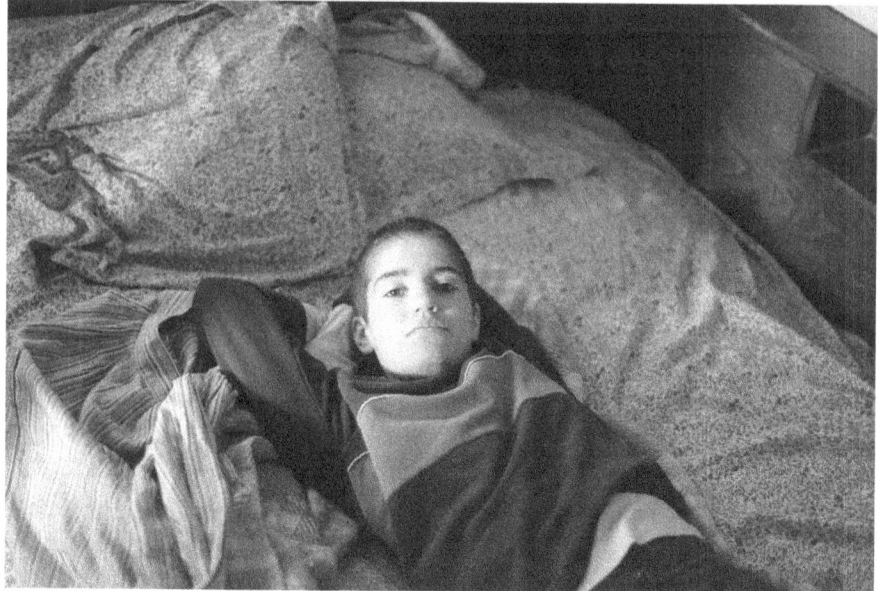

Figure 11.1   Doroteea Petre in *Ryna*

sign of femininity. When he ritualistically cuts her hair on the Danube river bank, the sequence is humiliating for onlookers (especially her mother) to watch. He represents an original variant of the castrating father, whose violent behaviour asks for appropriate reactions.

The rebellion of the daughter against her father is encouraged by a French anthropologist who comes to do research in the area. Their interaction arouses Ryna's femininity and her first shot at rebellion is represented by her attempt to recover her feminine attributes the day she dons a dress, earrings and a false pearl necklace to go to the marketplace. The signal for rebelling against the abusing father is given by the mother who, after a violent argument, runs away to Bucharest. Ryna follows her only after going through more humiliation, after suffering the trauma of being raped by the local mayor. The film revolves around the teenager whose body becomes an obsession for most of the male characters in the film. This obsession is depicted from a critical perspective: her body is not beautified through the strategic make-up, framing and lightening characteristic of mainstream cinema. The direction insists on the perception of women in a patriarchal society, 'as an erotic object for the characters within the screen story', without her becoming 'an erotic object for the spectator within the auditorium' (Mulvey 1975: 6–18), as in mainstream cinema. The importance of her body in the characters' interactions confirms what Ewa Grigar has written, that 'women artists, as a reaction to the crushing of individuality in the times of communism, now tend to use the woman's body "as a cipher" for the search for individual identity' (2007: 80–105).

All of Ryna's experiences caused by her body (even the moment when she is masturbating in her sleep) lead to her self-discovery and to her need to define her own identity. The feminine perspective assumed by the director offers the advantage of authenticity. The film can inspire a comparison with *4 Months, 3 Weeks and 2 Days* – whereas in Mungiu's film the drama is triggered by the arbitrary way in which the state regulated women's bodies (by outlawing abortions), in Ryna the heroine's suffering is similarly caused by the other people's decisions about her body.

Centred on the experiences of another teenager abused by men, *The World Is Mine* (2015), by Nicolae Constantin Tănase, follows closely the story of Larisa (Anamaria Guran), a sixteen-year-old girl from a poor family with a violent stepfather, in her desperate attempt to escape from an oppressive and hopeless space. A teenager with aggressive tendencies, Larisa flees home after stealing her mother's hidden money and faces tough experiences in trying to overcome social barriers by making herself accepted in the world of the rich. Larisa tries to seduce a handsome boy, but is humiliated by her rival, a bitchy schoolgirl with an influential father. Although she collides with the rough rules of the male-dominated society, the protagonist claims, in a voice-over, her determination to continue to fight for a better position in this world. As Jay Weissberg remarks in his review from *Variety*, 'Guran is a find, subtly registering Larisa's swing between insecurity and arrogance. You sense a full-blooded character whose eyes perceive almost every situation with ill-judged understanding' (2015).

Winner of a Special Mention at the Karlovy Vary Film Festival, *The World is Mine* displays characteristics that confirm the tendency of the new directors to minimise the influence of the New Romanian Cinema canons and to mix realism with genre conventions (mainly high-school films).

Happiness Lies Elsewhere

Often reflected by Romanian cinema, the obsession of Romanians to work or emigrate to the West in order to solve their material troubles defines an increasing number of female characters. Since statistics show that women earn on average 17 per cent less than men with the same qualifications for the same work, it comes as no surprise that the hope of a better life is linked to 'trying their luck elsewhere'. One of the films inspired by this reality is *The Other Irina*.

The film starts as the story of a young couple who have left the countryside trying to do better in the capital: Aurel (Andi Vasluianu) is a security agent at a shopping mall, and Irina (Simona Popescu) is an accountant, working without a contract for an Egyptian 'apartment-sized' firm. Close observation describes the hardships of adjusting to a hostile environment and the grey routine of a tiring life. Irina suddenly announces that she will be working in Cairo for three months and astutely rebuffs his objections by comparing him to her father, who 'kept Mum tied to the kitchen stove all her life'. He is so fond of her that he accepts, and fails to notice her new obsession about bigger breasts and the treatment with 'oriental herbs' to increase their size (showing the power of the media-standard 90–60–90 image). Before realising that his wife is trying to please another man's tastes, Aurel learns, shortly after leaving for Cairo for the second time, that Irina has committed suicide.

After her return in a sealed-up coffin from the so-called 'business trip', the man refuses to accept the conclusion of the police enquiry (suicide) and starts his own investigation to learn the truth about the woman's death. Vasluianu plays sincerely the male character's perplexity and stubborn refusal to believe that his wife planned to leave him for her Egyptian lover. He has to face harsh reproaches from Irina's father for 'letting her go, instead of making her a baby'. This accusation sums up perfectly the patriarchal mentality, which places the man in the role of 'producer', to the woman as 'reproducer'.[2] Centred on the man, *The Other Irina* nevertheless proposes a masculine perspective on women that differs from mainstream cinema.

For today's Romanian women, striving to find happiness in other spaces is a dangerous experience, as suggested by the film *Francesca*. It is the story of Francesca (Monica Bârlădeanu) a thirty-year-old kindergarten teacher faced with the decision to leave for Italy to find work and with the hesitations and motivation of doing so. Although she accepts a job for which she is overqualified by becoming the nurse of an elderly man with Alzheimer's in a small town near Milano, Francesca hopes to quickly save enough to start a private nursery school for the children of Romanians who work there. The members of her family have different reactions. Her remarried father tries to influence her decision by reminding her, in vulgar terms, of the anti-Romanian feelings of Italians and the obvious dangers: xenophobia and prostitution networks. Her mother, a woman who managed on her own after the divorce, encourages her to leave and be independent, to 'make a better life'. The young woman becomes a character acting under pressure (like most of the characters in New Romanian Cinema) when, before her departure, she tries to solve her boyfriend's financial problems: he is a small-time crook dealing with corrupt town council members and organised crime.

Beautiful Francesca is seen by most men as an attractive 'body'. The scene where Francesca gets the money to pay back her boyfriend's debts by borrowing from her godfather, who is highly placed in the business world, is quite significant. The godfather (Doru Ana) has a strange erotic fantasy: he asks her to say a childhood poem while sitting on his knees. Even if he goes no further,

Figure 11.2   Monica Bârlădeanu in *Francesca*

the price of his goodwill towards his 'favourite goddaughter' still appears as a cynical and grotesque gesture, described in a scene cultivating ambiguity and suspense through the *mise en scène*. The scene seems to confirm Laura Mulvey's idea that the woman is seen, in a patriarchal society, as a signifier for the male other, bound by a symbolic order in which a man lives out his fantasies and obsessions through linguistic command by imposing them on the silent image of a woman still tied to her place as bearer and not maker of meaning. (1975: 6–18)

Placed in the set of roadworks on the streets of old Bucharest, the heroine's walking through obstacles, in search of loans, is described following a neorealist strategy of close pursuit, as she's often filmed from the back, like the young women fighting to survive in the movies of Luc and Jean-Pierre Dardenne, especially *Rosetta* (1999). Her departure is a conclusion of an identity clarification process and an attempt, albeit a naïve one, to assert her own value in a male-dominated world.

Another film whose female main character tried to get a better life elsewhere is *First of All, Felicia*, directed by Răzvan Rădulescu and his Dutch wife, Melissa de Raaf. It represents Rădulescu's debut as a director, having already been acknowledged as an influential writer who wrote or co-wrote the scripts of films such as *Stuff and Dough*, *The Death of Mr Lăzărescu* (both by Cristi Puiu), *The Paper Will Be Blue* (2006) and *Boogie* (2008) (both by Radu

Muntean), *4 Months, 3 Weeks and 2 Days* by Cristian Mungiu, and so on. Rădulescu's exceptional talent for catching life-oozing dialogues is also confirmed by the apparently insignificant discussions between characters on the condition of emigrants, the opening of frontiers, illness and death.

In *First of All*, Felicia Rădulescu reinforces his ability to discover drama behind so-called 'banal' facts. During a visit to her parents in Romania, Felicia (Ozana Oancea), a forty-year-old woman who lives in the Netherlands, misses her flight. In the few hours previous to take-off, after she arrives late at the airport and runs from one desk to another to find a seat on another flight, Felicia goes through a small, albeit meaningful, crisis. During this crisis, she reconsiders her relationship with her family, with her well-meaning but nagging mother, and her ex-husband in the Netherlands. A divorced woman with an eleven-year-old son, Felicia has spent enough time abroad to find her mum's patronising attitude towards her seriously ill and weak-willed dad as well as towards herself to be over the top.

The clash between the heroine and the mother, who is 'irritating' her with her ideas, takes place after the moment where things seemed to have been 'sorted out' and the trip has been rescheduled for the next day. After two hours of uncertainty, of phone calls in which she tries to persuade her best friend or her ex-husband to pick up her son from summer camp, Felicia 'blows up' and finally finds the courage to reproach her mother for her authoritativeness. Felicia finally acts like an 'emancipated Western' woman. *First of All, Felicia* portrays women of different ages who, within the tensioned space of a family, are 'duelling' in defence of two opposite views of their place in society. Coming home from the Netherlands, a country with old feminist traditions, Felicia clashes head-on with a strong patriarchal mentality. Only suggested in Rădulescu's film, the absence of a feminist culture in Romania is an issue that deserves more attention in New Romanian Cinema.

Modern Women

Well-educated Romanian women are totally aware of gender inequality in the present day. This imbalanced situation is depicted by sociologist Vladimir Pasti:

> In today's Romanian society it's more convenient to be a man than a woman. As a man your income is higher, you do less housework, you have a privileged position in the family, you have less responsibilities towards your children, you are appreciated in society, you are more present in public life, can get involved in politics and participate in decisions regarding what's happening in society. (2003: 173)

Though they live in a world where a woman is seen as 'a person in the service of the man, the only true producer of events' (Grazzini 1980: v), some female characters of New Romanian Cinema, usually alumni of good universities, have the courage to question and oppose male dominance, and never abandon themselves to a victim mentality. One relevant movie describing this emancipation is the family drama *Tuesday, After Christmas* (Radu Muntean, 2010). Penned by Răzvan Rădulescu and Alexandru Baciu, *Tuesday, After Christmas* elicits middle-class characters, people with a way of life above material concerns. A sudden introduction into the story shows a naked couple, talking lazily among bed-sheets in the aftermath of sex. Paul (Mimi Brănescu) and Raluca (Maria Popistașu) are lovers and they strive to see each other every day, carefully hiding from Paul's family. This strategy seems good enough to prevent his comrade-wife (Mirela Oprișor) from suspecting anything. The drama is triggered accidentally, through an unforeseen change of schedule, when the two women meet at Raluca's dental surgery, where Mara, the couple's eight-year-old daughter, is a patient.

The moment of truth, in which the betrayed wife reacts with stupefaction, at first, and then with revolt and an honest outburst of fury, is a real highlight. The scene of the tense confrontation in *Tuesday, After Christmas* was somehow announced by the nocturnal dispute between spouses in *Boogie* (Radu Muntean, 2008), where the male-dominated relationship of the couple is obvious. Here the woman is on top of the situation and although she reels at receiving her husband's avowal that he is in love with another woman, she proves to be the stronger one eventually. The outrage and disgust she shows prove the full emancipation of a woman who does not envisage any compromise to 'save' her marriage. Determined to move forward, after the divorce, Adriana is strong enough to start a new life, without Paul. Mirela Oprișor offers an exceptional performance by portraying a hurt, outraged woman, for whom betrayal is harder to bear than the infidelity itself.

We find another interesting representation of modern women in Tudor Giurgiu's debut film *Love Sick* (2006). Inspired by Cecilia Rădulescu's book by the same name (she also wrote the script), the film, 'a double love story, tender and painful, almost luminous, but with dark shades' (Chirilov 2010: 21), tells us about the friendship turned into love between two female students at Bucharest University, two very different characters: provoking, sophisticated Kiki (Maria Popistașu), and naïve, nerdish country girl Alex (Ioana Barbu). Described with gentleness, without too many details of lesbian love, the relationship has the charm of first love, with long walks without a destination, small secrets and endless conversations. The love between the two is mostly suggested, not overtly exposed as in *La vie d'Adèle* (Abdellatif Kechiche, 2013). The first Romanian film to explicitly describe a lesbian love story, *Love Sick* brings onto the screen heroines for whom the human experience of their relationship is more important than the sexual one. Same-sex love is, for the heroines, a way of asserting their independence in a male-dominated society, as in Pedro Almodovar's films, which constantly criticise the sexist mentality in Spanish society.

Avoiding Melodrama: On Prostitution and Sacrifice

In the interview with the Romanian magazine *Film*, the Polish film critic Michal Oleszczyk makes a parallel between Italian Neorealism and New Romanian Cinema realism, by confessing how much he admires Romanian film directors because 'they avoided the trap of sentimentalism and melodrama, in which the Italians have fallen' (2015: 43). Several authors belonging to New Romanian Cinema confirm this remark with their movies, by dissolving melodramatic premises into austere social dramas.

After the film *If I Want to Whistle, I Whistle* (Florin Șerban, 2010) which features a realistic description of the environment in a prison for juvenile delinquents, another director belonging to the New Romanian Wave, George Bogdan Apetrei, makes a courageous incursion into the prison space in *Outbound* (2010). Sentenced for murder, the heroine is a 25-year-old woman, former prostitute Matilda (Ana Ularu), who receives twenty-four hours' leave to assist her mother's funeral. Her reconnection to normality and important people in her life is captured in fast forward.

Matilda has run away from home in her teens, only to become the property of a pimp who cynically exploits her, and has received a harsh sentence for apparently killing a customer who tortured her. She has an eight-year-old child who ended up in orphanage and we may guess she plans to start anew along with him. Her ex-pimp (Mimi Brănescu) refuses to pay her the money promised in exchange for leaving him out of the crime in her statement to the police. With unusual frankness, the betrayed woman advises the new girl rented by the hour to sadist customers to run away as quickly as possible from her 'protector'. Matilda mimics enthusiasm for a sex party that her ex-lover initiates with brutality only to use the opportunity to hit back and recuperate her money from the man who betrayed her.

The bleakest part of the film, in which Matilda tries to recuperate her son and flee the country, takes place in the post-apocalyptic set of a deserted outlying district, within the ruins of a former factory. The orphanage is a real horror shop where eight- to ten-year-olds smoke while watching cartoons on television. Matilda's decision to take back her child and together flee from the country shows that even a tough woman like her pays for being naïve. An early victim of abuse, the child has turned much too soon into a monster of indifference and who steals her money while she is asleep.

In suggesting that redemption is impossible for the woman who has accumulated so many mistakes, the film avoids the sort of melodramatic 'moral' found in typical examples of this genre, such as the tale of 'the fallen woman' who is described by Lea Jacobs as 'a woman who commits sexual transgression' (1991: X). Similar in many aspects to *If I Want to Whistle, I Whistle* (especially considering the absent mother character played by Clara Vodă), Apetrei's debut film refuses any kind of sentimental interval. At the same time, Matilda anticipates the vengeful Furiosa, the protector of oppressed women in *Mad Max: Fury Road* (George Miller, 2015), reinforcing the impression that newcomers to New Romanian Cinema are increasingly interested in including genre conventions in their movies.

In *Loverboy* (Cătălin Mitulescu, 2011), another young woman forced into prostitution becomes a character far from the usual image of a victim. Veli (Ada Condeescu), a country girl, falls in love with Luca (George Piștereanu), a 21-year-old man who makes young women fall for him so as to hand them over to prostitution networks. Luca, the 'loverboy', is a new kind of pimp inspired by the reality of sex trafficking in Romania in the 2000s. The charm of the young man in a leather jacket who recalled a young Marlon Brando could be lethal. Yet what we gradually find out about him (he has a mother who migrated to Italy and a senile grandfather whom he is taking care of) may well explain his indifference to suffering women.

Luca seems to change when he meets Veli, a very determined young woman he falls in love with. His transformation is depicted with poetical insertions, which explore with sensibility (thanks to the cinematographer Marius Panduru) the beauty of Danubian scenery. Nevertheless, Veli follows the other seduced girls into the prostitution business, but on her own terms, just like a modern geisha. Fabien Baumann notes the austere style in which the film catches this decision:

> Then, be it a romantic, a primordial or a nihilist decision, she'll do it. Three seconds after having accepted her future condition, in the same scene, with the same face, she offers a glass of water to her boyfriend's granddad. Nothing is underlined ... In life, violins don't play the moment you finish off your couple or your youth. (2011: 53)

The prostitute is surprisingly portrayed in this sad story about the loss of innocence and the need to cope with the brutality of the world. The heroine willingly becomes a prostitute, after having to choose between two male-dominated worlds: the poor family with a tyrant-father and the organised crime environment. The film privileges social motivations over sentimental reasons.

The Bechdel Test

Although feminist film theories propose many tools[3] for evaluating women's representation in cinema, a new procedure to examine the importance of female characters, the Bechdel test, is frequently used to establish the importance of women in cinematic narratives. Inspired by Alison Bechdel's comic strip book *Dykes to Watch Out For* (1986) this test is meant to assess the accuracy of female portrayal in movies. It includes a series of three requirements that a female character of the comic book claims must be fulfilled to convince her to go to see a movie: '1. the movie has at least two women characters; 2. who talk to each other; 3. about something other than a man'.[4] Liz Wallace developed the test by adding the condition that the female characters bear names. Although there are voices that criticise the test, arguing that it's a box office issue that would not allow a serious analysis of women's misrepresentation, there are many others to support it. For instance, Walt Hickey claims that 'passage of the test does not ensure the quality of writing, or depth of female roles, but it is the best test on gender equity in film we have' (2014).

Academic studies are increasingly interested in using the Bechdel test to assess the presence of women in films and it would be interesting to apply it to New Romanian Cinema films. Would the most awarded of New Romanian Cinema films pass it? We may bet on the successful testing of Cristian Mungiu's films, with their pairs of female protagonists facing all kind of adversities. In *4 Months, 3 Weeks and 2 Days*, the two friends risk their freedom and social position to perform an outlawed abortion during the last years of communism, and their dialogues are not focused on men, but on danger, rape, survival. The two young women from *Beyond the Hills*, heroines of tragic and harrowing exorcism story also face a crucial moment in their life together and talk about faith, Jesus Christ and their dreadful childhood, not about men. The in-depth depiction of the complicated relationship between the friends is based on a rigorous directorial strategy that David Bordwell appreciates:

> Alternating discreet hand-held takes with fixed shots staged in depth, making no concessions to impatience or easy response, *Beyond the Hills* recalls the sobriety of Dreyer's *Days of Wrath* and Bresson's *Les Anges du Péché*. It plays out in a rougher-textured, muddier world, but it's no less concerned with the dynamics of compassion and cruelty, dogmatism and eroticism. In each, a woman is ready to sacrifice herself for love. (2015)

On the other hand, the Bechdel test rules could suggest that Corneliu Porumboiu's movies misrepresent women simply because their narratives seldom include more than one female character. And this would be so wrong, especially because Porumboiu usually suggests women's superiority, as in the domestic conversation scene from *Police, Adjective* (2009), where the detective listens to his wife performing an expert analysis of the lyrics of a popular song. Another smart woman, the actress from *When Evening Falls on Bucharest, or*

Metabolism (2013) brilliantly rejects the attempts of the director (with whom she has an affair) to make her feel intellectually inferior.

We could try to apply the Bechdel test to a movie signed by a woman, Ana Lungu's debut feature *The Self Portrait of a Dutiful Daughter* (2015). The thirty-year-old protagonist has a name, Cristiana (Elena Popa) and a friend, Michelle (Iris Spiridon) with whom she shares her secrets. She has a lover, a doctor who is unfortunately married to another woman, and the friends talk about this, but their conversations also include other topics: her future career, the preparation of her PhD in earthquake engineering, the decoration of the apartment provided by her parents, her insomnia and her need to buy a dog.

The dog issue is, without irony, an important narrative device playing a double role. Cristiana's negotiations with her overprotecting father to get a thousand euros from him to buy a dog say much about her financial dependence and her immaturity. On the other hand, her need for a dog's company reveals the lack of affection in her life. Premiering at the Rotterdam Film Festival (2015), in a special selection of feminist films, *The Self Portrait of a Dutiful Girl* surely passes the Bechdel test. More importantly, it offers an in-depth analysis of a female category profile: young, emancipated middle-class women. It speaks in a subtle way about their frustrations and expectations, about difficulties in relationships and in assuming responsibility.

An ex-assistant to Cristi Puiu on *The Death of Mr Lăzărescu*, Ana Lungu learned from the herald of the New Romanian Cinema the rule of rigour in using careful observational strategies. Lungu's case deserves special attention, as it confirms the rightness of the profile of women's cinema described by Claire Johnston as 'a counter-cinema'. She claims that the emergency of a true women cinema's does not depend only on focusing on women's problems. 'It requires a revolutionary strategy based on an analysis of how film operates as a medium within a specific cultural system' (Johnston 1973: 25). As Cristi Puiu claims, 'an authentic women's cinema' is above all 'a mode of thinking cinema' (Puiu quoted in Gorzo 2012: 6)

NOTES

1. Bud Boetticher's opinion is quoted by Laura Mulvey in the essay 'Visual Pleasure and Narrative Cinema' (1975).
2. The distinction is made by Teresa de Lauretis (1989: 22, translated by Dana Duma).
3. Feminist theories and their tools are evaluated by Thomas Elsaesser and Matte Hagner in the chapter 'Cinema as Eye – Look and Gaze' (2010: 82–107).
4. The three requirements are quoted in the article dedicated to the Bechdel test, available at: <http://geekfeminism.wikia.com/wiki/Bechdel_test>, last accessed 10 August 2015.

12. TRACES OF GENRE IN NEW ROMANIAN CINEMA: A NARROW PATH FOR A SMALL ENTITY?

Andrea Virginás

GENRE USAGE: A CREATIVE CHOICE IN A 'SMALL' FRAMEWORK

When compared to global-reach major cinemas, most European national cinemas are small, defined by auteurism and arthouse poetics as dominant artistic practices,[1] and thus they constitute quite improbable milieus for genre filmmaking. In this context, I focus on contemporary films from New Romanian Cinema, which is one of the most successful cinemas to emerge from postcommunist Eastern Europe. New Romanian Cinema – as contributions to this volume demonstrate – has been described as neorealist, minimalist, post-Dogme. Furthermore, it has been linked to global slow cinema and the film-essay phenomenon. The important critical acclaim received by Romanian films as a 'new wave' of the new millennium has thus been dominated by auteurist and art film discourses (see the special editions of *Film Quarterly* in 2008 or *Film Criticism* in 2010, or indeed the recently published monographs by Nasta in 2013 or Pop in 2014).

The term 'small cinema' – a relatively new development in world film history – is introduced in *The Cinema of Small Nations* (2007b) edited by Mette Hjort and Duncan Petrie. Small national cinemas are defined primarily on the basis of geographical, social and economic criteria: territory, number of inhabitants, GNP per capita, as well as with regard to evidence of historical or current dependence on, or colonial subjugation by, a powerful foreign entity, usually an 'empire' (Hjort and Petrie 2007). Scandinavian cinemas were among the first to be used as case studies in developing the 'small cinema' concept, specifically Icelandic and Danish cinemas, but Hong Kong and Bulgarian cinemas were also theorised (Hjort and Petrie 2007). The following short summary of the discussion of New Romanian Cinema as a small cinema through Hjort and Petrie's theoretical grid, which I have developed in detail elsewhere (Virginás 2016), is an essential step towards the examination of genre in New Romanian Cinema.

In terms of its population (around 20 million) and area (237,500 square kilometres),[2] Romanian cinema is at the upper limits of what can be defined as a small nation cinema, similar to the examples of Taiwan or Burkina Faso, as described by Hjort and Petrie (2007). However, in terms of its recent GNP per capita (c. 8,000 USD in the period 2008–12,[3] comparable to Bulgaria or Tunisia), and its long history of subjugation by the Ottoman Empire, the Austro-Hungarian Monarchy, or as part of the Eastern Bloc, Romanian national cinema can certainly be labelled as a small cinema. Highlighting the importance of 'low GNP and domination' as 'facets' that refer to 'a situation requiring change', Hjort and Petrie argue that their model allows 'identifying strength in apparent weaknesses, and solutions that might be transferable' (2007: 7) – outcomes that would be corroborated by this examination of New Romanian Cinema. The term 'small cinemas', then, refers to film industries that – in accordance with such conditions – have an insignificant film output with regard to global film production.

Conversely, film genre – the other concept I am referring to here – is much wider in scope, as it allows narrative and iconographic categorisation of the majority of global film production. Film genres as filmmaking patterns have been associated with conventional filmmaking, defined by David Bordwell as 'classical mode of narration' (1985) associated with large studio-based film industries. Their target is a mainstream, nowadays global, audience, with Hollywood often mentioned as a paradigmatic example (Thompson and Bordwell 2002; Langford 2010).

On the basis of these streamlined definitions, we may infer that small cinemas do not produce genre films because they lack serious financial and industrial resources. Domestic audiences that are not accustomed to global genres is yet another obvious reason for this scarcity. Therefore, the typical prevalence of art and auteur filmmaking practices and aesthetic conventions in small national cinemas could be explained by the need to differentiate national film production from globalised mainstream filmmaking (Bordwell 2002, Neale 2002).

Moreover, the replacement of analogue film culture by digital platforms has induced fundamental changes in the evolution of film genres, highlighting and, in some cases, even initiating traditions different from those of Hollywood. Thanks to digitalisation, films from countries with a long history of studio-based commercial-genre filmmaking like Japan, Hong Kong or Bollywood (Balmain 2008, Bordwell 2011) have become accessible to a global audience. So have works from major European film-producing countries like France, Italy, Spain, Great Britain, Russia and Poland, which have been producing their fair share of genre films (Berghahn and Sternberg 2010, Ritzer and Schulze 2013). This colourful genre archive has provided templates for reproduction and imitation, facilitated by cheap digital postproduction possibilities, in most unlikely contexts, such as the peripheral cinemas of Nigeria/Nollywood, Tanzania or South Africa – which, in recent decades, have primarily produced genre films (Ritzer and Schulze 2013). Similarly, small national cinemas in Europe – left without adequate industry backing and desperate for audience attention after the fall of communism and the end of analogue filmmaking – have also turned to genre filmmaking despite the lack of infrastructure and tradition (Nestingen 2008; Imre 2012).

The first decade of New Romanian Cinema fits within the common paradigm of small cinemas as arthouse, auteur-driven, festival circuit cinema, and meeting formal postmodernist expectations by default. In such a context, the emergence of film genres can be considered out of the ordinary, a creative gesture – made possible thanks to extant conditions, as Isaac Getz and Todd Lubart put it, and allowing for the active pursuit of creative ideas, which 'represent a possible but risky solution to a bad situation' – as is the case with Romanian cinema (2009: 208). Their term 'unforeseeable availability' is a good one to describe the financial, technological, institutional and human resources at the disposal of New Romanian Cinema, which has been sustained by the ongoing interdependences of such production sites as (often) improvised studio backgrounds, classical theatre and non-commercial television. The disorganised, non-integrated modes of distribution – partly motivated by the linguistic fragmentation of domestic East European audiences – have posed further impediments. These audiences, and the Romanian audience in particular, have scarcely been subjected to long-term research, although such data would be essential for the balanced functioning of market-oriented genre cinema.

Thus Romanian filmmakers have had the choice either to carry on with the auteur-tradition, flaunting various poetic solutions (which would seem outdated even in the contemporary arthouse context), or to integrate certain genre elements while remaining within the confines of the auteur and arthouse discourse, a decision that would still allow their films to be included in the festival circuit. Lacking outspoken, Quentin Tarantino-style admiration for genre cinema or a French New Wave-inspired wish to transcend classical genre formulas, New Romanian filmic practice demonstrates a lucid acceptance of creative authorship, complemented by genre elements.[4] Paradoxically, appreciation of the resultant 'new ideas' needs a context that is possibly different from that of a small cinema, where knowledge of creative genre usage is hardly widespread.

Getz and Lubart identify the 'resource of knowledge' – which involves '[s]tored information on the task, knowledge of the task domain [in this case: film genres], and knowledge of domains remote from the task' (2009: 215) – as a condition for creative solutions. Small cinema filmmakers should appropriate 'a critical but not too extensive amount' of the 'knowledge of the task domain', since 'without the critical amount of task domain knowledge, every idea will seem "new"' (Getz and Lubart 2009: 215), and the arthouse impetus would not risk obliteration. However, 'with too much knowledge' filmmakers would be 'very likely to adopt the dominant perspective' and therefore produce full-blown genre films, 'thus impeding new ideas' (Getz and Lubart 2009: 215). In the process of applying their paradigm to the corpus of New Romanian cinema, I have identified two methods, the 'intertextual' and the 'allusive', which differ in the range of the 'knowledge of the task domain': that is whether the genre item referenced is one concrete film – a single item in the range of reference – or a genre cluster, consisting of several such examples.

The 'intertextual' method results in films that incorporate quotations from the original work without which their 'functioning' would be partial or even deficient. In other words, a small cinema work references a concrete film that is globally recognised, thanks to its high potential for self-reflexivity to a classical genre formula. This method is popular with Romanian and Danish directors,[5] and is most frequently used in melodrama, be it a 'female', like the woman's film,[6] or a 'male' one, like the gangster film. Radu Muntean's *Tuesday, After Christmas* (2010) has clear correspondences, as we shall see below, to the melodrama *Written on the Wind* (1956) by Hollywood director Douglas Sirk.[7] Corneliu Porumboiu's *When Evening Falls on Bucharest, or Metabolism* (2013) offers a less direct, but evident reference, to the melodrama *In the Mood for Love* (2000) by Hong Kong director Wong Kar-Wai. Finally, Florin Piersic Jr's gangster film, *Killing Time* (2012) includes a hard-to-miss intertextual reference to Quentin Tarantino's *Pulp Fiction* (1994) and its unforgettable main characters (see Figure 12.1). The deeply religious passive-aggressive Jules and the naïve, funny layman, Vince, are redesigned here as a tormented and reserved Bucharest killer-for-hire and his subordinate, a jovial fellow originating from Romania's poorest rural region, Moldova. This cultural transposition redefines fundamentally the blood-stained narrative of the Romanian film, which turns into a highly improbable treatise on the historical roots of regional differences in contemporary Romania.

The small cinema filmmakers in need of 'a critical amount of task domain knowledge' but 'not too much of it' illustrate the 'intertextual' method. Therefore, one film that works with the genre prototype is enough, but 'not too much' of it, when it comes to devising their own 'small cinema' version. By

Figure 12.1 *Pulp Fiction* and *Killing Time*: gangsters side by side

referencing these original works, primarily in their *mise en scène* and character construction, Muntean does not need to include every element of melodrama when construing his own love triangle and the ensuing family crisis. Neither does Porumboiu have to account for all of these details when crafting his version of an artist's creative and relational impasse with his muse. Nor does Piersic Jr have to account for all aspects of the latent enmity, energising the intimate relationship of well-known gangster buddies. Thus Romanian filmmakers profit from the global popularity of the originals, and the common genre expectations they induce – an important side-benefit of the 'intertextual' method.

Unlike the 'intertextual' method, the 'allusive' one suggests that the range of the 'task domain knowledge' is much wider than in the first case. This second method also involves the reference to existing models, yet not as a well-known specific example, but rather as an idea of a film genre. Through the 'allusive' method a film genre is referenced in its quality of 'a comparison class going beyond [concrete] movies actually made in the genre' (Laetz and McIver 2009: 158). Corneliu Porumboiu's *Police, Adjective* (2009), a film recalling Jean-Pierre Melville's universe,[8] is an example, but this method seems to be more common in Hungarian films that work with crime genre formulas. One might think of Attila Janisch's *After the Day Before* (2004), an explicit Hitchcockian thriller about wrongful deeds and crimes that remain hidden; Attila Gigor's *The Investigator* (2008), a crime film that embeds contemporary Hungarian middle-class reality within noir stylistics; or Márk Bodzsár's Tarantinesque *Heavenly Shift* (2013), which references, even in its colour-palette, the American director's films with his petty and funny criminals – but without actually quoting from them.

Relating back to Getz and Lubart's framework, the critical reception of these films demonstrates how the 'much wider knowledge of the task domain' – the main condition for the 'allusive' method – might generate, but also impede, new ideas. Porumboiu's police procedural would qualify as a successful application, mostly due to shifting the traditional emphasis of the genre from punishing the guilty to formulating guilt by questioning Romanian linguistic and legal frameworks. Its creativity is attested by its wide festival and critical success, contexts where components of Getz and Lubart's 'knowledge' are operational, while its poor domestic performance is partly because in the small Romanian market 'knowledge' of creative film genre usage is low or non-existent. The potential of the 'allusive method' to impede new ideas is exemplified by most of the aforementioned Hungarian crime films, which had minimal festival exposure and were generally condemned by Hungarian critics,[9] yet enjoyed wider domestic popularity. As already suggested, this leaves us with the paradox of small cinemas: their creative genre usage does not sit well with their domestic audiences.

In order to demonstrate the complex creative solutions devised by Romanian cinema as a representative of small European cinemas in creating genre-conscious films in spite of the obstructing factors discussed, I will offer below close readings of the above-mentioned Romanian melodramas and crime films.

'Real' Melodramas and Crime Films

It is important to emphasise the oppositional discursive positioning of genre films, oriented towards a heterogeneous, possibly global audience – be it a multiplex or a festival one – and of those emerging from small cinemas and targeting niche audiences. Discourses on major European film-producing countries in general, and on small European cinemas in particular, insist that their genre films are supposed to be 'more authentic' or 'more faithful to reality' than Hollywood, Bollywood or Hong Kong productions, which are often immersed in illusionary, fictional and extravagant audio-visual spectacles, offering a powerful escapist experience to their audiences. Unlike the spectacular, fictional universes of global genre production, Romanian filmmakers need to conform to expectations of producing reality on screen, which, determined by their small cinema status, is considered a must. Therefore, while illustrating the 'intertextual' method with melodramas, and the 'allusive method' with a crime film, I will pay special attention to the masterful artificial construction of reality effects in the New Romanian films under scrutiny.

Christine Gledhill's observation regarding 'excess of expression – hyperbolic emotions, extravagant gestures, high-flown sentiments, declamatory speech, spectacular settings and so on' (2005: 215) – capture the gist of the best known melodramas. Susan Hayward also speaks about the melodramatic, 'excessive *mise en scène*', 'surplus of objects and interior décor', a feature she attributes to the calibration of the classical genre for a female audience (2001: 215). Indeed, Kristin Thompson presents the concept of 'cinematic excess' in opposition to cinematic motivation and as the 'primary tool by which the work makes its own devices seem reasonable'. Once 'motivation fails, excess begins' (1977: 58).[10] Numerous examples of cinematic excess on all levels could be

Figure 12.2   *In the Mood for Love* and *When Evening Falls on Bucharest, or Metabolism*: lovers at a table

found in melodramas worldwide, reminiscent of the emotional whirlwind and extravagant appearance of female figures.

The extreme otherness of spectacular settings – like the aristocratic mansion in *Written on the Wind*, the Angkor Wat ruins in *In the Mood for Love* and the opera spectacle in Todd Haynes' HBO-miniseries, *Mildred Pierce* (2011) – becomes even more evident if we invoke the notion of 'crisis heterotopias' described by Michel Foucault as 'privileged or sacred or forbidden places reserved for individuals who are in a state of crisis with respect to society and the human milieu in which they live' (1998: 179). One striking difference between these global examples and the small cinema melodramas under scrutiny here is in the intensity and composition of cinematic excess, employed in the diegetic process leading up to 'crisis heterotopias'. In the global melodramas, these processes take the dramatic form of family quarrels, morphing into fights, and culminating in a tragic event (miscarriage, rape or murder). Their spectacular, seemingly unintended settings and excessively cluttered *mise en scènes*, as well as their elaborate frame composition, camera movements and editing effects, are much more obvious and striking than the cinematic means deployed in small cinema melodramas like the above-mentioned *Tuesday, After Christmas*, the Danish *A Soap* (Pernille Fischer Christensen, 2006) or the Hungarian *Down by Love* (Tamás Sas, 2004). When construing the 'crisis heterotopias', global melodramas privilege vertical movement in the diegetic space – for example, the spectacular staircases in *Written on the Wind* or the floating camera in *In the Mood for Love*. Small cinema melodramas, on the other hand, avoid vertical movement, most likely because of the claustrophobic flats where such scenes take place, and show affinity for a static point of view, for example during the spousal fight in *Tuesday, After Christmas*. In global melodramas, *mise en scène* is well lit by using heterogeneous sources of light, in contrast to the dimmed *mise en scène* in small cinema melodramas that uses very low or very high key lighting. Finally, while the liberating effect of these global 'heterotopias of crisis' is achieved – as in opera and theatre – by the inclusion of multidimensional aesthetic devices, the predilection of small

Figure 12.3 *Written on the Wind* and *Tuesday, After Christmas*: yellow patch in the mirror

cinema melodramas for two-dimensional framing, reminiscent of painting and mural friezes, creates a fundamentally opposite atmosphere of 'enclosure'.

A striking example is the Chinese restaurant sequence in *Metabolism*, where Paul, the neurotic film director, has a long and tense dinner conversation with Alina, the lead actress of the film he is shooting, who also happens to be his lover. The long take, filming the two in a generally static profile, moves between a close-up and a medium shot,[11] thus creating a painting-like structure – a frustratingly limited position in this doomed melodrama (see Figure 12.2).[12] In its arrangement, colour-scale and framing, this sequence is an evident reinterpretation of *In the Mood for Love*'s sensual restaurant scenes featuring the two melancholy protagonists. Yet it lacks Wong's fluid camera movements and evocative music, and the theatricality of Mrs Chan and Mr Chow alternating between being themselves and play-acting as their unfaithful spouses.

The penchant of small cinema melodramas for realist and minimalist aesthetics tones down their excessive drive since, as Thompson has it, '[s]trong realistic or compositional motivation' tends to foreground 'the perception of the narratively and stylistically significant' (1977: 57). However, since the genre framework of melodrama is predicated upon psychological crisis, spatial confinement and dominating *mise en scène*, in small cinema melodramas the repressed and ignored cinematic excess morphs into what – for the lack of a better term – I define as negative excess[13] or excessive scarcity.

In *Tuesday, After Christmas* the husband, bank clerk Paul, makes a confession to his wife, lawyer Adriana, about his five-month-old love affair with their daughter's dentist, Raluca. This happens on Christmas Eve, when the gift rush has calmed down. The pair is in their small, open-space living room, where their twenty-minute argument, prompted by Paul's confession, takes place. Paul and Adriana are shown predominantly in American shot, so the living room – because of the bright midday light coming through the window – may be observed in 'excessive' detail. In stark contrast to the couple's ongoing (melo)drama, the window opens onto a sunny street with people moving, cycling, carrying packages, yet the image of this festive world outside is blurry and its sounds are muffled due to considerations of verisimilitude. On the backdrop of this peaceful street view, the arguing couple in the room could be defined as another type of Foucauldian heterotopia, namely the 'heterotopia of compensation' (Foucault 1998: 184).[14]

There is a similarly structured shot at the end of the 'crisis heterotopia' sequence in *Written on the Wind*. Marylee, the psychotic sister, peers down from the first-floor balustrade to check up on the unfolding drama below, where her drunken brother Kyle is being kicked out of the mansion by his friend Mitch for having brutally punched his pregnant wife, Lucy (who miscarries as a result). In contrast to the blurred and muffled street view in Muntean's melodrama, what we see through the window is just as clear as the interior, not differing in size either, with the blue-black tree branches waving along with Marylee's body, bent over the balustrade. The long duration of the shot, emphasising Marylee's figure, dressed in pale lavender – paralysed by what she sees happening, silent and static – also enhances the significance of the blowing, dark trees framed by the window. While foreign to the classy interior, these trees are metaphoric expressions of the turmoil in the characters' souls. In Muntean's melodrama, on the other hand, while the window does not offer such a striking metaphoric correspondent, it does bear an equally important subtext. While in the former case human emotions are being directly compared to 'spectacular' blowing trees, thus creating excessive emotional charge from similarity, in the latter case human emotions are contrasted to the 'real' world, engaged in festive activities, yet the long shot and muffled sound subdue the emotional charge and generate negative excess.

As Adriana begins to move across the room, bursting in tears, lighting a cigarette, making Paul call Raluca, then literally beating him until he holds her still, the two-dimensional painterly effect of the kitchen sink – shown 'excessively' over and over again – gradually displaces the soothingly normalising effect of the window shots while the camera adjusts to the moving characters. At the end of the sequence, the painterly effect returns once again, with the camera lingering on the mirror after Paul has left the room. The change of framing from static and tight to fluid, is perfectly justified by the aesthetic choices: it reaches the mirror by panning towards it, but cannot move further or deeper. Moreover, the mirror, being particularly suitable for framed spectacles, reflects nothing but a square yellow decorative element on the wall. This mirror image, shown 'in excess' after the guilty husband leaves the scene of the crucial fight, is a convention already established in *Written on the Wind*, complete with the reflected yellow patch.

In Sirk's film, Kyle, the drunkard playboy-turned-good husband, resumes drinking and misses a formal dinner at home with Lucy, Mitch and Marylee. When he finally arrives, embarrassing the others, he is led upstairs by his serious and elegant wife. The lighting in their bedroom is multi-source, and shadows are thrown by strange objects: an Oriental-style screen, a plate with bright oranges, purple armchairs and a white sculpture. Lucy breaks the news that, against all odds, she is pregnant, thus awakening her husband's mad jealousy. He hits her, and then is thrown out by Mitch – the tumultuousness of this scene is emphatically conveyed by the famous strange-angle shot from the staircase discussed above. While Kyle runs through the hall, the camera pauses for a while on a mirror, which frames a vase of high yellow lilies, thus creating a moment of 'cinematic excess, based on form and duration' (Thompson 1977: 58–9). We witness in the same frame the guilty husband's departure and the mirror with the yellow patch of colour. Thus the narratively unmotivated scene in a 1955 melodrama, showing flamboyant yellow lilies in a spectacular vase, framed in an adjacent mirror for an excessively long period of time, is being transformed into a yellow patch of colour in a nondescript mirror, also shown for an excessive period of time in a 2010 Romanian melodrama (see Figure 12.3). This could be called a figuration of changes the genre of melodrama has undergone both historically (1950s/2010s) and canonically (global/small).

In contrast to the 'intertextual' method, the 'allusive' method – based on the entire iconography, dramaturgy and atmosphere of a genre as a template, rather than emulating symbolic moments as is the case with *Metabolism* or *Tuesday, After Christmas* – seems to be more suitable for crime films. Moreover, the penchant for 'more realistic, authentic' methods of investigation becomes a fundamental aesthetic principle: as we shall see, small cinema crime films rely heavily on analogue-type investigation techniques as opposed to the widespread use of digital techniques in global crime films.

In *Police, Adjective* the diegetic world is mostly constructed outside, on a street location that seems real – and is categorised as such by those familiar with Romanian postcommunist reality – bleak blocks of flats, unadorned sidewalks, rusty fences and an overall autumnal atmosphere. The static camera is positioned as an outsider, witnessing human figures that move in and out of its range. This mode is evocative of aesthetic standards of analogue photography as formulated by Matthew Biro apropos an analogue photographic series:

> [c]haracteristic of the Bechers' 'truthful' or 'objective' approach is their consistent choice of angles and viewing distances, which de-emphasise subjective shot decisions . . . Everything is done to reject the personality or particular sensibility of the photographer: the camera is consistently level with the middle of the subject; lighting is even and diffused; contrast is reduced to give all parts of the structure a similar weight and impact; and the background is de-emphasised. (2012: 354)

Similar associations of objectivity and truthfulness arise in connection with the real-time investigation sequence in Porumboiu's film, showcasing the visual choices as mentioned by Biro.

In the opening of *Police, Adjective*, we see two men walking one after the other through bleak streets, without their identities (of investigator and investigated, respectively) being revealed. The audience's genre expectations of what an investigation is and what a detective does while investigating provide a frame of reference, explaining the seemingly strange gestures of touching, sniffing and looking at a stub, which identify one of them as the detective, thus establishing an indexical as well as metonymical relationship to the entity under investigation.[15] This direct access to the trace of guilt evokes idealistic associations with truthfulness, authenticity and objectivity which, according to Biro, reside in analogue-type mediation and are endemic to 'its material basis as a chemically sensitised surface upon which light, reflected off real people and objects, has been captured in a direct and unmediated way' (2012: 354).[16]

A diametrically opposed scene from Sam Mendes' *Skyfall*, the 2012 James Bond sequel, constructs the diegetic space as an interior: a huge open office with white brick walls, furnished with desktops and screens on the wall. But even before the classical establishing shot – by the way absent from *Police, Adjective* – introduces the opening *mise en scène*, a close-up channels our attention to a huge screen, featuring red graphics that morph into 3D animation as the lines change shape and colour. In the next (counter?) shot we see two men trying to decipher the implications of the cluster-like graphic structure. One of the detectives, Q, feeds data into the system through the computer terminal, while referring to the Rubik's cube as a metaphoric correspondent of what we see on the screen. The other detective, Bond, is more pragmatic and, instead of trying to intuitively and/or metaphorically grasp the nature of the data cloud on the screen, concentrates on the floating groups of letters that he asks Q to align so as to form the discernible English word Granborough, the name of an old, now closed, London metro station.

Matthew Biro argues that 'objective', 'truthful', 'analogue' photography turns into 'subjective' – currently overwhelmingly identified with digital photography – because of the 'figure's mobile stance, lack of detail, and motion blur; the slightly low angle of the shot; and the photograph's overall emphasis on the process of human vision' (2012: 356–7). This might as well be a description of the scene, discussed above where Q and Bond watch the morphing, blurred digital replay of the evil deeds of Silva – the chief perpetrator – after he escapes from and attacks the MI6 headquarters. The digital trace has the detectives struggle to decipher it, while the camera-eye lingers over the scene, making the sequence resemble Biro's analysis of the digitally manipulated photographs of Andreas Gursky, which he likens to the process of (human) visual perception in their highly specific 'non-fixed', 'hovering', 'quasi-aerial point of view' (2012: 364–6).

The comparison between these two sequences, from a small Romanian police procedural and a global secret agent blockbuster, demonstrates two very different ways of media representation. An 'analogue cinematographic practice' is therefore connoted through fixed camera position and a wide-angle shot in the investigation sequence in *Police, Adjective*, while in *Skyfall* the hovering camera, showing blurred images in motion, signifies the 'digital cinematography' practice.

Conclusion

Through close readings of these film sequences, scenes and episodes in the light of genre and media theories, I have sought to demonstrate the possibility of construing a poetics of melodrama and the crime film, produced by small cinemas: a poetics that both relies on and deviates considerably from the mainstream canonical solutions of global genre models, predicated on asynchronous, and in many cases belated, engagement of small European cinemas with global genre tendencies. This process – as with New Romanian Cinema – has been enabled by the digital interconnectedness that complements the precarious position of small cinemas.[17] Furthermore, my analysis of genre activity in New Romanian Cinema has been informed by this tension between, on one hand, the liberating digital dissemination of local material globally and, on the other hand, the inevitable financial impediments and socio-cultural complications.

At the same time, by pointing to similarities among three small national cinemas (Romanian, Danish, Hungarian) and their divergences from mainstream global templates, I have implied that the geopolitical angle of the term 'postcommunist East European cinema' might be replaced with the more objectively descriptive notion of small (national) cinemas. Such a conceptual refinement foregrounds 'the theoretical currency of Eastern European cinemas for a globally conceived and interconnected film studies' (Imre 2012: 7). Yet it also allows not only for geographically defined and politically related traits to be established as common among 'postcommunist East European' cinemas, but also for textually based, formal and poetic similarities, which are predicated on similarities in the production, distribution and reception contexts of small national cinemas, to be emphasised.

Acknowledgements

This work was supported by two consecutive grants of the Romanian Ministry of Education, CNCS – UEFISCDI, PN-II-RU-PD-2012-3-0199 and PN-III-ID-PCE-2016-0418. The author wishes to thank Christina Stojanova and Corneliu Porumboiu for their indispensable help.

Notes

1. I use the phrase 'dominant artistic practice' in the sense Susan Hayward refers to 'dominant cinema' within a national cinema industry: 'all countries with a film industry have their own dominant cinema and this cinema constantly evolves depending on the economic and ideological relations in which it finds itself. Given the economic situation, the film industry of a particular country will favour certain production practices over others' (Hayward 2001: 93).
2. Numerical data originate from Romania's Wikipedia page.
3. The data originate from the World Bank website (see <http://data.worldbank.org/indicator/NY.GNP.PCAP.CD>, last accessed 30 October 2013): in the period of researching this topic (October–November 2013) data were available up to 2012. It must be mentioned that although different from a strict economic perspective, GNP (gross national product), GDP (gross domestic product) and GNI (gross national income) data are all significant for a country's economic strength and potential for investment in national film production. Thus, according to the World Bank, the estimated Romanian GDP for 2017 is about $212 billion dollars. See <https://data.worldbank.org/country/romania> (accessed 7 October 2018).
4. Stuart M. Kaminsky observes:

   > a consideration of any film should recognize: (a) that it is the creation of a person or a group of persons reflecting the contribution of that person or persons (authorship); and (b) that the film does not exist in a cultural vacuum; that it must, of necessity, have roots in other works which surround it or have appeared before it (genre). (Kaminsky qtd in Ritzer and Schulze 2013: 11)

5. My research examined Danish, Hungarian and Romanian examples as representatives of contemporary European small cinemas.
6. Danish Susanne Bier's comical melodrama, *Love is All You Need* (2012) is an explicit retake of UK Phyllida Loyd's musical comedy, *Mamma Mia!* (2008).
7. Born to Danish parents in Hamburg, Sirk had a prolific career in Nazi Germany before transferring to Hollywood. Sirk's 'Scandinavian' background is also acknowledged in contemporary film culture, see for example the tribute Aki Kaurismäki pays him in *Juha* (1999).
8. It was director Corneliu Porumboiu who, in a personal communication to the author, mentioned the French director's name (TIFF 2015, 4 June 2015, Q&A with the public in the festival lounge).
9. It needs to be mentioned that (dominant) Hungarian critical opinion has been changing fundamentally in the last two years, with genre films being more valued than in the past by a new (Y and Z) generation of younger critics.
10. Thompson differentiates between 'at least four ways in which the material of the films exceeds motivation': the specific form of a device, the duration of showing a device, the high frequency of showing a device (or similar devices), and finally the unmotivated repetition of a device (Thompson 1977: 58–9).
11. I thank Christina Stojanova for her suggesting that the composition might be seen as 'reminiscent of or directly referring to Yasujirō Ozu's static framing and editing manner'.
12. In a personal communication to the author, director Corneliu Porumboiu enforced the suggestion that 'he was thinking of melodramas in general' when writing the script of *Metabolism*, and also 'being quite fond of *In the Mood for Love*' (TIFF 2015, 4 June 2015, Q&A with the public in the festival lounge).
13. In Chapter 3, Ioana Uricaru also suggests that the minimalism of New Romanian

Cinema is related to melodramatic excess, however, where I, paying attention to textual genre elements, see (only) a difference in scale, she – relying on the concept of 'worldview' – sees a total opposition, 'arguing that [minimalism's] . . . opposition to melodrama comes not just from the stripping down of the generically understood elements of excess, but from a worldview that rejects the myth of melodrama'.

14. 'Or, on the contrary, creating a different space, a different real space as perfect, as meticulous, as well-arranged as ours is disorganized, badly arranged, and muddled. This would be the heterotopia not of illusion but of compensation' (Foucault 1998: 184).
15. On the same occasion director Corneliu Porumboiu formulated that he thought of *Police, Adjective* explicitly as a crime film, with Jean-Pierre Melville's 1950s–1960s French policiers a (possible) template he had in mind (TIFF 2015, 4 June 2015, Q&A with the public in the festival lounge).
16. Such a parallel to be drawn between truthfulness (to the real), objectivity, and analogue-type mediation seems even more plausible if one situates it in the context of the Romanian director's already examined *Metabolism*: during the starting discussion between filmmaker Paul and his lead actress Alina, the differences between film recorded on the celluloid filmic strip, making full use of analogue technologies in filmmaking, and the current digital possibilities – which Paul considers much below the (aesthetic and philosophical) possibilities of the preceding paradigm – are developed.
17. As Ib Bondebjerg and Eva Novrup Redvall observe:

> [w]e can no longer lock ourselves in the national cinema box. A global, digital revolution has already taken place. The audience knows it and acts accordingly. The national film cultures need to get moving and to find new ways of taking both traditional and new platforms into consideration in a national, regional and global perspective – the future is already here. (2011: 12)

PART V

NATIONAL/PLACE AND TRANSNATIONAL/SPACE

13. KITCHEN ENCOUNTERS: SCENES OF FACE-TO-FACE DIALOGUE IN FILMS OF THE NEW ROMANIAN CINEMA

Mircea Deaca

The Cognitive Model

A setting – or a scene – in film can be constructed by the audience in the manner of creating a model of designed space. One such model is the diegetic space where characters have conversations that move the narrative forward, and David Bordwell dedicates a long discussion to the narrative function of face-to-face dialogue (2005: 208). As diegetic space, the kitchen has a descriptive function since it allows certain aspects of the scene to be ignored, while others – like dialogue – to be privileged.

The kitchen space has a schematic aspect and, as a cognitive model, evokes a cultural body of knowledge that defines the viewer's expectations of actions to be performed – a particular cinematography makes certain aspects of the scene prominent. This kind of cultural analysis has been around since Hans Robert Jauss published his studies on the transmission of 'cultural norms' and on the 'model of social interaction' in literature, using the motif of the 'nursing home' (1978). In his 2012 essay 'What's Eating the Romanian "New Wave"?', Doru Pop proposed an inquiry into the 'motivations and techniques' of the way Romanian movie makers deal with the issue of 'taste', and 'food and food consumption as social practice' in scenes with characters sitting around a table. Following Torben Grodal's theoretical investigations (2009: 259–68), the sentiment of realism is a perceptual complexity, generated by the merging of agglomeration of particular – or unique – actions and gestures, of characters with gestures, considered schematic and caricature-like. Additionally, several features of the cinematographic style facilitate the perception of realism: the use of canonical perspective on the objects represented, the mediation of the emotional appraisal of the situation, and the quality of imperfect perception (subjective filters). The realist style thus described is also, for us, a defining feature of New Romanian cinema minimalism. One has to note, however, that when in excess, schematicity invites allegorical reading.

In film, the kitchen has a twofold advantage. It allows the dramatic unfolding of face-to-face dialogue and gives the audience the opportunity to access characters' intimate world. In short, an analysis of kitchen scenes gleans specific aspects of cultural anthropology as it evokes the cultural values invested: the *eros* and the *agape*. *Agape* is understood here as gathering together, tying social and emotional bonds with human beings inside and outside the family. *Agape* facilitates the manifestation of *Eros*, which involves relationships based on intimacy and love within the couple and their children. Scenes around the table are prototypical in the discursive assessment of values that tie the extended family circle, and determine whether the guest, the stranger or the intruder are admissible – or not. Thus the motif of gathering around the kitchen table reveals the intimate space of an affective, tighter and isolated (insulated) relationship. Here, members of the family show their 'true' face and abandon role playing that is practised in the office or even the dining room or lounge when in the company of guests who are not family.

An example of a typical kitchen scene appears in Radu Muntean's *Tuesday, After Christmas* (2010) – cameraman Tudor Lucaciu frames the family in a classical wide aspect ratio of 2.35:1, in a medium shot – capturing the family threesome at the table: the daughter, the wife and the husband, with the father figure as the protagonist of the drama, located in the middle of the compo-

Figure 13.1   *Tuesday, After Christmas*

sition. Building on the schematic perception of this canonical scene of the 'kitchen', we can compare and contrast its several occurrences in Romanian films, released between 2000 and 2010.

Children's Viewpoints

In *Tales from the Golden Age* (2009) Cristian Mungiu (as a screenwriter) adapts to screen a series of anecdotes – part of communist-era urban folklore – most of which take place in the kitchen. In the manner of theatrical comic tradition, the child is cast as a focaliser, justifying the 'innocent' point of view of the family's misfortunes, unfolding during a communist-era Christmas celebration. Since Oleg Mutu's versatile cinematography – he went on to become one of the most sought-after cameramen of New Romanian Cinema – was designed deliberately in the style of official films made before 1989, its parodic aspect becomes immediately apparent to the audience, which clings with delight to the incongruous juxtaposition of communist-period settings and a narrative which would have been unthinkable to film during communism. As a postmodern pastiche, the film is steeped in an irony inherent in children's-point-of-view narratives, which usually feature not-so-bright adults and see them through the lens of deliberately old-fashioned cinematography.

In *Outbound* (Bogdan George Apetri, 2010) the kitchen, as shot by Marius Panduru – yet another prominent New Romanian Cinema cameraman – is the locus of emotional unmasking, where brother and sister can indulge their animosities while the parents are away. In *How I Spent the End of the World* (Cătălin Mitulescu, 2006) the director juxtaposes children's everyday life with the historical changes taking place during the 1989 Revolution. By using a narrative that approximates a child's point of view – thanks again to Panduru's skilful cinematography – he is able to play up the contrast between the march of history and family life, nestled in the intimate emotional playground of the kitchen.

Serial Kitchen(s)

In Constantin Popescu Jr's short film, *The Apartment* (2004), an anonymous character leaves his apartment on the fourth floor of a grey communist-era prefab building each morning to take the garbage out, while his wife makes breakfast in the kitchen. One day, the man leaves on a business trip, but in fact returns through the building backdoor, and takes the elevator to an eighth-floor apartment where his mistress lives. Next morning the character repeats the garbage routine, while his mistress prepares the meal. Once again, he takes the elevator, but mistakenly rings the doorbell of his own apartment, only to find himself face to face with his wife, an encounter shown in a series of shot/

counter-shot singles of their astounded faces, with the camera focusing on the man's ridiculous slippers, borrowed from the mistress.

This short minimalist film proves, as Dominique Nasta writes, to be 'a universal, prototypical tale of an adulterous episode with a tragicomic conclusion' (2013: 146). Nasta indicates the schematic structure of the film, which is 'totally devoid of dialogue' and where 'the film's entire meaning needs to be decoded by way of recurring visual elements but also with the help of a very effective soundscape'. Nasta concludes that, due 'to the musical message, the tragicomic conclusion further creates a purely aesthetic, albeit universal kind of film emotion' (2013: 146). Minimalist style imposes an allegorical reading, so the film reads like a fable of a certain human condition, where scarcity of detail schematises the content represented, and the sound further cues such a reading. The anonymity of the anti-hero, living a ritualised and repetitive life in serialised grey flats – part and parcel of the modern urban landscape – indicates that anyone could be in his position.

The establishing shot of the cube-shaped kitchen (cameraman Mihai Mălaimare Jr) is split into two by a dark pillar, situated in the forefront of the frame. Jean Baudrillard (1976: 156) talked about the symbolic role of an interdictive bar for emasculating desire. In a similar fashion, the dark pillar in the kitchen impedes the view and emasculates the scopic desire of the spectator by interdicting transparency and obstructing the gaze. The spectator is formally positioned in front of the image, as the character is within the diegesis. The protagonist is profiled in a dorsal posture, lit against the window – or *contre-jour* – which allows us to see him as a shadow. We are, however, unable to see

Figure 13.2 *The Apartment*

what he sees, yet can guess that this is the blurred image of a standard prefab apartment, like those overlaying the dull urban landscape. The couple at the table is framed in a medium lateral shot, which emphasises the symmetrical line drawn between them. Their gestures and postures indicate the burden of the effort – eating in silence is not a feast, the food is not being enjoyed, they are just feeding themselves. *Agape* is absent.

The cinematographic style of *The Apartment* eschews editing and narrative motivation through visual tension. The absence of dialogue indicates an absence of *eros*: no sharing or feasting in a leaden *agape*. The frame is either inside the kitchen container – keeping its distance from the opaque composition – or avoids the 'best view' – the most informative vantage point – on the scene. The close-ups, and especially the extreme close-ups, enhance the autonomous objects in an alienating Bressonian vein, in which the camera, from inside the scene, adopts points of view that are constantly impeded by obstacles and obstructions.

Typical situations invite an allegorical and a realist interpretation, as concomitant alternative readings. The event depicted is not specifically identified as reflecting life in present-day or communist-era Romania. Most of us are aware that the anecdote of the adulterous husband and the confusion created by the identical prefab apartments became an urban legend long before 1989. But, in more than one sense, 'today' is like 'yesterday'. The human condition circa 2004 remained unchanged after 1989. So it could easily be said that Popescu's film depicts life in a generic communist landscape, which amounts to a universal Orwellian dwelling thanks to the ambivalence of the minimalist documentary realism of its cinematographic style and the fable-like/allegorical nature of its subject matter.

Pharmakon Thriller

In *The Death of Mr Lăzărescu* (Cristi Puiu, 2005), the anti-hero is the victim of an obscure malady and the carelessness of the medical system. In the introductory shots of the film, Mutu's perceptive camera avoids entering the untidy, dimly lit kitchen, and spares us the details of this kitchen where the character feels protected – or trapped and alone – unable to stay in touch with other human beings. Through the curtain behind his back, the silhouette of a closed window frame emerges, solidly blocking access to the outside world. At the end of the episode, the character is framed dorsally – at the doorstep, surrounded by dark walls – contemplating the interior of the kitchen, and is then reframed advancing through the darkness of the corridor. The kitchen is an intimate space, full of signs and symbols of the past, and its minimalistic and schematic setting cues a symbolic reading of the character, trapped in a room that has only one exit: into the dark hallway as a passage unto death. These initial shots reveal, in a nutshell, the character of the narration that will unfold during the remaining two hours of the film. Once again, there is no *agape*, no *eros*, no dialogue, no passion and no movement. The kitchen is the antechamber of the hero's infernal journey, and from the very beginning he is the walking dead, shackled by a predetermined fate. The camera keeps a distance from his intimate space as if, symbolically, it is situated in another chamber, in another space. The distance/dissonance between the order of reality, or the film diegesis, and the order of art, exemplified by the brilliant cinematic discourse, will become a trademark of Puiu's films.

In *Aurora* (2010), for example, the use of a shaky hand-held camera by cinematographer Viorel Sergovici heightens the subjective aspect of the narration, which deliberately avoids most revealing POV shots, refusing the audience access to the intimate space of the protagonist. The masking frame of the door, situated in the foreground of his kitchen, obscures the view permanently, and the space is never revealed as Viorel, the psychotic killer, takes refuge in the room. He doesn't go into this room to eat or to communicate by telephone with the outside world, which he rarely does anyway. This intimate space epitomises his secretive mental life and his reluctance to be seen. In most kitchen scenes, Sergovici depicts Viorel in a dorsal position, the camera mirroring his mental disposition by allowing very little exposure of his face or eyes, thus concealing expression of his inner feelings. This ambiguity is enhanced by Viorel often turning his back on the camera or the camera veering away from profiling his face. Elsewhere I have called this cinematographic trope a 'psychotic camera' (Deaca 2013). It means that the camera, albeit 'involved' in the events, offers an imperfect perception, always missing the point of narrative interest in the evolving situation; it is a camera that has difficulties coping with reality.

Viorel is trapped in his own mental processes, which remain inaccessible to the audience. The spectator's identification with the camera's POV does, however, give access to a certain mental point of view of the character, manifested as an unsuccessful desire to see. Nevertheless, through this partial display, the framing constantly teases scopic interest without granting it full satisfaction. Like the protagonist, we are under the spell of a guilty desire to see the crime. We are in a state of regression, like the Freudian child who peeps through the keyhole at the primal sexual scene in his parents' bedroom. For the audience, which craves to see violence and murder, the dissociation between perverse voyeuristic compulsion and imposed abstention construes a moral dilemma. Attraction and repulsion are the two drives of the *cognitive dissonance*, generated by a *psychotic camera* that, as in *Mr Lăzărescu*, always seems to be in the other room, the dark and deep room of the psyche. It incites a desire to see and at the same time keeps a discrete distance that teases our moral involvement in the scene. That which is eluded by an ellipsis – the crime – is not remembered by the psychopath, who keeps reality at a comfortable distance since his mind, and his moral judgement with it, are in 'another room'. The audience is thus formally positioned in a psychotic position, and has to rationally resolve the dilemma of this cognitive dissonance. Overbearingly attracted by the violent diegesis, we have to construct – in order to secure our own moral alibi – a rationale, justifying the guilty act of seeing. A psychotic gap is opened between what one actually does – 'I see a crime' – and what one says – 'I see a film about crime'. These mutually excluding behaviours generate a mechanism that is meant to create a reflective distance and reduce cognitive dissonance. Michael Haneke induces a similar audience reaction to *Benny's Video* (1992) and *Funny Games* (1997). This surely is not Brechtian *verfremdungseffekt*, but rather a way of provoking the viewer's frustration. It could be argued that Puiu – like Haneke – refuses to resolve the tension created by the tripartite strain of diegesis/frame/camera, and 'irritates the spectator's moral and aesthetic judgement without offering any answers' (Metelmann 2010: 169).

In a scene from Puiu's first film, *Stuff and Dough* (2001), the cinematographer Silviu Stavilă – known for his work on Lucian Pintilie's films, starting from 1998 – shows the characters cramped in a small kitchen, each occupied with a different, swiftly reframed action: moving objects, eating, talking. This frantic activity is centred on a mute grandmother who is being fed and, in contrast to the bodies moving around, is totally inert. This nervousness of the camera is a discursive *mise en abyme* of sorts for the general existential confusion of the characters, who will face dangerous uncertainties during their impending journey: from the obscure intentions of their employer (is he a friend or a foe?), to the contents of the parcel he consigns to them to deliver in the capital, to having no clue, during the voyage, of their assailants' identities. As a consequence, neither camera nor protagonists are in an optimally informed or informing position, although they seem to be trying hard to cope with a constantly changing situation. All that is achieved, however, is a grasp of only fragments that raise more questions than answers. Yet while a shot from the protagonist POV captures what seems to be an accidental view of the assailants' corpses, there is nothing casual about this within the aesthetic system of Puiu and Stavilă, since violence and death – no matter how inexplicable and opaque – are part of their hero's journey to maturity.

During the epilogue, the protagonist is seen back in the family kitchen, this time alone with his mother. Confused and quiet, he fails to respond to her questions about the trip. The slower rhythm and the reframing of his eyeline underscore his alienation – he has emerged as an adult with a singular narrative position out of the magma of characters and narrative possibilities that were cramped in the kitchen scene at the beginning of the film.

Puiu's protagonist suffers from the aggression of the villainous drug dealer, which he internalises by becoming an accomplice to a roadside massacre; he is, however, unable to talk or act on it since he is trapped inside the event, not unlike Haneke's characters in *Caché* (2005) or *Amour* (2012). Evil is pervasive and the enemy is dwelling both outside and inside the hero. We, as spectators, are similarly trapped as we, too, are witnesses to the unfolding unfortunate deeds and misdemeanours, and are thus accomplices to the villainy effected. And yet since we are trapped in 'the other room', we are unable to undo what is being done. One could say that Puiu – like Haneke – attempts a thaumaturgical operation by suffusing our audience-body with the poisonous cure of self-reflective distance, provoked by immediate encounters with violence. Such is the benefit of Derrida's *pharmakon*, the poisonous cure or the curing poison of conscious tragic awareness in a parable mode.

The Father Figure: Home Alone

The kitchen is the privileged dwelling of 'old age' – usually represented by a derelict founder of the family and an impersonation of the ancient social order. In *Loverboy* (Cătălin Mitulescu, 2011) a symbolic father figure, as exhausted as the values he represents, occupies the foreground of the kitchen scenes. In *Medal of Honor* (Călin Peter Netzer, 2009), a victim of his own beliefs and misguided actions, the father also takes refuge in the kitchen. Curiously enough, the young protagonist of Corneliu Porumboiu's *When Evening Falls on Bucharest, or Metabolism* (2013) is the son who occupies the absent father's position both on narrative level – as a Pygmalion, educating his young actress – and on level of visual composition. The son, a symbolic representative of the new generation, is however unable to cope with the full-blown existential and creative crisis he is faced with, and craves the help and nurture of a mother figure.

Another of Porumboiu's characters, the anti-hero of *Police, Adjective* (2009), is also profiled alone in his kitchen. He is a police officer confronted with a moral dilemma. He has either to mechanically apply an absurd law and arrest a young boy, who is guilty of a minor offence, with dramatic and disproportionate consequences for the adolescent's later life, or let him go, in direct violation of the strict police code. The police superior, however, menacingly manipulates the protagonist into making the arrest, forcing him to abandon his principles. By reducing him from a human being with a conscience to an insignificant 'adjective' in the symbolic order, the police boss neuters the protagonist psychologically and eliminates him as an Oedipal threat to his position as a father figure.

Repetitively, the protagonist is framed by Panduru in his kitchen, in a frontal close-medium shot. Eating alone late at night is part and parcel of his profession, but it also happens to be the attribute of the father figure or the *pater familias* in traditional societies, who also eats alone while his women folk and offspring serve him hand and foot, or sit obediently around. In Porumboiu's film, however, this ritual acquires a different dimension: the introverted protagonist is pondering alone at the table, although towards the end of the film, he is seen briefly – cramped in a close-medium shot – having dinner with his wife. She does not offer advice or the moral support he so badly needs, but remains a passive eyewitness to his moral agony. Doru Pop also notes that the 'father figure' is increasingly absent or derelict – 'merely simulacra of their authority' – in the New Romanian Cinema, and his avatars 'appear in circumstances that void them of relevance and representativeness' (2010: 29). One such 'void of relevance' derelict father is old man Pișcoci from Porumboiu's *12:08 East of Bucharest* (2006). Shown by Panduru in medium shot alone in his kitchen, he is staring blankly at a street lamp outside his window. A few years later, Panduru would apply this framing in *Police, Adjective* to depict the existential anguish of the young policeman, sitting in his grey kitchen alone with his moral dilemma.

In Pintilie's *Niki and Flo* (2003), two father figures confront each other: the ex-colonel Niki: 'An old-fashioned patriot ... [who] represents the alienated subject, pathetic and marginalised, highly paradoxical because he is nostalgic, like many others, for the Communist times' and Flo, 'a pure product of a certain category of post-Communist Romanians: vulgar, eccentric, aggressive, seizing any opportunity, any small upstart job to make money and have fun' (Nasta 2013: 113–14). Their battleground is Niki's family kitchen, into which Flo nonchalantly intrudes whenever he pleases. Niki's kitchen is a kind of shrine of intimate memorabilia from his previous life, which was spent in a world that has suddenly ceased to exist. Significantly, throughout the film, Stavilă frames Niki at the edges of the familial kitchen – usually laterally, in the forefront or in the background. In the final scene, however, which takes place in the kitchen of his nemesis Flo, Niki makes a sudden appearance in the middle of the frame, and in a medium-long shot. Reframed to a medium close-up and in the foreground, he is seen killing Flo with a hammer, as retribution for betraying and humiliating him. A subsequent empty shot of the window enhances the metaphoric momentum, which culminates in Niki's blank stare at the camera. Thus the two kitchens and Niki's framing amount to figurative externalisation of two conflicting mentalities. The old father kills the imposter, but remains stuck at a dead end. Pintilie thus sets the stage for the alienated protagonists that will populate the up-and-coming New Romanian Cinema. *Agape* and *eros* melt into confrontation and conflict, into *agone*.

Next Stop Paradise

Following this line of thought, it is interesting to look at the evolution of the role of the intimate kitchen space in Pintilie's previous films. A director who came to national and international renown in the 1960s, within the truly classical narrative of *Sunday at Six* (1965), Pintilie weaves a romantic theme along with a socio-political one, and renders the dilemma of love *versus* social activism in a modernist vein by juxtaposing the dream of freedom with the grounding of familial comfort that is associated with the kitchen (Nasta 2013: 86).

Thirty years later, Pintilie returns to the kitchen as an intimate space of family values and paternal/maternal comfort in his 1998 contemporary drama, *Next Stop Paradise* (Nasta 2013: 107). The kitchen here is the place where the couple, Norica and Mitu, live through their moments of bliss and love, and where Stavilă's camera follows their dialogue in tight, single shots. The intimacy of the shots is emphasised by the minimalist setting of the kitchen, coloured in abstract, dirty white, and by glimpses of a distant outside view seen through the window. The metaphoric interpretation is additionally encouraged by a commercial photograph of a brightly coloured rural landscape hanging on the kitchen wall. It serves both as a diegetic poster and a subjective flash-forward image, providing with its speculatively optimistic imagery yet another contrast to the desolation of the kitchen setting. For Pintilie, mental and cinematographic processes mirror each other, therefore the kitchen – as an intimate container – can be read as an analogue to the *camera lucida*; a mental image processing data that bridges moments in time. For Pintilie, therefore, *agape* and *eros* are qualia of the human theatre, where characters take refuge. It is not the place here to elaborate on the repressed Hollywood entertainment imaginary that comes back to haunt New Romanian Cinema films as displaced desire, not unlike consciously denegated material (in a Freudian sense), which returns as an imaginary subjective image of 'paradise lost'.

Kitsch Warzone

In *Everybody in Our Family* (2012), Radu Jude and his cinematographer, Andrei Butică, choose the kitchen as the principal setting to emphasise 'a conflict that spirals out of control, eventually into absurd violence' (Nasta 2013: 148). In what comes through as a collective hysterical breakdown, family bonds unravel, revealing in ugly detail the dissolution of *agape* and *eros*. The kitchen is actually only part of the dramatic stage, which comprises the otherwise spacious apartment. It however remains visually incoherent as the camera follows tightly the protagonist – or rather his visually fragmented body – from one congested room to another as he pursues his targets. Framing displays an affinity to slightly canted angles (higher or lower than human vantage point). Thanks to the hand-held camera shots, quick reframing in close proximity allows more emphasis on swift changes in tone and mood, and enhances perceptual realism. Continuity editing is also thrown into disarray for the sake of getting a better grasp of a family torn apart. The cinematographic disturbances, along with the claustrophobic *mise en scène*, mirror the evolving familial pandemonium. The audience is further assaulted by the plenitude of details and moving shapes – a visual expression of chaos, matters spinning out of control – which complicate our ability to focus, thus replicating the confused mental state of the protagonist.

The Mother Figure

In Cristian Nemescu's short film *Marilena from P7* (2006), the plot involves the 'derelict underground Bucharest milieu, where an intolerant pimp ... indulges in youth exploitation and corrupt money dealing' (Nasta 2013: 214). Here the kitchen is once again a family container, lacking any outside aperture (the window is closed and no profiling of the door is visible since the entrance is occupied by the camera). As in other similar scenes, it is usually a female who does the kitchen work (cooking, washing), stuck inside the narrow space of the room. Nemescu's character replays the *topos* of the nurturing mother – caring, advising and confident – whose warm presence lets the hero confess or discharge his erotic/identity crisis. Realism is generated here by typical action in a typical setting, while the camera incessantly pans between the upset mother, the guilty father and the son, but does not change its fixed position at the door. Father and son are positioned in childlike poses in front of the furious matriarch. The analytical editing keeps the pace by carefully selecting cuts that are most revealing of this comedy of familial anxieties.

In *Mr Lăzărescu*, Mioara, the medical assistant who escorts Marius Dante Lăzărescu on his last journey towards death, becomes his guide not only through hell – like Dante's Virgil – but also, like Beatrice, is there to take him on his post-mortem spiritual journey through heaven. And even if she is never profiled in the kitchen, the Dantesque intertext is interpreted in light of the Romanian Orthodox cultural context. Thus Mioara, as an archetypal version of the ideal feminine – the Virgin Mary – is not seen as the beautiful virginal maiden Beatrice, but as a mother-like, nurturing figure.

The Domesticated Mother

The mother figure, whether she is a wife or biological mother, usually takes one of two dramatic functions in New Romanian cinema. She either epitomises a source of comfort, an accomplice, participant, or witness of her man-folk crises, or is the supportive mother who feeds, does laundry and irons clothes. Obviously, this dichotomy is far from ingenuous, but its emphatic repetition brings out an ironic attitude towards male chauvinism in a still patriarchal society. Thus the domesticated mother, an enduring helper in time of crisis and a silent maidservant – or both – is a simultaneously realistic and ironic presence. The packed oblong space of the kitchen, profiled in *12:08 East of Bucharest*, seems to come straight from a silent cinema comedy. Though with difficulty, suggested in their gestures and postures, husband and wife co-habit this dimly lit container and, in the absence of *eros* and *agape*, remain confined to their own domestic chores. The other couple in the film – the TV channel director and his wife – enact another comedic trope. The husband, seated, is entirely focused on his phone conversation, while the wife, standing, keeps serving him the meal. There is no eye contact between the two. The woman acts like a servant, taking care of her 'master'. Similarly, Viorel's mother-in-law in *Aurora* is seen in the role of maidservant – peeling potatoes while talking to her murderous ex son-in-law – which in some perverse way could have suggested to Viorel's psychopathological mind a reason to treat her as an expendable asset.

The mother figure occupies the kitchen scenes in *Stuff and Dough*, where she appears mostly to comfort and alleviate her son's crisis. In *Everybody in Our Family*, the protagonist's mother tries unsuccessfully to mediate the conflict between father and son, but all she manages is to either offer them cookies in the climactic scene, or engage in the generic act of even more cooking. In Pintilie's *Sunday at Six*, the mother performs the same generic act of stuffing people with cakes, which seems to be intrinsic part of her conservatism and, by extension, the reason for the weakness of her husband and son. Since the cultural model of the domesticated mother suggests her confinement to the kitchen, where she is allowed only a limited number of stereotypical actions that appear out of place in the context of modern life, she is consequently depicted either with irony or, as in Mungiu's films, eschewed altogether.

A Change of Paradigm: Mutter Courage

The mother figure takes centre-stage in Călin Peter Netzer's film, *Child's Pose* (2013), which profiles forcefully the dramatic dilemma of an active and strong-willed mother, who is confronted with a family crisis that she is incapable of coping with. The mother transcends the traditional role of supporter, helper and nurturer, and becomes the heroine of the film, thanks to the shift of her narrative position from passive and restricted to active subjectivity. In one scene, for example, while alone in the kitchen, she walks aimlessly around, devising an action plan. This dramatic decision clearly demonstrates that she is no longer the typically passive 'mama' who serves meals to her men-folk – usually ironised anti-heroes – along with moral and emotional comfort. The cinematographic style of Netzer and Andrei Butică - reflects eloquently the paradigmatic change in representation of the mother in New Romanian Cinema: she is now capable of making decisions and implementing them, and 'conquers' the kitchen, that masculine space of reclusion and nurturing, turning it into action headquarters. Furthermore, the conquest gives her licence to the cinematographic foreground, where she might engage in face-to-face exchanges with other important characters and move the action forward. This, in turn, affects the way she is being shot. The cinematographic style abandons conversations, framed in static medium and long-medium shots (as iconic *tableaux figés* resembling old family photos), the axis of action becomes drawn along the lyrically symbolic window–door line (outside *versus* inside), yet clearly in the classical narrative – continuity – style. This new type of heroine becomes associated with an international, Hollywood – capitalist, if you will – style of cinema. Her exchanges are framed in rigorous over-the-shoulder or single shots that capture the intensity of meaningful dialogues conducted by a strong female figure. The proverbial minimalism of New Romanian Cinema is abandoned for the sake of a new cinematographic ideology that leaves behind the mythology of the father figure. Moreover, along with the cinematographic conventions, Netzer discards the ideologies that motivate them, embracing a feminine approach to conflict and reconciliation as a new cinematographic paradigm. The film can thus be seen as an allegory of how Romanian society could attain reconciliation with its cultural identity, rooted in traditional rural society. Mediation of sensitive political, social and psychological issues seems to have become a prerogative of empowered, strong women.

Conclusion

The kitchen as dramatic stage, discussed so far, reveals a cultural model of the larger contextual drama of urban alienation and moral dilemmas, of anti-heroes, abandoned or domineering fathers, and of incessantly nurturing, domesticated mothers. It is a stage where directors challenge national cinematic tropes by ironising characters and ridiculing social and textual clichés. Their realism, understood as typical characters in typical circumstances, allows both allegorical and realist readings that could also serve an educational purpose. The audience is thus invited to reflect on values and principles governing not only past Romanian history but contemporary life as well. Thrillers like Mungiu's *4 Months, 3 Weeks and 2 Days* (2007) and *Beyond the Hills* (2012), and Puiu's *The Death of Mr Lăzărescu* and *Aurora*, have made such a serious impact thanks to their original exploration of the relationship between camera/frame and the depicted diegetic world. Moreover, Netzer's *Child's Pose* proposes a radical break with the traditional cinematographic paradigm, depending on intertextual references to films. The minimalist (realist) style purposefully sustained for the film 'festival' circuit (see Pop 2010: 29) has indeed been a successful tactic used by a small national cinema to differentiate itself from the dominant mode of classical narrative (or Hollywood) style, and to attract interest as an exotic 'art cinema', telling stories about an alien reality. The goal has been achieved and Netzer – as a member of a new generation – abandons minimalism altogether, and initiates a change of the cinematographic style and of characters that are increasingly consistent with the international classical narrative film style.

Acknowlegements

I would like to thank the editorial staff for encouraging the progress of this project. I would particularly like to thank Dominique Nasta for the stimulating conversations and Christina Stojanova for her careful reading and comments on earlier drafts of this chapter.

14. NEW ROMANIAN CINEMA: GEOGRAPHY AND IDENTITY

Marian Țuțui and Raluca Iacob

PRELIMINARIES

As incredible as it may seem nowadays, in the 1980s Romanian cinema was held in some kind of disrepute, despite the fact that it had received nine awards at major film festivals in Cannes, Venice and Berlin between 1939 and 1989. However, accolades for Romanian films were sporadic, and therefore this cinema was generally overlooked. The repeated successes of Romanian films since the early 2000s have radically changed this perspective. Critically, Romanian cinema is currently evaluated as a source of cinematic excellence, which is reflected in Steven Zeitchik somewhat anecdotal statement in the *Los Angeles Times* that 'Romanians can't make a bad film. It's, like, illegal in their country. Or at least not in their DNA' (2010). He goes on to say that 'film-makers from the small Eastern European nation have swept into the south of France every May and put far bigger, more storied film cultures to shame, the US and the fiercely proud host country among them' (Zeitchick 2010).

The consistent presence of Romanian films on the international festival circuit facilitates a better understanding of their historical and cultural nuances. Although New Romanian Cinema directors systematically avoid spectacular, exotic and picturesque depictions, they manage to be distinct and successful in tackling contemporary topics and situations, thus addressing a wider market, beyond the confines of their national borders. Meanwhile, Western critics have become more familiar with the context of New Romanian Cinema, while

Romanian critics have been – increasingly – acting as mediators, contributing to a better understanding of their cinema and its aesthetics. Doru Pop, for example, points out the similarities between recent Romanian films and Italian neorealism (2014: 55). Mihai Fulger (2013), on the other hand, traces the influence of the Dardenne Brothers or Michael Haneke in recent Romanian films. In general, the focus on New Romanian Cinema realism also takes precedence in the works of Rodica Ieta (2010) or Alex Leo Șerban (2010). And the fact that a few of the high-profile films– such as *The Death of Mr Lăzărescu* (2005), *California Dreamin'* (2007), and *Of Snails and Men* (2012) – have, indeed, been inspired by vexatious real events, recorded in the local press, is yet more proof of the importance of this critical debate.

In a study on Danish cinema, Birger Langkjaer points out four types of cinematic realism,[1] and notes that Danish cinematic realism is mostly about the way 'personal space is . . . defined within a given social space' (2002: 38). In this light, it could be said that New Romanian Cinema reflects Langkjaer's taxonomy of a realism of recognition – that is, it is realistic from both a stylistic and narrative perspective, as well as from the audiences' perception of representation of reality – and also in the ways in which these films negotiate the position of the individual within a specific social environment. This passion for realism, so to speak, could be explained through the background and worldview of the filmmakers. Born in the late 1960s and 1970s, most New Romanian Cinema filmmakers have spent their formative years in the late 1980s and 1990s, that is, during the last years of Ceaușescu's regime and the most challenging times of the ensuing transitional period. However, they have succeeded somehow in remaining more objective and emotionally detached, and this has allowed them to reflect critically on contemporary Romanian society without the virulent cynicism of their older colleagues. It took twelve years from the 1989 Revolution, however, until directors like Cristi Puiu, with *Stuff and Dough* (2001), were able to make notable films about serious sociopolitical issues that reflected on the country's communist past or its troubled transition to a market economy, thus marking the advent of a new direction in Romanian cinema. This is significant for our argument here, as filmmakers of the New Romanian Cinema have come to accept their country's peripheral identity, which is aptly reflected in the geographical locations and characters of their films. Not coincidentally, during the journey from Constanța to Bucharest in *Stuff and Dough*, the discussion between the two young friends reverts to differences between life in Western Europe and Romania. We find similar topics being discussed in Radu Muntean's *Boogie* – also known as *Summer Holiday* – (2008) or in Călin Peter Netzer's *Medal of Honor* (2009), while Cristian Mungiu's *Occident* (2002) addresses the topic of immigration to the West. These conversations and references invariably bring to light the perceived or real marginalisation of characters, rendering their peripheral condition palpable for both national and international audiences. Marginality is depicted through authentic and profound stories of marginalised dwellers in the Bucharest outskirts, like those in Bogdan George Apetri's *Outbound* (2010), about the inhabitants of an insignificant little village situated 'where the map bends' in *California Dreamin'*, or about a small border town in *Morgen* (2010).

Romania's historical, cultural and geopolitical peripheral position towards Western Europe, and its ideological entrenchment under communism, created conditions of dependency, aggravating rather than decreasing the disparity with the centre of global power. Romanian films reflect these conditions by focusing on minor destinies of ordinary people in everyday situations, as they face numerous challenges in a society in continuous transformation.

Historically – as noted by Larry Wolff (1994) and Maria Todorova (1997) – the West European perspective, has always attributed a position of alterity to Eastern Europe, resulting in its marginalisation, which in time has been internalised by the local population. Romania's self-perception as an unimportant Balkan country has been pervasive throughout its history. Romanian intellectuals like Costică Brădățan and Aurelian Crăiuțu suggest that Romanian identity 'for many reasons – linguistic, geographical, political – has been consumed by, and obsessed with, understanding and dealing with its marginal condition' (2012: 726). Brădățan and Crăiuțu further claim that 'in the very process of struggling with their "complex of marginality", Romanians define themselves' as marginal (2012: 726), arguing that the very self-perception as 'marginal' forms a part of the national identity construction.

The continuous successes of Romanian films on the international festival and distribution circuit have ensured an unvarnished and authentic perspective on their environment as a form of the filmmakers' self-marginalisation. Reflecting on similar issues in his book on Emir Kusturica, Goran Gocić talks about 'ethnocinema' as a manifestation of 'local colours via a conscious "art cinema" style, applied according to Western standards' (2001: 6). He also notices that ethnocinema is prompted by a kind of conditional appropriation: 'if "ethnofilms" satisfy certain production and aesthetic criteria, Eastern (European) artists could be included in the Western canon, even to the extent that they redefine it' (Gocić 2001: 5–6). Moreover, Romanian anthropologist Florin Poenaru, in drawing some parallels between New Romanian Cinema and post-war European art cinemas, observes that recent Romanian films display an '(auto)colonial character', by offering to 'Western audiences as well as [to] any knowledgeable observer, what they expect and are ready to see' (2014: 153).

Going even further, Dina Iordanova suggests that the success and appeal of Romanian cinema to international audiences stems from its acceptance of the country's liminality and position of insignificance and the openness of the filmmakers to 'talk[ing] sincerely about difficult subject matters' (2014: 262). Since the condition of marginality could be either ascribed or internalised, we argue that Romanian films, in acknowledging and rendering the marginal status of the society they represent, offer multiple examples of marginality, concerning both the geographies represented on screen and the identities of its characters.

I: Mapping the Geography of New Romanian Cinema

A visual representation of the Romanian space in recent films delineates a map that usually concentrates on narratives set in or around Bucharest and other more provincial cities. These films offer a bleak perspective, lacking any sort of scenic or glamorous panoramas. Instead, they focus on presenting an unvarnished reality of everyday life in contemporary Romania. Despite focusing their geographical concentration around urban hubs, these films underline the marginal condition of the characters and their position on the peripheries of their locations.

Bucharest *versus* the Provinces

Most films belonging to New Romanian Cinema have their action taking place in Bucharest.[2] This choice can be explained by financial decisions (maintaining low costs in the context of limited budgets) but also by the projection of the capital as a metonymic reference to the entire national space. One way – embraced by other Balkan cinemas – to expand this limited territorial and social geography is through cinematic journeys enabling rapid familiarity with new places and people, as in one of the best known Turkish films, Yilmaz Güney's *The Way* (1982), or Fatmir Koçi's *Tirana Year Zero* (2001), the harbinger of the New Albanian Cinema. Following this line of thought, it is therefore not accidental that New Romanian Cinema was inaugurated by a road movie, Puiu's *Stuff and Dough*, which tells the story of a journey from Constanța to Bucharest and back again, to deliver a package of drugs. Besides capturing urban and rural landscapes from a moving car, the film also observes the interactions between the protagonist Ovidiu and his friend Vali as they engage in a discussion about differences between life in the West and that in their own country, thus allowing for a glimpse into the motivations of these otherwise nice kids to undertake such a dangerous trip.

California Dreamin' is about an internationally and politically significant journey, so to speak, which again juxtaposes Western – in this case American – and local Romanian values. The story, inspired by real events, is set in 1999, when a zealous station master of a small provincial town 'where the map bends' delays for five days a NATO train staffed with US personnel carrying

GEOGRAPHY AND IDENTITY

Figure 14.1 *Stuff and Dough*: on the way to Bucharest

strategic weapons during the war in Kosovo, and neither local, nor central administration are able to break his ideologically motivated stubbornness and allow the train to move on.

One way to move beyond the social and geographical space of Bucharest is through films set in the provinces. Concerned with depicting their native environs, two prominent Romanian filmmakers – Corneliu Porumboiu and Marian Crişan – set their first films in their hometowns.[3] Furthermore, in addressing the conditions of marginalisation, other filmmakers are able to emphasise the marginal condition of their characters who live in small Southern Romanian towns.[4]

URBAN *VERSUS* RURAL LANDSCAPES

Apart from films that take place at the seaside and along the Danube,[5] the natural landscape is almost entirely absent. And even when present, it is usually relegated to the background, is banal, and perpetuates the mundane and dreary urban landscape while mirroring the faces of the characters. According to Lucian Georgescu (2011), the futility of travelling in Romanian films is determined by the fact that the 'cinematic narration is today closed inside city walls' and there is no possibility for horizontal escape, as society has developed into a 'territory of urban verticals' (2011: 131). Similarly, he explains a preference for the sweeping views of cinematic landscapes that is associated with road movies: 'through the windshield of a moving car the surroundings look alive and populated', but once the journey ends, one is up for the shock of 'the desolate surrounding landscape' (2011: 131). In his view, this endemic juxtaposition is signified by the virtually interchangeable prefab block of flats in *Stuff and Dough* and in Adrian Sitaru's *Hooked* (2008), featured usually as the starting point of a journey (2011: 146).

In *12:08 East of Bucharest* (2006) a tracking shot – placed between the introduction of the three main characters and the ensuing TV show – helps transition, according to Porumboiu, the individual stories to the TV show, but also captures a fragment of the town (Rus and Filippi 2014). The one-minute scene follows the car, containing the three protagonists, through side streets, between grey apartment buildings on one side and concrete garages on the other, and reveals a sleepy, cloudy glimpse of an afternoon in a small provincial town. The car veers into the main street and the film jump-cuts to the talk show inside the TV station, revealing – despite its shabbiness – the pretentiousness of this space that is to be recognised as 'the centre'. Not coincidentally, the film ends by emphasising the metaphor of centre–periphery dynamics as it shows the street lanterns turning on in succession, from the centre to the periphery.

The deliberately vague identifications of film locations sabotage their usage as geographical landmarks, of towns and places represented on screen, and further solidify what has already become a generic landscape of auteur post-communist cinema. Only in films like *Occident* or *Child's Pose* (2013) do we get a glimpse of different environments, like the new luxury mansions that belong to wealthy individuals. This, along with a shared plot-line (a tragic traffic accident and attempt to avoid the consequences), makes *Child's Pose* so similar to Paolo Virzi's *Human Capital* (2013).

Landscapes and Soundscapes

Mapping the spaces of New Romanian Cinema is not limited solely to the geography of their locations, but also includes the space of the film frame, as the films' visual and aural specificities constitute the aesthetics of the New Romanian Cinema.

For Dominique Nasta, for example, Cristian Nemescu's graduating film *C Block Story* (2003) is 'extremely convincing' due to its 'noisy, block-of-flats, "kitchen sink" neorealist atmosphere' (2013: 214). In *12:08 East of Bucharest* she again notices the 'shabby interiors, describing the post-Communist poverty-stricken environment through stage-like frontal views inside three ordinary provincial apartments' (Nasta 2013: 167). Marilena Iliesiu explains the role of the ubiquitous dilapidated concrete blocks of flats, built under communism and since fallen into ugly disrepair – in New Romanian Cinema, and in East and Central European films in general. She describes these buildings as 'ground by a superficial disease (degraded, patched, cracked walls) but also by a profound one, of their function', as in this framework the buildings not only represent a reflection of the social status of the characters, but are also their 'sensorial extension: the building is an extension of the epidermis' (Ilieşiu 2011: 155).

One cannot but agree with Doru Pop, who claims that, in aiming for mimetic authenticity, the films of New Romanian Cinema avoid picturesque and natural landscapes, and opt for the 'absence of extra-diegetic sound (or non-diegetic soundtrack)' (2014: 109). Dominique Nasta emphasises how such absence is perfectly counterbalanced, and even becomes an asset, in one of Sitaru's short films, *Waves* (2007), in which '[the] audience witnesses a foreign tourist's mysterious disappearance amidst the Black Sea waves' during the climactic scene. Despite the film's anti-minimalist visual style – most critics consider minimalism the style of choice of New Romanian Cinema – the 'sound mixing is very realistic and results in the development of autonomous auditory "channels"', combining direct sound with 'dialogue, crowd noises, entertaining French music, radio football commentaries and mobile phone conversations'. This realistic representation is used to give a genuine sense of Romanian society at the turn of the century (Nasta 2013: 149–50).

II: The Periphery Without

Just like mapping their geographical and stylistic positions, mapping the identities of characters living on the margins, with minor destinies and of little historical impact, foregrounds a perception of periphery through domestic and public social spaces. Generally confined to the enclosed spaces of their immediate environments (homes, shops, restaurants, offices, cars), these characters usually confront the drama of their existence between four walls. A recurrent trope in Romanian films is that of characters sitting around a table and eating, present in most (if not all) Romanian films of the last two decades (Chirilov 2011). The impact of these mealtime scenes is rooted in their capacity to convey the power of everyday realism through ethnographic observations of routine actions, which transforms the 'ordinary' into something noteworthy.

The importance of food, eating, feeding others and being fed, is present in *Stuff and Dough, The Paper Will Be Blue* (2006) or *First of All, Felicia* (2009), where the mothers fuss over the protagonists' need to eat before leaving home. The caring mother is a compelling metaphor of the traditionally matriarchal East European, or rather Balkan, society. Stemming from its self-perception as a hospitable people, the sharing of food represents a cultural gesture of building rapport with others, which is specifically significant in the case of foreigners. In *Morgen*, one of the first things Nelu does after bringing the illegal Kurdish immigrant to his home is to offer him food. In *Occident*, the most important event for Michaela's family when hosting Luigi – her Mozambique-born Italian suitor – is the preparation of a multiple-course sit-down meal. In *California Dreamin'*, Doiaru – despite his animosity towards Americans – welcomes Captain Jones, who has come to negotiate their departure, with traditional food and drinks.

In *4 Months, 3 Weeks and 2 Days* (2007), Otilia's inner tension becomes almost palpable as the camera remains fixed on her, centre-framed at the head of the table, just sitting there silently, barely touching the food, during the birthday dinner for her boyfriend's mother (Chirilov 2011; Pârvulescu 2009). Echoed in the convent refectory episode from Mungiu's next film, *Beyond the Hills* (2012), this scene exemplifies two important aspects of the New Romanian Cinema table scenes – the ability to create a sense of (often false) community, and the capacity to provide the space for conflicts to unfold. The dinner table thus becomes a microcosm of social interactions.

The process of eating foregrounds the everydayness of life by stretching the fabric of cinematic time, illustrating what has been noted as another central characteristic of New Romanian Cinema, that of being part of the 'slow cinema' trend (Jaffe 2014). In *Police, Adjective* (2009), for example, the protagonist Cristi sits at the kitchen table in his cramped apartment, eating his dinner on his own and in silence, while his wife is in front of the computer listening to music.

Another narrative trope found in Romanian cinema, in general, is that of scenes set within the confined spaces of cars, while in traffic – in both feature-length films, like *Stuff and Dough* and *Hooked*, as well as in a number of short films. Nae Caranfil uses this trope in *Philanthropy* (2002), when the worldly 'screenwriter of the underworld' educates the naïve high-school teacher about making a quick profit on a car journey around Bucharest. From the car races in Muntean's *The Rage* (2002), to the recurring car scenes in *When Evening Falls on Bucharest, or Metabolism* (2013), the vehicle represents a source of income, a way of travelling between places, and, as seen in *Child's Pose*, a plot device that triggers the existential crisis of its main characters. In *Horizon* (2015) the car represents a lifeline for a family running a hotel in a remote location. But it is also the locus of conflict, as the husband, Lucian – distrustful of (the local Mafioso) Zoli's intentions with his wife – starts an argument with him while on the road and is forced to return home on foot, while Zoli and Lucian's wife continue their journey to the city.

Domestic Spaces

Like the space in the car, domestic space contains and regulates social interactions and relationships within families, between friends, but also between neighbours, tracing the social dynamics inside apartment buildings. As noted above, the tattered exteriors of communist pre-fabs represent a staple of New

Romanian Cinema urban landscapes, yet it is equally worth examining the interiors of these buildings as veritable laboratories for social and psychological interactions. The apartment building is a mappable environment, encompassing points of access and exit, staircases and other communal areas, charting and organising the relations among its inhabitants. Generational differences and distinctions based on social and economic status, personalities or outlooks, structure these relations and offer a condensed snapshot of wider societal dynamics. As Ruxandra Cesereanu observes, the 'mixture of so many social classes, crammed like a jar of preserves, can have explosive consequences'. In her view, communal living has produced – under both communism and post-communism – a very specific mode of existence, a 'Tower of Babel, in which almost nobody gets along, and [nobody] respects anyone else' (2004).

The awkward sides of communal living are eloquently exemplified in *The Death of Mr Lăzărescu*. While waiting for the ambulance to arrive, the title character asks his neighbours for a pill, which they offer along with 'friendly' criticism of his drinking habits, his slovenly home, and his attachment to his three cats. And yet they will not accompany him to the hospital: the wife voices her complaints, accusing him of being a bad influence on her husband, thus 'othering' Lăzărescu as a member of a different group who is used to hard spirits, and creating a clear distinction between 'us' and 'them'. While living just across the hallway from each other, the financial, social and cultural chasm between Lăzărescu and his neighbours could not be more evident. The wife's tirade sums up the challenges of communal living in close quarters, which inevitably leads, as Cesereanu suggests, to intolerance.

Alone and feeble, Lăzărescu is the epitome of the marginal subject, left at the mercy of strangers and increasingly disjointed as the narrative progresses and his condition worsens. His loneliness is accentuated when, after calling the ambulance, he has only the cats to tell that he is not feeling well. Carted from one emergency ward to another, he is inviting ever diminishing concern due to his age, his alcoholic breath, and because he happens to fall ill on a night heavy in traffic accidents. Curiously, the director refuses to show any Bucharest landmarks during Lăzărescu's nocturnal journey, focusing instead on the inside of the moving vehicle, where the sole companions of a dying old man are two strangers – the paramedics.

III: The Periphery Within

In her book on contemporary Turkish cinema, Asuman Suner describes the provinciality in Turkish films as a condition, 'a mode of feeling', of 'sensing that life is elsewhere', rather than a specific locality (2010: 84). She also claims that the 'province recognises its provincial status only when it becomes aware of another mode of life that excludes itself' (Suner 2010: 84). In Suner's observation, the centre represents an elusive target, an imaginary construction, towards which the periphery always gravitates. As noted above, the physical locations in New Romanian Cinema are scattered either on the peripheries of Bucharest, or in the provinces. Puiu's films *The Death of Mr Lăzărescu* and *Aurora*, for example, are part of a planned series of 'six stories from the outskirts of Bucharest' (as an homage to Éric Rohmer's 'Six Moral Tales'), thus emphasising the significance of the periphery in Romanian cultural consciousness.

In his empirical study on the self-image of Serbians from different social strata, Zala Volčič observes that his respondents, working under the assumption that culturally specific symbols and self-exoticising representation are what foreigners pay for, seem inclined to use stereotypical images of the Balkans for profit (2005). This, however, creates what Volčič describes as 'confused despair', manifested in catering both to (usually) imaginary Western expectations, and to people's low self-esteem as minor, insignificant players in a globalised world. Similarly, in *California Dreamin'*, the mayor, the locals, even the central administration, are willing to stereotype themselves in the hope of gaining some political or financial advantage. The mayor invites the Americans to a party organised in their honour, and held at Hotel Dallas (in nearby Slobozia), which is a replica of the Dallas soap opera ranch (Nasta 2013: 218). The locals stage the show *Mystery of Dracula* for foreigners, featuring a man in a Dracula costume and a dozen scantily clad young women as his assistants. The scene satirises two aspects of internalised marginality: first, the uncritical acceptance of a dominant cultural influence (the reproduction of a culturally specific image, that of the American ranch); and second, the reproduction of stereotyped images with a local flavor.

California Dreamin' is probably the most conspicuous satire of the inferiority complex of Romanians, stemming from the juxtaposition of their culture vis-à-vis the unfathomable centre, and exposed in feeble attempts to redress the country's position internationally. The prologue, set during the Second World War, introduces Doiaru as a child, fleeing his home alongside his family during an Allied air raid. As Nasta points out, Doiaru – who considers himself a 'surviving metaphor of the damage caused by the Second World War' (2013: 217) – resents the American troops because of his 'troubled childhood'. His resentment also sums up the 'disillusionment shared by millions of Romanians' (2013: 218). According to a widespread belief from the immediate post-war years, the Americans were expected to save Romania from the Soviets – hence the anti-communist motto 'The Americans are coming!' Ironically, in the film Monica (Doiaru's daughter) receives a note reading 'The Americans have arrived' – unfortunately, almost half a century too late.

When Doiaru initially intercepts the Americans at the train station, and Jones informs him that they are on an international peacekeeping mission,

Figure 14.2 *California Dreamin'*: Captain Jones meets station master Doiaru

Doiaru responds: 'Fuck USA, fuck NATO, fuck Bill Clinton and those pricks in Bucharest. This is my train station.' Doiaru's autarchic rule of the small town, and especially of the train station, comes in stark contrast to the political dynamics between the two countries. The clash between their two cultures is made grotesquely evident at the very beginning of the film – the viewer sees things from the point of view of the marines, as on their way to the train station the convoy passes through the impoverished peripheries of Constanţa, passing dilapidated buildings on roads full of potholes, a funeral procession, and a few teenagers playing football among clothes on a drying line in a courtyard.

The presence of foreigners creates a referent against which collective identities become visible, as entrenched mores are exposed through wit, irony and the satirical outlook adopted by Romanian filmmakers. Besides the American marines in *California Dreamin'*, other foreign referents are: the illegal Kurdish immigrant in *Morgen*, the Chinese shop owner in *12:08 East of Bucharest*, the French men in *Of Snails and Men*, or the Mozambique-born Italian suitor in *Occident*. In his capacity as another foreign referent, Carfin, the escaped Gypsy serf from *Aferim!* (2015), whom Constandin is tasked with capturing, tells Constandin and his son about his travels with his previous owners through Vienna and Paris: 'The world? Big and beautiful, not like here.' While not a foreigner per se, but a deprived Rom, Carfin's well-travelled experience allows him to distinguish between the centre (Western Europe) and the periphery (the Balkans) and note the latter's deficiencies due to its projected and self-perceived marginality.

Instead of Conclusion: Widening the Map

The tensions arising from living in societies in transition are often rendered by East European filmmakers as extraordinary, even as absurdist juxtapositions, which in turn become sources of irony and black humour. Thus the realist, almost documentary, minimalist style of New Romanian Cinema often times is peppered by a dose of black humour and irony (Stojanova 2013b).

As Porumboiu admitted, 'a special kind of humour, an absurd humour' (Horton *et al.*, 2007) is common to Balkan filmmakers. To be sure, Kusturica's influence can be traced in 'Turkey Girl', Mungiu's episode from the omnibus film *Lost and Found* (2005). Tatiana, the main character, is at the age of her first idyll, but is still attached to her turkey, which she considers a special creature, and cannot accept her father's intention to offer it as a present to the doctor who will operate on her mother. Her affection for the turkey is strongly reminiscent of the analogical passion of the teenager Perhan for his turkey in *Time of the Gypsies* (1988). In the short fiction *C Block Story*, the main character has the unusual gift of provoking short-circuits and power outages, which again allude to Perhan, with his telekinetic powers. In *How I Spent the End of the World* (2006), the narrative is delivered from the points of view of a teenage girl and her little brother, which allows Cătălin Mitulescu to reconstruct 1989 with a mixture of humour, nostalgia and freshness of perception, similar not only to those of Kusturica, but also of Jiří Menzel. Thus he has the boy, Lalalilu, dreaming of receiving a wheel of cheddar cheese from Ceaușescu himself, which later materialises on the real-life family breakfast table. And the scene where he imagines making a huge balloon of chewing gum looks like it comes straight out of a Kusturica film. Such stylistic and modal approaches have never been explored by Romanian cinema before, with perhaps the notable exception of Caranfil's *Sundays on Leave* (1993).

On the other hand, the influence of the New Romanian Cinema on other Balkan cinemas is becoming increasingly noticeable. In the documentary *Sofia's Last Ambulance* (2012) by Bulgarian Ilian Metev, one could, for example, trace the influence of *The Death of Mr Lăzărescu*.[6] Considering the fictional world of Puiu's classic as a model of reality that in turn inspired Metev's gritty documentary might seem absurd, but Genoveva Dimitrova's observation to this effect is not only flattering, but also true (2012). And it would not be a stretch to say that the universe created by the films of New Romanian Cinema does not simply mirror, but rather creates, a model of reality, whose influence on young Balkan filmmakers – in terms not only of aesthetics, but also of general thematic direction – is further acknowledged by Jurica Pavičić in his writing about post-Yugoslav films (for example Pavičić 2011). In his view, Romanian cinema represents a 'political gesture', a way of rendering a different (Balkan) cinema that would challenge the Kusturica-like Balkan style, which is seen as politically regressive and auto-colonial. The influence can be noted, suggests Pavičić, in the films of Croatian directors Dalibor Matanić, and more specifically his film *Mother of Asphalt* (2010), or in Tomislav Radic's

Three Stories about Sleeplessness (2008), as well as in *Ordinary People* (2009) by Serbian filmmaker Vladimir Perišić (2011: 208, 264).

It should be noted that Romanian directors have increasingly resorted to co-productions lately, flaunting transnational topics – a predictable move, prompted by the need to reach international markets under the pressure of the inevitable globalisation processes. One of the successes of Romanian cinema, *Aferim!*, could be defined as a Balkan Western placed in the nineteenth century. Co-produced by Bulgaria and featuring Bulgarian folk costumes, it is a shared Balkan fable about the 'clash of civilizations' in Samuel Huntington's terms, as well as an exemplary instance of transnational cinema.

In conclusion, it could be said that the films of New Romanian Cinema have drafted a distinct map of their country that – although far from picturesque – is truly memorable, and thanks to the persistent international successes of Romanian films, has come to epitomise the Balkans and Eastern Europe.

Acknowledgement

We would like to express our gratitude to Christina Stojanova and Dana Duma, for offering great insight and helpful expertise that greatly helped improve an earlier version of this chapter.

Notes

1. Langkjaer proposes four types of realism: 'perceptual realism', specific for media, which uses the same intuitive skills towards mediated content as they would towards their physical environment; the second category refers to a 'realism of style', encompassing audio-visual aesthetics; 'narrative realism'; and 'realism as recognition' that can refer to social, cultural, psychological or emotional elements (2002: 18–20).
2. Films set in Bucharest include: Mungiu's *Occident*, Puiu's *The Death of Mr Lăzărescu*, *Aurora*, Muntean's *The Rage*, *The Paper Will Be Blue*, Mitulescu's *How I Spent the End of the World*, Netzer's *Medal of Honor* and *Child's Pose* (2013), Radu Jude's *The Happiest Girl in the World* (2009), Tudor Giurgiu's *Love Sick* (2006), Porumboiu's *When Evening Falls on Bucharest, or Metabolism*. Also, some well-known short films are located in Bucharest, including Mitulescu's *Traffic* (2004), Puiu's *Coffee and Cigarettes* (2004), or Nemescu's *C Block Story* (2003), Sitaru's *The Cage* (2010) and *Lord* (2010).
3. Porumboiu's films *12:08 East of Bucharest* and *Police, Adjective* mirror his hometown of Vaslui, while Crișan's *Morgen* and *Rocker* (2012) are set around his hometown in Western Transylvania.
4. Nemescu's *California Dreamin'*, Giurgiu's *Of Snails and Men*, Tudor Cristian Jurgiu's *The Japanese Dog* (2013) and Jude's *Aferim!*.
5. *Ryna* (2005) is about a girl raised as a boy and confined to isolation in the Danube delta. *A Good Day for a Swim* (2007) and *The Waves of the Danube* take place in Black Sea resorts. *Silent River* (2011) and *Oxygen* (2010) evoke two tragic episodes of the communist period, as people try to escape by swimming across the Danube.
6. At the film's premiere at Cannes in 2012, film critics saw similarities with Puiu's film. Jay Weissberg describes the film as a 'nonfiction version' of the Romanian film,

through the 'trio's heroic soldiering on in the face of a practically nonexistent infrastructure' (2012). Besides a vein of similar cinematic styles (*Sofia's Last Ambulance* could be classified as a 'direct cinema' documentary, and *The Death of Mr Lăzărescu* as new realist cinema), the two films are also connected by the quotidian accounts of health care professionals.

15. THE 'TRANSNATIONAL TURN': NEW URBAN IDENTITIES AND THE TRANSFORMATION OF CONTEMPORARY ROMANIAN CINEMA

Doru Pop

The Difficulties of the National Cinema Marketplace

The Romanian film industry was developed as part of 'the national cinema', and under the national communism of Nicolae Ceauşescu the films produced were concerned mostly with the so-called 'national epic' (with grandiose historical costume dramas). These films, together with a couple of 'national comedies', generated incredible revenues. According to the data of the Romanian Film Centre, the first top ten Romanian movies, in terms of viewership, were all produced before 1989 and the top five had each surpassed sales of thirteen million tickets. After 2000, when internationally successful Romanian films appeared, although they were no longer nationalistic, they were a part of 'national cinema'. Even acclaimed productions, Cristi Puiu, *The Death of Mister Lăzărescu* (2005) or Cristian Mungiu *4 Months, 3 Weeks and 2 Days* (2007), tell 'Romanian' stories and are clearly located in a recognisable national context. These films, although relatively well received at home, did not match the popularity of the previous generation of filmmakers. Mungiu's film, albeit rewarded with the highest prize in Cannes, had a little over 100,000 viewers in Romania, yet it fared well abroad, with almost 300,000 admissions in France and over 700,000 tickets sold in Spain. Therefore, it could be surmised that Romanian filmmakers clearly suffered from the collapse of Romanian film distribution and the dismantling of the national film industry.

Recently there was a relevant increase of the total revenues from cinema tickets sales in Romania: according to the European Audiovisual Observatory in 2013 the total sales increased 13.8 per cent; the country is still among the lowest ranked European markets in terms of cinema admissions. Compared to the Europe-wide revenue of 6.3 billion euros, Romania's market share is merely 2.8 per cent, with an estimated 9 million assessed viewers bringing in 36.3 million euros (data estimated for 2013). The staggering increase in Romanian film exports, which reached an impressive 90 per cent of admissions to the EU market during 2006–7, has decreased since 2010–11, with a total of 2.3 million viewers in the member states (for the 1996–2012 period). Moreover, the national film industry is suffering deeply from a lack of resources, since most viewers prefer American-made productions, with international blockbusters accounting for more than 90 per cent per cent of tickets sold in Romania. To make things even worse, in 2013 domestic earnings decreased again, from 880,000 euros in 2012 to 671,000 euros. According to the data provided by the Romanian Council for Competition, the lion's share of the market (almost 90 per cent) goes to blockbusters and highly popular commercial films, while independent productions have limited access to screenings. Even successful films like *4 months, 3 Weeks and 2 Days*, which managed to attract an impressive 975,158 viewers in the EU, drew domestically a mere 89,662.[1] Thus in 2014 a single Hollywood production, Martin Scorsese's *The Wolf of Wall Street*, dominated the national admissions in the first half of the year and was able to attract more viewers (over 295,000) than all the Romanian films that year combined![2]

The key argument of this study then, is to examine how these changes in the film marketplace have influenced recent Romanian cinema and its gradual transformation. I use the emergent transnational film theory, and authors like Hamid Naficy, who explains a transnational cinematic style that he calls 'accented cinema' in terms of the political and ideological aspects of transnationalism and postcolonialism (Naficy 2001). Although I am more interested in transnational cinema in terms of thematic and identity formation issues, rather than in its distribution or production, as I pointed out in another study (Pop 2014), Romanian cinema must be seen as part of a European filmmaking industry owing to its financing structure and its implicit audiences. Therefore, I am rejecting the argument, put forward by Halle, for whom transnational cinema is made possible by 'supranational funding mechanisms', which in turn lead to the development of a 'transnational orientation for audio-visual production, expanding dramatically the popular orientation, and bolstering pan-European structures of synergistic cooperation' (2010: 304). The 'multicultural logic' designed to undermine the 'national specificity', suggested by Halle (2010: 306), is not supported by argumentation since he makes no clear distinction between the transcultural and the transnational. Halle argues that there are three aesthetic levels of transnational cinema that stem from either a disregard for the actor's ethnicity or from their reliance on the English language and are bolstered by the use of well-known literary texts and transnational topics. These elements, in my view, are not sufficient to make a movie 'transnational', but can make it 'transcultural'.

My contention is that contemporary Romanian cinema is changing from a national to a transnational film industry and, more importantly, that directors are increasingly agglutinated into a cosmopolitan identity that flaunts the values of a transnational lifestyle, and sometimes of a transnational elite. The main purpose of this chapter is to map the most important transformations brought about in current Romanian filmmaking and to show how some of the writer-directors – who in the early 2000s concentrated on topics and narratives deeply rooted in a specifically national experience, thus creating a truly European cinema – are now being sidelined by new searches for means of expression that move beyond local, regional and even international relevance. Looking for wider contexts and audiences, Romanian filmmakers are gradually becoming part of transnational cinema. The chapter, then, is intended to create a framework to explain the reorientation of recent Romanian cinema, and to envision its possible future developments.

Hollywoodisation and Genrefication

The signs of a widespread genrefication were visible in the Romanian film industry even before 1989, when Romanian films, often mimicking popular genres, borrowed from international cinema cultures. The grand historical epic films made by Sergiu Nicolaescu were offshoots of the famous peplum genre movies in Italian cinema, while comedies of the same era were using easily recognisable narrative schemes from gangster parodies and other popular cinematic productions in Italian cinema, like the Transylvanian Westerns of Dan Pița or Mircea Veroiu. This was a period when the Romanian filmmakers reached the highest commercial success – the most viewed productions of all times, in Romania, are Sergiu Nicolaescu's films *Uncle Marin, the Billionaire* (1979), with almost 15 million tickets sold, followed by *Michael the Brave* (1970) and *The Dacians* (1966) with almost 13 million viewers each. This process of productive emulation was slowed down by budget reductions, yet it continued after 1989 when Romanian national cinema came clearly under the globalised influence of Hollywood cinematic practices.

Although some authors (see Sarkar in Ďurovičová and Newman 2010) claim that transnational cinema is part of the current globalisation of cinema industry, I would argue that the internationalisation of Romanian cinema had already begun in the early 2000 and, to refer to my work on the subject (Pop 2014: 13–15), Romanian directors of the post-2000 generation developed their own international co-productions, influencing regional and international cinemas. Yet co-productions do not make the Romanian film industry transnational – they rather make it part of global cinema, an altogether different aesthetic phenomenon. A global cinema, be it influenced by Hollywood or, more generically, by a global blockbuster culture, differs from transcultural cinema, which is characterised by de-localised narratives and settings. An extremely relevant example for this trend is Nae Caranfil's film *Closer to the Moon*, which obtained its national financing in 2007, went into production in September 2011, and was released only in 2014. The film tells the story of the unique bank robbery in Stalinist Romania and casts famous American and British actors like Mark Strong, Vera Farmiga, Christian McKay and Tim Plester. The film, with dialogues entirely in English, albeit set in Bucharest in late 1959, uses the communist past in an attempt to reach global audiences. Although released both in the US and internationally, the film had only 18,400 viewers in Romania.[3]

Closer to the Moon is representative of the new film industry development in Romania, where numerous films are made possible because of the availability of international co-production resources. Although performed by international stars who speak English, this international mix is still a Romanian production, part of Romanian national cinema, since the story takes place during the Stalinist regime in Bucharest and refers to a particular cultural context. *Closer to the Moon* might be internationally relevant but is national in its scope. And although the co-production of a Romanian company (Mandragora Movies), an Italian group (Rainier), a French firm (Denis Friedman) and a Polish financing group (Agresywna Banda), it does not exhibit any traits of transnationalism. The international cast and the internationalisation of the formal cinematographic devices, if not based on relevant content, remain attempts to globalise the national.

Figure 15.1   *Closer to the Moon*: the first post-1989 international film, starring Mark Strong and Vera Farmiga

Thus following Palacio's convincing theoretical explanation of transnational cinema as a type of cinema that has lost its 'nationality' (2013: 37), such co-productions could be defined as environments in which crossing over from the national to the transnational can take place, bringing forth new forms of expression, yet the universe of meanings, which addresses wider audiences and is cross-cultural by nature, is not necessarily transnational.

Another tendency is shown by more recent productions, like Alexandru Maftei's *Miss Christina* (2013), which points to the penchant of Romanian filmmakers for blockbuster genres. Maftei, in his efforts to make different films than those of the generation represented by Puiu or Mungiu, is betting on genre cinema for innovation. His film, marketed as the 'first Romanian horror movie', premiered on Halloween and claimed to be a new beginning for the national film industry. Unfortunately, the reinvention of the genre was bogged down by an awful mélange of Hitchcock meets Dracula and the Exorcist, with ill-adjusted elements from Child's Play, and attracted about 26,000 viewers in 2013. The most important defect of this production, its insufficient funding, is made obvious by its artistic deficiencies. Based on Mircea Eliade's eponymous novel, the story takes place at a country estate belonging to the Moscu family. Egor, a young painter, arrives there and promptly falls in love with a strange woman who turns out to be an undead creature killed during the peasant revolution of 1907. Regrettably, the entire fantastic narrative is undermined by total lack of visual verisimilitude. Theatrical displays, poor special effects and artificial backdrops are cluttered by impossible and excessive dialogue. Actually most relevant information is presented verbally, with the visuals reduced to decontextualised sequences. In his efforts to create a true 'Romanian horror', Maftei manages to create a sometimes grotesque caricature thereof, with ill-constructed characters and story, that lacks credibility. Without suspense and sustained tension building, *Miss Christina* is a disappointment for genre renewal as well as for the expectations of Romanian blockbuster cinema.

Another trope of the global popular culture is the romantic comedy, more specifically the mainstream American 'romcom' (McDonald 2013). A relevant illustration is *Love Building* (aka *Alt Love Building*, 2013), a romantic comedy, directed by Iulia Rugină, one of the young female directors of New Romanian Cinema. The film became the second most viewed Romanian film in 2013, with about 27,400 paying viewers in cinemas, a remarkable achievement for a debut movie. As schematic and melodramatic as it might appear, *Love Building* exploits some of the most important conventions of a genre that has mostly been ignored in recent Romanian cinema. Relevantly enough, Rugină has cast three of the best-known male actors of the Romanian New Wave cinema: Dragoș Bucur and Alexandru Papadopol (who both appeared in Cristi Puiu's *Stuff and Dough*), and Dorian Boguță (known from The Death of Mr Lăzărescu). *Love Building* looks very much like a typical Hollywood production, using clichés employed in films like *Couples Retreat* (Peter Billingsley, 2009) or *Hope Springs* (David Frankel, 2012).

More importantly, the film brings to focus social relations and social contexts no longer linked to a narrow, national specificity. Bucur plays Silviu, a cynical sexologist; Papadopol is Cristian, a shy couple-psychotherapist; and Boguţă's Valentin is also a group psychotherapist and personal development specialist. Between the three of them, they are monitoring the problems of fourteen different couples. The couples are also socially 'globalised' in their dysfunctions. Having been in a relationship for four years, for example, Eugen plays computer games and is addicted to gadgets, while Dana is extremely bossy; Claudia and Emil, in a relationship for over eight years, grapple with problems of infidelity and jealousy; Andreea and Mihai have been in a relationship for more than two years, but his dependency on his mother causes problems; Melania and Ioana, in a homosexual relationship for about a year, are confronting alcohol issues, and so on. The movie, which is placed in a summer retreat that could be located at any resort around the world, shows generic human relationships in an oversimplified context, which has appeal for a global audience.

Sweet Little Lies (2012), directed by Iura Luncaşu (who has specialised in soap operas for Media Pro Films), is another production that features social groups so far ignored by art films of the New Wave generation. Like *Love Building*, it presents new professions and the recently established job marketplace in Romania. This otherwise aesthetically irrelevant comedy depicts the love mishaps of a hacker and an IT manager, which takes place in call centres and online, and offers a glimpse at other professional activities like career advisors and PR specialists, gigolos and chocolate shop owners (of French origin). The main characters conduct their love lives online while leading a superficial existence in shallow urban spaces (coffee shops, taxi cabs) contextualised in a globalised Bucharest. Regrettably, the scenario falls into the trap of the online dating genre conventions, with borrowed elements from Ernst Lubitch's *The Shop around the Corner* (1940), and the poster mimics the famous *You've Got Mail* (Nora Ephron, 1998).

Perhaps the most interesting illustration of the globalisation trend in recent Romanian cinema is Cristina Iacob's first feature film, *#Selfie* (2014), which was extremely well received by Romanian audiences, reaching over 81,000 viewers in only two months.[4] Filmed like a road trip, I consider that *#Selfie* marks the completion of a full circle in the evolution of Romanian contemporary cinema. From the road trip in Cristi Puiu's *Stuff and Dough* (2001), which marked the beginnings of the New Wave cinema, to this teenage flick, full of gags, Romanian filmmaking moved from national to international, then to global and now to transnational cinema.

This movie is emblematic of the ultimate integration of global themes, subjects and stories in Romanian national cinema. If the New Wave films were focusing on the disenfranchised social margins, the directors of this 'New Cinema' are increasingly interested in a youth culture with no links to Romanian society, one that could be easily identified. Furthermore, by applying star system practices – for example, casting pop/dance stars like Alex Velea and Andrei Maria aka Smiley – #*Selfie* uses Romglish (the pidgin version of Romanian) as a common 'langue', where expressions like 'epic genre' (epic gen) confirms the advent of a globalised generation.

Indeed, while these films depict economic realities and human relations marking the transformation of Romanian society, and on another level reflect changes in the imaginary of the community, they are nothing but manifestations of the internationalisation and globalisation of media discourses, and could therefore not be described as transnational films. In other words, they are no longer the reflection of a limited national identity, but have become part of the globalised, internationally standardised audio-visual media imagery.

Clinging to the National: Subjects and Stories

While the films discussed above demonstrate a clear disengagement from national themes, locations and historical relevance, the core of what is called 'national cinema' is alive and well in Romania. As pointed out by Martha Nochimson, a 'national film culture' entails the desire of filmmakers to put into cinematic language particular 'national' stories (2010: 14) that are deeply linked to national canons (literary, artistic). The extant national cinema is surely different from the nationalist Romanian cinema of the ideologically obsolescent communist period, but it is still associated with the artistic expression of culturally specific historical and social traits related to idiosyncratic national traumas. The best example of Romanian national cinema is certainly *Beyond the Hills* (Cristian Mungiu, 2012), made using the cinematic tools of the New Wave, yet it remains intrinsic part of the national cinema, since it delivers a narrative totally immersed in a national context. The participants (the nun Voichița and her friend Alina), the environment (a remote Orthodox monastery), the problems faced (exorcism, faith) are all deeply national in scope. It is at this juncture that we note the divide between a national cinema, dealing with themes meant to facilitate understanding of a national psyche, and the transnational cinema. Unlike the nationalistic representations of a gloriously monolithic national identity, a national cinema allows a glimpse into social problems like prostitution, exploitation or authority.

Sometimes recent works, belonging to this trend, recycle themes and issues in locally contextualised narratives. Such is the case of *The Unsaved* (2013) by Andrei Gruzsniczki, which looks back to communist Romania as a source of inspiration and is a metaphorical reiteration of an argument already made by the films of Mungiu and Porumboiu. Using black and white aesthetics, the director places his story in 1984, when the Securitate and the Communist Party are still in charge of the lives of Romanians. The same is true of two other productions from 2013, Stere Gulea's *I'm an Old Communist Hag* and *Roxanne*, by Valentin Hotea. In both films the recent past – be it memories of a self-proclaimed 'communist hag' or the drama of a man who finds out a dark truth from the Securitate files –haunts the present-day national imaginary. An even more explicit movie is Nicolae Mărgineanu's *White Gate* (2014), which is not much different from his remarkable tales about the communist regime, *Bless you Prison* (2002), which takes place in one of the most sinister labour camps of Stalinist Romania.

These films do not break any new ground, but repeat aesthetic and narrative tropes, already established by Romanian filmmakers when dealing with the recent (mostly communist) past, and with moral issues linked to serious local social problems, in particular those with potential for expressing globally valid questions. Interesting cases to point are *Of Snails and Men* (2012) by Tudor Giurgiu or *Chasing Rainbows* (2012) by Dan Chişu, which are centred on nationwide problems like the protracted transition to a market economy, and are situated in locally specific peripheral urban and social spaces: these films are examples of a nation-centred filmmaking.

Even *The Japanese Dog* (2013), a feature film debut of the promising young director Tudor Cristian Jurgiu, relies heavily on regional identities. The story is anchored in the popular national narrative about the dramatic fate of old and lonely parents whose children have emigrated, and has an internationalised twist. The elderly main character, Costache Moldu (played by Victor Rebengiuc), is trying hard to cope with the consequences of the flooding of his already derelict home. Costache's biggest problem, however, is that his son Ticu lives now in Japan and, when he returns with his wife and son, it becomes obvious that he is totally estranged from his father. This circumstantial internationalisation – familiar from other New Romanian Cinema films like *Medal of Honor* (2009), where Rebengiuc plays Ion Ion, an old man whose son lives in Canada – is counterbalanced by extremely narrow shots of the typical poor Romanian village looming in the background. Such productions could also be described as multinational films, where the specificities of an ethnic group are reflected in the perceptions of another ethnic group or individuals.

The 'Transnational Turn'

Three movies reveal important changes in contemporary Romanian cinema, indicating a trend towards the creation of a transnational urban identity: Radu Muntean's *Tuesday, After Christmas* (2010), Călin Peter Netzer's *Child's Pose* (2013) and Corneliu Porumboiu's *When Evening Falls on Bucharest, or*

Metabolism (2013). These aesthetically accomplished movies are indicators of the 'transnationalisation' of New Romanian Cinema, sharing several key characteristics: limited references to local or national identities; reduced background information on characters and events; transnational themes, characters and narratives that are decreasingly linked to a particular cultural milieu.

The first profound modification is made visible in their settings, which I would define as 'transmutation of the kitchen sink'. As noted in my booklength study on the Romanian New Wave, many directors from the new generation have used interior *mise en scènes* to visualise their characters' degradation along with the deterioration of their social and psychological conditions. Physical surroundings, featuring decrepit kitchens, enclosed rooms in blocks of flats, even sordid bathrooms, have been shaped to reflect the characters' state of mind. Such, among many, is the case with Puiu's *The Death of Mr Lăzărescu* (2005) and Porumboiu's *12:08 East of Bucharest* (2006), where kitchens and bathrooms in a working-class prefab building are used as the bleak backdrops of human tragedies.

Among the earliest indications of the ongoing transformation of cinematic social identities is reflected in the *mise en scène* of *Tuesday, After Christmas*. Its urban interiors suggest not only a different social milieu – that of the urban middle class of well-to-do doctors and their working surroundings – but also foregrounds a certain decontextualised, nationally non-specific identity. A simple sequence analysis shows that most scenes from Muntean's film take place in culturally non-specific social environments. The first scene takes us to a private space – a bedroom – lacking any culturally contextualising elements. The second scene takes place in a shopping mall with no references to a particular geographical or cultural place either. The third scene happens in a fancy car where father and daughter are caught in traffic, and the urban space they pass through shows no local references. The subsequent sequence evolves in a dentist's office, where the protagonist's mistress, Raluca, works. Time and again, the film takes us to completely neutral urban spaces, thanks to both their chromatic colour design and to external references. This is also the case with later sequences, where, at a restaurant, we witness two couples, the protagonist Paul Hanganu, his wife, Paul's friend Cristi and his young lover, who are engaged in a long conversation. There is no visual referencing to any local or national specificity; moreover, the jokes at the table all allude to international contexts, such as the fact that the father of Enrique (Iglesias) is also a singer, making fun of the international music listened by older generations. Clearly, this kind of approach facilitates the construction of the amorous triangle and the development of a narrative that is open to an audience beyond the confines of the national cinema circuit. It must also be noted that this film shows stark contrast with a 'national' film like Mircea Daneliuc's *Fed Up* (1994), where similar backdrops (hospital, urban spaces) and actions (infidelity, driving) are involved, yet their presentation demonstrates an exaggerated concern with localisation of the narrative.

Radu Muntean's most recent film, *One Floor Below* (2015) shows how the internationalisation of movie production influences the narrative content and leads to genrefication. This thriller, financed by national cinema institutions from four countries (France, Germany, Sweden and Romania), follows a crime mystery storyline. And, although it takes place in a Bucharest neighbourhood, the film exposes the moral dilemma of a typical middle-class man, one that can be found in an urban context anywhere in the world. The boring everyday routine of Sandu Pătrașcu, a car sales and transactions broker, is disrupted by a homicide next door. Not willing to become a witness in a trial, Pătrașcu (played by Teodor Corban, one of the most important actors of the New Wave) is nonetheless watching from a distance the man who he believes to be the murderer. This presumed killer, an Alan Bates look-alike, is a young yuppie: an IT and computer games specialist. Just as in *Tuesday, After Christmas*, all characters in Muntean's thriller are petty-bourgeois, leading unremarkable urban lives. And although the director manages the build-up to the final denouement, creating a noteworthy fight scene between the two men where authenticity and realism are at their best, the rest of the film is heavily dependent on the stereotypes of the 'suspense thriller'.

The Romanian director simply recontextualises Hitchcockian techniques – with several indirect references to classics like *Shadow of a Doubt* (1943) and *Rear Window* (1954) – and exercises his ability to keep the viewer in a constant uncertainty, relying mostly on the 'whodunnit' plot cliché. Striving to reinvent the genre – Muntean claims his film is an anti-thriller – he actually does nothing new, but skilfully applies the well-worn 'red herring' and the 'unsuspected killer' techniques. As a result, the director achieves, on one hand, a remarkably strange and troubling atmosphere in which he brilliantly constructs the apparent normalcy of a murder. On the other hand, by placing his narrative in a de-contextualised space, he generates a precarious sense of reality.

Similar intentions and consequences are discernible in *Metabolism*, whose minimalist *mise en scène* and spatial neutrality transcend the limitations of a national cinema. Porumboiu develops a meta-narrative about filmmaking, not unlike Truffaut's *Day for Night* (1973), whose deliberate de-contextualisation is facilitated by driving foreign brand cars at night, moving through an anonymous urban space, complete with generic steel and glass buildings, non-specific ads and street signs. This process is further emphasised by an important discussion between the central character – the film director – and his main actress that takes place in a Japanese restaurant amidst the minimalist scenery of wall paintings, and reaches its absolute realisation in one of the final scenes, which features endoscopic images of the protagonist's intestines.

The abandonment of the old Romanian-made Dacia automobile for newer, mostly foreign, models is yet another external sign of the changes taking place both in life and on screen. Just like in *Tuesday, After Christmas*, where the adulterous father drives his daughter in a foreign-made car, in *Child's Pose* all the characters are well off and drive expensive, foreign-brand cars. The central dramatic event of the movie is a tragic car accident caused by a powerful Audi 8 driven by Barbu, the son of Neli, who drives an even more powerful BMW X5. Furthermore, the most important conversation in the film, placed at its climax, attributes the traffic tragedy to competition between car manufacturers.

Along with neutral urban identities, Netzer is also a master of depicting a cosmopolitan way of life. The opening scene in *Child's Pose* places the story in a nationally non-specific urban interior where two well-off, middle-aged women are engaged in conversation. One of them is Neli (played by the remarkable Luminița Gheorghiu), Barbu's overprotective mother and the film's protagonist. Relevantly enough, their clothes and accessories, including smart phones and jewels, not only place them in the highest socio-economic bracket, but also betray their positions of control. The second scene takes us to a party where managers and ministers, celebrities, realtors and doctors are amusing themselves in a luxurious environment. Here, as in *Tuesday, After Christmas*, there are no cultural markers except the Romanian language spoken to indicate a prevalent national identity in this generic urban gathering. The guests dance to Italian music, drink French champagne and Campari orange and enjoy the services of private cleaning personnel who take care of them and their sumptuously decorated living quarters.

Figure 15.2 *Child's Pose*: Luminița Gheorghiu as mother from Romanian new social elites

Neli, an interior design decorator – a job that is not atypical in postcommunist Romania – is married to a highly paid doctor and surrounded by influential people who complete this portrayal of the transition to transnationality, not only in film but also in reality. For example, Neli, who buys her son Nobel prize-winning novels, is totally unaware of contemporary Romanian writers, although she considers herself a patron of the arts – the news of Barbu's accident reaches her at a socially well-heeled event at the opera.

This phenomenon could be best described by what Mette Hjort calls 'modernising transnationalism' (2010: 24), meaning the creation of a cinematic cultural space that does not belong to the national, but exists beyond the limitations of specificity. This 'modernised transnational space' allows movement from one narrative level to another, since neither space nor time are localised. Such neutralised urban spaces and the implicit minimalistic *mise en scènes* make national (Romanian) identity indistinguishable from other national identities. The resultant cosmopolitan identities and behaviours, then, along with the urban life and spaces they represent become undistinguishable from other European identities, life and urban spaces, and thus acquiesce with a transnational imaginary, which Netzer's film amply illustrates. Indeed, it subtly implies that where transnational contexts and transnational values are part of the narrative, transnational world views are invariably foregrounded.

Interestingly enough, Ewa Mazierska and Laura Rascaroli suggest that the creation of a 'new city' opens up discussions about a 'postmodern cinema' (2003: 15–16). The new cityscape does not flaunt a specific national identity and cannot be localised, even if it is inhabited by apparently national or local themes and subjects. It is in this city that 'the shedding of national differences and the acquisition of uniform, transnational or post-national identities' occurs (Mazierska and Rascaroli 2003: 6). In Netzer's film, the 'new city' is clearly populated by the nouveau riche (Romanian) elite, which is no longer bound by common cultural or ethnic traits, and where class division remains the most visible maker. Thus in stark contrast with the dire social circumstances of the family of the boy Barbu accidentally kills, whose apartment is a cosmopolitan designer gem with an interior staircase and indistinct furniture of industrial colours and shapes, adorned with technological gadgets and appliances that could be found in any urban interior around the world and point to a lifestyle that is completely nationally non-specific. Curiously enough, while the victim's family are living in a poor rural context – where the final, dramatic unravelling of both Neli and Barbu takes place – it is also de-territorialised. Or, in accordance with Milja Radovic's description of the transnational (2014), this is the communication space between the otherwise mutually exclusive national and global.

One of the most relevant cosmopolitan spaces used in recent Romanian cinema is epitomised by the mushrooming shopping malls across the country.

The Romanian cultural and socio-economic environment was totally transformed from penury to affluence by the 'shopping mall' culture. The mall accelerates the loss of national identity, which is eloquently illustrated by the second scene from *Tuesday, After Christmas*. The action takes place in a shopping mall, but for more than five minutes the viewer is denied information about the specificity of the location, which could have been in any city or country around the world. Most importantly, the generalised shopping mall space acquires a narrative function, made explicit in one of the key scenes in *Child's Pose*. Here the dynamics between the global and national spaces become indicative of the dynamics between the characters' personas and their hidden, private identities. As Barbu, Bogdan Dumitrache comes through as the quintessential imbalanced young man confronting a disturbed older generation, personified by Vlad Ivanov in the memorable role of the demonic arriviste, Dinu Laurenţiu. Dinu sets the tragedy in motion, yet shows no signs of morals and remorse, and his rationalist explanation for his irrational behaviour takes us not only into the depths of his character but also into the depths of an individualistic society. Dinu, as well as Barbu, are no longer manifestations of national identities, but epitomes of transnational character traits, reflecting a profoundly disturbing and ubiquitous psychological phenomenon that is intelligible to contemporary audiences everywhere.

This is why *Child's Pose*, awarded with some of the most important prizes at the Berlin Film Festival (Best Film, FIPRESCI) confirms the general transnational trend discussed here. In a masterful display of filmmaking, it sums up the best traits of recent Romanian cinema. Yet it also captures Romanian cinema in the process of moving away from the locally and nationally identifiable subjects and themes, which until recently constituted its core, towards non-specific situations and universal themes. An eloquent illustration of this shift is the Christmas celebration in Muntean's film, which does not reference the trauma of communism but suggests contemporary consumerism – in sharp contrast with Porumboiu's movie (*12:08 East of Bucharest*, 2006) about whether or not the Romanian revolution, which tragically ended on Christmas night, happened or not. Netzer's film is no longer about a case that is specific to Romanian society, as it is with Mr Lăzărescu, but rather a story that anybody around the world can relate to. The directors, who became known as 'the young Romanian filmmakers', have since matured both aesthetically and conceptually and, I would argue, are now entering a new phase, one inspired by and fuelling the transnational imaginary, which would allow them to move beyond the specific identity of national filmmakers. The type of transnational cinema they are now involved in is no longer related to national issues, and yet it is not a part of a global tendency. Following the anthropological perspective suggested by Liehm and Liehm (1977), a radical idea in itself, I would define the nature of their transnational cinema as art that transcends the cultural barrier (1998: 245). While these directors depict a transnational space, create transnational identities, and are using transnational discourses and narratives, these are means of expression allowing them to go beyond their individual culture and, moreover, to transcend international cultural barriers.

The films discussed above belong to a transnational aesthetic that should be seen, as Newman eloquently puts it, as being 'above the national but below the level of the global' (2010: 10). My understanding of their 'transnationality' is along the fault lines, suggested by Natasa Ďurovičová and Kathleen Newman (2010: x): distinct from the international and the global, the transnational presupposes a spatial and personal identity that cannot be particularised to a given national cultural canon. A transnational cinema allows the translatability of stories, scenes and spaces into other cultural contexts without the need for reinterpretation. In this respect, transnational cinema refuses the national while also resisting assimilation into a global, standardised representation. In other words, when featuring urban space, which can be easily recognised, the transnational space is in clear contrast with global space. Such is the case with the Romanian middle class described in these films. According to their social appearance they share typical bourgeois traits (lifestyle, clothes), yet their individual narratives are transferable into any other cultural context, with a wider relevance than that allowed by the simple 'stereotypical' discourses of genre movies. This is a cinema that is not focused on the particular, nor dependent on any national social group (albeit belonging to a neo-liberal, or mostly liberal social stratum that allows them a certain freedom of movement), and indicates a clear shift from the localist dimension, and even from national problems, to a magnitude capable of generating transnational connections. Offering viewers such transparent identities, placed in environments beyond the fixations of the national, recent Romanian cinema features some of the most important transnational characteristics: neutral urban spaces, cosmopolitan themes and problems, and social identities that are part of a transnational form of capitalism.

Last but not the least, these films can be described as 'transnational' not merely because they result from the co-production system of making movies, or, as in the case of Abbas Kiarostami's most recent films, as bi-products of a transnational political option of the directors. Without leaving their Romanian contexts, these films belong to forms of expression that are no longer national; nor are they generic enough to be part of a global cinema. They are transnational films, made for transnational audiences, which places the most recent Romanian cinema in another paradigm altogether.

NOTES

1. The information included here is extracted from the European Audiovisual Observatory, available at <http://www.obs.coe.int> and <http://lumiere.obs.coe.int> (accessed 15 July 2014).
2. Information available at <http://www.cinemagia.ro/stiri/cu-21-mai-multe-bilete-vandute-arn cinematografe-26038/> (accessed 15 July 2014).
3. Information extracted from the website <www.cinemagia.ro> (accessed 15 July 2014).
4. Information available at <http://www.cinemagia.ro/stiri/cu-21-mai-multe-bilete-vandute-arn cinematografe-26038/> (accessed 15 July 2014).

PART VI

OVERVIEW

16. HISTORICAL OVERVIEW OF ROMANIAN CINEMA

Christina Stojanova

Romanian Cinema as National Cinema

The New Romanian Cinema has compelled academics, journalists and critics to once again reconsider the concept of national cinema in a new light. Indeed, concepts like peripheral, accented, diasporic and local cinema along with those of global, transnational and world cinema, have thrown into question the very idea of national cinema. Nonetheless, as Laszlo Strausz writes, while 'contemporary Romanian films are doubtlessly part of a phenomenon which, when coupled with the lack of domestic attention, can be described as transnational, the best [d]iachronic interpretive framework for New Romanian Cinema [remains] the national' (2017: 5). Therefore the ensuing historical overview of Romanian cinema from its inception to the early 2000s excavates the cultural, socio-political, institutional and aesthetic origins of the NRC as part of the Romanian national cinematic tradition, but also highlights the roots of its transnationality by pointing to long-standing connections with European – Western as well as Eastern – cinemas and cultures. Moreover, the overview regards Romanian cinema as a result of the intricate interactions between the nation state and the intelligentsia at crucial historical junctures – most notably, after the establishment of communism in 1944, and after its fall in 1989 – thus setting the stage for its current reshaping by the NRC movement.

In his essay 'National Belonging', Canadian film scholar Jerry White proposes a renewed approach to national cinema that avoids the mistakes of national cinema scholarship from the 1980s and 90s, and embeds the national into the transnational (White 2004: 222–3). His definition of national cinema first envisions the 'presence of national identity' through which a sense of belonging is established – possibly but not necessarily linked to the 'unified territory' of a nation state (2004: 225–7). Next, White postulates evidence of film production 'output', constituting a 'sustained and diverse' tradition,[1] accomplished by 'a community reasonably considered to be a nation' (ibid.). And last, he assumes a state funding apparatus as indispensable since it ensures 'a more secure production infrastructure (or at least the potential for such an infrastructure)' (2004: 227). He also stipulates conditions for the transnational moment in national cinemas, predicated on diasporic directors working abroad, and immigrants working within a country's multicultural milieu.

White's first criterion remains the most elusive since the issue of national belonging and national identity in the cinemas of Eastern Europe[2] was decided by two principal agents – the state and the intelligentsia – under political and ideological duress, both internal and external. Relative newcomers to the European family of nations as a result of bloody conflicts,[3] Eastern European elites saw culture – and film – as a powerful tool for facilitating their national and social integration, additionally complicated by belated modernisation and industrialisation. Back then – not unlike now:

> weary of the steadily growing gap between the advanced Western European societies and the backwardness of their own, Eastern European intellectuals and artists found a much needed contentment in art, the only place where they could compete as equals with their Western counterparts. (Stojanova 2000)

The works of art, towering well above achievements in other walks of life, nurtured Eastern European intelligentsia's belief in its mission as a bearer of pure transcendence and as the moral conscience of the nation, while in fact it was consolidating as a proxy elite class with powerful social and political interests, which led to what Hungarian-born scholars George Konrad and Ivan Szelenyi define as the 'crisis of self-knowledge' from the era of the 'rational redistributive societies' (1979: 46–54).[4] Exacerbated by severe ideological clashes between nationalism, fascism and communism throughout the 1920s and 1930s, this crisis reached its peak during the communist era of 'life in lies', which Václav Havel believed was 'far worse than a simple conflict between two identities ... and a challenge to the very notion of identity itself' (qtd in Stojanova 1999: 105–69).

HISTORICAL OVERVIEW OF ROMANIAN CINEMA

THE EARLY YEARS

Since its inception in the late 1890s – the first screening is believed to have taken place on 27 May 1896 in Bucharest – Romanian cinema has been 'linked to the unified', albeit often contested, territory of a nation state, housing several ethnic and cultural traditions.[5] Not unlike its Bulgarian and Serbian counterparts,[6] Romanian films emerged relatively late, around the early to mid-1910s, although according to Nasta, film records of local events from the late 1890s still exist thanks to the omnipresent Pathé cameramen (2013: 7). According to Manuela Cernat's 1982 official Romanian film history, Romanian cinema endured through the 1920s mostly as a promotional vehicle for Romanian theatre professionals like Constantin T. Theodorescu, who founded several film companies (1910–12), and whose eclectic documentary *reportages* and travelogues were typical of this chaotic stage of film production.[7]

The official beginning[8] of Romanian national cinema is marked by the well-preserved *Independence of Romania*, made in 1912 by theatre actor and director Aristide Demetriade and produced by his colleague Grigore Brezeanu. Known as the first Eastern European Nationalist blockbuster,[9] it focuses on the liberation of Romania from the Ottomans as a result of the Russian–Turkish wars in the late 1800s, and dwells on an episode in which a large contingent of Romanian volunteers fought for their country's independence alongside the Russians. It was also a precursor of things to come, as in the 1960s and 1970s, the nationalist blockbuster or the Nationalist Epic would become a privileged official genre of Romanian cinema. Paradoxically, it was Nae Caranfil's *The Rest is Silence* (2007) – a meta-cinematic and self-reflexive remake of Demetriade's original – that put the Nationalist blockbuster to rest.

EARLY ROMANIAN CINEMA AND THE STATE

The role played by the state of the Kingdom of Romania – a constitutional monarchy (1881–1947) – in the early years of Romanian cinema was almost non-existent as film production itself was cottage and, to quote Croft, overwhelmingly 'cultural'.[10] As in the other Axis countries, the state was expected to provide funding – very generous in Hungary, much less so in Bulgaria and Romania – before and during the Second World War (Stojanova 1999: 171). Following democracies like Britain, which saw the potential of cinema as a propaganda tool back in 1914, the Romanian state established the Photographic and Cinematographic Service of the Romanian Army (PCSRA) in November–December 1916. It became 'one of the earliest state-run production companies in the world that specialized in documentary films', which helped lay the foundations of production base, and boosted technical staff professionalism, mostly that of cameramen (Aitken 2013: 774).

The PCSRA was followed by inconsistent and sporadic protectionist measures, designed to encourage a national film production, the most serious one being the introduction in 1934 of the progressive (for its time) National Cinema Fund (1934),[11] which entailed deducing 1 RON from each ticket sold and 10 RON from each ten metres of film stock imported (Uricaru 2012: 429).[12] After PCSRA became independent in 1937, on 1 September 1938 the Romanian government created the National Office of Cinema (Oficiul Naţional al Cinematografiei or ONC), which took over 'the activity of producing newsreels on Romanian and foreign affairs' (Aitken 2013: 774).

The establishment of the ONC, with film director Paul Călinescu at its helm, benefited from the renewed interest in state-subsidised production infrastructure, which accounted for what Croft (1998) calls 'mixed' or rather non-market-based funding of the 'sustained and diverse' film tradition during the interwar period and beyond. As Konrad and Szelenyi have it, the pre-1989 Eastern European economies 'fundamentally and qualitatively' differed from the Western European '19th century self-regulating market' (1979: 95), due to their above-mentioned 'rational redistributive' nature, where the power to dispose of surplus product, or of 'teleological distribution', was based on special knowledge, and delegated to the state apparatus and its loyal intelligentsia (1979: 42–8).

Early Romanian Cinema and the Intelligentsia

The prolonged and difficult Romanian national and social integration during the last 160 years of the 'early rational redistributive society' (1800–1947), sheds additional light on the state deference towards arts and culture and its rapport with the intelligentsia. Since the interwar national integration was vehemently contested along the lines of 'territorial statehood, ethnicity, language, and religion', Romanian nation-builders were faced with 'an arduous process of elite bargaining', in which the role of the intelligentsia – albeit riddled with ideological, social and ethnic controversies – was instrumental (Iordachi and Trencsényi 2003: 418–19). After all, the few institutions of political and cultural modernity were the 'creation of a handful of Romanian intellectuals' (ibid.). In its turn this resulted in 'pre-eminence of the executive [stratum], excessive centralization of the administration, factionalism of the parties', and 'a political system, characterized by low-level participation', which have come to chronically plague Romanian society (Iordachi and Trencsényi 2003: 421). Furthermore, the over-politicised schism within intelligentsia between nativist-traditionalists and pro-Western modernisers, dating back to the literary circle Junimea from the second half of the nineteenth century, was exacerbated over the years and led either to the 'culpabilising' of world-famous Romanian humanist scholars and philosophers like Mircea Eliade, Emil Cioran or Constantin Noica – part of the so-called 'young generation' (tânăra generaţie) from the late 1920s and 1930s – or to glorifying them as 'cultural models' rather than viewing their work as evidence of 'the self-destruction of Eastern European cultural avant-garde, which identified with 'Western political modernity' (Iordachi and Trencsényi 2003: 435).

The growing popularity of cinema as mass entertainment threw into high relief these endemic tensions since, as Eliade wrote in 1957, the 'active classes' of the region undoubtedly 'belonged to the "modern" world', while the majority of the population 'still maintained its attachment to a traditional and half-Christian spiritual universe' (Eliade 1972: 160). In his view, these peculiarities allowed for the coexistence of two layers of culture, whereas Western modernity never succeeded in obliterating the traditional Eastern and Balkan core – at least not until the violent communist takeover – and remained constantly challenged by it.

Against this backdrop, the battle for the survival of modest local film production against the sophisticated Western European – mostly German and Hollywood imports[13] – was played out, and its concerns inform the 1935 collection *The Factory of Fairy Tales or Elements of a Philosophy of the Cinema (Uzina de basme sau Elementele unei filosofii a cinematografului)* by prominent film critic and essayist Ion F. Cantacuzino (Cernat 1982, Nasta 2013). Among the first attempts to analyse the links between cinema and a predominantly peasant society, the collection brings to light the fact that early Romanian cineastes – like their Eastern European counterparts – were either idealistic aesthetes or down-to-earth pragmatists. The former, while enthusiastic advocates of cinema as a new form of 'high' – 'seventh' – art or 'tenth muse',[14] were also fierce critics of its popularity as a 'low' fairground entertainment. The latter, on the other hand, saw cinema as a form of public service and education, promoting folk customs, the beauty of nature and healthy lifestyles, but also as a vehicle of militarist and nationalist propaganda.

Cinema as 'High' Art

The beginnings of Romanian cinema fall far short of the high standards of Romanian interwar literature, which reached its peak with Liviu Rebreanu's *The Forest of the Hanged (Pădurea Spânzuraţilor,* 1922, published in English in 1931). To this day, it remains a powerful pacifist work, whose exquisite style and captivating narrative rivals its contemporaneous masterpiece, Erich Maria Remarque's *All Quiet on the Western Front* (1930). As Pop asserts, '[t]he true recognition of national Romanian moviemaking came only in 1965', when Liviu Ciulei was awarded the Best Director prize in Cannes, for his remarkable black and white transposition of the novel (2014: 2).

Indeed, as demonstrated below, the great Romanian interwar literature was a powerful – albeit contentious – lifeline for 'artistic' Romanian cinema from its very beginning. Thus Rebreanu's[15] novel *Ciuleandra* (1927), named after a Gypsy dance known to bring its participants into a trance, was co-produced as *Faded Dreams* (1930) by German director Martin Berger. Best known for his Expressionist[16] film *The Wife's Crusade* (1926), starring Conrad Veidt, Berger was obviously attracted by the socio-melodramatic bent of the story about a village girl, seduced and then killed by her city suitor. Seeing Romanian literature as a source of exoticism, associated at that time with all things Eastern European, Berger also filmed the popular novel *A Mill Was Floating Down the Siret...* (1925) by Mihail Sadoveanu– yet another interwar literary giant – with the title *Storm of Love* (1929).[17]

The work of the most popular Romanian playwright of that time, Ion Luca Caragiale, was adapted for screen only twice before the Second World War.[18] His tragic-comedy *The False Accusation*, filmed by Gheorghe Popescu in 1926, was followed in 1943 by the extremely successful adaptation of his comedy *A Stormy Night*. Produced by Ion F. Cantacuzino and directed by Jean Georgescu, it was a crowning achievement of the ONC, and 'the first internationally acclaimed Romanian box-office hit' (Nasta 2013: 11).

Figure 16.1 *A Stormy Night*

Cinema as Public Service and Propaganda

Treating cinema as an educational tool could be defined as 'a compromise between the enlightenment fervor of the Leftist intelligentsia and the elitism of the conservative *literati*' (Stojanova 2005a: 224), best illustrated by the number of publications[19] devoted to '[t]he pressure to regulate cinema and put it to public use', which, according to Cernat, 'began mounting in the early 1910 [sic]' (1982: 19). One of these publications, *The Appeal of Cinema* (*Chiemarea cinematografului*, 1915), penned by police inspector G. Olărașu and writer C. Rauleț, emphasised the 'aesthetic and social-educational importance of the new medium' (ibid.). At the same time CIPETO, a Cinema for All society, founded by G. Brezeanu 'aimed at "instructing and educating the public through cinema"' (ibid.).

The so-called 'art documentaries' were a form of ideological compromise practised by the interwar intelligentsia, split in the 1930s along nationalist, as well as pro-fascist and pro-communist lines. Best known for their conservationist and ethnographic, but mostly patriotic bent, are the 1929 *Drăguș, the Life of a Romanian Village* by Paul Sterian and Nicolae Argintescu-Amza and certainly Paul Călinescu's *The Land of the Motzi* (1938).[20] Produced by the ONC, the latter became the most famous pre-Second World War Romanian film thanks to its Best Documentary award from the 1939 Venice Film Biennale. Replete with not-so-subtle chauvinism and in tune with the general sentiment of Romanian intelligentsia, it eulogised countryside mystique, most likely under the influence of its narrator, the writer Sadoveanu, whose own prose is marked by a penchant for folkloric mysticism.[21]

The combination of nationalist fervour and state subsidies brought about the nationalist blockbuster *Ecaterina Teodoroiu* (1930). Devoted to the bravery of its eponymous heroine, who joins the war first as a nurse, then as a foot-soldier, and is killed in a 1917 battle as a platoon commander, the film was 'the most popular WWI film in interwar Romania', but also 'the first sung and spoken Romanian war film' (IEFWW, see note 22). Directed by Ion Niculescu-Brună, it was heavily reliant on the reconstructed documentary of the First World War on the same topic,[22] and its footage, 'totaling more than 20,000 metres, filmed by Romanian cinematographers between 1916 and 1919' (IEFWW).

Curiously enough, the Romanian Axis alliance inspired few films, and most of them were documentaries. The best known fiction film is the Italian-Romanian co-production *Odessa in Flames*, whose remastered copy was premiered at the 2011 Transylvania International Film Festival. Made in 1942 by Italian director Carmine Gallone, it exalted the fascist (German and Italian) liberators of Moldova from Soviet occupation. The film was co-produced by the ONC under the auspices of its new director, the increasingly controversial Ion F. Cantacuzino. While Cantacuzino's early publications bespoke the idea of cinema as a public service, proclaiming the 'cultural orientation of the ONC [and] favouring art documentaries and screen versions of literary classics', after April 1941 (once at the helm of the ONC, which was already 'at the disposal of the army general staff'), his position became openly propagandistic (Cernat 1982: 35).[23]

The Sustained and Diverse Tradition of Pre-war Romanian Cinema

It is clear that during its first fifty years of existence, Romanian cinema meets White's requirements for a sustained and diverse national cinematic output. According to Cernat, during that period, fifty feature-length narrative films – thirty silent and twenty talkies – were produced semi-commercially or independently.[24] Although most of them are lost, and their production details are either absent or contradictory, it is safe to conclude that, with the very few exceptions noted above, interwar fiction films were made by short-lived companies located in big cities like Bucharest, Sibiu, or Iasi, but mostly in Cluj (or Kolosvár until 1919), which remains to this day one of the busiest cultural hubs in Romania.

A solid number of mostly state-subsidised 'art documentaries' were also produced, although no firm figures are available. Moreover, as Liehm and Liehm write, 'as far back as the 1920s, Aurel Petrescu and Marin Iorda had been experimenting in the field of animation',[25] thus meeting White's requirement for existence of avant-garde and non-commercial works. Overall, despite its humble beginnings, early Romanian cinema offers a surprising variety of genres. Liehm and Liehm cite Georgescu and Jean Mihai as the best-known interwar Romanian film directors (1977: 22). And while the former, as discussed above, specialised in comedies of manner penned by local playwrights, the latter – best known for his films *Manasse* (1925) and especially for the 'stirring' *Lia* (1927) – with his painstaking attention to Jewish tradition – preceded by almost a decade the golden age of Polish Yiddish cinema (ibid.).

Generally speaking, popular Romanian cinema branched in two genre directions – the national blockbuster and the melodrama. The well-documented successes of *Independence of Romania* and *Ecaterina Teodoroiu* inspired few other works, none of them as successful.[26] Yet the trend survived in works of what Marian Țuțui calls a 'typically Balkan' (2011: 156) genre about anti-Ottoman rebels, known as Haidouks (outlaws).[27]

Understandably, the melodramas were most numerous since Romanian cinema, under the influence of imports, drew heavily on melodramatic themes and plots from the national literature. And although Cernat points to three films as quintessential melodramas – Brezeanu's *Fatal Love* (1911), Ion Sahighian's *Symphony of Love* (1928) and *A Memorable Night* (1939) – all films from the period, regardless of genre, were made in melodramatic mode.

In film, as in literature and theatre, melodrama served diametrically opposite ideological purposes, ranging from right-wing nationalism to populism and proletarian socialism. This quintessential 'contending discourse' of modernism enabled 'spectators to negotiate change in a period of industrial growth and socio-economic instability, through the use of contrast, humour and irony' (Bratton 1994: 38–49).

Strangely enough, despite the general craze for the supernatural prompted by German Expressionism in the 1920s and by Hollywood monsters in the 1930s, early Romanian cinema remained aloof from 'the many species of blood-sucking, flesh-eating, and sexually disturbing creatures of the night, disruptive of harvest, livestock, and family life', with which Romanian folklore teems (Stojanova 2005a: 222). Perplexing also is its indifference to tales of the sinister and the demonic, spawn by literary masters, which remained unchanged even after the unprecedented success of Alfred Halm's *The Gypsy Girl in the Alcove* (1923),[28] based on the mystical novel by the famous Moldavian writer Radu Rossetti about 'the forbidden love of a spell-casting gypsy slave for the son of a nobleman and their mysterious and violent death' (Cernat 1982: 24).

Notwithstanding the sporadic successes of the nascent popular cinema, the notion that film could be more than an ideologically controlled vehicle for national integration – or, for that matter, a new-found form of high art – seems not to have been considered seriously by the state or the intelligentsia. Thus – despite its potential as cross-class entertainment on a par with radio and football/soccer – early Romanian cinema did not succeed in its role as a force for social integration. Yet the major trends in its development forestalled the evolution of Romanian communist cinema as regulated, high-brow cinema, with an educational and propagandist bent.

Romanian Cinema under Communism

The People's Republic of Romania was established on 30 December 1947,[29] and a new economic-political system of a 'modern rational redistributive society' – or communism[30] – was introduced, along with one-party communist rule. The second era in the evolution of Romanian national cinema began after the signing of Decree 303 for 'Nationalization of the film industry and the regulation of commerce in cinematic products' on 2 November 1948. In this way the cinema of communist Romania – like the cinemas across Eastern Europe – falls under Croft's industrial category of totalitarian cinema, 'centralized and maximally controlled' by the state. This transformation was made possible by the wholesale imposition of the Soviet institutional and ideological model.[31] And the most decisive battle for the creation of a Soviet-type society was to be waged in the name of total destruction of Romanian *ancienne* society and its replacement with a new, 'totalized' one. According to Agnes

Heller, such a 'totalized' society, where 'social and system integration' merge into one, and the 'will of the sovereign determines the entire socio-economic and ideological-political structure', is a major priority of the totalitarian state (1987: 247).[32] Cinema was to play a major role in the totalising of Romanian society and was therefore destined to become 'the most important art', as Lenin's famous dictum went.

Establishing Communist Institutional and Ideological Infrastructure

The first phase of the construction of *Centrul de producție cinematografică Buftea* (the Buftea Film Studio) was completed by 1956. As most of the emergent Eastern European film studios, it was a replica of the Soviet Mosfilm studios.[33] It provided a solid professional base that would help realise the goal of the communist regime 'to turn the factory of dreams into a school for the nation', proclaimed in the introduction of the Romanian cinema nationalisation decree (Cernat 1982: 39). Indeed, as Dana Duma points out, some historians even insist that 'the actual history of a national cinema begins with the setting-up of a film industry and of the organization of an adequate production', and therefore 'consider all movies, made before the foundation of the Buftea Studios, as an extended 'prehistory' of Romanian cinema' (personal correspondence 2017).

The imported ideological software – a rigidified version of Socialist Realism, known as Zhdanovism[34] – proved very useful in facilitating the cultural domination of Eastern Europe. Based on Zhdanov's three 'spirits' or 'essences', remindful of Neoplatonic ideas – the Communist Party spirit (*partiinost'*), People's spirit (*narodnost'*) and Ideological Spirit (*ideinost'*) – Zhdanovism 'mandated pragmatic rules for representation of official myths by means of art' (Stojanova 1999: 217–39).

Understandably, the Romanian pre-Second World War intelligentsia – habitually 'anti-Russian and anti-Soviet' (Liehm and Liehm 1977: 139) – was silenced under the new regime, and its members were either purged or decimated by emigration. Those who remained retreated in internal exile – that is, kept a very low profile – in order to survive (Nasta 2013: 19). Thus a relatively small number of radicalised communist party officials and proponents of all things Soviet took charge of Romanian cultural industry by placing 'film distribution immediately under political supervision' (Stoil 1974: 101). Clearly, Romanian viewers were not shown avant-garde works by Eisenstein, Dovzhenko or Vertov, or even the sincerely naïve, but captivating Socialist Realist works from the 1930s like *Counter-plan* (1932). They were treated mostly to works made during the most severe Zhdanovist period (1946–54), known as *malokartinie* (or restricted film production), justified by Stalin's aphorism 'fewer films, but masterpieces'. A quintessential example of this lore is *Miners of the Don* (1951) – a 'utopian story about the transformed life of Donetsk's miners after the introduction of new technology' (Liehm and Liehm 1977: 64). The intense propagation of Soviet cinema was however only the tip of the massive ongoing operation to reset the national cultural code, which was much better served by locally produced films.

The Totalitarian Genre Paradigm as Means of System Integration

During the immediate post-war years (1945–8), Romanian film production resumed 'sluggishly' with several 'primitive comedies and musicals' made by a 'few private companies' (Liehm and Liehm 1977: 140). The truly Zhdanovist creations began to appear after the ONC morphed into a new state film organisation, which produced twenty-seven features between 1949 and 1956. As Nasta writes, 'veterans resurfaced, directing sheer propaganda',[35] along with new directors, who 'also appeared on the scene' (2013: 13).[36]

These early films could be seen as a rough blueprint whose modifications would dominate Romanian – and Eastern European – communist cinema until its collapse in 1989. The Romanian film industry was still under construction, yet Zhdanovist principles – although never officially inaugurated at a filmmakers' conference as they were elsewhere across Eastern Europe – were already restructuring national film production along the lines of the Soviet hierarchy of genres. At that time, films 'about building of socialism' came third in importance – after films about the Great Patriotic War and Biopics – and also followed an internal hierarchy. Thus works 'about building of the 'new socialist industry' were 'more important than those about new socialist villages or agriculture', while the ones about 'scientists and the scientific-technological revolution' – were privileged over films 'for entertainment' – that is, comedies, children and youth films and family dramas – which had the 'lowest artistic priority' (Kenez 1992: 161).

Stoil proposes a similar hierarchy of official or administrative genres, but like other attempts at a detailed genre taxonomy of communist cinema, his endeavour to specify the corpus descriptively is overdetermined.[37] Yet it is clear that these genres reflect the thematic plans of the studio administration, and therefore represent topic-oriented 'forms of ideological communication', as is any 'meaningful genre activity, destined to enforce a single pre-determined reading' (Altman 1987: 2). Moreover, when scrutinised in hindsight and *en masse*,[38] official films coalesce into a mega genre or *totalitarian genre paradigm* (Stojanova 1999: 263–4). In addition to flaunting 'identifiable historical or contemporary themes, and stock characters, selected in accordance with the dominant esthetic doctrine (Zhdanovism and its derivative, which closely follow the fluctuating Party priorities)', the works belonging to the *totalitarian genre paradigm* consistently deploy 'narrative structural patterns of apprenticeship and confrontation, thus ensuring the presence of *exemplary rules of action, dual value system, doctrinal intertext* as principal modal traits' (ibid., original emphasis). Understandably, these official films were made in the 'excessively obvious' classical Soviet style of the 1930s, quite like that of classical Hollywood (Bordwell qtd in Stojanova, ibid.).

In this light, the history of Eastern European cinema in general – and of Romanian in particular – could be seen in terms of compliance with, or deviations from, this mega genre paradigm, most often by degree and very rarely – in kind. Any negotiation of its thematic, narrative or modal traits and its stylistic obviousness, amounts to a displaced dialogue between society and the system – epitomised by the cineastes and the ideological apparatchiks, respectively – whose outcome reflects the political situation in the country. Negotiations were next to impossible during the regime's initial (1945–56), or terroristic, 'classical phase' (J. Kornai qtd in Stojanova 1999: 87), as well as during the Czechoslovak 'normalisation' after the Prague Spring defeat in 1968 – and, for that matter, after Ceaușescu's July 1971 theses, enforcing 'methods of indoctrination used by Mao's Cultural Revolution' (Nasta 2013: 27).

Overwhelmingly, the filmmaking process during the post-terroristic phase from the late 1950s onwards is underwritten by what Antonin Liehm calls 'the new social contract', described by the regime's commitment 'to guarantee some basic degree of well-being and safety, while the citizens, in exchange, [agree] to put up with the system's injustices' (1980: 43). The post-terroristic phase also features rare moments when negotiations yielded both artistic freedom and generous state financing, which made the Czechoslovak New Wave possible during the Prague Spring (1963–8). The Yugoslav Novi Film, known as the 'black series' – while made possible thanks to the film industry decentralisation in the early 1950s – was a reflection of the Yugoslav ideological liberalisation (late 1960s to early 1970s). Both movements ended with most of their films banned, their directors purged and their national film industries reverting to the dominant normative aesthetics.

It was during the protracted post-terroristic phase that 'indigenous totalitarianism finally established its undeniable historicity and legitimacy' (Havel qtd in Stojanova 1999: 95), which led to some positive outcomes in the relentless bickering between apparatchiks and cineastes, and even resulted in a number of short-lived film schools, cycles and clusters of films that undermined various aspects of the *totalitarian genre paradigm*.[39] As the famous Polish director Krzysztof Kieslowski comments:

> [T]o try is simply a duty. I am trying all the time. I believe in trying. There is also the matter of pressure. I believe that if my colleagues and I present

ten scripts, they may all be rejected ten times, but the eleventh time one of them at least will be accepted. (Bren 1986: 132)

Thanks to such tenacity, Eastern European film auteurs became increasingly successful internationally in the 1960s and 1970s and – in the best traditions of Eastern European intelligentsia – emerged as the moral conscience of their nations. This phenomenon is all the more remarkable against the backdrop of the growing self-confidence of Eastern European regimes as legitimate historical subjects – demonstrated most unabashedly by Ceaușescu's Romania and Tito's Yugoslavia – which put additional pressure on cinema as an instrument of national(istic) as well as of system integration. Yet because of the rapid evolution of the international film language at that time, complying wholesale with the *totalitarian genre paradigm* became a serious formal liability, which auteurs like Ciulei, Pița, and especially Pintilie and Daneliuc, sought to negotiate. Therefore their hard-fought attempts at frustrating the paradigm in its most sensitive, contemporary manifestations – seen by the regime as an indispensable tool in its push towards total system integration[40] – cannot be underestimated.

The Valley Resounds (1950): A Paradigmatic Construction of Socialiasm Film

Since the wartime experience of Romania – an Axis country, defeated along with Bulgaria and Hungary – was far from inspiring like that of Poland or Yugoslavia, cultural ideologues focused on the Construction of Socialism genre.[41] Thus Paul Călinescu, the former head of the ONC and award-winning documentarian, was entrusted with the direction of *The Valley Resounds* (1949). The film, like other Eastern European works from that time,[42] adheres to the letter of the *totalitarian genre paradigm*, and construes a template of the New Society and the New Man, whose influence would be felt one way or another well into the 1980s.

According to Russian film historian Irina Mjagkova, Călinescu wanted to make a documentary film about the enthusiasm of the brigadier movement, popular across Eastern Europe, which he encountered when filming the construction of the Agnița-Botorka pipeline and the Jiu mining valley railway, but[43] 'made the fatal mistake in agreeing to suggestions from above that he ignore the rich, socially conscious post-war Romanian literature' (1993: 110–15).

The film exemplifies what David Bordwell calls a 'narrative and stylistic economy of "redundancies"', typical of the 'tendentious narrative' of official genres and their stock characters (1985: 57). The Villain, for example, is an Enemy of the People, a mean, ugly man whose elegance, along with his education – he is a foreman – implies a bourgeois background and ideological unreliability. The good-looking, sweet tempered and wealthy heir, Niko, is the stock Hesitant Hero. A pivotal character in any tendentious or authoritarian narrative, the Hesitant Hero – according to Susan Suleiman – should undergo either a 'positive' or a 'negative' apprenticeship, with the former representing a movement from ignorance to knowledge about Marxist–Leninist ideology and its practical implementation, while the latter entails a movement towards the retrograde delusions of bourgeois values (1992: 63–99). Understandably, Niko moves towards an enlightened acceptance of the new collective way of life, and then to action in its name under the guidance of his ideological mentors, represented by a group of exemplary – young and handsome – communists, and unobtrusive (but also handsome) Securitate[44] agents. Niko graduates to a Positive Hero by unmasking the Villain and his cronies – and their predictable sabotage schemes, involving a landslide, a wagon accident and a poisoning of the water supply. Moreover, to further emphasise the dual value system and the doctrinal intertext, Niko's positive apprenticeship is contrasted to the negative one of a couple deluded brigadiers who, by following the Villain's false mentorship, end up in disgrace.

Obviously, a character like Niko serves best the goals of system integration because of his unequivocal acceptance of the communist economic and political agenda, and his categorical rejection of any traditional – and therefore reactionary – personal concerns. In aesthetic terms this means domination of socialist content over national form – a Zhdanovist dictum, translated literally in the film by making the brigadiers – in the name of equal multi-ethnic representation – wear cumbersome folklore costumes from various Romanian regions. This faux pas notwithstanding, the featured folkloric songs and dances are the film's highlights, and the only moments when Călinescu is evidently in his element.

The Valley Resounds provides a perfect example of what Regine Robin calls the 'impossible aesthetics' of Socialist Realism – taken *ad absurdum* by Zhdanovism – namely, the 'irresolvable frictions' between its 'fictional' artistry and 'functional' didacticism, which ultimately grind the narrative flow to a halt (1992: 298). Indeed, Călinescu's film – like its contemporaneous Soviet films – resembles a *tableau vivant*, made at times worse by accidentally captured moments of authenticity that threaten the controlled message, a process also known as 'the revenge of the *écriture*' (Suleiman 1992: 201). A case in point is the representation of women, whose narrative presence is strictly functional – or didactic. Instead of casting the New Socialist women brigadiers as sexless, butter-fresh girls 'of the people', Călinescu has selected actresses whose 'bourgeois' chic disrupts the ideological consistency of the film. Additionally, regardless of the effect they might have had at the time,[45] his trademark visual improvisations make the film look today like a mean-spirited parody of its own genre.

HISTORICAL OVERVIEW OF ROMANIAN CINEMA

Negotiating the Paradigm: Liviu Ciulei

By the mid-1950s, Romanian cinema reached a level of professional sophistication similar to that of the developed Eastern European national cinemas with rich pre-war traditions. An eloquent evidence of this is *Eruption* (1957), an accomplished rendition of the Construction of Socialism genre by Liviu Ciulei. Although debutant, he had already accumulated considerable experience as a film actor and production designer. His acting debut was in the melodrama *In Our Village* where, as Liehm and Liehm have it, '"socialism" takes the place of "God"' (1977: 142). This was followed by participation in Negreanu's epic social duology[46] (which Ciulei also designed), meant to prove that the communist victory was a long-cherished dream of the oppressed classes. While these films share the melodramatic sentiment of leftist pre-war literature, *Alarm in the Mountains* (1955), Negreanu's second venture into the Spies and Saboteurs genre,[47] was Ciulei's first serious encounter with the proclivity of Zhdanovist normative aesthetics for always telling the same story about agents of the *ancienne* regime, who try – of course unsuccessfully – to disrupt the building of communism. His previous experience notwithstanding, with its moody atmosphere his debut has more in common with masterful Czechoslovak renditions of the Construction of Socialism genre like Jiří Weiss' *Predators* (1948) and Ladislav Helge's *The Great Solitude* (1959) than with its Romanian contemporaries.

The film follows Anca to her first job, which is assigned by the state, as all professional appointments were under communism. Her further exemplary actions as a drilling specialist in an oilfield promote official policies, which encourage gender equality and university graduates taking jobs in the provinces. Despite the fact that her mostly male colleagues seem not to trust her expertise, and life in the newly built settlement is hard for a big city girl – she decides to stay. Yet her positive apprenticeship seems to be prompted not so much by the Party representative's terse mentorship, but by existential reasons related to her 'bourgeois' past.

The predictable plot is amply compensated by Grigore Ionescu's expressive visuals of dark metal oil rigs, encroaching towards the whitewashed wooden houses of a nearby poor village, thus creating a metaphor of progress *versus* agrarian backwardness, further visualised by panning shots of crosses over graves of socialist labour heroes killed in the line of duty. A final oil eruption, shattering drills and wooden houses, is cross-cut with a succession of close-ups of the heroine and her brigade with their oil-covered faces, thus sealing Anca's positive transformation as well as the fate of the villagers, who are now left with no choice but to join the oilfield workforce.

Under obvious Neorealist influence, Ciulei succeeds in destabilising the *totalitarian genre paradigm* aesthetically, but also structurally, through flashbacks revealing Anca's previous luxurious lifestyle, which was provided by her much older, rich, married lover whom she has left behind, refusing to be treated as a plaything. However, the flashbacks and the trendy allure of Eva Cristian as Anca problematise her image of a monolithic Positive Heroine, capable of sacrificing her private life for the public good. Moreover, the flashbacks are originally meant to establish the dual value system of the *totalitarian genre paradigm* by playing up communist over bourgeois values, yet – as another revenge of the *écriture* – bring about the forbidden pleasures of decadent escapism.[48] Such forays into illicit bourgeois lifestyles and banned intimate desires, albeit rare for Construction of Socialism films, were common occurrence in the Spies and Saboteurs genre, and particularly in period genres, including Resistance Fighter and Nationalist Epic films, contributing immensely to their popularity in the 1960s and 1970s.

Three years later, Ciulei made *The Waves of the Danube* (1959), the first Romanian Resistance Fighter film, devoted to the inconsequential Romanian anti-fascist Resistance. The main plot about a Resistance fighter, posing as a hired hand in order to smuggle arms for the Resistance, is comparable to the remarkable body of Yugoslav, Bulgarian and Polish Resistance Fighter films from that time and, like them, deploys the structure of confrontation as better suited to the Manichean duality of the doctrinal intertext because of its 'predilection for narratives of antagonism' (Robin 1992: 251). The Positive Hero, Toma, an 'emblematic figure' of the Resistance, 'is on the right track from the start' as he cheats his way into the boat, operated by the Hesitant Hero – the soldier Mihai (played by Ciulei), and then steers it against a German barge, carrying ammo to the front (Robin 1992: 251). However, this standard Resistance Fighter narrative is complicated by the personal drama, played out in the *huis clos* of the boat, and threatens to destroy the didactic message. The presence of Mihai's unusually sexy bride, Ana, and her obvious attraction to Toma explains why Mihai fails to undergo the typical positive transformation. Consumed with jealousy, but also with doubts as to whether Toma's mission is worthy of violating his soldier's oath, Mihai joins the struggle too late and is therefore killed. Despite his failure as Mentor, Toma wins both the girl and the battle, but walks into the sunset alone, following his higher priorities. All things considered, the film has aged quite well thanks to Mihai's psychologically ingenuous presence – yet another case of revenge of the *écriture* – which dwarfs the didactic bore Toma, and thereby his message.

When Ciulei turned to Rebreanu's famous novel *Forest of the Hanged*, he had already proven his ideological reliability, and was therefore deemed worthy of a generous budget for filming a notable literary classic. As the most successful Romanian film until the mid-2000s, *Forest of the Hanged* asserted the cinematic potential of Romanian interwar literature and, moreover, thanks to Ciulei's knack for the psychological authenticity of tragedy, counts among

Figure 16.2 *The Forest of the Hanged*

the few antecedents of the existentialist realism of New Romanian Cinema discussed in the Introduction.

The characters – entangled in the cobweb of contradictory professional, ideological and ethnic allegiances plaguing the Austro-Hungarian army – are brought in tune with post-Second World War existentialist universalism. Ciulei's own interpretation of captain Otto Klapka – the Austro-Hungarian officer of Czech origin who triggers the moral awakening of the main (anti) hero, Apostol Bologa, a lieutenant of Transylvanian-Romanian origin – is a case in point. Steering Klapka away from omniscient Zhdanovist Mentors like Toma, Ciulei portrays him as the conflicted, world-weary and sceptical alter ego of Victor Rebrengiuc's inexperienced philosophy student Bologa, whose 'actions are marked by tragic spiritual isolation' (Stringer 1997: 39). Therefore Bologa's move from the ignorance of an obedient Austro-Hungarian soldier, ready to condemn a fellow soldier to death, to knowledge of Austro-Hungarian militarism and its callous nature is justified not in Zhdanovist but in existentialist-psychological terms. And, as Kierkegaard would have it, Bologa accepts the responsibilities for his moral choice to side with fellow Romanians across enemy lines and, when tried for high treason, chooses death despite the sympathies of the court.

While communist ideologues would have liked to see Bologa's end as a triumph of Romanian nationalism, Ciulei and Rebengiuc emphasise their hero's calm withdrawal from life, as he 'acknowledges death as freedom' beyond 'anxiety of death and pettiness of life', and as the only chance 'to become himself' in a war whose only point is indiscriminate destruction of life (Heidegger qtd in Lavine 1985: 332). Yet the *mise en scène* of the finale dampens this existentialist reading and, paradoxically for its time, presents Bologa's final supper as a self-sacrificial passage to Christian Orthodox martyrdom.

Romanian Cinema in the 1960s and 1970s: Sustained and Diverse Tradition

Liviu Ciulei's remarkable film appeared during a period of modest cultural relaxation – or rather diversification – associated with the last years in office of the Romanian leader Gheorghe Gheorghiu-Dej, who died in 1965. Thanks to Dej's crafty politics, a possibility for a nationally specific, Romanian road to communism emerged, which explains the varied cinematic production at that time.

According to Liehm and Liehm, the projected annual production in the mid-1960s hovered around '15 fiction films, 25 animated cartoons, 76 newsreels, and 150 documentaries' (1977: 257–353). And, as Nasta notes, 'almost half of the [fiction] film production in the late 1960s and early 70s consisted of adaptations' of classics like Caragiale, Rebreanu, Sadoveanu, or contemporaries 'such as Mihail Sebastian and Ion Agârbiceanu' (2013: 20). Indeed, only a year after Ciulei's success at Cannes, Mircea Mureşan filmed Rebreanu's novel *Răscoala*. This story about the 1907 peasant uprising in Botoşani, suppressed in a most horrific way, was to bring him the Best First Film Award at Cannes in 1966. The proliferation of period films and literary adaptations was accompanied by successful works in children's film and animation – also considered ideologically safe across Eastern Europe. Elisabeta Bostan, one of the few Romanian women directors and a prolific champion of cinema for children, debuted successfully with her 1965 *Memories of My Childhood*, and renowned Ion Popescu-Gopo won the 1957 Best Short Film Palme d'Or for his animation *A Brief History*.

It was at that time that French filmmakers, along with other westerners, became interested in working in Romania.[49] Among them were Henri Colpi and Louis Daquin, left-leaning directors captivated by socialist interwar writer Panait Istrati,[50] who was called 'the Maxim Gorky of the Balkans' by his friend and mentor Romain Roland. The young Henri Colpi made *Codine* (1963)[51] and Louis Daquin – *Baragan Thistles* (1957). This mythopoetic trend was further inspired by Sadoveanu and Agârbiceanu, whose screen adaptations – *The Hatchet* (1969), directed by Mureşan, and *Stone Wedding* (1972) and *Lust for Gold* (1974), directed by Dan Piţa and Mircea Veroiu – brought more international recognition to Romanian cinema. The eclectic formal and ideological pedigree of these works – on one hand interwar symbolism and naturalism, and, on the other, various trends of poporanism,[52] nationalism and socialism – allowed Romanian filmmakers to circumvent the 'revolutionary romanticism' and 'historical optimism' of the dominant normative aesthetics, and take advantage of the brief revival of national folklores in Eastern Europe during the 1960s and early 1970s, along with the so-called 'cinema of poetics' (Holloway 1989). Seeped in Romanian legends of lust, revenge and retribution, and shot against gorgeous landscapes, these films feature extraordinary characters in extraordinary circumstances, male as well as female, driven by intoxicating, destructive passions, and culminating in violent death. Romanian cinema's newly found fascination with death, seen from an abstract – even transcendental – perspective, was an artistically attractive and relatively safe way of resisting the party line. True, traditional rural life, still thriving and vibrant, was presented in these films in a stylised fashion, but their harsh mysticism posed a coded defiance of the new eschatological myth of a radiant communist future, and offered a preview of the very real horrors yet in store for Romanian people, especially in the countryside.

Even more fascinating is the wide variety of genre films from this time, pointing to a nascent brand of vibrant popular cinema. Albeit dismissed by Liehm and Liehm (1977: 353), the 1960s saw the production of two versatile Romanian Communist musicals, Manole Marcus' *I Do Not Want to Get Married* (1961) and Andrei Călărașu's *Vacation on the Black Sea* (1963).[53] Marcus later made *The Power and the Truth* (1972), based on a script by Titus Popovici,[54] one of the most prolific and successful Romanian scriptwriters. Nasta describes it as a 'codified' biography of Ceaușescu and a 'sequel to *The Valley Resounds*', where the 'hymn to Dej and Lenin' is replaced by a 'tribute to Ceaușescu' (2013: 29–31). With *The Actor and the Savages* (1975), also scripted by Popovici, and inspired by the life of the famous interwar entertainer Constantin Tănase, Marcus takes to another level his mastery of the musical comedy,[55] and forestalls the metaphoric-allegorical energy of *Mephisto* (1981), István Szabó's Oscar winning fable about the fateful incompatibility between artistic freedom and political compromise under a totalitarian regime.

Masters of the Paradigm: Nicolaescu, Năstase and the Nationalist Epic

It is difficult to pinpoint the date when the propagandistic zeal of the Nationalist Epics of the 1960s – inspired by Gheorghiu-Dej's home-grown nationalism – adapted to the 1970s' prothocronist slogan 'we have been here for more than two thousand years', raised by Ceaușescu's July 1971 theses (Nasta 2013: 27). The rekindled ideological stagnation was facilitated by the so-called 'decentralization' of Centrala România Film in 1972, resulting in seven film-producing studios run by four 'production houses' or units, also common to the Hungarian, Czechoslovak and Bulgarian film industries since the 1960s.[56] While the model demonstrated organisational efficiency, it gave little ground for optimism since the units facilitated internal control – and fostered self-censorship – thus regulating the creative process from within. Yet again, they exposed loopholes and systematic contradictions, which gave filmmakers more room for negotiations with the powers-that-be (Stojanova 1999: 357–9).

In this light, the transformation of the Nationalist Epic into ideologically the most favoured genre is instructive. Indeed, in Romania, as well as in Poland and Bulgaria, the penchant for period adaptations, based on national literary classics, was encouraged by authorities and eagerly sought after by filmmakers due to the generous budgets and the prestige these productions commanded. Moreover, while the Construction of Socialism genre was propelled by system integration concerns, the structure of confrontation and the duality of the doctrinal intertext of the historic 'them' *versus* the historic 'us' of the Nationalist Epic accomplished vital national integration tasks. Above all, it ascertained the legitimacy of communist rule in a 'baroque', even decadent manner, much better liked by the viewers than the populist antics of the anti-Ottoman fighters, the outlawed Haidouks,[57] let alone the straightforward Zhdanovist chastity – and historical falsity – of the Resistance Fighter genre. Albeit slower-paced and psychologically oriented, the genre was as conservative as its Hollywood counterpart.

The trend was set in 1963 by Lucian Bratu with *Tudor* – a story about Tudor Vladimirescu, an early nineteenth-century leader of Wallachian uprising against the Ottomans. It was, however, Sergiu Nicolaescu, Romania's quintessential official director, who became the uncontested master of the Nationalist Epic. Fellow of the so-called 'champions of the box-office' from the mid-1960s (Cernat 1982: 85), Nicolaescu came to prominence with the lavish Romanian-French co-production *The Dacians* (1966).[58] Based on a script by Popovici and French scriptwriter Jacques Rémy and featuring French star Marie-Jose Nat, it endorsed *avant la lettre* Ceaușescu's obsession with Dacian heritage and protochronism.[59] Thanks to the unlimited budget, full access to unpaid Romanian army recruits as extras, the meticulous design of costumes and settings, and above all to the contribution of Popovici with whom he was to make eight films, Nicolaescu directed yet another fancy co-production, *Michael the Brave* (1970), known as the 'most expensive film of the Communist era' in Romania (Nasta 2013: 28). The domestic success of *The Dacians* and *Michael the Brave* was so great that Liehm and Liehm describe it as a 'sociological phenomenon' (1977: 351).

Along with its second[60] and third[61] parts, made by other directors, *The Dacians* was highly praised for evoking the 'struggle for ethnic unity of a race whose permanence and Latinity in South-Eastern Europe for the last two thousand years' is considered an 'ethnic miracle' (Cernat 1982: 61). Also a handsome actor, starring in most of his films, Nicolaescu went unabashedly through known and lesser known monarchs, including *William the Conqueror* (1982) and *Carol I* (2012) – Romania's last king – whose role he played two years before his death in 2014.[62]

It is important to note that – while monitored with trepidation by the authorities – box office success was generally considered a sell-out by critics. Thus while Mircea Drăgan was a runner-up in the 'box office championship' thanks to his Nationalist Epics and particularly Spies and Saboteurs films, they became just a footnote in his official biography. What ranked him 'no. 1 among Romanian filmmakers' according to official film critics, were his 'social-political frescoes', devoted to the heroic struggles of the Jiu Valley miners in the 1920s (Cernat 1982: 88). Nevertheless, his five-film series, known as *B.D.*, or *Brigada Diverse* (1970–1), ridiculing the otherwise untouchable Romanian police (or militia) in the style of the 1960s French films about the hilariously incompetent Inspector Juve (Louis de Funès), have enjoyed lasting – and after the July 1971 theses, a sort of alternative – popularity.

If the Dacian trilogy responded to nation-building concerns, Doru Năstase's *Vlad the Impaler* (1979), as a quintessential Nationalist Epic helming Năstase's otherwise short career of six period films – strongly implies that Ceaușescu the Conducător (or leader) is part of the formidable succession of Romanian rulers. Năstase's representation of Dracula as a Romanian national hero, struggling to unite his country in the face of internal and foreign foe, resulted in a bland, pseudo-historical rendition of 'facts' culled from the life of the infamous ruler. Despite its questionable aesthetic values, the film does a good job justifying Ceaușescu's atrocities yet to come, evoking the favourite communist myth of 'historical necessity'. Indeed, Năstase seems to have stumbled upon the method in Vlad's madness and, as Draculean specialists Radu Florescu and Raymond T. McNally suggest, has pointed to irrational terror that, 'as a means of social integration and political control', has been around since the dawn of time (1973: 210, note 35).

Vlad the Impaler: The True Life of Dracula (1978) was advertised as an expression of official indignation with Western Draculiana,[63] 'brought to a head by state-induced chauvinistic fervor, anti-Western sentiment, and general fear and compliance' (Stojanova 2005a: 227). This 'removal of Dracula from the nocturnal domains of horror and death to the brightly lit terrain of the *Nationalist Epic*' constituted a significant political and psychological feat (ibid.). Indeed, as Karen Jaehne has wittingly put it, 'the major history lesson ... is that Vlad Țepeș was faced with betrayal and rancor in the ranks no less complex than that of a modern Romanian ruler, for example Ceaușescu!' (1980: 38).

Rejecting the Paradigm: Lucian Pintilie

It is during the relative ideological relaxation of the 1960s that Lucian Pintilie emerged as a truly dissident Romanian director. His first significant film, *Sunday at Six* (1965), an off-shoot of the Resistance Fighter genre, belongs to the 'cinema of poetics', associated predominantly with Resistance Fighter films made in the mid-1960s across Eastern Europe[64] as a form of 'negotiated experiments with high modernist form and style within the confines of the dominant normative aesthetics' and characterised by 'new ways of processing black and white footage; nuanced acting style; and free-moving, subjective camera' (Stojanova 1999: 336). Unlike the monolithic Positive Heroes, victorious even in their death, the underground activists Radu and Anca come through as fragile, both physically and emotionally and, apart from a few sunlit episodes showing their shy intimacy, they are overwhelmed by persecution, betrayal and finally death. It is no wonder that the director, as Nasta writes, was 'criticized by hard-line Communist colleagues' for 'lack of transparency in depicting the illegal cause' (Nasta 2013: 85). The officially endorsed pre-eminence of the ideological is subverted, in favour not of the psychological as in *The Waves of the Danube*, but in that of the sensual materiality and raw emotionality brought on by the 'brute facticity of objects in real world', permeating French existentialist literature and cinema (McArthur 1999: 191). The inevitable tensions of art cinema narration created by the uneasy coexistence of realism, authorial expressivity and psychological subjectivity are elegantly resolved through the ambiguity of an 'almost surrealist atmosphere and evocations of flashbacks and visions', where the plot 'unfolds in a peripheral way' (Liehm and Liehm 1977: 346).

The fragmented structure of the film rhymes with Radu's fragmented consciousness, torn between private and public loyalties and a growing existential guilt for Anca's death, and brings him to the point when he, like Bologa, would embrace death willingly by stepping into the trap set for him. Yet if at the end of his quest Rebengiuc's Bologa matures, Dan Nuţu's Radu gradually unravels and instead of the display of bravery that is mandatory for the genre, reveals the immaturity of a confused eternal boy – or *puer aeternus*, as the founder of analytical psychology Carl Gustav Jung would have it. While the proliferation of this psychological type, popularised by youth movements and New Wave cinemas from the 1960s, is explained by the growing post-Second World War culture of 'momism',[64] in Romanian – as well as in Eastern European – context it is additionally predicated by the infantilising totalitarian state. Thus the Resistance hero Radu becomes a harbinger of the *pueri aeterni*, whose omnipresence during the subsequent three decades would reflect the growing power of the state.

***

Towards the end of the 1960s, the evolution of Romanian cinema was stalled, and thenceforth, until the very end of the 1980s, attempts to negotiate the dominant normative aesthetic were conducted mostly on the terrain of period literary adaptations. The strategic sphere of contemporary cinema came under even closer scrutiny after the banning of Pintilie's next film, *Reconstruction* aka *Reenactment* (1968), regarded 'as Romanian cinema's unique "dissident film"' (Nasta 2013: 88). Indeed, its modernist take on the sensitive Delinquent Youth genre – a scrupulous reconstruction of a drunken restaurant brawl staged by the police and involving two of the participants, one of whom gets accidentally killed in the process – amounts to a dangerously transparent metaphor of Romanian society. The two naïve detainees – the contemplative Nicu and his witty friend Vuică – undergo a transformation under the pressure of the coercive system, yet a negative one, turning them within less than twenty-four hours into a killer and his victim. The system itself is represented by symbolic stand-ins of various social strata, involved in this unusual disciplining process. Consequently the Prosecutor, who oversees the reconstruction, is a cold careerist and a blasé dandy, while his aide, the policeman, is a good man of obviously peasant origin, but too eager to please his boss. In a self-critical twist, Pintilie casts the cameraman and his assistant – members of the so-called creative intelligentsia — as servile pawns, whose professional zeal at times surpasses that of the prosecutor. The only person of conscience on site is Professor Paveliu, who however is a psychological wreck and a drunk, signifying the intelligentsia's poor standing as a mouthpiece for the regime; he is therefore lamentably inefficient champion of the boys. Like all the others, the professor is seen as what Soviet dissident Aleksandr Zinoviev calls *homo soveticus* – a mediocre, survival-obsessed being, product of decades of communist social engineering (1986: 185). The cruel reality of this notion is reinforced at the film's finale: after manifesting their sycophant obedience to the Prosecutor and his cronies, the crowd pouring out from a nearby stadium, turns into a surreal mob. The football fans first harass the fatally wounded Vuică – who, in a Pietà-like manner and under a Bee Gees tune, dies in Nicu's hands – and then redirect their aggression to Nicu, thus pushing him even deeper into his guilt-driven desperation, symbolised by the mud and rain. It is this unflattering take on Romanian communist society – officially lauded as most advanced and altruistic – that trumps Pintilie's sarcastic portrayal of the authorities and constitutes the film's most insufferable offence.[65]

Circumventing the Paradigm: Piţa, Daneliuc and the 'Old' Wave

The meta-cinematic techniques of Pintilie's *Reconstruction*, along with the provoked quasi-documentary situation of shooting a film or a TV reportage, inspired three films in the early 1980s – *Microphone Test*, *A Girl's Tear* and *Sequences* – which became signature works of the 'old' wave, and encouraged a significant NRC following. Thus authentic footage for internal militia use, taken in 1959 and documenting the reenactment of a bank hold-up attempt by six young members of communist nomenclature, was used in Alexandru Solomon's documentary *The Great Communist Bank Robbery* (2004). It also served as a base in Caranfil's high-budget, Hollywood-star studded *Closer to the Moon* (2013). A number of NRC directors followed the spirit if not the letter of Pintilie's technique – Porumboiu in *12:08* and *When Evening Falls on Bucharest, or Metabolism* (2013); Jude in *The Happiest Girl in the World*, Gabriel Achim – in *Adalbert's Dream* (2011).[67]

The 'old wave', also known as 'the 1970s generation', came to prominence in 1971, thanks, as Duma writes, 'to the success of *Water Like a Black Buffalo*, a documentary about the catastrophic floods of the 70s' (personal correspondence, 2017). The film – a collective debut of nine graduates[68] of the National University of Theatre and Cinema (IATC) – became, as Căliman writes, 'a promotional manifesto for its young directors and cameramen ... described also as the "flood generation"' (qtd in Duma, ibid.). And although after the ban of *Reconstruction* it was impossible for contemporary subjects to be tackled creatively, 'old' wave films nonetheless succeeded in dragging the normative aesthetic pomp – flaunting protagonists who are superior to others and to the environment – to the realism of what Northrop Frye calls 'low mimetic' or 'ironic' narrative modes,[69] where the characters' power to act and influence their regimented environment is like ours – that is, next to none.[70]

After their successful breakthrough in the 1970s with the mythopoetic Agârbiceanu adaptations, the tandem Piţa–Veroiu – both students of Victor Iliu[71] – turned to official genres, diversifying them psychologically and stylistically. Hence the eponymous Filip from *Filip the Kind* (1974) – Piţa's contribution to the Delinquent Youth genre – undergoes a predictable positive apprenticeship which, after aberrant social explorations, brings him back to his father's working-class fold. The film however preserves the overall background authenticity of 'bleak, miserable Romanian city life', along with glimpses of 'hookers' who are interrogated by Securitate for 'dating Italians, the quintessential coveted Westerners in the 1970s' (Nasta 2013: 48). Similarly, Veroiu's *Seven Days* (1973) – a Spies and Saboteurs film – is immersed in a 'melancholy atmosphere', reflecting the 'oppressive loneliness after office hours' of a militia major investigating an industrial spy' (Cernat 1982:96). Piţa and Veroiu wrapped up the decade with three period comedies inspired by

Sergio Leone's spaghetti Westerns, about imaginary Wild West adventures of Transylvanians.

The most consistently iconoclastic representative of the 'old' wave is undoubtedly Mircea Daneliuc, an unusually gifted auteur who wrote the scripts for his films and played the main role in half a dozen of them, and whose career was riddled with difficulties and censorship bans (Nasta 2013: 57–72). His moody debut *Long Drive* (1974), followed by *Microphone Test* (1980), and *The Cruise* (1981) – along with Piţa's *Contest* (1982) and *Sand Cliffs* (1983) – form the 'old' wave's core, marking its radical aesthetic and ideological break with the *totalitarian genre paradigm*. The metaphysical implications of their 'political narratives', potentially more subversive than *Reconstruction*, expose the falsities of the doctrinal intertext alongside the profoundly destructive 'effects of history on the individual' (Elsaesser qtd in Pop 2014: 16). Therefore it could be argued that the most important achievement of the 'old' wave is its psychologically diverse portrayal of Romanian society from the late 1970s and early 1980s.

A parallel discussion of *Contest* and *The Cruise* highlights them as precursors of the principal stylistic and conceptual approaches of New Romanian Cinema[72] – the tragic-ironic and the comedic-ironic. Deployed here to contrasting renditions of an organised recreational trip inspired by Plato's 'ship of fools' allegory,[73] these approaches call into question the ethics behind the pre-eminence of the collective over the individual as a basic principle of communism. In tune with the paradigmatic Eastern European fable about a dream-turned-nightmare, the featured trips quickly degenerate from a celebration of physical stamina and *esprit de corps* into a blatant display of selfishness and intolerance, all the more daunting in the face of collectivist manipulation, demanding hypocrisy and 'administrative enthusiasm', as Dostoyevsky had it (1871: 55). Fittingly, Piţa construes the 'all too human' egoism of his characters as tragically ironic by situating them within a mythological narrative structure, while Daneliuc plays up the comically ironic incongruities of his quasi-documentary observations and their official interpretation.

The meticulously designed architectonics of *Contest*, timed within the Aristotelian 'one revolution of the sun', confines its eight orientation competition contestants within an uncanny reality of a forested terrain where mysterious paramilitaries are at work on imminent explosions. Following his penchant for 'eclectic aestheticism' (Liehm and Liehm 1977: 35), Piţa intersperses the terse narrative with recurring images of a white horse,[74] ruins, and mist, encoding the longing for an absent God[75] by introducing the enigmatic Kid as a Christ-like figure of sorts. Shortly after the Kid materialises on his bike to guide the contestants' bus into the orientation site, everyone begins to avail themselves of his supernatural powers to guide, protect and heal. In Jungian terms, the Kid could be seen as a manifestation of the positive aspect of the *puer aeternus* archetype[76] – a 'divine boy or youth associated with light' and signalling renewal – in contrast with middle-aged males, who are portrayed as a negative collective *senex*, symbolising a rigidified, 'controlling and blocking paternalistic power' (Von Franz 1993: 310).

Interestingly enough, both *Contest* and *The Cruise* defy the hypocrisy of officially sanctioned gender equality. Piţa deploys inflated male socio-psychological types who flaunt a collective, 'shallow, brittle, conformist "all *persona*" type of personality', riddled with fear from authorities (Stevens 1990: 43). The secondary role of the three women in his film reflects the occulted misogyny of communist societies, and their externalised 'shadow' (in the Jungian sense) – associated with chaos, unbridled instincts, inebriation and vanity – foregrounds male ineptitudes, but also lampoons the stereotypically chaste and bland female representation in official cinema. Hence the very public affair of the Boss's Wife with the Bus Driver exposes her husband's marital, but also professional impotence, while the Handsome Male's game of seduction with the office Femme-fatale bares his unabashed narcissism. The middle-aged female Gossip and a couple of interchangeable minor male administrators, always at each other's throats, act as fillers in this acerbic office drama.

The moral aloofness of the group is laid bare by the blood-curdling, off-screen screams of a young woman, when their initial impulse to help her is swiftly dampened by the Boss's suggestion that this is just a hallucination. Eager to leave, they also remain indifferent when the Kid is sent back on a senseless errand to the site where explosions are already in progress, and where he stumbles upon the body of the brutally raped young woman. Having failed to awaken the contestants' confused collective consciousness – caught between the false idols of communism and the absent, or dead, God – the Kid vanishes into the evening fog.

Daneliuc's satirical rendition of the 'ship of fools' parable is spread over the few days needed to cover the distance between Calafat and Cernavoda on a dilapidated Danube barge. During this supposed celebration of their amateur achievements, the young participants from all over the country spend their nights at random dorms along the river, and their days rowing alongside the barge, which houses the cruise headquarters. Proca, the middle-aged party functionary and cruise organiser, and his assistant, Dr Velicu, act as 'controlling and blocking' *senes irati*. In addition to fostering denunciations and intrigue, they keep cancelling dances – and any unsanctioned diversion activities – to allegedly prevent undesirable sexual encounters and anarchy, all the while bickering with each other and flirting around.

The participants' reaction to this petty harassment, camouflaged as munificence, is also intriguing, with the young women more aware of the ongoing power struggle, yet more likely to support the administration rather than the few short-lived attempts at challenging it.[77] Generally passive and prone to cynicism – sure signs of *puer aeternus* immaturity and irresponsibility – the young men become enterprising only when pursuing sex, evading chores or showing off drinking polluted Danube water. And the ship – that is, the barge – sails on, without anything getting properly done and with everyone unhappy, yet sticking together.

As a truly self-effacing ironist, Daneliuc 'pretends to know nothing', and lets the events unfold, as 'natural occurrences' and in blatant opposition to the doctrinal catchphrases from Proca's daily log that he reads at the finale. Essentially, none of the participants in this seemingly never-ending, anti-climactic and disturbingly realistic portrayal of Ceaușescu's Romania is worthy of sympathy. For Daneliuc – like Pița – sees this 'human degradation' as a result of 'bad choices', and the characters as 'accomplices in their own destruction' (Stojanova 2013a: 171).

Captivating portrayals of mature grown-ups who actually get things done are hard to find in 'old' wave films,[78] a notion reinforced by the characters Daneliuc plays in his own films. The Reporter (*Long Drive*), the Cameraman (*Microphone Test*), and the Intellectual (*The Cruise*) are part of the intelligentsia and therefore doubly emasculated by the regime – first through its institutions, the family and the mandatory army service – and then via its totalitarian ideology.

Rebengiuc's middle-aged doctor, Hristea from *Sand Cliffs*, a highlight in his career from the 1980s, is a refreshing exception to the omnipresent *pueri*. The unsympathetic Doctor with his arrogant sense of entitlement, is the driving force behind Pița's attempt to repeat the success of *Contest* by means of another socially acerbic metaphor with metaphysical meaning, based on a psychological duel between a *senex* and a mysterious *puer*. However Vasilie, unlike the Kid, is a much more sinister personage, not a guardian but an exterminating angel, who taunts, lures and ultimately destroys the Doctor, thus foreshadowing the downfall that authoritarian father figures would suffer during the subsequent couple of decades.[79]

Romanian Cinema in the 1980s: The Return of the Paradigm and its Metaphoric-allegorical Challenges

With a rapid turn of the censorship screw, the 'old' wave came to an end after the ban of *Sand Cliffs*. Pița's comeback with *Paso Doble* (1985) and *White Lace Dress* (1988) was damaged by the frictions between the 'functional' didacticism and 'fictional' aesthetics, which, although somewhat mitigated by the conspicuously expensive set designs and costumes, failed to justify ideologically or aesthetically, let alone morally, their high budgets. Against the bleak backdrop of an impoverished country, these posh melodramas look like naïve renditions of Ceaușescu's propaganda at its most delusional, or as its hyperbolised caricature.

After his less-than-successful psychological thriller *The End of the Night* (1982), whose glum young prosecutor as the stock Positive Hero, tries to deal with the idiosyncrasies of communist justice, Veroiu – and after yet another few insignificant period films – left Romania in 1986. Filming contemporary subjects in 1980s Romania had undoubtedly become impossible if all the 'old' wave masters could showcase were socially and emotionally castrated *pueri* and *puelli*, controlled by party functionaries cum Mentors, like the factory foreman in *Paso Doble* or the old Prosecutor in *The End of the Night*. This crisis came to a head in Anghel Mora's *Reserve at the Start* (1988), where the dramatic conflict is reduced to a 'struggle between the good and the better' – an aphorism attributed to Stalin – that is, between the good sportsman and his better replacement who, under the wise guidance of the coach as omnipotent Mentor, wins the day. The irresolvable tensions between the 'functional' and the 'fictional' thus bring Mora's narrative to a standstill, taking, *mutatis mutandis*, Romanian contemporary cinema all the way back to *The Valley Resounds*.

During this period, the social and psychological complexity of great literary works – considered until then more or less immune – also became subject to strict censorship, forestalling the metaphoric-allegorical encoding of otherwise prohibited subjects across Eastern Europe.[80] Building on the psychological tradition of literary adaptations from the 1960s and 1970s, this trend in Romania relied as much on the *double entendre* of its Aesopian language as – thanks to the generous budgets – on the sumptuous 'retro' style. With the disappearance of the historic socio-ideological context, it is now difficult to determine which of these works required decoding, and which were just a form of stylish escapism, all the more so as many of them fall into both categories.

The films that Daneliuc, Pița and Veroiu each made about the impossible love of a much older man for a younger woman, are a case in point – while they do transpose prohibited metaphysical and humanist ideas into interwar Romanian society, they also interlace them with erotic decadence. In psychological terms, this narrative situation captures the authors' Pygmalion complex – that is, the frustration of their creative potential by the repressive regime. In Veroiu's *Adela* (1985), based on opera libretto by Garabet Ibrăileanu, the fascination of a middle-aged doctor with a girl he has known since childhood is abruptly severed despite their strong mutual attraction. Pița – after *Chained Justice* (1984), a visually exclusive black and white Historical Revolutionary film – adapted Sadoveanu's 1930s classic *The Place Where Nothing Ever Happens*. Following the original, the film *The Last Ball in November* (1989) tells the story of a country boyar and his younger female protégée, who – despite their passionate love – are undone by inaction on the eve of the fateful 1940s. Yet even such a bold insinuation to Ceaușescu's Romania as the 'place where nothing ever happens' was outdone by Daneiuc's radically nihilist

Glissando (1982), based on Cezar Petrescu's novel *The Dream Man* (*Omul din vis*). Harking back to the intricate symbolism of high modernism, its oneiric imagery is strung around the protagonist's obsession with a portrait of a young woman, believed to be his mother's. Unlike the reflexive male protagonists of Veroiu and Pița, Daneliuc's Ion Teodorescu goes all the way to mould his mentally fragile girlfriend after the portrait, which eventually destroys her.

Although Daneliuc had to fight hard for this eccentric vision (Nasta 2013: 57–68), his next film *Jacob* (1988), based on Geo Bogza's bleak eponymous novel, was even more problematic. Arguably one of the darkest films made in communist Romania, *Jacob* is a harbinger of the post-1989 naturalistic-nihilist trend. It is still impressive, thanks to Dorel Vișan's tragic hero, whose demise climaxes in the long finale when – after a series of exquisitely shot efforts to get off the cable cart he has mounted in order to get home faster on Christmas Eve – his Jacob falls to the frozen ground. The reference to the biblical Jacob's dream about climbing a ladder to God as a way of deliverance is presented here as defiance of God. Such a Nietzschean twist solicits little sympathy and upsets the 'moral and political encoding' of the film as a metaphor of 'a dead end [and] the apocalyptic condition for the Romanian people in general', as Nasta has it (2013: 66). And rather upholds a metaphysical reading, suggesting that the resilient Jiu valley miner has remained earth-bound and unredeemed. In Jungian terms, the damaged masculinity of mythological patriarchs – while symbolising obsolescence of the collective consciousness – presages socio-cultural renewal. However, the return of Jacob's rough machismo in post 1989 films indicates that this renewal might not necessarily be a positive one, as Vișan's own roles of a brazen (post)communist apparatchik demonstrate in Daneliuc's own *The Snails' Senator* (1995), and in its tribute, Tudor Giurgiu's NRC film *Of Snails and Men* (2012).

✳ ✳ ✳

Nominally part of the 'flood generation', Stere Gulea is a standalone director whose relatively small body of work yields an inordinate number of significant films. His principal *œuvre*, *The Moromete Family* (1986) – was followed by the versatile and much discussed *University Square* (1991),[81] an internationally popular documentary about the 1990 anti-communist demonstrations. Most recently, Gulea made *I'm an Old Communist Hag* (2013) – a tour de force of Luminița Gheorghiu, the NRC fetish actress from the older generation. It is a bold comedic-ironic take, through the eyes of the middle-aged heroine, on the incongruities between the great expectations in the wake of communist downfall and the current realities.

The Moromete Family, not unlike *Jacob*, stands apart from the intellectual sophistication of the metaphoric-allegorical trend because of its focus on impoverished rural and working-class Romanians. Gulea subverts the *totalitarian genre paradigm* aesthetically via its modernist-expressionist black and white visuals, but mostly with the help of his unusual protagonist. Based on Marin Preda's novel (1955/1957), which is considered among the most important works of Romanian post-Second World War literature, the film focuses on the disintegration of an interwar peasant family, triggered by the sons' rebellion against their patriarch of a father, Ilie Moromete (in the brilliant interpretation of Victor Rebengiuc). By selling the horses and pocketing the money in the hope of starting a new life in the city, Ilie's three sons reject his unquestionable patriarchal authority but also his hard work and frugality, as equally disposable values of the old consciousness.

Ilie cuts a contradictory father figure – a cunning braggart, he caves in before the powerful and pontificates among the weak; and he is an archetypal blocking *senex*, who 'combines [the] opposites into a single ambiguous image of seductive and paralyzing power', associated with the reactionary *ancienne* regime (Jung 1989: 65). By way of the sons' rebellion, Gulea does point to Marxist class consciousness as the only form of new consciousness, yet from today's vantage point this seems like a substitution of one kind of patriarchal oppression with another.[82]

The psychologically and socially castrating effect of a demonic mother has a long pedigree in Romanian art, as demonstrated by the tragic fate of young men from the mythopoetic films, and by the self-inflicted suffering of sons who refuse to let off their mothers – as Bogdan Dumitrache's characters in the NRC films *Best Intentions* (2011) and *Child's Pose* (2013) testify. Gulea's ominously complex father figure, however, while relatively new to Romanian cinema at that time, reappeared with a vengeance in Pintilie's *The Oak* (1992), and then in New Romanian films like Jude's *The Happiest Girl in the World* (2009) and *Everybody in Our Family* (2012), and certainly in Popescu's *Principles of Life* (2010).

Romanian Postcommunist Cinema in the 1990s – East Meets West

The radical transition in the 1990s from a totalitarian, centrally planned system towards a democratic, free-market one, resulted in a drastic reduction of film production in Romania – as across the postcommunist space,[83] and a massive closure of film theatres.[84] And while the immediate postcommunist aftermath, as Duma suggests, was 'marked by high hopes for a renewal, based on real freedom (no censorship!)', the 'film landscape remained mostly sad' (personal correspondence, 2017). She quotes Andrei Gorzo (2007) on the 'primitive notions of entertainment' and the 'weakened professional standards all around' of Romanian cinema under communism, and its postcommunist confusion with 'the newly found freedom to show sex and use swear words, and to get hysterically angry'. According to Duma, the 'euphoria ... lasted from May 1991 to April 1992', when 'eight feature premieres were theatrically released' – with 'only three directors returning to filmmaking reasonably quickly' (ibid.).

Far from unique to Romanian cinema, this dire picture could be explained by the unexpected transposition of Eastern European filmmakers from privileged 'teleological distributors' to independent artists with little to no financial support. The abdication of the state and the collapse of the 'modern redistributive society' exacerbated the filmmakers' crisis of self-knowledge, and reinforced old delusions about the omnipotent West. This early postcommunist obsession, reflected in film, was a natural reaction to Ceaușescu's isolationist protochronism. It was also an intrinsic part of the ongoing East *versus* West debate about geopolitical and cultural allegiances, which Iordachi and Trencsényi considered the 'central dilemma of Eastern European intellectual history', and a 'blueprint' for any 'reading of Romanian culture' (2013: 416–17).

The changing cinematic landscape in the 1990s falls roughly into two major cycles of films with discernible nativist and Western influences on formal, thematic and socio-political levels. The first cycle, called elsewhere the Quest for the Lost Viewer, rehabilitates entertainment cinema by overhauling the interwar Nationalist Epic and resuscitating Melodrama – virtually non-existent during communism due to its 'bourgeois' sentimentality – and brings in new hybrid genres like the Mafiosi Thriller[85] by borrowing heavily from international renditions of the gangster and thriller genres (Stojanova 2005c). The second cycle, or the Quest for Truth, reflects the moods of guilt and betrayal

Figure 16.3   *The Oak*

unleashed by the regime's collapse, and additionally forms two general tendencies on the basis of style and ideological priorities – the realistic-descriptive, which points to enlightenment-inspired Western values as the sole alternative to the postcommunist impasse – and the naturalistic-nihilist, where the Western gaze is tangibly present as the new-found significant other.

Pintilie's *The Oak* and Pița's *Luxury Hotel* (1992), despite their prestigious awards and experimental narratives – predicated on the intermedial folding of time in the former, and on the metaphoric-allegorical encoding of a totalitarian state as a five-star hotel in the latter – were side-tracked by realistic-descriptive films like Gulea's *Fox: Hunter* (1993) and *State of Things* (1995), Pintilie's own *Afternoon of a Torturer* (2001) and certainly Radu Mihăileanu's *Traitor* (1993).[86]

Among these works, *The Earth's Most Beloved Son* (1993) by Șerban Marinescu stands out for its unique representation of the intelligentsia's crisis of self-knowledge under communism. The film follows closely Marin Preda's eponymous novel, which was banned shortly before his mysterious death in 1980. Its protagonist Victor Petrini is a philosophy professor, who is arrested on trumped-up charges at the onset of terroristic totalitarianism, a period hitherto strictly tabooed. As is typical of the realistic-descriptive trend, the film foregrounds the intelligentsia's self-image as a perennial scapegoat by absolving its tragic hero of personal responsibility, and blames the ubiquitous brutality on circumstances and forces that are considered deeply foreign to the otherwise humane national character.[87]

Against all odds, Petrini survives the labour camp, and even kills his tormentor, who – in a graphic scene – has assaulted him sexually. The murder goes somehow unnoticed and Petrini is released after the death of Stalin, casually marked by his portrait with a black ribbon across mounted on a Danube barge. Once out of prison, Petrini is unable to start a new life since Romania has turned into a prison in its own right, where the price for survival is betrayal – his beautiful young wife has divorced him, married a party functionary, and alienated his child. After catching his new love Suzy – a colleague – sleeping with their boss, Petrini abandons her although she was obviously forced into the act, and the film's finale shows him before the altar of an empty church, defying God.

Yet another paradigmatic Eastern European fable of guilt and betrayal, *The Most Beloved* portrays the tragic entrapment of pre-war intellectuals forced to choose between Professor Paveliu's humiliating opportunism and Petrini's righteousness, influenced by Nietzsche via Emil Cioran, whom he often quotes.[88] The transcendence of Petrini's quest is surmised in the film's epitaph by Nietzsche, '[T]here is nothing without love' (Nietzsche 1984: 252). Even so, he never forgives his former wife or claims his estranged child, and has little to offer his ailing mother but a pack of Kent cigarettes. Petrini's set of values, hinged on strong will and lack of remorse, include neither humble love for one's fate – or *amor fati* as Nietzsche has it – nor the 'human, all too human' love for another human being. And although for Suzy he is the 'most beloved among the earthlings', Petrini leaves her to wallow in a world that is epitomised by Rebengiuc's lascivious boss urinating on the apartment building door. What Petrini seeks is sublime love for love's sake, unattainable by earthlings, not unlike the famous 'life for life's sake' espoused by the 1930s mystical-existentialist school of Trăirism, whose ideas seduced Romanian intellectuals in their early youth. And while Eliade, Eugène Ionesco and Cioran emigrated, the fate of those who stayed behind, such as Constantin Noica, is uncannily similar to Petrini's. Moreover, the fact that the Nietzsche-influenced[89] ideas of Trăirism were espoused by the ultra-nationalist and Anti-Semitic Iron Guard[90] has triggered a protracted debate over the interwar legacy of Romanian intelligentsia, providing yet another reason for its crisis of self-knowledge.

The film does point to Petrini's firm determination to resist collaboration in shaping the *faux* communist-nationalist consciousness, but his lack of compassion defeats any ethical pursuits. And then again, as is typical of the realistic-descriptive trend, *The Most Beloved* implies cathartically that the suffering, no matter how horrible, is now (circa 1993) over, and the 'return' to civilised Europe is imminent.

***

The contemporary subject matter and dreary subjective long takes of the naturalistic-nihilist trend represent the flip side of the realistic-descriptive one. All the more so, as it interprets the postcommunist crisis not as a result of a failed experiment, imposed from abroad, but as an innate metaphysical breakdown that has brought Eastern Europe to a complete social and moral stupor. Formally, this trend turns the *totalitarian genre paradigm* on its head, exhibiting a quintessentially *enantiodromic*[91] reaction to communist values and ideals. Rooted in the Czechoslovak New Wave[92] and having inspired some of the boldest dissident works across the region,[93] during the 1990s and early 2000s the trend produced a steady flow of films,[94] defined post-factum as miserabilist.[95] Strausz explains the success of such speculative self-exoticising or 'self-colonizing'[96] works at international film festivals with the need of the West 'to breathe a sigh of relief', knowing that these 'barbaric communities' whose 'social-ethical standards are blurred' are 'at a safe distance from the civilized and enlightened hubs of cultural exchange' (2017: 243).

Worth noting here is *Everyday God Kisses Us on the Mouth* (2001), which both cajoles and transcends the shock-based rapport of the naturalistic-nihilistic trend with the Western 'other'. Its director, Siniṣa Dragin – part of the generation caught in-between the veterans and the New Romanian directors – offers a black and white vision of the 1990s confused zeitgeist, saturated with long-forgotten Romanian mythopoetic symbolism. As is common to the trend, the protagonist Dumitru is an underdog from the social margins, a butcher by profession and a convicted killer. A comparison between Dumitru and another serial killer, Viorel, from Puiu's *Aurora* (2010) yields intriguing observations about their radically different positioning with regard to the Western gaze. The metaphysical implications of Dragin's film create a circular world of diabolical retribution populated by morally ambiguous characters, complicit in their own demise. Dragin, however, harnesses the film's self-exotisising – or miserabilist – potential via horror genre tropes, thus universalising the feelings of guilt and betrayal. On the other hand Puiu – true to the testimonial realism of the NRC narratives – bypasses any obsequiousness to the viewers, Eastern or Western, and compels them to grasp the 'depressingly bland social reality' from Viorel's 'psychologically colour-blind' point of view (Stojanova 2010).[97]

The mature attitude to the West initiated by Cristian Mungiu's *Occident* actually dates back to the self-ironic satire of *The Snails' Senator*, which helped Daneliuc put to rest the miserabilist self-exotisising of postcommunist Romania he launched with *The Conjugal Bed* (1993) and *Fed Up* (1994). An uncontested early master of representing the complex rapport with the West is Nae Caranfil, also part of the 1990s – or the in-between – generation. Because of their unassuming lyricism, humour and genre heterogeneity, his *Sundays on Leave* (1993) and *Asphalt Tango* (1996) are known as 'dramedies'.[98] Along with *Niki and Flo*, his works foster an understanding of the West as neither panacea nor arbiter, but as an aloof observer of the evolving Eastern European drama: a realisation whose crown achievement is the NRC gem Cristian Nemescu's *California Dreamin'* (2007).

The blame-and-guilt game – which is still being played out across the postcommunist space with self-colonising and miserabilist extravagances – was brought to an end by the New Romanian Cinema. It seems that the near-death experience of postcommunist cinemas in the 1990s have nurtured the *sui generis* maturity of the NRC directors, and has motivated their qualitatively new approach to life, as well as their poetics, encoding simultaneously the metaphysics of experience and the ironic ambiguity of its representation. They have since emerged as representatives of what Karl Mannheim calls 'free-floating (*freischwiebende*) intelligentsia', capable of overcoming 'the ideological conditions of its activity', of being 'independent of particular interests in society', and of advancing 'a higher, more real, more objective kind of (self) knowledge' (qtd in Konrad and Szelenyi 1979: 7–8). Responsible 'moral and rational agents', courageous enough to contrast 'ideas and free minds to ideological mentalities', the New Romanian Cinema directors have thus bestowed a unique voice to the frustrated denizens of our postmodern times (Havel 1993: 5–6).

Notes

1. Predicated on 'feature-length narrative (commercial), feature-length and short narrative (semi-commercial/independently produced), documentary (independent or government-subsidised), avant-garde (fully non-commercial), political/Third Cinema' (White 2004: 226).
2. For justification of the usage of 'Eastern Europe', see endnote 1 of the Introduction.
3. Romania, Bulgaria, and Serbia emerged as independent nations as a result of the Russian-Turkish wars from the second half of the nineteenth century, while Czechoslovakia, Poland and later Yugoslavia came into being thanks to the post-First World War peace treaties.
4. Konrad and Szelenyi discern three periods in the development of the 'rational redistributive societies' – traditional (up to 1700s); early (from 1700s to the communist take-over); and modern redistributive societies or socialism proper (1947–89) (1979: 39–45) – characterised along the lines of their capacity for growth/stagnation; level of independence/coordination; legitimised control over the surplus product and its determination; and the type of commodity relations (1979: 47–54).
5. Greater Romania (1918–40) consisted of:

    different historical provinces: the former principalities of Moldavia and Wallachia (unified in 1859); the former Ottoman province of Dobrudja (annexed in 1878); the former Russian province (1812–1918) of Bessarabia; the former Austrian province (1775–1918) of Bukovina; and territories that were part of the Hungarian half of the Habsburg Monarchy, such as Transylvania, Banat, Maramures, and the Partium. (Iordachi and Trencsényi, 2003: 418–19)

6. *Bulgaran is Gallant*, recognised as the first Bulgarian film, premiered in 1915, although director Vasil Gendov claims the date was 22 June 1910 (Kurdjilov 1987: 62–3). The first Serbian film, *In the Kingdom of Terpsichore* was made in 1906, but the best known one – *The Life and Deeds of the Immortal Leader Karadjordje* – appeared in 1911. See <hwww.kinokultura.com/specials/8/jankovic.shtml> (last accessed December 2016).
7. The passionate cinephiles Yanaki and Milton Manaki were of Aromanian (Romanian) origin, but their prolific legacy of ethnographic actualities made between 1904 and 1921 has been claimed by most countries that were formerly part of the Ottoman Empire. Only recently have they been recognised as part of Romanian film heritage (Țuțui 2011: 112–23).
8. Most historians point to the 1911 melodramas *Fatal Love*, directed by Brezeanu, and *Spread Yourselves, Daisies*, co-directed with Demetriade – now lost, like the first Romanian fiction films.
9. Released on the eve of the tragic Balkan War of 1913, the film was shot with 80,000 extras (supplied for free by the Ministry of War with full equipment). The production, placed under 'the cultural patronage of the Bucharest National Theatre', was subsidised mostly by the state and enjoyed real success all over Europe (Cernat 1982:15–16).
10. Croft discerns 'eight varieties of nation-state cinema', grouped around three major modes: '*industrial* – US cinema, Asian commercial successes, other entertainment cinemas, totalitarian cinemas; *cultural* – art cinemas, American Art, international co-productions, art for socialist export; *political (anti-state)* – Third cinemas, Sub-state cinemas' (1998: 389).
11. The recently defunct archival section of Romanian Film Centre (CNC) website, cited by Uricaru, used also to claim that the Film Fund was initially disbursed by

the Cinematographic Service within the Ministry of Tourism (August 1936). And that soon after (August 1937), it was the cinematography department of the Propaganda Ministry, which came to be 'in charge of the production, dissemination, propaganda, control and censorship of cinema'; however, this information is impossible to cross-reference now.

12. Similar to the *avance sur recette* (or *aide seléctive*), introduced in the 1960s by the French government, and considered the main reason for the consistent success of French national cinema (Hayward 2005: 38).
13. For details on the virtual cinematic war, waged between Germany and Hollywood in Romania, see Barbara A. Nelson (2009: 295–319).
14. Czech literature professor Vaclav Tille laid the foundations of film aesthetics in his book *Kinema* in 1908, and in 1924, the Polish literary critic and novelist Karol Irzykowski published *The Tenth Muse* (*Dziesiata Muza*), one of the first serious theoretical studies on film art (Stojanova 1999: 171).
15. Rebreanu's novels *The Uprising* aka *Blazing Winter* (1932) and *Ion* (or *The Lust for the Land, the Lust for Love*) (1920) were filmed under communism.
16. Lupu Pick, a Romanian-born filmmaker and actor, made the famous German *Kammerspiel* film *New Year's Eve* (1924).
17. According to Nasta, Berger's adaptations were 'complete flops' (2013: 10).
18. Cernat claims that J. Georgescu's first film, *Millionaire for a Day* (1924) is also based on Caragiale, which is impossible to cross-reference (1982: 27).
19. *Cinematograful și Educatia* (*The Cinema and Public Education*, 1912) by C. Iordachescu; *De la fotografie la cinematograf* (*From Photography to Cinema*, 1914) by M. Demetrescu, etc. (Cernat 1982: 19).
20. Professor Dmitrie Gusti, the founder of the Monographic Sociological School in Bucharest and film director, was in 1929 among the first to initiate the usage of educational- patriotic documentaries for sociological research (Cernat 1982: 31).
21. Sadoveanu's œuvre, based on Romanian historical legends and myths, generated eight adaptations between 1953 and 1989.
22. Citing Cernat (1982: 21), the International Encyclopedia of the First World War (IEFWW) refers to this film as *Our War*, but does not give a Romanian title or the name of the director. See <http://encyclopedia.1914-1918-online.net/article/filmcinema_south_east_europe>, last accessed 31 October 2017.
23. *Romania and the Fight against Bolshevism* (1941) and *Our Holy War* (1942), were both produced by ONC under Cantacuzino (who scripted the former, and directed the latter).
24. Referring to Florian Potra, Duma suggested in personal correspondence that 'there were the 80 full-length feature films made up until 1948, joined by 15 more titles by 1955 (all in all less than 100)'.
25. According to Liehm and Liehm, 'there still exist today about 15 of their small compositions in which drawings and caricatures come to life' (1977: 22).
26. According to 'The Report on Censorship', published in the 'reliable film journal' *Cinema* (No. 26, 15 January 1926), Sahighian's *Duty and Sacrifice* (1925) was made 'for military and patriotic youth education' (Cernat 1982: 116).
27. Most notably, Horia Igiroșanu's trilogy - *Iancu Jianu* (1928); *Outlaws* (1929); *Ciocoii* (1931).
28. Made by Austrian-German director Alfred Halm and co-produced by Romania, the Netherlands and Germany, it was 'the first Romanian film to break post-WWI box office records' (Cernat 1982: 24).
29. On 12 September 1944, with Soviet troops on its soil, Romania signed the Armistice Agreement, and joined the Allied powers. After the Communist

government won a fraudulent majority in Parliament on 19 November 1946, the monarchy was abolished.
30. For justification of the usage of 'communism', see endnote 2 of the Introduction.
31. Created at the October 1944 conference in Moscow, in this so-called 'naughty document' Stalin and Churchill agreed that the Soviet influence in Romania would be 90%; 75% in Bulgaria; 50% in Hungary and Yugoslavia, and so forth.
32. Nonetheless, Heller believes that by the mid-1980s, only Soviet society was fully totalised because of its successful merge of system integration and social integration. The other Eastern European societies – due to various 'systematic flaws' – avoided full totalisation (1987: 247).
33. So were the Koliba in Bratislava, the Boyana Studio in Sofia, Bela Balazs in Budapest, and Koshutnyak in Belgrade. The only exception was Barrandov in Prague, which was modelled after the German UFA.
34. The protracted debate over the theory and methodology of Socialist Realism was streamlined in 1946 by Soviet ideologue Alexander Zhdanov, who turned it into a militant dogma.
35. Jean Georgescu with *In Our Village* (1951) and Jean Mihai with *Ionut's Brigade* (1954).
36. Victor Iliu with *Mitrea Cocor* (1952), and Dinu Negreanu – with *The Bugler's Grandsons* (1953) and *The Sun Rises* (1954).
37. On the basis of over thirty years of official film production in Albania, Bulgaria, Romania and Yugoslavia, Stoil defines the following administrative genres: (1) history (with four sub-genres: commemorative, humanising, proto-revolutionary, historical fantasy); (2) anti-fascism; (3) spies, criminals and detectives, and (4) rural development (1984: 58–62).
38. The original genre approach, developed in my doctoral dissertation, is based on 450 official fiction films from seven countries, made between 1948 and 1989.
39. While leaving intact all other aspects of the paradigm, the Polish School from the 1950s was still accused of 'formalism' for substituting high-key lit photographic realism with a low-key expressionist atmosphere. Conversely, the Polish Cinema of Moral Anxiety from the late 1970s openly questioned the 'exemplary rules of action, dual value system, and doctrinal intertext'. Also in the 1970s, the Hungarian 'documentary fictions' and the Bulgarian Migration Cycle, while strictly abiding by the requirement to show exemplary workers and peasants, sabotaged the doctrinal intertext by featuring them in hyperrealistic mode as existentially frustrated subjects.
40. In 1974, in his most notorious push towards system integration, Ceaușescu launched the 'systematization' project to double the number of cities by 1990, forcing people into industrial-agricultural complexes: a manipulation of space that Strausz describes by way of Foucault as ideological coercion (2017: 30–8).
41. Henceforth my own taxonomy of official genres is referenced: *Contemporary* – (1) Construction of Socialism, (2) Spies and Saboteurs, (3) Children's, (4) Delinquent Youth, (5) Family Drama. *Historical* – (1) Nationalist Epic, (2) Historical (Bio) Revolutionary, (3) Battalia, (4) Partisan, (5) Resistance Fighter, (6) Holocaust (Stojanova 1999: 266–80).
42. *A Great Opportunity* (Czechoslovakia, 1949); *First Take-off* (Poland, 1951); *Dawn Over the Homeland* (Bulgaria, 1952).
43. In Mjagkova's view, scriptwriter M. Ștefanescu handled the 'brigadier movement' in the 'standard for literature and theatre... epic way', throwing in 'every possible propaganda concern', expressed in 'heavy-handed theatrical dialogue' (1993: 110–15).
44. Communist secret police.
45. Călinescu had a good reason to try hard, lest the new regime go after him for

Romania and the Fight against Bolshevism (Mjagkova 1993: 110–15; Aitken 2013: 775).
46. See endnote 36.
47. The first being *Life Triumphs* (1951).
48. In the role of Nina, Anca's unreformed bourgeois friend, Ciulei audaciously cast Lica Gheorghiu, the daughter of Gheorghe Gheorghiu-Dej, Romanian Communist Party leader and head of state (1944–65).
49. Western producers were attracted to Eastern Europe by the affordable prices of highly professional labour and modern facilities. René Clair's *The Lace Wars* (1965) and Terence Yong's *Mayerling* (1968) are amongst the best known co-productions with Romania (IMDb).
50. His most famous novel, *Kira Kiralina* (1923) – a steamy story of debauchery and repentance – was filmed in the USSR (1928) and Romania (2014).
51. Best Script Award at Cannes in 1963.
52. This was a turn-of-the century Romanian version of populism, with a major influence on interwar literature in terms of moral responsibility and depiction of debilitating poverty in a naturalistic manner, propagated by the famous literary journal *Viața românească*. Another journal, *Sămănătorul*, insisted that peasantry is the only 'positive class'. A third literary circle around the journal *Gîndirea* looked to the peasantry for inspiration in proclaiming mysticism and nationalism (*Encyclopedia of Literature* 1987: 338–9, translation CS).
53. Dana Ranga's excellent documentary *East-Side Story* (1997), devoted to communist musicals made between 1930s and the early 1970s, includes long excerpts from both films.
54. Popvici scripted *The Waves of the Danube*, *The Forest of the Hanged* and *Michael the Brave*, and also worked with Mureşan and Piţa.
55. For more, see Nasta (2013: 33–4).
56. The Polish film industry had four film units in 1948, and eight *zespoly* ten years later. The Yugoslav version of these units were the 'temporary' collective enterprises that facilitated the famous self-managed Yugoslav filmmaking from 1953 until the collapse of the country.
57. Between 1966 and 1981, Dinu Cocea made five films and one TV series in this genre.
58. Thanks to his position as 'an important Party official for Romanian Film', he 'managed to set up a deal with Columbia-Warner, dubbing the film in English and distributing it in forty countries and eighteen TV channels' (Nasta 2013: 29).
59. Katherine Verdery describes protochronism as '[t]he most paradigmatic cultural phenomenon of the Ceauşescu regime, which asserted that all major achievements of European culture and society were invented by Romanians (qtd in Iordachi and Trencsényi 2003: 417).
60. *The Column* (1968) – an illustrious co-production with West Germany, starring Antonella Lualdi and Amedeo Nazzari – was Drăgan's only film to please the authorities.
61. Gheorghe Vitanidis' *Burebista* (1980) was about a Dacian war leader who ruled 'the first centralized Dacian state' between 80 and 44 bc (Cernat 1982: 62).
62. Contemporary lore, usually Spies and Saboteurs films, constitutes a lesser known, but very popular side of his 51-film filmmaking career.
63. The hysteria came to a head when American actor George Hamilton was refused a Romanian visa for his portrayal of Dracula in Stan Dragoti's 1979 Hollywood comedy, *Love at First Bite* (Stojanova 2005: 227).
64. Prominent examples include *The Passenger* (Poland, 1964), *Birds and Greyhounds* (Bulgaria, 1969), *Closely Watched Trains* (Czechoslovakia, 1966).

65. Marie-Louise Von Franz cites Philip Wylie's book *Generation of Vipers* (1942) to explain the 'highly regressive' tendency of young men to avert responsibility with the overprotectiveness of their mothers, but also of Western civilisation (Von Franz 1993: 318).
66. Pintilie's subsequent film *Why Are the Bells Ringing, Mitică?* (1982), based on the eponymous play by Caragiale, was banned until 1990 because of transparent allusions to knowable characters and survival tactics that were popular in Ceaușescu's Romania.
67. For discussion of this trend, see Strausz (2017: 51–82).
68. Youssouff Aidaby, Andrei Cătălin Băleanu, Pierre Bokor, Iosif Demian, Stere Gulea, Roxana Pană, Dan Pița, Dinu Tănase, Mircea Veroiu.
69. For more on Frye's narrative modes, see endnote 42 of the Introduction.
70. Yvette Bíró also notes a 'downward' move from the romantic pathos of Polish, Hungarian, Czechoslovak and Yugoslav films made in the late 1950s to early 1960s, to the irony of those made in the late 1960s and 1970s. Her impressionistic approach however construes irony as authorial attitude (to all things official) rather than as a dramatic mode (1983: 28–55).
71. Author of the famous *Mill of Luck* (1955), an adaptation of Ioan Slavici's eponymous 1881 masterpiece about greed and lust, recently contemporised by the NRC film *Horizon* (2015).
72. See 'Towards a Definition of the Existentialist Realism of New Romanian Cinema' in the Introduction.
73. The Yugoslav classic *Who Is Singing Over There?* (1980) applies the same structure with prophetic meaning for the fate of the federation. A diverse ethnic group on a Belgrade-bound bus on 6 April 1941 is hit by a German bomb amidst a heated argument with the two Gypsies on board, sparing the Gypsies but destroying their attackers.
74. Nasta calls it 'the Eastern European paradigmatic white horse' (2013: 49).
75. A sentiment Béla Tarr's apocalyptic *Satantango* (1994) would reiterate in a decidedly bleaker manner.
76. According to Jung, archetypes consist of positive and negative aspects.
77. Tora Vasilescu has ingenuously captured common types of female opportunism in Daneliuc's films.
78. With the arguable exception of the drivers' duo in *Long Drive* (1974), whose success in sabotaging the Construction of Socialism genre paradigm is proven by the three-year delay in its release.
79. See Pop (2014: 120–9).
80. Prominent examples of this trend include: Bulgaria – *The Unknown Soldier's Patent Leather Shoes* (1979); Hungary – *The Red and the White* (1967), *Red Psalm* (1972), *Hungarian Rhapsody* (1979), *Mephisto* (1981), *Colonel Redl* (1985), *Hanussen* (1988); Poland – *The Wedding* (1973); and certainly, films by Andrey Tarkovsky and Emir Kusturica.
81. See Chapter 9 for detailed discussion of the film.
82. In the modern world, as post-Jungians argue, changes of the collective consciousness are increasingly imposed without much consideration of 'the superior spontaneity of the collective unconscious', whose manifestations are relegated only to art and dreams (Rowland 2005: 5).
83. Twenty-three features were produced in 1989; 12 in 1994 and six in 1997, according to <www.obs.coe.int> (accessed May 2018).
84. Six hundred and twelve theatres were closed in 1989, 391 in 1994, and 432 in 1997, according to <www.obs.coe.int> (accessed May 2018).
85. Popular mostly in Russia and Poland.

86. Mihăileanu came to international renown with the Holocaust film *Train of Life* (1998) and *The Concert* (2009).
87. Prominent examples of this trend include: Bulgaria – *The Camp* (1990), *After the End of the World* (1998); Germany – *Lost Landscape* (1992); Czech Republic – *The Fortress* (1994), *Thank You for Each New Morning* (1994), *Cozy Dens* (1998); Hungary – *Outpost* (1994) and the last part of *Sunshine* (1999); Poland – *The Convert* (1994) and *The Temptation* (1995).
88. In her famous essay 'Thinking against Oneself: Reflections on Cioran', Susan Sontag remarks Nietzsche's 'undeniable consequences for Cioran' (1969: 81).
89. '[T]he influence of Nietzsche [on the Balkans] is as important in the artistic realm as it has been prominent in the sphere of philosophy and religion' (Miller 1915: 299–300).
90. A far-right movement, later a political party in Romania (1927–41).
91. Borrowed from Heraclitus, the term signifies 'an essential characteristic of all homeostatic systems' pertaining to 'the inherent compensatory tendency of all entities, pushed to the extreme, to go over to their opposite' (Stevens 1990: 140).
92. The omnibus film *Pearls of the Deep* (1965), *Report on the Party and the Guests* (1966), *The Firemen's Ball* (1967).
93. Bulgaria – *The Rabbit's Death* (1982), *A Woman of 33* (1982); Poland – *Golem* (1980), *The War of the Worlds* (1983); the Yugoslav Black series.
94. Bulgaria – *Exitus* (1989), *Late Full Moon* (1997); Czech Republic – *Traps* (Věra Chytilová, 1998); Hungary – *Child Murders* (Ildiko Szabo, 1992); Poland – *The End of the World* (1993), *Polish Death* (1994); almost all post-Yugoslav films from the 1990s.
95. For discussion of miserabilism, see endnote 24 of the Introduction.
96. Coined by Bulgarian scholar Alexander Kiossev in 1999, the term signifies 'a core of self-imposed, voluntary identification, formed by Eastern European nationalisms following the West's image of the region' (qtd in Imre 2014: 121).
97. For more on these two films, see Chapter 8 in this volume.
98. For analyses of Caranfil's films see Nasta (2013: 122–4), Strausz (2017: 122–3), and Chapter 6 in this volume.

COMBINED BIBLIOGRAPHY

Agnew, Vanessa (2004), 'Introduction: What Is Reenactment?' *Criticism*, 46: 3, pp. 327–39.
Aitken, Ian (2013), *The Concise Encyclopedia of the Documentary Film*, London: Routledge.
Altman, Rick (1987), *The American Film Musical*, Bloomington: Indiana University Press.
Anghelescu, Şerban (2005), 'The colours of transition', *Martor*, 10, pp. 12–6.
Arendt, Hannah (2006 [1963]), *Eichmann in Jerusalem: A Report on the Banality of Evil*, London: Penguin Classics.
Aristotle (1961), *Poetics*, New York: Hill and Wang.
Arvon, Henri (1973), *Marxist Aesthetics*, Ithaca: Cornell University Press.
Bardan, Alice (2012), 'Aftereffects of 1989: Corneliu Porumboiu's *12:08 East of Bucharest* (2006) and Romanian Cinema', in Aniko Imre (ed.), *The Blackwell Companion of Eastern European Cinema*, Malden, MA: Wiley-Blackwell, pp.125–47.
Balázs, Béla (2010), *Early Film Theory: Visible Man and The Spirit of Film*, New York and Oxford: Berghahn Books.
Balmain, Colette (2008), *Introduction to Japanese Horror Film*, Edinburgh: Edinburgh University Press.
Baudrillard, Jean (1976), *L'échange symbolique et la mort*, Paris: Gallimard.
Baudrillard, Jean (1994), *The Illusion of the End*, Stanford: Stanford University Press.
Baumann, Fabien (2011) 'La manière roumaine d'étirer le temps', *Positif*, 608, October.
Bechdel, Alison (1986), *Dykes to Watch Out for*. Ithaca, NY: Firebrand Books.
Bellour, Raymond (2007 [1984]), 'The Pensive Spectator', in David Campany (ed.), *The Cinematic*, London: Whitechapel and Cambridge, MA: MIT Press, pp. 119–23.
Berghahn, Daniela, and Claudia Sternberg (ed.) (2010), *European Cinema in Motion: Migrant and Diasporic Film in Contemporary Europe*, Basingstoke: Palgrave Macmillan.

Biro, Matthew (2012), 'From Analogue to Digital Photography: Bernd and Hilla Becher and Andreas Gursky', *History of Photography*, 36: 3, pp. 353–66.
Bíró, Yvette (1983), 'Pathos and Irony in Eastern European Films', in David W. Paul (ed.), *Politics, Art and Commitment in the East European Cinema*, London: Palgrave Macmillan, pp. 28–55.
Blyth, Mark (2013), *Austerity: The History of a Dangerous Idea*, Oxford: Oxford University Press.
Bogue, Ronald (2003), *Deleuze on Cinema*, New York: Routledge.
Bolter, Jay David and Grusin, Richard (1999), *Remediation: Understanding New Media*, Cambridge, MA and London: MIT Press.
Bondebjerg, Ib and Eva Novrup Redvall (2011), 'A Small Region in a Global World: Patterns in Scandinavian Film and TV Culture', *Think Thank* website, <http://cemes.ku.dk/research/research_literature/workingpapers/scandinavian_cinema-final_lrl_.pdf> (accessed May 2017).
Bonitzer, Pascal (2000 [1971]), 'Deframings', in David Wilson (ed.), *Cahiers du Cinéma: History, Ideology, Cultural Struggle*, London: Routledge, pp. 197–204.
Bordwell, David (1981), *The Films of Carl Theodor Dreyer*, Berkeley, Los Angeles and London: University of California Press.
Bordwell, David (1985), *Narration in the Fiction Film*, Madison: University of Wisconsin Press.
Bordwell, David (2002), 'The Art Cinema as a Mode of Film Practice', in Catherine Fowler (ed.), *The European Cinema Reader*, London: Routledge, pp. 94–102.
Bordwell, David (2005), *Figures Traced in Light: On Cinematic Staging*, Berkeley: University of California Press.
Bordwell, David (2006), 'An appetite for artifice', Observations on Film Art, 25, December, <http://www.davidbordwell.net/blog/2006/12/25/an-appetite-for-artifice/> (accessed 13 September 2018).
Bordwell, David (2011), *Planet Hong Kong: Popular Cinema and the Art of Entertainment*. Madison: Irvington Way Institute Press.
Bordwell, David (2015), 'National cinemas. Eastern Europe', Observations on Film Art, <http://www.davidbordwell.net/blog.category/national-cinemas-eastern-europe/> (accessed 13 August 2015).
Boym, Svetlana (n.d.), 'Nostalgic Technology: Notes for an Off-modern Manifesto', <http://www.svetlanaboym.com/manifesto.htm> (accessed 15 August 2015).
Brădățan, Costică (2005), 'A Time of Crisis – A Crisis of (the Sense of) Time: The Political Production of Time in Communism and its Relevance to the Postcommunist Debates', in *East European Politics and Societies*, 19, pp. 260–90.
Brădățan, Costică and Aurelian Crăiuțu (2012), 'Introduction: The paradoxes of marginality', *European Legacy*, 17: 6, pp. 721–9.
Bratton, Jacky (1994), 'The Contending Discourses of Melodrama', in Jacky Bratton, Jim Cook, Christine Gledhill (eds), *Melodrama: Stage, Picture, Screen*, London: British Film Institute, pp. 38–49.
Bren, Frank (1986), *World Cinema 1: Poland*, London: Flicks Books.
Brooks, Peter (1976), *The Melodramatic Imagination: Balzac, Henry James, Melodrama, and the Mode of Excess*, New Haven: Yale University Press.
Brophy, Phil (2007), 'How Sound Floats on Land', in Daniel Goldmark, Lawrence Kramer, Richard Leppert (eds), *Beyond the Soundtrack: Representing Music in Cinema*, Berkeley: University of California Press, pp.136–48.
Brown, Wendy (2003), 'Neo-Liberalism and the End of Liberal Democracy', *Theory & Event*, 7: 1.
Burch, Noël (1990), *Life to those Shadows*, Berkeley, Los Angeles and London: University of California Press.

Camus, Albert (1946), *The Stranger*, New York: Vintage.
Caranfil, Tudor (1988), *În căutarea filmului pierdut*, Bucharest: Meridiane.
Cardullo, Bert (2012), *European Directors and Their Films: Essays on Cinema*, Plymouth: The Scarecrow Press.
Casetti, Francesco (2011), 'Back to the Motherland. The Film Theatre in the Postmedia Age', *Screen*, 52: 1, Spring, pp. 1–12.
Cavell, Stanley (1971), *The World Viewed: Reflections on the Ontology of Film*, New York: Viking.
Centrul Național al Cinematografiei (Romanian Film Centre) Results (2014), *Rezultatele Concursului de proiecte cinematografice, Sesiunea II 2014*, <http://cnc.gov.ro/?page_id=1584> (accessed 15 August 2015).
Centrul Național al Cinematografiei (Romanian Film Centre) (2015), 'General Overview 2010–2014', <http://cnc.gov.ro/wp-content/uploads/2015/05/III_Exploatare_2014.pdf> (accessed 15 August 2015).
Cernat, Manuela (1982), *A Concise History of Romanian Film*, Bucharest: Editura științifică și enciclopedică.
Cesereanu, Ruxandra (2004), 'Viața la bloc sau România la borcan?', *Revista 22*, 8 June, <http://www.revista22.ro/viata-la-bloc-sau-romania-la-borcan-923.html> (accessed 6 March 2016).
Chevrier, Jean-François (2003), 'The Adventures of the Picture Form in the History of Photography', in Douglas Fogle (ed.), *The Last Picture Show: Artists Using Photography, 1960–1982*, Minneapolis: Walker Art Center, pp. 113–28.
Chion, Michel (1994), *Audio-Vision: Sound On Screen*, New York: Columbia University Press.
Chirilov, Mihai (2007), 'You Can Run, But You Cannot Hide: New Romanian Cinema', in Christina Stojanova and Dana Duma (eds), *Kinokultura*, Special Issue 6, May, <http://www.kinokultura.com/specials/6/romanian.shtml> (accessed May 2018).
Chirilov, Mihai (2010), 'Love Sick', in *Aperitiff: The New Romania Cinema*, special issue, Cluj: Transylvania International Film Festival, p.21.
Chirilov, Mihai (2011), 'Stop-cadre la masă', in Cristina Corciovescu and Magda Mihăilescu (eds), *Noul Cinema Românesc: De la tovarășul Ceaușescu la domnul Lăzărescu*, Iași: Polirom, pp. 10–31.
Cockrell, Eddie (2006), 'Taxidermia', *Variety*, <https://variety.com/2006/film/markets-festivals/taxidermia-1200518771/> (accessed March 2017).
Collinson, Diané (1985), 'Ethics and Aesthetics Are One', in *British Journal of Aesthetics*, 25: 3, pp. 266–72.
Cosmescu, Corina (2013), 'La mulți ani, maestre! Petre Geambașu, la 70 de ani', *Adevărul*, 6 November, <http://adevarul.ro/entertainment/celebritati/petre-geambasu-70-ani-artrebui-existe-echitate-muzica-veche-muzica-mai-noua-1_5279c6a4c7b855ff56c0e5f9/index.html> (accessed 15 March 2016).
Crețulescu, Andrei (2011), 'Nu mișcă nimeni. Noul cinema românesc, gen', in Cristina Corciovescu and Magda Mihăilescu (eds), *Noul Cinema Românesc: De la tovarășul Ceaușescu la domnul Lăzărescu*, Iași: Polirom, pp. 54–73.
Critchley, Simon (2009). 'Being and Time, Part 2: On "mineness"', in *The Guardian*, available at <https://www.theguardian.com/commentisfree/belief/2009/jun/15/heidegger-being-time-philosophy> (accessed 23 September 2018).
Croft, Stephen (1998), 'Concepts of National Cinema', in John Hill and Pamela Gibson (eds), *The Oxford Guide to Film Studies*, Oxford: Oxford University Press, pp. 385–94.
Czach, Liz (2012), 'Acting and Performance in Home Movies and Amateur Film', in Aaron Taylor (ed.), *Theorizing Film Acting*, New York: Routledge, pp. 152–66.

Dánél, Mónika (2015), *Spectactors – Between Watching and Playing in the Reenactments of the 'Televised Revolution'*, manuscript, conference presentation (Play, Perform, Participate, Utrecht, 16–18 April).
Deaca, Mircea (2013), *Postfilmic Cinema: Notes and Readings about Contemporary Film*, Timisoara: Editura Brumar.
De Lauretis, Teresa (1989), *Differenza e indifferenza sessuale*, Firenze: Estro Editrice.
Deutsch, Stephen (2003), 'Music for Interactive Moving Pictures', in Larry Sider, Dianne Freeman and Jerry Sider (eds), *Soundscape: The School of Sound lectures 1998–2001*, London: Wallflower, pp. 28–34.
Dimitrova, Genoveva (2012), 'Боде очите, но няма болка', *Kultura*, 43: 2705, 14 December, <http://www.kultura.bg/bg/article/view/20396> (accessed 2 January 2016).
Dogme 95 (1995), *The Vow of Chastity*, <http://www.dogme95.dk/the-vow-of-chastity/> (accessed 15 August 2015).
Dostoyevsky, Fyodor M. (1871), *Demons* («Бесы»), <http://rvb.ru/dostoevski/01text/vol7/29.htm> (accessed May 2017).
Duma, Dana (2013), 'Nae Caranfil and "Maximalist" Aesthetics', *Close Up: Film and Media Studies*, 1: 1, pp. 20–31.
Ďurovičová, Natasa and Kathleen Newman (eds) (2010), *World Cinemas, Transnational Perspectives*, New York: Routledge.
Eagleton, Terry (2014), *Culture and the Death of God*, New Haven and London: Yale University Press.
Eliade, Mircea (1972), *Zalmoxis, the Vanishing God: Comparative Studies in the Religions and Folklore of Dacia and Eastern Europe*, Chicago: University of Chicago Press.
Eliade, Mircea (1987), *The Sacred and the Profane: The Nature of Religion*, San Diego: Harcourt Brace Jovanovich.
Elleström, Lars (2014), *Media Transformation: The Transfer of Media Characteristics among Media*, London: Palgrave Pivot.
Elsaesser, Thomas (2005), *European Cinema: Face to Face with Hollywood*, Amsterdam: Amsterdam University Press.
Elsaesser, Thomas and Hagner, Matte (2010), *Film Theory: An Introduction through the Senses* (first edition), London: Routledge.
Encyclopaedia of Literature (*Литературная Энциклопедия*) (Volume 5) (1987), Moscow: State Publishing House, pp. 338–9.
Ferencz-Flatz, Christian (2013), '*Aurora*, Elements from an Analysis of a Misunderstanding' in *Close Up*, 1:1, Bucharest: UNATC Press, pp. 32–42.
Ferencz-Flatz, Christian (2015), *Incursiuni fenomenologice în noul film românesc*, Cluj Napoca: Tact.
Filimon, Monica (2017), *Cristi Puiu*, Chicago: University of Illinois Press.
Filippi, Gabriela and Andrei Rus (2014), 'Despre imaginea de film cu Marius Panduru', in *Film Menu*, <https://filmmenu.wordpress.com/2014/09/30/interviu-marius-panduru/> (accessed 25 August 2015).
Fisher, Greg (2013), 'The Art of the City: Liverpool', in *Pergyll Productions Official Wordpress Blog*, 14 September, <https://peryglproductions.wordpress.com/2013/09/14/the-art-of-the-city-liverpool/> (accessed 28 October 2016).
Flusser, Vilém (1990), *Television Image and Political Space in the Light of the Romanian Revolution*, Lecture held on 7 April, in Budapest. <https://www.youtube.com/watch?v=QFTaY2u4NvI&feature=channel_video_title> (accessed 25 August 2015).
Florescu, Radu and Raymond T. McNally (1973), *Dracula: A Biography of Vlad the Impaler, 1431–1476*, London: Robert Hale.
Foucault, Michel (1998), 'Different Spaces', in James D. Faubion (ed.), *Aesthetics,*

Method, and Epistemology: Essential Works of Foucault 1954–1984, New York: The New Press, pp. 175–85.
Frampton, Daniel (2006), *Filmosophy*, London: Wallflower.
Fried, Michael (1980), *Absorption and Theatricality: Painting and Beholder in the Age of Diderot*, Chicago: University of Chicago Press.
Fried, Michael (1967), 'Art and Objecthood', *Artforum*, 5: 10, pp. 12–23.
Frye, Northrop (1990 [1957]), *Anatomy of Criticism*, Princeton: Princeton University Press.
Fulger, Mihai (2006), *Noul val în cinematografia românească (New Wave In Romanian Cinema)*, Bucharest: Grupul Editorial Art.
Fulger, Mihai (2011), 'Despre moarte, numai de bine', in Cristina Corciovescu and Magda Mihăilescu (eds), *Noul Cinema Românesc*, Bucharest: Polirom, pp. 104–27.
Fulger, Mihai (2013), 'Moartea doamnei Laurent – Amour', *Observator Cultural*, 661, 15 February, <http://www.observatorcultural.ro/articol/kinobservator-moartea-doamnei-laurent-2/> (accessed 6 March 2016).
Georgescu, Lucian (2011), 'Portretul unui popor vegetal. Despre tema drumului', in Cristina Corciovescu and Magda Mihăilescu (eds), *Noul Cinema Românesc: De la tovarășul Ceaușescu la domnul Lăzărescu*, Iași: Polirom, 129–53.
Getz, Isaac and Todd Lubart (2009), 'Creativity and economics: current perspectives', in Tudor Rickards, Mark Runco and Susan Moger (eds), *The Routledge Companion to Creativity*, London: Routledge, pp. 206–21.
Gledhill, Christine (2005), 'Signs of Melodrama', in Christine Gledhill (ed.), *Stardom: Industry of Desire*, London: Routledge, pp. 210–34.
Gocić, Goran (2001), *The Cinema of Emir Kusturica: Notes from the Underground*, London, New York: Wallflower.
Goldsmith, Leo (2008), 'Stuff and Dough', *Reverse Shot*, Issue 22, 23 April, <http://reverseshot.org/reviews/entry/82/stuff_and_dough> (accessed 15 March 2016).
Gorzo, Andrei (2007), 'The Critic s Perspective in *The Young, the New, the Daring*', edited by Adriana Grădinaru and Dragoș Tudor, Bucharest: Romanian Culture Institute.
Gorzo, Andrei (2012), *Lucruri care nu pot fi spuse altfel. Un mod de a gândi cinemaul de la André Bazin la Cristi Puiu*, Bucharest: Humanitas.
Gorzo, Andrei (2013), 'Concerning the Local Precursors of the New Romanian Realism', *Close Up*, 1: 1, Bucharest: UNATC Press, pp. 4–11.
Gorzo, Andrei and Andrei State (eds) (2014), *Politicile filmului: Contribuții la interpretarea cinemaului românesc contemporan*, Cluj-Napoca: Editura Tact.
Grodal, Torben (2009), *Embodied Visions: Evolution, Emotion, Culture, and Film*, Oxford: Oxford University Press.
Grazzini, Giovanni (1980), *Eva dopo Eva, Gius*. Roma-Bari: Laterza Figli Spa.
Grigar, Ewa (2007), 'The Gendered Body as Raw Material for Women Artists of Central Eastern Europe after Communism', in Janet Elise Johnson and Jean C. Robisnon (eds), *Living Gender after Communism*, Bloomington: Indiana University Press, pp.80–105.
Groys, Boris (2004), 'The Post-communist Condition', in Maria Hlavajova and Jill Winder (eds), *Who if not we should at least try to imagine the future of all this? 7 episodes on exchanging Europe*, Amsterdam: Artimo, pp. 163–70.
Halle, Randall (2010), 'Offering Tales They Want to Hear: Transnational European Film Funding as Neo-Orientalism', in Rosalind Galt and Karl Schoonover (eds), *Global Art Cinema New Theories and Histories*, Oxford: Oxford University Press.
Hames, Peter (2001), 'I Am a Tool: An Interview with Ian Svankmajer', *Sight and Sound*, 11: 10, October, pp. 26–8.
Hames, Peter (2005), *The Czechoslovak New Wave*, London: Wallflower.

Hames, Peter (2008), 'ágnes Kocsis: *Fresh Air (Friss Levego*, 2006)', in *Kinokultura*, Special Issue 7 on Hungarian cinema, <http://www.kinokultura.com/specials/7/friss.shtml> (accessed March 2017).
Havel, Václav. *Summer Meditations*, New York: Vintage Books, 1993.
Hayward, Susan (2001), *Cinema Studies: The Key Concepts*, London: Routledge.
Hayward, Susan (2005), *French National Cinema*, London: Routledge.
Hayward, Susan (2013), 'Postmodernism' in *Cinema Studies: The Key Concepts*, New York: Routledge, pp. 284–94.
Heidegger, Martin (1962 [1927]), *Being and Time*, New York: Harper.
Heller, Agnes (1987), 'An Imaginary Preface to the 1984 Edition of Hannah Arendt's *The Origins of Totalitarianism*', in Ferenc Feher and Agnes Heller, *Eastern Left, Western Left: Totalitarianism, Freedom and Demo*cracy, Atlantic Highlands: Humanities Press International.
Heredero, Carlos (2008), 'Realismo y Metáfora: *4 meses, 3 semanas, 2 días*, de Cristian Mungiu', in *Cahiers du Cinéma, España*, 8, January, pp. 22–3.
Hickey, Walt (2014), *The Dollar and Cents Case against Hollywood's Exclusion of Women*, <http://fivethirtyeight.com/features/the-dollar-and-cents-case-against-hollywoods-exclusion-of-women/> (accessed 2 August 2015).
Hjort, Mette and Duncan Petrie (eds), (2007) *The Cinema of Small Nations*, Edinburgh: Edinburgh University Press.
Hjort, Mette (2010), 'On the plurality of cinematic transnationalism', in Natasa Ďurovičová and Kathleen Newman (eds), *World Cinemas, Transnational Perspectives*, New York: Routledge, pp. 12–32.
Holloway, Ronald (1989), 'Bulgaria: A Cinema of Poetics', in Daniel J. Goulding (ed.), *Post New Wave Cinema in the Soviet Union and Eastern Europe*, Bloomington: Indiana University Press, pp. 215–48.
Horton, Andrew James, Dan Georgakas and Angelike Contis (2007), 'Is There a Balkan Cinema? A Filmmakers' and Critics' Symposium', *Cineaste*, 32: 3 (Summer), <www.cineaste.com/articles/is-there-a-balkan-cinema.htm> (accessed 20 August 2015).
Hutcheon, Linda (1994), *Irony's Edge: The Theory and Politics of Irony*, London and New York: Routledge.
Iacob, Raluca (2015), *Projecting Peripheries: Allegories of Marginality in Post-Communist Romanian Cinema*, Doctoral Dissertation, St Andrews: University of St Andrews.
Ieta, Rodica (2010), 'The New Romanian Cinema: A Realism of Impressions', *Film Criticism*, 34: 2/3, pp. 22–38.
Ilieşiu, Marilena (2011), 'România 2000: o poveste în spaţiu şi timp', in Cristina Corciovescu and Magda Mihăilescu (eds), *Noul Cinema Românesc: De la tovarăşul Ceauşescu la domnul Lăzărescu*, Iaşi: Polirom, pp. 155–79.
Imre, Anikó (ed.) (2012), *A Companion to Eastern European Cinemas*, Malden: Wiley-Blackwell.
Imre, Anikó (2014), 'Postcolonial Media Studies in Postsocialist Europe', in *boundary 2*, 41: 1, pp. 113–34.
Iordachi, Constantin and Balázs Trencsényi (2003), 'In Search of a Usable Past: The Question of National Identity in Romanian Studies, 1990–2000', in *East European Politics and Societies*, 17: 3, pp. 415–53.
Iordanova, Dina (ed.) (2006), *The Cinema of the Balkans*, London: Wallflower.
Iordanova, Dina (2014), 'Unseen Cinema: Notes on Small Cinemas and the Transnational', in Lenuţa Giukin, Janina Falkowska and David Desser (eds), *Small cinemas in global markets: genres, identities, narratives*, London: Lexington Books, pp. 259–70.

Jacobs, Lea (1991), *The Wages of Sin: Censorship and the Fallen Woman Film 1928–1944*, Wisconsin: University of Wisconsin Press.
Jaehne, Karen (1980), 'The True Life of Dracula' in *Cineaste*, 10: 3, (Summer).
Jaffe, Ira (2014), *Slow Movies Countering the Cinema of Action*, London: Wallflower.
Jauss, Hans Robert (1978), 'La douceur du foyer', in Hans Robert Jauss, *Pour une esthétique de la reception*, Paris: NRF, Gallimard, pp. 263–29.
Johnston, Claire (1973), 'Women's Cinema as Counter Cinema', in Claire Johnston (ed.) *Notes on Women's Cinema*, London: Society for Education in Film and Television, reprinted in Sue Thornham (ed.) (1999), *Feminist Film Theory: A Reader*, New York: New York University Press.
Joseph, Branden W. (2007), 'The Tower and the Line: Toward a Genealogy of Minimalism', *Grey Room*, no. 27, Spring, pp. 58–81.
Judd, Donald (1965), 'Specific Objects', *Contemporary Sculpture: Arts Yearbook 8*, New York: Art Digest, pp. 74–82.
Jung, C. G. [1959] (1977), *The Collected Works of C. G. Jung*, London: Routledge and Kegan Paul.
Jung, Carl Gustav (1980/1990), *Collected Works*, vols 7–9 (second edn), Princeton: Princeton University Press.
Jung, Carl Gustav (1989), *Aspects of the Masculine*, edited by John Beebe, Bollingen Series, Princeton, NJ: Princeton University Press.
Kaplan, E. Ann (2005), *Trauma Culture: The Politics of Terror and Loss in Media and Literature*, New Brunswick: Rutgers University Press.
Kaceanov, Marina (2008), 'On the New Romanian Cinema', *POV* magazine, 25 (March), <https://pov.imv.au.dk/Issue_25/section_3/artc6A.html> (accessed January 2018).
Kurdjilov, Petar (1987), *Bulgarian Feature Films – An Annotated Illustrated Filmography* – Volume I (1915–48) (in Bulgarian and English). Sofia: Dr Peter Beron State Publishing House.
Kearney, Richard (2003), *The Wake of Imagination: Toward a Postmodern Culture*, New York, Routledge.
Kenez, Peter (1992), *The Birth of the Propaganda State: Soviet Methods of Mass Mobilization 1917–1929*, New York: Cambridge University Press.
Kim, Ji-Hoon (2009), 'The Post-Medium Condition and the Explosion of Cinema', *Screen*, 50: 1, Spring, pp. 114–23.
Király, Hajnal (2015), 'Leave to Live? Placeless people in Contemporary Hungarian and Romanian Films of Return', *Studies in Eastern European Cinema*, 6:2, pp. 169–83.
Kirsten, Guido (2015), 'Fictions of everydayness: Focalization Patterns and Narrative "Reality Effects" in *Police, Adjective* and Other Films from the Romanian New Wave', <http://www.photogenie.be/photogenie_blog/article/fictions-everydayness> (accessed 14 November 2016).
Konrad, George and Ivan Szelenyi (1979), *Intellectuals on the Road to Class Power*, Brighton: Harvester Press.
Kosciejew, Richard John (2014), *The Treadmills of Time*, Bloomington: Author House.
Kotlyarenko, Eugene (2010), 'Colossal Cinema: The Films of Pedro Costa', in *Art in America Magazine*, 25 March, <http://www.artinamericamagazine.com/news-features/previews/pedro-costa-criterion-collection/> (accessed 28 October 2016).
Kovács, András Bálint (2007), *Screening Modernism: European Art Cinema, 1950–1980*, Chicago and London: University of Chicago Press.
Lacan, Jacques (2004), *The Four Fundamental Concepts of Psychoanalysis*, London and New York: Karnac.
Laetz, Brian and Dominic McIver Lopes (2009), 'Genre', in Paisley Livingston and

Carl Plantinga (eds), *The Routledge Companion to Film and Philosophy*, London: Routledge, pp. 152–61.

Lang, Brent (2014), 'Lisandro Alonso Named Lincoln Center Filmmaker in Residence', in *Variety*, 24 June, <http://variety.com/2014/film/news/lisandro-alonso-lincoln-center-1201245477/> (accessed 28 October 2016).

Langford, Barry (2010), *Film Genre: Hollywood and Beyond*, Edinburgh: Edinburgh University Press.

Langkjaer, Birger (2002), 'Realism and Danish Cinema', in Anne Jerslev (ed.), *Realism and 'reality' in Film and Media*, Copenhagen: Museum Tusculanum Press, University of Copenhagen, pp.15–40.

Lavine, T. Z. (1985), *From Socrates to Sartre: The Philosophic Quest*, New York: Bantam.

Lazzarato, Maurizio (2012), *The Making of the Indebted Man: an Essay on the Neoliberal Condition*, Cambridge MA: MIT Press.

Lewy, Guenter (2008), 'Introduction: Dostoyevsky's Proposition', in *If God Is Dead, Everything Is Permitted?* New Brunswick: Transaction Publishers.

Liehm, Antonin (1980), 'Milan Kundera: Czech Writer', in William Edward Harkin and Paul I. Trensky (eds), *Czech Literature since 1956: A Symposium*, New York: Bohemica.

Liehm, Mira and Antonin J. Liehm (1977), *The Most Important Art: Soviet and Eastern European Film After 1945*, Berkeley: University of California Press.

McArthur, Colin (1999), 'Mise-en-scène degree zero: Jean-Pierre Melville's *Le Samouraï* (1967)', in Susan Hayward and Ginette Vincendeau (eds), *French Film: Texts and Contexts*, London: Routledge, pp. 189–200.

McDonald, Tamar Jeffers (2013), *Romantic Comedy: Boy Meets Girl Meets Genre*, New York: Wallflower.

MacDougall, David (1998), *Transcultural cinema*, Princeton: Princeton University Press.

McGuire, William and Richard F. C. Hull (eds) [1959] (1977), 'The "Face to Face" Interview', in *C. G. Jung Speaking*, Princeton: Princeton University Press, pp. 424–39.

McKay, Ryan and Harvey Whitehouse (2015), 'Religion and Morality', in *Psychological Bulletin*, 141: 2 (March), p. 447.

Margulies, Ivone (1996), *Nothing Happens: Chantal Akerman's Hyperrealist Everyday*, Durham, NC: Duke University Press.

Marie, Michel (2003), *The French New Wave: an artistic school*, Malden, MA: Blackwell.

Martel, Frédéric (2001), 'France's Film Subsidy System', in *Correspondence: An International Review of Culture and Society*, 8 (Spring/Summer), p. 8.

Massino, Jill (2007), 'Women, Welfare and the Self in Post-Socialist Romania', in Angela Brintlinger and Natasha Kolchevska (eds), *Beyond Little Vera: Women's Bodies, Women's Welfare in Russia and Central/Eastern Europe*, Columbus: Ohio State University.

Mazierska, Ewa and Laura Rascaroli (2003), *From Moscow to Madrid: Postmodern Cities, European Cinema*, London: I. B. Tauris.

Meštrović, Stjepan (1994), *The Balkanization of the West: The Confluence of Postmodernism and Postcommunism*, New York: Routledge.

Metelmann, Jörg (2010), 'Fighting the Melodramatic Condition. Haneke's Polemics', in Roy Grundmann (ed.), *A Companion to Michael Haneke*, Chichester: Wiley-Blackwell, pp. 168–86.

Mihăilescu, Magda (2010), 'Tragedia realităţii violate', in Cristina Corciovescu and Magda Mihăilescu (eds), *Cele mai bune 10 filme româneşti ale tuturor timpurilor stabilite prin votul a 40 de critici*, Bucureşti: Polirom, pp. 10–7.

Miller, William (1915), 'The Balkans: Roumania, Bulgaria, Servia and Montenegro', *Bulletin of the American Geographical Society*, 47: 4, available at <www.jstor.org/stable/201494> (accessed 25 March 2014).
Mjagkova, Irina (1993), 'At Home amongst Wolves: A History of the Romanian Film 1946–1960', in *From Yalta to Malta*, Moscow: Isskustvo Publishing House, pp. 110–15.
Monk, Ray (2005), *How to Read Wittgenstein*. New York: W. W. Norton.
Morrey, Douglas (2008), 'Open Wounds: Body and Image in Jean-Luc Nancy and Claire Denis', *Film-Philosophy*, 12:1, pp. 10–30. <http://www.film-philosophy.com/2008v12n1/morrey2.pdf> (accessed 15 August 2015).
Mulaem, Shlomo (2017), 'Nonsense and Irony: Wittgenstein's Strategy of Self-refutation and Kierkegaard's Concept of Indirect Communication', in *Tópicos, Revista de Filosofía*, 53, pp. 203–27.
Mulvey, Laura (1975), 'Visual pleasure and the Narrative Cinema', *Screen*, 16: 3, Autumn, pp. 6–18, <https://wiki.brown.edu/confluence/display/MarkTribe/Visual+Pleasure+and+Narrative+Cinema> (accessed 15 August 2015).
Mulvey, Laura (2006), *Death 24 x a Second: Stillness and the Moving Image*, London: Reaktion Books.
Naficy, Hamid (2001), *An Accented Cinema: Exilic and Diasporic Filmmaking*, Princeton: Princeton University Press.
Nancy, Jean-Luc (2008), *Corpus*, New York: Fordham University Press.
Naremore, James (2010), 'Police, Adjective', in *Film Quarterly*, 63: 4, Summer, pp. 18–20.
Nasta, Dominique (1991), *Meaning in Film: Relevant Structures in Soundtrack and Narrative*, Bern: Peter Lang.
Nasta, Dominique (2007), 'The Tough Road to Minimalism: Contemporary Romanian Film Aesthetics', in *Kinokultura* (special issue on Romanian cinema), <http://www.kinokultura.com/specials/6/nasta.shtml> (accessed 25 August 2015).
Nasta, Dominique (2013), *Contemporary Romanian Cinema: The History of an Unexpected Miracle*, London, New York: Wallflower.
Nasta, Dominique (2014), 'Usages de la musique chez les cinéastes migrants et diasporiques', in *Musiques de Films: Nouveaux enjeux*, Bruxelles: Les Impressions nouvelles, pp. 60–71.
Neale, Steve (2002), 'Art Cinema as Institution', in Catherine Fowler (ed.), *The European Cinema Reader*, London: Routledge, pp. 103–20.
Nelson, Barbara A. (2009), 'Hollywood's struggle for Romania, 1938–1945', *Historical Journal of Film, Radio and Television*, 29: 3, pp. 295–319.
Nestingen, Andrew (2008), *Crime and Fantasy in Scandinavia: Fiction, Film, and Social Change*, Seattle: Washington University Press.
Newman, Kathleen (2010), 'Notes on Transnational Film Theory. Decentered Subjectivity, Decentered Capitalism', in Natasa Ďurovičová and Kathleen Newman (eds), *World Cinemas, Transnational Perspectives*, New York: Routledge.
Nietzsche, Friedrich (1984), *Human, All Too Human*, translated by Marion Faber and Stephen Lehmann, Harmondsworth: Penguin.
Nochimson, Martha P. (2010), *World on Film: An Introduction*, Chichester: Wiley-Blackwell.
Oleszczyk, Michal (2015), 'Redefinirea realismului', an interview with Michal Oleszczyk by Dana Duma, in *Film*, 1: 43.
Paech, Joachim (2000), *Artwork – Text – Medium: Steps en Route to Intermediality*, <http://www.uni-konstanz.de/FuF/Philo/LitWiss/MedienWiss/Texte/interm.html> (accessed 15 February 2011).
Palacio, Manuel (2013), 'The Hard Route to Europeanness. The Case of the Series Pepe

Carvalho', in Manuel Palacio and Jorg Türschmann (eds), *Transnational Cinema in Europe*, Munster: LIT Verlag.
Pasti, Vladimir (2003), *Ultima inegalitate: Relatiile de gen in Romania*, Iasi: Polirom.
Pavičić, Jurica (2011), *Postjugoslavenski film: stil i ideologija*, Zagreb: Hrvatski filmski savez.
Pârvulescu, Constantin (2009), 'The Cold World behind the Window: *4 Months, 3 Weeks and 2 Days* and Romanian Cinema's Return to Real-Existing Communism', *Jump Cut*, 51, < http://www.ejumpcut.org/archive/jc51.2009/4months/index.html> (accessed 6 March 2016).
Père, Olivier (2012), 'Why Romanian Cinema is Great', in *Olivier Père* blog, 19 July, <https://olivierpere.wordpress.com/2012/07/19/6660/> (accessed February 2018).
Pethő Ágnes (2003), *Múzsák tükre: Az intermedialitás és az önreflexió poétikája a filmben*, Miercurea Ciuc: Pro-Print.
Pethő Ágnes (2011), *Cinema and Intermediality: The Passion for the In-Between*, Newcastle upon Tyne: Cambridge Scholars Publishing.
Pethő, Ágnes (ed.) (2012), *Film in the Post-Media Age*, Newcastle upon Tyne: Cambridge Scholars Publishing.
Pethő, Ágnes (2015), '"Housing" a Deleuzian "Sensation": Notes on the Post-Cinematic Tableaux Vivants of Lech Majewski, Sharunas Bartas and Ihor Podolchak', in Ágnes Pethő (ed.), *The Cinema of Sensations*, Newcastle upon Tyne: Cambridge Scholars Publishing, pp. 155–85.
Pethő Ágnes (2015b), 'Between Absorption, Abstraction and Exhibition. Inflections of the Cinematic Tableau in the Films of Corneliu Porumboiu, Roy Andersson, and Joanna Hogg', in *Acta Universitatis Sapi-entiae: Film and Media Studies*, 10.
Peucker, Brigitte (2007), *The Material Image: Art and the Real in Film*, Stanford: Stanford University Press.
Pipolo, Tony (2010), *Robert Bresson: A Passion for Film*, New York: Oxford University Press.
Pisters, Patricia (2003), *The Matrix of Visual Culture: Working with Deleuze in Film Theory*, Stanford: Stanford University Press.
Poenaru, Florin (2014), 'Noul val din perspectiva colonială', in Andrei Gorzo and Andrei State (eds), *Politicile filmului: Contribuții la interpretarea cinemaului românesc contemporan*, Cluj-Napoca: Tact, pp.151–71.
Pop, Doru (2010), 'The Grammar of the New Romanian Cinema', *Acta Univ Sapientiae, Film and Media Studies*, 3, pp.19–40.
Pop, Doru (2012), 'What's Eating the Romanian "New Wave"?' *Ekphrasis*, 1, pp. 58–67.
Pop, Doru (2014), *Romanian New Wave Cinema: An Introduction*, Jefferson: McFarland.
Popescu, Cristian Tudor (2011), *Filmul surd în România mută, Politică și propagandă în filmul românesc de ficțiune (1912– 1989)*, București: Polirom.
Puiu, Cristi (2017), *Interview* (unpublished), by Christina Stojanova, March, Sofia.
Radovic, Milja (2014), *Transnational Cinema and Ideology: Representing Religion, Identity and Cultural Myths*, London: Routledge.
Rajewsky, Irina (2005), 'Intermediality, Intertextuality, and Remediation: A Literary Perspective on Intermediality', in *Intermédialités: histoire et théorie des arts, des lettres et des techniques*, 6, Montréal: Presses de l'Université de Montréal, pp. 43–64.
Riding, Alan (2007), 'The Cameras Were Ready, the Revolution Wasn't', *New York Times*, 3 June.
Ritzer, Ivo and Peter W. Schulze (2013), 'Genre Hybridisation. Global Cinematic Flows', in Ivo Ritzer and Peter W. Schulze (eds), *Genre Hybridisation: Global Cinematic Flows*, Marburg: Schüren Verlag, pp. 9–38.

Robin, Régine (1992), *Socialist Realism: An Impossible Aesthetic*, Stanford: Stanford University Press.
Rogozanu, Cristi (2012), 'Noul Cinema Românesc și lucruri care chiar nu pot fi spuse altfel', *Vox Publica: Realitatea.Net*, 24 November, <http://voxpublica.realitatea.net/politica-societate/noul-cinema-romanesc-si-lucruri-care-chiar-nu-pot-fi-spuse-altfel-87420.html> (accessed 15 March 2016).
Roman, Marina (2010), 'Priză directă la realitate', in Cristina Corciovescu and Magda Mihăilescu (eds), *Cele mai bune 10 filme românești ale tuturor timpurilor stabilite prin votula 40 de critici*, București: Polirom, pp. 170–7.
Rothman, William (1990), 'Virtue and Villainy in the Face of the Camera', in Carole Zucker (ed.), *Making Visible the Invisible: An Anthology of Original Essays on Film Acting*, Metuchen: The Scarecrow Press, pp. 28–43.
Rowland, Susan (2005), *Jung as a Writer*, New York and London: Routledge
Rus, Andrei and Gabriela Filippi (2014), 'Interviu: Căutările lui Corneliu Porumboiu', in *Film Menu*, 17 (November), <https://filmmenu.wordpress.com/2014/11/30/interviu-film-menu-corneliu-porumboiu/> (accessed 6 March 2016).
Schahadat, Schamma (2009), 'Postmodernism – Postcommunism. Literature from Eastern Europe between Two Cultures of Post', in *Translating Society* conference papers, <http://www.translating-society.de/conference/papers/3/> (accessed 25 August 2015).
Schoonover, Karl (2012), *Brutal Vision: The Neorealist Body in Postwar Italian Cinema*, Minneapolis: University of Minnesota Press.
Scott, A. O. (2008), 'In film, the Romanian New Wave has arrived', in *The New York Times*, 19 January, <https://www.nytimes.com/2008/01/19/arts/19iht-fromanian.1.9340722.html> (accessed January 2018).
Siegel, Amy (2003), 'Violations, Indiscretions and Narrative Expectation in Film Sound', in Larry Sider, Dianne Freeman and Jerry Sider (ed.), *Soundscape: The School of Sound lectures 1998–2001*, London: Wallflower, pp. 138–49.
Smith, Craig S. (2005), 'A Casualty on Romania's Road Back from Atheism', *New York Times*, 3 July, < http://www.nytimes.com/2005/07/03/world/europe/a-casualty-on-romanias-road-back-from-atheism.html?_r=0> (accessed 14 November 2016).
Smith, Jeff (1999), 'Movie Music as Moving Music: Emotion, Cognition and the Film Score' in Carl Platinga and Greg Smith (eds), *Passionate Views: Film, Cognition and Emotion*, Baltimore: John Hopkins Press, pp. 146–52.
Sobchack, Vivian (1991), *The Address of the Eye: A Phenomenology of Film Experience*, Berkeley: University of California Press.
Sontag, Susan (1969), *Against interpretation, and other essays*, New York: Dell.
Stanca, Adriana (2014), 'Topul filmelor românești care au adus cei mai mulți spectatori în sălile de cinema în ultimii cinci ani. Care este producția carea a vândut doar 3 bilete', in *Gândul*, 20 April, <http://www.gandul.info/magazin/topul-filmelor-romanesti-care-au-adus-cei-mai-multi-spectatori-in-salile-de-cinema-in-ultimii-cinci-ani-care-este-productia-care-a-vandut-doar-3-bilete-12414103> (accessed 28 October 2016).
Stanford Encyclopedia of Philosophy (2014), *Authenticity*, <https://plato.stanford.edu/entries/authenticity/index.html#note-2> (accessed May 2018).
Stevens, Anthony (1990), *On Jung*, London: Routledge.
Stewart, Garrett (1999), *Between Film and Screen: Modernism's Photo Synthesis*, Chicago: University of Chicago Press.
Steyerl, Hito (2009), 'In Defense of the Poor Image', in *E-flux Journal*, 10, pp. 1–9, <http://www.e-flux.com/journal/in-defense-of-the-poor-image/> (accessed 12 August 2015).

Stoil, Michael J. (1974) *Cinema beyond the Danube: The Camera and Politics*, Metuchen, NJ: The Scarecrow Press.
Stoil, Michael Jon (1982), *Balkan Cinema: Evolution after the Revolution*, Ann Arbor, MI: University of Michigan Research Press.
Stojanova, Christina (1998), 'Le film de genre américain dans le cinéma post-communiste: "Le Mafiosi Thriller"', in *Ciné-Bulles*, 17: 2, pp. 38–43, <https://www.erudit.org/culture/cb1068900/cb1119772/34363ac.pdf> (accessed May 2018).
Stojanova, Christina (1999), *The Eastern European Crisis of Self-Knowledge (1948–1989): The Relationship Between State and Society as Reflected in Eastern European Film – A Genre Approach*, Doctoral Dissertation, Montreal: Concordia University.
Stojanova, Christina (2000), 'Ars Longa, Politica Brevis', published as 'Ars Longa, Politica Brevis: A Kelet-Európai Mozi Legújabb Történetének Tengerentúli Vázlata', in *Filmkultura*, <www.filmkultura.hu/regi/2000/articles/essays/keleteuropa.hu.html> (accessed January 2017).
Stojanova, Christina (2005a), 'Beyond Dracula and Ceausescu: Phenomenology of Romanian Cinematic Horror', in Steven J. Schneider and Tony Williams (eds), *Horror International*, Detroit: Wayne State University Press, pp. 220–34.
Stojanova, Christina (2005b), 'Fragmented Discourses. Young Cinema from Central and Eastern Europe', in Anikó Imre (ed.), *East European Cinemas*, London and New York: Routledge, pp. 213–27.
Stojanova, Christina (2005c), 'Post-Communist Cinema: The Politics of Gender and Genre', in Linda Badley, R. Barton Palmer and Steven Schneider (eds), *Traditions in World Cinema*, Edinburgh: Edinburgh University Press, pp. 95–114.
Stojanova, Christina (2010), 'The New Vicissitudes of *Auteur* Cinema in Central and Eastern European Cinema: Karlovy Vary 2010', *KinoKultura*, 30, <http://www.kinokultura.com/2010/30-stojanova.shtml> (accessed 15 March 2016).
Stojanova, Christina (2013a), 'The Damnation of Labor in the Films of Béla Tarr', in Ewa Mazierska (ed.), *Work in Cinema: Labor and the Human Condition*, New York: Palgrave Macmillan, pp. 169–87.
Stojanova, Christina (2013b), 'Ethics is the New Aesthetics', in *Close Up: Film and Media Studies*, 1: 2, pp. 22–40.
Stojanova, Christina (2016), 'Eticul, răul şi urâtul şi cei prinşi la mijloc: Note despre trei filme româneşti din NCR la TIFF', in *Film: Revistă trimestrială de cinema a Uniunii Cineaştilor din România*, 3: 13, pp. 37–41.
Stojanova, Christina and Dana Duma (2007) (eds), *Kinokultura*, Special Issue 6: Romanian Cinema, May, <http://www.kinokultura.com/specials/6/romanian.shtml> (accessed December 2016).
Stojanova, Christina and Dana Duma (2012), 'New Romanian Cinema between the Tragic and the Ironic', in *Film International*, 10: 1, pp. 7–21.
Strausz, László (2017), *Hesitant Histories on the Romanian Screen*, Basingstoke: Palgrave Macmillan.
Stringer, Julian (1997), '"Your Tender Smiles Give Me Strength": Paradigms of Masculinity in John Woo's *A Better Tomorrow* and *The Killer*', in *Screen*, 38: 1, pp 25–41.
Suleiman, Susan R. (1992), *Authoritarian Fictions: The Ideological Novel as a Literary Genre*, Princeton: Princeton University Press.
Suner, Asuman (2010), *New Turkish Cinema: Belonging, Identity and Memory*, London: I. B. Tauris.
Szabados, Béla and Christina Stojanova (eds) (2011), *Wittgenstein at the Movies: Cinematic Investigations*, Lanham: Lexington Books.
Şerban, Alex Leo (2006), *De ce vedem filme?* Bucharest: Polirom.

Șerban, Alex Leo (2010), 'Romanian Cinema: From Modernity to Neo-Realism', *Film Criticism*, 34: 2/3, pp. 2–21.
Ștefănescu, Bogdan and Sanda Foamete (2013), 'Narratives of the Emerging Self: Romania's First Years of Post-totalitarian Cinema', in Catherine Portuges and Peter Hames (eds), *Cinemas in Transition in Central and Eastern Europe after 1989*, Philadelphia: Temple University Press, pp. 161–96.
Thompson, Kristin (1977), 'The Concept of Cinematic Excess', *Ciné-Tracts: A Journal of Film, Communications, Culture and Politics*, 1: 2, 54–64, <http://library.brown.edu/cds/cinetracts/CT02.pdf> (accessed 24 August 2015).
Thompson, Kristin and D. Bordwell (2002), *Film History: An Introduction* (second edn), New York: McGraw-Hill.
Todorova, Maria (1997), *Imagining the Balkans*, New York: Oxford University Press.
Trocan, Irina (2011), *Andy Warhol și alte suprafețe*, in *Film Menu*, 13 (December), Bucharest: UNATC Press, pp. 49–52.
Truffaut, François (1954), 'A Certain Tendency of the French Cinema', *Cahiers du Cinéma*, 1 in English (originally published in French in *Cahiers du Cinéma*, 31), available at <www.newwavefilm.com/about/a-certain-tendency-of-french-cinema-truffaut.shtml> (accessed 23 September 2018).
Turcuș, Claudiu (2014), 'Receptarea Noului Cinema Românesc și Aurora lui Cristi Puiu', in Andrei Gorzo and Andrei State (eds), *Politicile filmului: Contribuții la interpretarea cinemaului românesc contemporan*, Cluj-Napoca: Editura Tact, pp. 281–98.
Țuțui, Marian (2011), *O scurtă istorie a filmului românesc /A Short History of Romanian Cinema*, Bucharest: Noi Media Print.
Uricaru, Ioana (2008), 'Dopo la Rivoluzione: media, cinema e campionatura storiografica', in Nicoleta Neșu (ed.), *Romania Culturale Oggi – Quaderni di Romania Orientale*, Roma: Bagatto Libri, pp. 393–401.
Uricaru, Ioana (2012), 'Follow the money: financing contemporary cinema in Romania', in Anikó Imre (ed.), *A Companion to Eastern European Cinemas*, Hoboken: Wiley-Blackwell, pp. 427–53.
Uroskie, Andrew V. (2014), *Between the Black Box and the White Cube: Expanded Cinema and Postwar Art*, Chicago, London: University of Chicago Press.
Vincze, Teréz (2013), *Szerző a tükörben: Szerzőiség és önreflexivitás a filmművészetben*, Budapest: Kijárat Kiadó.
Virginás, Andrea (2011), 'New Filmic Waves in Hungarian and Romanian Cinema: Allegories or Stories about Flesh?', *Acta Universitatis Sapientiae: Film and Media Studies Journal*, 4, pp. 131–41.
Virginás, Andrea (2016), 'Funding un/popular films in Hungary and Romania: a recent history', in Jana Dudková and Katarina Mišíková (eds), *Transformation Processes and New Screen Media Technologies*, Bratislava: Academy of Performing Arts, Institute of Theatre and Film Research, The Slovak Academy of Sciences.
Voinescu, Sever (2008), 'Nae Caranfil, un maximalist – *Restul e tăcere*', <http://agenda.liternet.ro/articol/7549/Alex-Leo-Serban-Sever-Voinescu/Nae-Caranfil-un-maximalist-Restul-e-tacere.html> (accessed 25 August 2015).
Volčič, Zala (2005), 'The Notion of the "West" in the Serbian National Imaginary', *European Journal of Cultural Studies*, 8: 2, pp. 155–75.
Von Franz, Marie-Louise (1987), *C. G. Jung Speaking: Interviews and Encounters*, Princeton: Princeton University Press.
Von Franz, Marie-Louise (1995), *Shadow and Evil in Fairy Tales*, Boston and London: Shambhala.
Von Franz, Marie-Louise (1993), *Psychotherapy*, Boston and London: Shambhala.
Weissberg, Jay (2012), 'Review: "Sofia's Last Ambulance"', *Variety*, 25 May, < http://

variety.com/2012/film/markets-festivals/sofia-s-last-ambulance-1117947641/> (accessed 28 March 2016).
Weissberg, Jay (2015), *The World Is Mine*, <http://variety.com/2015/film/festivals/the-world-is-mine-review-1201534720> (accessed 12 August 2015).
White, Jerry (2004), 'National Belonging', in *New Review of Film and Television Studies*, 2: 2, pp. 211–32.
White, Rob (2010), 'Cristi Puiu Discusses Aurora', *Film Quarterly*, 64: 2, pp. 4–7.
Williams, Linda (2014), *On the Wire*, Durham: Duke University Press.
Wittgenstein, Ludwig (1984), *Culture and Value*, Chicago: University of Chicago Press.
Wittgenstein, Ludwig (2015 [1922]), *Logico-Philosophicus*, <http://people.umass.edu/klement/tlp/> (accessed May 2018).
Wolff, Larry (1994), *Inventing Eastern Europe: The Map of Civilization on the Mind of the Enlightenment*, Palo Alto: Stanford University Press.
Wolf, Werner (2002), 'Intermediality Revisited: Reflections on Word and Music Relations in the Context of a General Typology of Intermediality', in Suzanne M. Lodato, Suzanne Aspden and Walter Bernhart (eds), *Essays in Honor of Steven Paul Scher and on Cultural Identity and the Musical Stage*, Amsterdam and New York: Rodopi, pp. 13–34.
Young, Benjamin (2004), 'On Media and Democratic Politics: Videograms of a Revolution', in Thomas Elsaesser (ed.), *Harun Farocki: Working on the Sightlines*, Amsterdam: Amsterdam University Press, pp. 245–60.
Zeitchik, Steven (2010), 'Cannes 2010: Those Romanians are at it again', *Los Angeles Times Blogs*, 13 May, <http://latimesblogs.latimes.com/movies/2010/05/cannes-film-festival-romanian-tuesday-after-christmas.html> (accessed 20 August 2015)
Zinoviev, Alexander (1986), *Homo Sovieticus*, Boston, New York: The Atlantic Monthly Press.
Žižek, Slavoj (1996), 'I Hear You with My Eyes, or The Invisible Master', in Renata Saleci and Slavoj Žižek (eds), *Gaze and Voice as Love Objects*, Durham: Duke University Press, 90–5.
Žižek, Slavoj (2002), *Welcome to the Desert of the Real! Five Essays on September 11 and Related Dates*, London and New York: Verso.

FILMOGRAPHY OF THE NEW ROMANIAN CINEMA

Sundays on Leave (*E pericoloso sporgersi*), Romania/France, 1993. Director and screenplay: Nae Caranfil; Cinematography: Cristian Comeagă; Actors: Marius Florea Vizante, Coca Bloos. **Critics Award,** Montpellier Mediterranean Film Festival, 1993

Asphalt Tango (*Asfalt tango*), Romania/France, 1996. Director: Nae Caranfil; Screenplay: Nae Caranfil, Stephan Levine; Cinematography: Cristian Comeagă; Actors: Charlotte Rampling, Mircea Diaconu, Ion Fiscuteanu

The Firemen's Choir (*Corul pompierilor*), Romania, 2000 (**short**). Director and screenplay: Cristian Mungiu; Cinematography: Oleg Mutu; Actors: Doru Ana, Mircea Diaconu, Valeriu Andriuță

Stuff and Dough (*Marfa și banii*), Romania, 2001. Director: Cristi Puiu; Screenplay Răzvan Rădulescu, Cinematography: Silviu Stavilă; Actors: Alexandru Papadopol, Dragoș Bucur, Luminița Gheorghiu, Răzvan Vasilescu. **Special Jury Award,** Cottbus, 2001

Everyday God Kisses Us on the Mouth (*În fiecare zi Dumnezeu ne sărută pe gură*), Romania, 2001. Director: Sinișa Dragin, Screenplay: Ioan Cărmăzan, Sinișa Dragin; Cinematography: Alexandru Solomon; Actors: Dan Condurache, Horațiu Mălăele, Ana Ciontea. **Grand Prix Tiger Award,** Rotterdam, 2002

Occident, Romania, 2002. Director and screenplay: Cristian Mungiu, Cinematography: Vivi Drăgan Vasile; Actors: Alexandru Papadopol, Dorel Vișan, Coca Bloos, Gabriel Spahiu, Doru Ana, Tora Vasilescu. **Grand Prix and Titra Prize,** Mons Film Festival, 2003

The Rage (*Furia*), Romania, 2002. Director: Radu Muntean; Screenplay: Ileana Constantin, Radu Muntean, Mircea Stăiculescu; Cinematography: Vivi Drăgan Vasile; Actors: Dragoș Bucur, Dorina Chiriac, Andi Vasluianu. **Romanian Union of Filmmakers Award for Best Actor** (Dragoș Bucur), 2003

Philanthropy (*Filantropica*), Romania, 2002. Director and screenplay: Nae Caranfil;

Cinematography: Vivi Drăgan Vasile; Actors: Mircea Diaconu, Gheorghe Dinică, Mara Nicolescu. **Special Jury Prize**, Wiesbaden, 2002

C Block Story (Poveste de la scara C), Romania, 2003 (**short**). Director and screenplay: Cristian Nemescu; Cinematography: Liviu Marghidan; Actors: Lucian Ciurariu, Maria Dinulescu. **Special Mention** at the Berlin InterFilm Festival, 2003

Maria, Romania 2003. Director: Peter Călin Netzer, Screenplay: Gordan Mihic, Peter Călin Netzer; Cinematography: Mihail Sarbusca; Actors: Diana Dumbravă, Horațiu Mălăele, Luminița Gheorghiu, Șerban Ionescu. **Jury's Special Award**, Best Actress (Diana Dumbravă) and Best Actor (Șerban Ionescu), Locarno, 2003

Niki and Flo (Niki Ardelean, colonel în rezervă), Romania/France, 2003. Director: Lucian Pintilie, Screenplay: Cristi Puiu, Razvan Radulescu, Cinematography: Silviu Stavilă, Actors: Victor Rebengiuc, Razvan Vasilescu, Coca Bloos

Traffic (Trafic), Romania, 2004 (**short**). Director: Cătălin Mitulescu; Screenplay: Cătălin Mitulescu, Andreea Vălean; Cinematography: Marius Panduru; Actors: Maria Dinulescu, Andi Vasluianu, Bogdan Dumitrache. **Palme d'Or for Shorts**, Cannes Film Festival, 2004

Coffee and Cigarettes (Un cartuș de Kent și un pachet de cafea), Romania, 2004 (**short**). Director and screenplay: Cristi Puiu; Cinematography: Oleg Mutu; Actors: Victor Rebengiuc, Mimi Brănescu. **Golden Bear**, Berlin Film Festival, 2004

A Trip to the City (Călătorie la oraș), Romania, 2004 (**short**). Director and screenplay: Corneliu Porumboiu, Cinematography: Bogdan Tălpeanu; Actors: Constantin Diță, Ion Săpdaru. **Best Short Film**, Karlovy Vary International Film Festival, 2004

The Apartment (Apartamentul) Romania, 2004 (**short**). Director and screenplay: Constantin Popescu; Cinematography: Mihai Malaimare Jr; Actors: Laura Ilica, Dana Nedelcu, Nicodim Ungureanu. **Best Script**, Anonimul International Independent Film Festival 2004

The Death of Mr Lăzărescu (Moartea domnului Lăzărescu), Romania 2005. Director: Cristi Puiu; Screenplay Răzvan Rădulescu, Cristi Puiu; Cinematography: Oleg Mutu; Actors: Ion Fiscuteanu, Luminița Gheorghiu, Gabriel Spahiu. **Best Film, Un Certain Regard – A Certain Talent Prize**, Cannes Film Festival, 2005

Ryna, Romania, 2005. Director: Ruxandra Zenide; Screenplay: Marek Epstein, Andreea Valean, Ruxandra Zenide; Cinematography: Marius Panduru; Actors: Dorotheea Petre, Valentin Popescu. **Special Jury Award**, Cottbus, 2005

The Tube with a Hat (Lampa cu căciulă), Romania, 2006 (**short**). Director: Radu Jude; Screenplay: Florin Lăzărescu; Cinematography: Marius Panduru; Actors: Gabriel Spahiu, Marian Bratu. **Best International Short**, Sundance Film Festival, 2007

Marilena from P7 (Marilena de la P7), Romania, 2006. Director: Cristian Nemescu; Screenplay: Cristian Nemescu, Tudor Voican; Cinematography: Andrei Butică, Liviu Marghidan; Actors: Mădălina Ghițescu, Gabriel Spahiu, Andi Vasluianu. **Best Short Film, Audience Award**, Transylvania International Film Festival, 2006

12:08 East of Bucharest (A fost sau n-a fost), Romania, 2006. Director and screenplay: Corneliu Porumboiu, Cinematography: Marius Panduru; Actors: Mircea Andreescu, Teodor Corban, Ion Săpdaru, Luminița Gheorghiu. **Camera d'Or**, Cannes 2006

How I Spent the End of the World (Cum mi-am petrecut sfârșitul lumii), Romania, 2006. Director: Cătălin Mitulescu; Screenplay: Cătălin Mitulescu, Andreea Vălean; Cinematography: Marius Panduru; Actors: Dorotheea Petre, Mircea Diaconu, Bogdan Dumitrache. **Best Actress** (Dorotheea Petre), **Un Certain Regard – A Certain Talent Prize**, Cannes Film Festival, 2006

The Paper Will Be Blue (Hârtia va fi albastră), Romania, 2006. Director: Radu Muntean; Screenplay: Răzvan Rădulescu, Radu Muntean, Alexandru Baciu; Cinematography: Tudor Lucaciu; Actors: Paul Ipate, Dragoș Bucur, Andi Vasluianu, Ion Sapdaru. **Best Direction Award**, Cottbus, 2006

Love Sick (*Legături bolnăvicioase*), Romania, 2006. Director: Tudor Giurgiu; Screenplay: Răzvan Rădulescu, Cecilia Ştefănescu; Cinematography: Alexandru Sterian; Actors: Maria Popistaşu, Ioana Barbu, Tudor Chirilă. **Grand Prix for Photography**, Montreal International Film Festival, 2006

Waves (*Valuri*), Romania, 2007 (**short**). Director and screenplay: Adrian Sitaru; Cinematography: Adrian Silişteanu; Actors: Clara Vodă, Adrian Titieni, Şerban Pavlu. **Best Short**, Las Palmas Film Festival, 2009

A Good Day for a Swim (*O zi bună de plajă*), Romania, 2007 (**short**). Director: Bogdan Mustaţă; Screenplay: Cătălin Mitulescu; Cinematography: Barbu Bălăşoiu; Actors: Florin Sinescu, Okan Kaya. **Golden Bear**, Berlin Film Festival, 2007

4 Months, 3 Weeks and 2 Days (*4 luni, 3 săptămâni şi 2 zile*), Romania, 2007, Director: Cristian Mungiu; Screenplay: Cristian Mungiu, Răzvan Rădulescu; Cinematography: Oleg Mutu; Actors: Anamaria Marinca, Vlad Ivanov, Luminiţa Gheorghiu. **Palme d'Or and International Critics Prize, FIPRESCI**, Cannes Film Festival, 2007

California Dreamin', Romania, 2007. Director: Cristian Nemescu; Screenplay: Cristian Nemescu, Tudor Voican; Cinematography: Liviu Marghidan; Actors: Răzvan Vasilescu, Maria Dinulescu, Andi Vasluianu, Gabriel Spahiu. **Grand Prix, Un Certain Regard – A Certain Talent Prize**, Cannes Film Festival, 2007

Hooked aka *Angling* (*Pescuit sportiv*), Romania, 2008. Director and screenplay: Adrian Sitaru; Cinematography: Adrian Silişteanu; Actors: Adrian Titieni, Ioana Flora, Maria Dinulescu. **Special Jury Award** (Silver Alexander) and **Best Actress (ex-aequo)** (Maria Dinulescu and Ioana Flora), Thessaloniki Film Festival, 2008

Summer Holiday aka *Boogie*, Romania, 2008. Director: Radu Muntean; Screenplay: Radu Muntean, Alexandru Baciu, Răzvan Rădulescu; Cinematography: Tudor Lucaciu; Actors: Dragoş Bucur, Anamaria Marinca, Mimi Brănescu. **Gopo Awards** for Best Director, Best Actor (Dragoş Bucur) and Best Actress (Anamaria Marinca), Romania, 2009

The Happiest Girl in the World (*Cea mai fericită fată din lume*), Romania, 2009. Director: Radu Jude; Screenplay: Radu Jude, Augustina Stanciu; Cinematography: Marius Panduru; Actors: Şerban Pavlu, Andi Vasluianu, Andreea Bosneag. **CICAE Award**, Forum, Berlin International Film Festival, 2009

The Other Irina (*Cealaltă Irina*), Romania, 2009. Director: Andrei Gruzsnitki; Screenplay: Andrei Gruzsnitki, Ileana Muntean, Mircea Stăiculescu; Cinematography: Vivi Drăgan Vasile; Actors: Andi Vasluianu, Vlad Ivanov, Gabriel Spahiu, Dragoş Bucur. **Best Romanian Film**, Transylvanian International Film Festival, 2009

Police, Adjective (*Poliţist, adjectiv*), Romania, 2009. Director and screenplay: Corneliu Porumboiu; Cinematography: Marius Panduru; Actors: Dragoş Bucur, Vlad Ivanov. **FIPRESCI** and **Un Certain Regard – A Certain Talent Prize**, Cannes Film Festival, 2009

Medal of Honor (*Medalia de onoare*), Romania, 2009. Director: Călin Peter Netzer; Screenplay: Tudor Voican; Cinematography: Liviu Mărghidan; Actors: Victor Rebengiuc, Mimi Brănescu, Gabriel Spahiu. **Jury's Special Award** (Silver Alexander), **FIPRESCI Award, Best Screenplay, Best Actor** (Victor Rebengiuc), Thessaloniki Film Festival, 2009

Francesca, Romania, 2009. Director and screenplay: Bobby Păunescu; Cinematography: Andrei Butică; Actors: Monica Bârlădeanu, Dorian Boguţă, Luminiţa Gheorghiu, Doru Ana, Theodor Corban, Gabriel Spahiu. **FIPRESCI Prize**, Gijon International Film Festival, 2009

First of All, Felicia (*Felicia, înainte de toate*), Romania/France/Croatia/Belgium, 2009. Director and screenplay: Răzvan Rădulescu and Melissa de Raaf; Cinematographer: Tudor Lucaciu; Actors: Ozana Oancea, Vasile Mentzel, Ileana Cernat. **Best Screenplay, Best Actress** (Ozana Oancea), Transylvanian International Film Festival 2010

Tales from the Golden Age (Amintiri din epoca de aur), Romania/France, 2009. Screenplay: Cristian Mungiu; Directors: Hanno Höfer; Razvan Marculescu; Cristian Mungiu; Constantin Popescu; Ioana Uricaru; Cinematography: Liviu Marghidan; Oleg Mutu; Alexandru Sterian; Actors: Teodor Corban, Vlad Ivanov, Gabriel Spahiu. **Best Film**, Gopo Sound and Audience Awards Romania, 2010

The Cage (Colivia), Romania, 2010 (short). Director and screenplay: Adrian Sitaru; Cinematography: Adrian Silişteanu; Actors: Clara Vodă, Adrian Titieni. **DAAD Award for Short Films**, Berlin Film Festival, 2010

Lord, Romania, 2010 (short). Director and screenplay: Adrian Sitaru; Cinematography: Adrian Silişteanu; Actors: Sergiu Costache, Andreea Samson. **Bayard d'Or Award**, Namur Film Festival, 2010

Oxygen (Oxigen), Romania, 2010 (short). Director and screenplay: Adina Pintilie; Cinematography: Marius Iacob; Actors: Cezar Antal; Adriana Mocca; Gabriel Spahiu. Nominated Best Documentary, Jihlava International Film Festival, 2011

Aurora, Romania/France/Switzerland/Germany, 2010. Director and screenplay: Cristi Puiu; Cinematography: Viorel Serghovici; Actors: Cristi Puiu, Clara Vodă; Luminiţa Gheorghiu. **East of West Award and Crystal Globe** (Best Cinematography), Karlovy Vary International Film Festival, 2010

Tuesday, After Christmas (Marţi după Crăciun), Romania, 2010. Director: Radu Muntean; Screenplay: Radu Muntean, Alexandru Baciu, Răzvan Rădulescu; Cinematography: Tudor Lucaciu; Actors: Mimi Brănescu, Mirela Oprişor, Maria Popistaşu, Dragoş Bucur. **Grand Prix Asturias** (Best Film), Best Actor (Mimi Brănescu), Best Actress – ex-aequo (Maria Popistaşu, Mirela Oprişor), Gijon International Film Festival, 2010

If I Want to Whistle, I Whistle (Eu când vreau să fluier, fluier), Romania/Sweden/ Germany, 2010. Director: Florin Şerban; Screenplay: Cătălin Mitulescu, Florin Şerban; Cinematography: Marius Panduru; Actors: George Piştereanu, Ada Condeescu, Clara Vodă. **Alfred Bauer Award**, Silver Bear (Jury Grand Prix), Berlin Film Festival, 2010

Morgen, Romania/France/Hungary, 2010. Director and screenplay: Marian Crişan; Cinematography: Tudor Mircea; Actors: András Hatházi, Yilmaz Yalcin, Elvira Rîmbu. **Don Quijote Award, Ecumenical Jury and Special Jury Prize**, Locarno International Film Festival, 2010

Outbound (Periferic), Romania/Austria, 2010. Director: Bogdan George Apetri; Screenplay: Bogdan George Apetri, Cristian Mungiu, Ioana Uricaru, Tudor Voican; Cinematography: Marius Panduru; Actors: Ana Ularu, Andi Vasluianu, Ioana Flora, Mimi Brănescu, Ion Săpdaru. **Golden Alexander** (Bogdan George Apetri), Best Actress (Ana Ularu), Hellenic Association of Film Critics Award, Thessaloniki International Film Festival, 2010

Principles of Life (Principii de viaţă), Romania, 2010. Director: Constantin Popescu; Screenplay: Alexandru Baciu, Răzvan Rădulescu; Cinematography: Liviu Marghidan; Actors: Vlad Ivanov, Rodica Lazăr. **Best Director**, Transylvanian International Film Festival, 2011

Silent River (Apele tac), Romania/Germany, 2011 (short). Director: Anca Miruna Lăzărescu; Screenplay: Bianca Oana, Anca Miruna Lăzărescu; Cinematography: Christian Stangassinger; Actors: Andi Vasluianu, Cuzin Toma. **Best Short Film**, Gopo Awards, Bucharest, 2012

Best Intentions (Din dragoste cu cele mai bune intenţii), Romania/Hungary/France, 2011. Director and screenplay: Adrian Sitaru; Cinematography: Adrian Silişteanu, Mihai Silişteanu; Actors: Bogdan Dumitrache, Adrian Titieni, Clara Vodă. **Best Director, Best Actor** (Bogdan Dumitrache), Locarno International Film Festival, 2011

Loverboy, Romania/Sweden/Serbia, 2011. Director: Cătălin Mitulescu; Screenplay:

Cătălin Mitulescu, Bogdan Mustață, Bianca Oana; Cinematography: Marius Panduru; Actors: George Piștereanu, Ada Condeescu, Clara Vodă. **Heart of Sarajevo – Best Actress** (Ada Condeescu), Sarajevo International Film Festival, 2011

Adalbert's Dream (*Visul lui Adalbert*), Romania, 2011. Director: Gabriel Achim; Screenplay: Gabriel Achim, Cosmin Manolache; Cinematography: George Chiper; Actors: Gabriel Spahiu, Doru Ana, Ozana Oancea. **Best First Feature Film**, Gopo Awards, 2013

Rocker, Romania/Germany/France, 2012. Director and screenplay: Marian Crișan, Cinematography: Tudor Mircea; Actors: Dan Chiorean, Alin State, Ofelia Popii. **Best Actor** (Dan Chiorean), **New Names Competition**, Vilnius International Film Festival, 2013

Beyond the Hills (*După dealuri*), Romania/France/Belgium, 2012. Director and screenplay: Cristian Mungiu; Cinematography: Oleg Mutu; Actors: Cosmina Stratan, Cristina Flutur, Luminița Gheorghiu, Teodor Corban. **Best Screenplay, Best Actress** (Cosmina Stratan, Cristina Flutur), Cannes International Film Festival, 2012

Everybody in Our Family (*Toată lumea din familia noastră*), Romania/Netherlands, 2012. Director: Radu Jude; Screenplay: Radu Jude, Corina Sabău; Cinematography: Andrei Butică; Actors: Șerban Pavlu, Gabriel Spahiu, Sofia Nicolaescu. **Heart of Sarajevo – Best Film**, Sarajevo International Film Festival, 2012

Of Snails and Men (*Despre oameni și melci*), Romania, 2012. Director: Tudor Giurgiu; Screenplay: Ionuț Teianu; Cinematography: Vivi Drăgan Vasile; Actors: Andi Vasluianu, Monica Bârlădeanu, Dorel Vișan. **Special Jury Award** (Tudor Giurgiu), Warsaw International Film Festival, 2012

Domestic, Romania/Germany, 2012. Director and screenplay: Adrian Sitaru; Cinematography: Adrian Silișteanu; Actors: Adrian Titieni, Ioana Flora, Clara Voda. **Best Art Direction**, Gopo Awards, 2014

I'm an Old Communist Hag (*Sunt o babă comunistă*), Romania, 2013. Director: Stere Gulea; Screenplay: Stere Gulea, Vera Ion, Lucian Dan Teodorovici Cinematography: Vivi Dragan Vasile; Actors: Luminița Gheorghiu, Marian Râlea, Ana Ularu. **Nominated in three categories, Gopo Awards**, 2013

The Escape (*Quod erat demonstrandum*), Romania, 2013. Director and screenplay: Andrei Gruzsniczki, Cinematography: Vivi Dragan Vasile; Actors: Sorin Leoveanu, Ofelia Popii, Florin Piersic Jr, Tora Vasilecu. **Golden Taiga (Best Film)**, Spirit of Fire Debut Film Festival, Russia, 2014

Child's Pose (*Poziția copilului*), Romania, 2013. Director: Călin Peter Netzer; Screenplay: Răzvan Rădulescu, Călin Peter Netzer; Cinematography: Andrei Butică; Actors: Luminița Gheorghiu, Bogdan Dumitrache, Vlad Ivanov, Ilinca Goia, Mimi Brănescu. **Golden Bear, FIPRESCI Award**, Berlin International Film Festival, 2013

When Evening Falls on Bucharest, or Metabolism (*Când se lasă seara peste București sau Metabolism*), Romania/France, 2013. Director and screenplay: Corneliu Porumboiu; Cinematography: Tudor Mircea; Actors: Bogdan Dumitrache, Diana Avrămuț, Alexandru Papadopol, Mihaela Sârbu. **Nominated for the Golden Leopard**, Locarno International Film Festival, 2013

It Can Pass through the Wall (*Trece și prin perete*), Romania, 2014 (**short**). Director: Radu Jude; Cinematography: Marius Panduru; Actors: Gabriel Spahiu, Sofia Nicolaescu. **Best Short**, Gopo Awards Bucharest 2015

The Japanese Dog (*Câinele japonez*), Romania, 2013. Director: Tudor Cristian Jurgiu; Screenplay: Ioan Antoci, Tudor Cristian Jurgiu; Cinematography: Vivi Dragan Vasile; Actors: Victor Rebengiuc, Șerban Pavlu, Laurentiu Lazar. **Best Film (New Names Competition)**, Vilnius International Film Festival, 2014

The Second Game (*Al doilea joc*), Romania, 2014. Director and screenplay: Corneliu

Porumboiu; Actors: Corneliu Porumboiu, Adrian Porumboiu. **Best Romanian Feature Film**, Transylvania International Film Festival, 2014

One Floor Below (*Un etaj mai jos*), Romania/Sweden/France/Germany, 2015. Director: Radu Muntean; Screenplay: Alexandru Baciu, Radu Muntean, Răzvan Rădulescu; Cinematography: Tudor Lucaciu; Actors: Teodor Corban, Ioana Flora, Vlad Ivanov. **Best Actor** (Teodor Corban), **Best Screenplay**, Seville European Film Festival, 2015

The Treasure (*Comoara*), Romania/France, 2015. Director and screenplay: Corneliu Porumboiu; Cinematography: Tudor Mircea; Actors: Toma Cuzin, Adrian Purcărescu. **Un Certain Regard – A Certain Talent Prize**, Cannes Film Festival, 2015

Graduation (*Bacalaureat*), Romania/France/Belgium, 2015. Director and screenplay: Cristian Mungiu; Cinematography: Tudor Panduru; Actors: Adrian Titieni, Maria Drăguş, Lia Bugnar, Vlad Ivanov. **Best Director**, Cannes Film Festival, 2015

Aferim!, Romania/Bulgaria/France/Czech Republic, 2015. Director: Radu Jude; Screenplay: Radu Jude, Florin Lăzărescu; Cinematography: Marius Panduru; Actors: Teodor Corban, Toma Cuzin, Luminiţa Gheorghiu, Victor Rebengiuc, Şerban Pavlu, Gabriel Spahiu. **Silver Bear (Best Director)**, Berlin International Film Festival, 2015

Horizon (*Orizont*), Romania, 2015. Director and screenplay: Marian Crişan; Cinematography: Oleg Mutu; Actors: András Hatházi, Rodica Lazar, Zsolt Bogdán. **Best Music, Romanian Union of Filmmakers Award**, 2015

The Last Day (*Ultima zi*), Romania, 2016. Director: Gabriel Achim; Screenplay: Gabriel Achim, Cosmin Manolache; Cinematography: George Chiper; Actors: Doru Ana, Mimi Brănescu. **Best Romanian Feature Film**, Transylvania International Film Festival 2016

Sieranevada, Romania/France/Bosnia-Herzegovina/Croatia/Republic of Macedonia, 2016. Director and screenplay: Cristi Puiu; Cinematography: Barbu Bălăşoiu; Actors: Mimi Brănescu, Bogdan Dumitrache. **Best Feature Film, Best Director**, Chicago International Film Festival, 2016

Dogs (*Câini*), Romania/France/Bulgaria/Qatar, 2016. Director and screenplay: Bogdan Mirică; Cinematography: Andrei Butică; Editing: Roxana Szel; Actors: Dragoş Bucur, Gheorghe Vişu, Vlad Ivanov. **FIPRESCI Prize, Un Certain Regard – A Certain Talent Prize**, Cannes International Film Festival, 2016

Ana, mon amour, Romania/Germany/France, 2017. Director: Călin Peter Netzer; Screenplay: Călin Peter Netzer, Cezar Paul-Bădescu, Iulia Lumânare; Cinematography: Andrei Butică; Actors: Diana Cavallioti, Mircea Postelnicu. **Silver Bear – Outsanding Artistic Contribution** (Dana Bunescu, editor), Berlin International Film Festival 2017

Pororoca, Romania/France, 2017. Director and screenplay: Constantin Popescu; Cinematography: Liviu Marghidan; Cast: Bogdan Dumitrache, Iulia Lumanare, Constantin Dogioiu. **Best Actor** (Bogdan Dumitrache), East–West Golden Arch, Eurasian Film Award, Moscow, 2018

I Do Not Care If We Go Down in History as Barbarians (*Îmi este indiferent dacă în istorie vom intra ca barbari*), 2018. Director and screenplay: Radu Jude; Cinematography: Marius Panduru; Editing: Cătălin Cristuţiu; Cast: Gabriel Spahiu, Şerban Pavlu. **Crystal Globe (Best Film)**, Karlovy Vary International Film Festival, 2018

GENERAL FILMOGRAPHY

2001: A Space Odyssey, Stanley Kubrick, UK/USA: Metro-Goldwyn-Mayer (MGM), Stanley Kubrick Productions, 1968.
The Actor and the Savages (*Actorul și sălbaticii*), Manole Marcus, Romania: Casa de filme 4, 1975.
Adela, Mircea Veroiu. Romania: Casa de filme 4, 1985.
The Afternoon of a Torturer (*După-amiaza unui torționar*), Lucian Pintilie, France/Romania/Gabon: Filmex, YMC Productions, 2001.
After the Day Before (*Másnap*), Attila Janisch, Hungary: Euròfilm Stúdió, 2004.
After the End of the World (*Sled kraja na sveta*), Ivan Nitchev, Bulgaria/Germany/Greece: BNT, Hellenic Radio and Television, Marathon Films, Meta BM-4, Saxonia Media Filmproduktion, 1998.
Alarm in the Mountains (*Alarmă în munți*), Dinu Negreanu, Romania: Studioul cinematografic București, 1955.
All Quiet on the Western Front, Lewis Milestone, USA: Universal Pictures, 1930.
Amour, Michael Haneke, Austria/France/Germany: Les Films du Losange, X-Filme Creative Pool, Wega Film, France 3 Cinéma, Canal+, 2012.
Andrei Rublev, Andrei Tarkovsky, USSR: Mosfilm, 1966.
Anna's Meetings (*Les rendez-vous d'Anna*), Chantal Akerman, France/Belgium/West Germany: Centre du Cinéma et de l'Audiovisuel de la Fédération Wallonie-Bruxelles, 1978.
Auditions for a Revolution (**short**), Romania: Irina Butea, 2006.
The Autobiography of Nicolae Ceaușescu (*Autobiografia lui Nicolae Ceaușescu*), Andrei Ujica, Romania: ICON production, Centrul Național al Cinematografiei (CNC), Societatea Româna de Televiziune, 2010.
Baragan Thistles (*Ciulinii Bărăganului*), Louis Daquin, Romania: Studioul cinematografic București, 1957.
B.D., or *Brigada Diverse* (*Diverse Brigade* aka *Brigade Miscellaneous*), Mircea Drăgan,

Romania: Studioul cinematografic București, 1970–1.
Benny's Video, Michael Haneke, Austria/Switzerland: Bernard Lang, Langfilm, Wega Film, 1992.
Beyond the Bridge (*Dincolo de pod*), Mircea Veroiu, Romania: Casa de filme 1, 1976.
Birds and Greyhounds (*Ptizi I hrutki*), Georgi Stoyanov, Bulgaria, 1969.
Bless you Prison (*Binecuvântată fii, închisoare*), Nicolae Mărgineanu, Romania: Ager Film, 2002.
Boiler Room, Ben Younger, USA: New Line Cinema, 2000.
Bonnie and Clyde, Arthur Penn, USA: Warner Brothers, 1967.
A Brief History (*Scurtă istorie*), Ion Popescu-Gopo, Romania: Studioul cinematografic București, 1957.
The Bugler's Grandsons (*Nepoții gornistului*), Dinu Negreanu, Romania: Studioul cinematografic București, 1953.
Bulgaran is Gallant (*Bulgaran e galant*), Vassil Gendov, Bulgaria, 1915.
Burebista, Gheorghe Vitanidis, Romania: Casa de filme 5, 1980.
Caché, Michael Haneke, France/Austria/Germany/Italy: Les Films du Losange, Wega Films, Bavaria Film, BIM Distribuzione, 2005.
The Camp (*Lagerat*), Georgi Djulgerov, Bulgaria: Boyana Film, 1990.
Carol I (*Carol I – Un destin pentru România*), Sergiu Nicolaescu, Romania: MediaPro Pictures, 2008.
Chained Justice (*Dreptate în lanțuri*), Dan Pița, Romania: Casa de filme 1, 1984.
Chasing Rainbows (*Și caii sunt verzi pe pereți*), Dan Chișu, Romania: DaKino, 2012.
Child Murders (*Gyerekgyilkosságok*), Ildiko Szabo, Hungary: Hétföi Mühely, 1992.
Children of the Decree (*Născuți la comandă: Decrețeii*), Florin Iepan, Răzvan Georgescu, Romania/France: TVR, Arte, SubCultUra, 2005.
Cigarettes and Coffee, Jim Jarmusch, USA/Japan/Italy: Asmik Ace Entertainment, BIM Distribuzione, Smokescreen Inc, 2003.
Ciocoii, Horia Igiroșanu, Romania: Clipa Film, 1931.
Closely Watched Trains (*Ostre sledované vlaky*), Jirí Menzel, Czechoslovakia: Barrandov film studio, 1966.
Closer to the Moon (*Mai aproape de lună*), Nae Caranfil, Romania/USA/Italy/Poland/France: Mandragora Movies, Agresywna Banda, Denis Friedman Productions, 2013.
Codine (*Codin*), Henri Colpi, Romania/France: Studioul cinematografic București, Como-Films, Les Tamara, Unifilm France, 1963.
Colonel Redl (*Oberst Redl*), István Szabó, Hungary/Yugoslavia/West Germany/Austria: MAFILM Objektív Filmstúdió, Manfred Durniok Filmproduktion, Mokép, Zweites Deutsches Fernsehen (ZDF), Österreichischer Rundfunk (ORF), 1985.
The Column (*Columna*), Mircea Drăgan, Romania: Studioul cinematografic București, 1968.
The Conjugal Bed (*Patul conjugal*), Mircea Daneliuc, Romania: Alpha Films International, 1993.
The Concert (*Le concert*), Radu Mihăileanu, France/Italy/Romania/Belgium: Oï Oï Oï Productions, Les Productions du Trésor, France 3 Cinéma, EuropaCorp, Castel Films, Panache Productions, 2009.
Contest (*Concurs*), Dan Pița, Romania: Casa de filme 3, 1982.
The Convert (*Zawrócony*), Kazimierz Kutz, Poland: Ikam Ltd, 1994.
Counter-plan (*Vstrechnii*), Sergei Yutkevich, Fridrik Ermler, Soviet Union: Lenfilm, 1932.
Couples Retreat, Peter Billingsley, USA: Universal Pictures, 2009.
Cozy Dens (*Pelíšky*), Jan Hřebejk, Czech Republic: Ceská Televize, Total HelpArt (THA), 1998.
The Cruise (*Croaziera*), Mircea Daneliuc, Romania: Casa de filme 3, 1981.

GENERAL FILMOGRAPHY

The Dacians (Dacii), Sergiu Nicolaescu, Romania/France: Studioul cinematografic București, Franco-London Film Paris, 1966.
The Waves of the Danube or *The Danube Waves (Valurile Dunării)*, Liviu Ciulei, Romania: Studioul cinematografic București, 1959.
Dawn Over the Homeland (Utro nad rodinata), Anton Marinovich, Stefan Syrchadjiev, Bulgaria: Boyana Film, 1952.
Day for Night (La nuit américaine), François Truffaut, France/ Italy: Les Films du Carrosse, 1973
Down by Law, Jim Jarmusch, USA/West Germany: Black Snake, Grokenberger Film Produktion, Island Pictures, 1986.
Down by Love (Szerelemtől sújtva), Tamás Sas Hungary: Budapest Film, 2004.
Drăguș, the Life of a Romanian Village (Drăguș, viața unui sat românesc), Paul Sterian, Nicolae Argintescu-Amza, Romania: Seminarul de sociologie al Universității din București, 1929.
Duty and Sacrifice (Datorie și sacrificiu), Ion Șahighian, Romania: Studioul foto-cinematografic al Armatei Române, 1925.
The Earth's Most Beloved Son (Cel mai iubit dintre pământeni), Șerban Marinescu, Romania: Societatea Electronum, Trustul Express, 1993.
East-Side Story, Dana Ranga, Germany/France: Anda Film, Canal+, DocStar, Westdeutscher Rundfunk (WDR), 1997.
Ecaterina Teodoroiu, Ion Niculescu-Brună, Romania: Soremar Film, 1930.
The End of the Night (Sfârșitul nopții), Mircea Veroiu, Romania: Casa de filme 4, 1982.
The End of the World (Kraj swiata), Maria Zmarz-Koczanowicz, Poland, 1993.
Eruption (Erupția), Liviu Ciulei, Romania: Studioul cinematografic București, 1957.
Exitus, Krassimir Krumov, Bulgaria: Boyana Filmstudio, 1989.
Faded Dreams (Verklungene Träume), Martin Berger, Germany/Romania: Martin Berger Film, 1930.
The False Accusation (Năpasta), Eftimie Vasilescu, Romania: România Film, 1926.
Fatal Love (Amor fatal), Grigore Brezeanu, Romania: București, 1911.
Fed Up (Șoapte de amor aka *Această lehamite)*, Mircea Daneliuc, Romania: Alpha Films International, 1994.
Filip the Kind (Filip cel bun), Dan Pița, Romania: Casa de filme 3, 1974.
The Firemen's Ball (Hoří, má panenko), Miloš Forman, Czechoslovakia/Italy: Barrandov Film studio, Carlo Ponti Cinematografica, 1967.
First Take-off (Pierwszy start), Leonard Buczkowski, Poland: Wytwórnia Filmów Fabularnych, 1951.
The Forest of the Hanged (Pădurea spânzuraților), Liviu Ciulei, Romania: Studioul Cinematografic București, 1965.
The Fortress (Pevnost), Drahomíra Vihanová, Czech Republic/France, 1994.
Fox: Hunter (Vulpe – vânător), Stere Gulea, Romania/Germany: Filmex Romania, Ecco-Film Berlin, 1993.
Funny Games, Michael Haneke, Austria: Wega Film, 1997.
Get Shorty, Barry Sonnenfeld, USA: MGM, 1995.
A Girl's Tear (O lacrimă de fată), Iosif Demian, Romania: Casa de filme 5, 1980.
Glissando, Mircea Daneliuc, Romania: Casa de filme 3, 1982.
Golem, Piotr Szulkin, Poland: Film Polski, Zespol Filmowy Perspektywa, 1980.
The Great Communist Bank Robbery (Marele jaf comunist), Alexandru Solomon. Romania: Les Films d'Ici, Libra Film, ZDF/Arte, BBC, FR2, 2004.
A Great Opportunity (Velka Prilezitost), K. M. Wallo, Czechoslovakia: Ceskoslovensky Státní Film, 1949.
The Great Solitude (Velka samota), Ladislav Helge, Czechoslovakia: Barrandov Film studio, 1959.

The Gypsy Girl in the Alcove (*Țigăncușa de la iatac*), Alfred Halm, Germany/Romania: Spera Film, Rador Film, 1923.

Hanussen, István Szabó, Hungary/West Germany/Austria: Hungarofilm, Mafilm, Mokép, Central Cinema Company Film (CCC), Objektív Filmstúdió Vállalat, Zweites Deutsches Fernsehen (ZDF), 1988.

The Hatchet (*Baltagul*), Mircea Mureșan, Romania: Studioul cinematografic București, IDI Cinematografica Roma, 1969.

Heavenly Shift (*Isteni műszak*), Márk Bodzsár Hungary: Unió Film, Sparks, Hungarian National Film Fund, 2013.

Hiroshima mon amour, Alain Resnais, France/Japan: Argos Films, Como Films, Daiei Studio, Pathé Entertainment, 1959.

Hope Springs, David Frankel, USA: Columbia Pictures, 2012.

Human Capital (*Il capitale umano*), Paolo Virzi France: Indiana Production Company and Motorino Amaranto, 2013.

Hungarian Rhapsody (*Magyar rapszódia*), Miklós Jancsó, Hungary: Objektiv Film, 1979.

The Hunt (*La caza*), Carlos Saura, Spain: Elías Querejeta Producciones Cinematográficas S. L, 1966.

I Do Not Want to Get Married (*Nu vreau să mă însor*), Manole Marcus, Romania: Studioul cinematografic București, 1961.

I, You, He, She (*Je, tu, il, elle*), Chantal Akerman, France/Belgium: Paradise Films, 1976.

Iancu Jianu, Horia Igiroșanu, Romania: Clipa Film, 1928.

Independence of Romania aka *Independence War* (*Independența României*), Aristide Demetriade, Grigore Brezeanu, Romania: Filmul de artă Leon M. Popescu, 1912.

In Our Village (*În sat la noi*), Jean Georgescu, Romania: Studioul cinematografic București, 1951.

In the Kingdom of Terpsichore (*U carstvu Tepsihore*), Ernest Bošnjak, Serbia, 1906.

In the Mood for Love (*Fa yeung ning wa*), Kar-Wai Wong, Hong Kong/China: Block 2 Pictures, Jet Tone Production, Paradis Films, 2000.

The Investigator (*A nyomozó*), Attila Gigor, Hungary/Sweden/Ireland: Anagram Produktion, Fastnet Films, Inforg Stúdió, KMH Film, 2008.

Ion: The Lust for the Land, the Lust for Love (*Ion: Blestemul pământului, blestemul iubirii*), Mircea Mureșan, Romania: Casa de filme 5, 1980.

Ionuț's Brigade (*Brigada lui Ionuț*), Jean Mihail, Romania: Studioul cinematografic București, 1954.

Jacob (*Iacob*), Mircea Daneliuc, Romania: Casa de filme 5, 1988.

Juha, Aki Kaurismäki, Finland: Sputnik, 1999.

Killing Time, Florin Piersic Jr, Romania: Kinosseur, Elefant Film, 2012.

Kira Kiralina, Boris Glagolin, USSR: VUFKU, 1928.

Kira Kiralina, Dan Pița, Romania: Castel Film, 2014.

Kino Caravan (*Caravana cinematografică*), Titus Muntean Romania/Germany: Libra Film, FilmKombinat, 2009.

Kolya, Jan Sverák, Czech Republic/UK/France: Biograf Jan Sverak, Pandora Cinema, Portobello Pictures, Space Films, 1996.

The Lace Wars (*Les Fêtes Galantes*), René Clair, France/Romania: Gaumont International, Studioul cinematografic București, 1965.

The Land of the Motzi aka *The Country of Motzi* (*Țara Moților*), Paul Călinescu, Romania: Oficiul Național Cinematografic, 1938.

La notte, Michelangelo Antonioni, Italy/France: Nepi Film, Sofitedip, Silver Films, 1961.

The Last Ball in November (*Noiembrie, ultimul bal*), Dan Piţa, Romania: Casa de filme 4, 1989.
Late Full Moon (*Zakasnjalo palnolunie*), Eduard Zakhariev, Bulgaria: Eduard Zahariev Films, 1997.
Le Petit Soldat, Jean-Luc Godard, France: Société Nouvelle de Cinématographie (SNC), 1963.
Lia, Jean Mihail, Romania: Indro-Film, 1927.
The Life and Deeds of the Immortal Leader Karadjordje (*Život i dela besmrtnog vozda Karadjordja*), Ilija 'Čiča' Stanojević, Kingdom of Serbia: Pathé-Frères, 1911.
Life Triumphs (*Viaţa învinge*), Dinu Negreanu, Romania: Romfilm, 1951.
The Lives of Others (*Das Leben Der Anderen*), Florian Henckel von Donnersmark. Germany: Wiedemann and Berg Filmproduktion, 2006.
Liviu's Dream (*Visul lui Liviu*), Corneliu Porumboiu, Romania: Universitatea Nationala de Arta Teatrala si Cinematografica 'I. L. Caragiale' (UNATC), 2004.
Long Drive (*Cursa*), Mircea Daneliuc. Romania: Casa de filme 1, 1974.
Lost Landscape (*Verlorene Landschaft*), Andreas Kleinert, Germany: Von Vietinghoff Filmproduktion GmbH, 1992.
Love at First Bite, Stan Dragoti, USA: Melvin Simon Productions, 1979.
Love Building aka *Alt Love Building*, Iulia Rugină, Romania: DaKino, 2013.
Love is All You Need (*Den skaldede frisør*), Susanne Bier, Denmark/Sweden/Italy/France/Germany: Zentropa Productions, 2012.
Lust for Gold (*Duhul aurului*), Dan Piţa, Mircea Veroiu, Romania: Casa de filme 1, 1974.
Luxury Hotel (*Hotel de lux*), Dan Piţa. Romania: Solaris Film, Parnasse Production Paris, Romania Film, 1992.
Mad Max: Fury Road, George Miller, USA: Warner Brothers, 2015.
Mamma Mia! Phyllida Loyd, USA/UK/Germany: Universal Pictures, 2018.
Manasse, Jean Mihail, Romania: Naţional Film, 1925.
Margin Call, J. C. Chandor, USA: Before the Door Pictures, 2011.
Mayerling, Terence Young, UK/France: Les Films Corona, Winchester Productions, 1968.
Meanders (*Meandre*), Mircea Săucan, Romania: Studioul cinematografic Bucureşti, 1966.
A Memorable Night (*O noapte de pomină*), Ion Sahighian, Romania: Ciro Film, 1939.
Memories of My Childhood (*Amintiri din copilărie*), Elisabeta Bostan, Romania: Studioul cinematografic Bucureşti, 1965.
Mephisto, István Szabó, Hungary/West Germany/Austria: Mafilm, Objektiv Film, Manfred Durniok Filmproduktion, 1981.
Michael the Brave (*Mihai Viteazul*), Sergiu Nicolaescu, Romania/France/Italy: Studioul cinematografic Bucureşti, 1970.
Microphone Test (*Probă de microfon*), Mircea Daneliuc, Romania: Casa de filme 3, 1980.
Mildred Pierce, Todd Haynes, USA: HBO Killer Films John Wells, 2011.
Mill of Luck (*La Moara cu noroc*), Victor Iliu, Romania: Studioul cinematografic Bucureşti, 1955.
Millionaire for a Day (*Milionar pentru o zi*), Jean Georgescu, Romania, 1924.
Miners of the Don (*Donetskie shakhtyory*), Leonid Lukov, USSR: Kinostudiya imeni M. Gorkogo, 1951.
The Mirror – The Beginning of Truth (*Oglinda – Începutul adevărului*), Sergiu Nicolaescu, Romania: Star Film, 1994.
Miss Christina (*Domnişoara Christina*), Alexandru Maftei, Romania: Abis Studio, 2013.

Mitrea Cocor, Victor Iliu, Romania: Studioul cinematografic București, 1952.
The Moromete Family (*Moromeții*), Stere Gulea, Romania: Casa de filme 1, 1987.
Mother of Asphalt (*Majka asfalta*), Dalibor Matanić, Croatia: Kinorama, Hrvatska Radiotelevizija, 2010.
New Year's Eve (*Sylvester*), Lupu Pick, Germany: Rex-Film GMBH, 1924.
Next Stop Paradise (*Terminus Paradis*), Lucian Pintilie, France/Romania: MK2 Productions, Filmex, 1998.
The Oak (*Balanța*), Lucian Pintilie. France/Romania: MK2 Productions, Parnasse Production, Les Films du Scarabée, Studio of Cinematographic Creation of the Romanian Ministry of Culture, 1992.
Odessa in Flames (*Odessa in fiamme* aka *Catușe roșii* aka *Odessa în flăcări*), Carmine Gallone, Italy/Romania: Grandi Filmi Storici, Oficiul Național Cinematografic, 1942.
One Hundred Lei (*100 de lei*), Mircea Săucan, Romania: Studioul cinematografic București, 1973.
Ordinary People (*Obični ljudi*), Vladimir Perišić, Serbia/Netherlands/France/Switzerland: TS Productions, Arte France Cinema, Trilema, Prince Film, 2009.
Our Holy War (*Războiul nostru sfânt*), Ion Cantacuzino, Romania: Oficiul Național Cinematografic, 1942.
Outlaws (*Haiducii*), Horia Igiroșanu, Romania: Clipa Film, 1929.
Outpost (*A részleg*), Peter Gothar, Hungary/Romania: Domino Film, Hunnia Filmstúdió, MTV Drámai Stúdió, Neuropa, 1994.
Palindromes, Todd Solondz, USA: Extra Large Pictures, 2004.
Paso Doble (*Pas în doi*), Dan Pița, Romania: Casa de filme 4, 1985.
The Passenger (*Pasazerka*), Andrzej Munk, Poland: Zespol Filmowy, 1964.
Pearls of the Deep (*Perlicky na dne*), Vera Chytilová, Jaromil Jires, Jirí Menzel, Jan Nemec, Evald Schorm, Czechoslovakia: Filmové studio Barrandov, 1965.
Polish Death (*Polska smierc*), Waldemar Krzystek, Poland: Skorpion Art Film, Telewizja Polska (TVP), 1994.
The Power and the Truth (*Puterea și adevărul*), Manole Marcus, Romania: Studioul cinematografic București, 1972.
Predators (*Dravci*), Jiří Weiss, Czechoslovakia: Ceskoslovenský Státní Film, 1948.
Pulp Fiction, Quentin Tarantino, USA: Miramax, A Band A Part, Jersey Films, 1994.
The Rabbit's Death (*Smartta na zaeka*), Anri Kulev, Bulgaria: Boyana Film, 1982.
Rear Window, Alfred Hitchcock, USA: Paramount Pictures, 1954.
Reconstruction (*Reconstituirea*), Virgil Calotescu, Romania: Filmstudio, Ministry of Internal Affairs of the Romanian People's Republic, 1960.
Reconstruction/The Re-enactment (*Reconstituirea*), Lucian Pintilie, Romania: Studioul Cinematografic București, 1970.
The Red and the White (*Csillagosok, katonák*), Miklós Jancsó, Hungary/USSR: Mafilm, Mosfilm, 1967.
Red Psalm (*Még kér a nép*), Miklós Jancsó, Hungary: Játékfilmstúdió, 1972.
Report on the Party and the Guests (*O slavnosti a hostech*), Jan Nemec, Czechoslovakia: Filmové studio Barrandov, 1966.
Reserve at the Start (*Rezerva la start*), Anghel Mora. Romania, 1988.
The Rest is Silence (*Restul e tăcere*), Nae Caranfil, Romania: Domino Film, Realitatea Media, 2007.
Romania's Independence (*Independența României*), Aristide Demetriade, Romania: Societatea Filmul de Artă Leon Popescu, 1912.
Romania and the Fight against Bolshevism (*România în lupta contra bolșevismului*), Paul Călinescu, Romania: Oficiul Național Cinematografic, 1941.
Rome, Open City (*Roma città aperta*, Roberto Rossellini, 1945), Roberto Rossellini, Italy: Minerva Film SpA, 1945.

Rosetta, Luc Dardenne, Jean-Pierre Dardenne, France/Belgium: Les Films du Fleuve, 1999.
Roxanne, Valentin Hotea, Romania: Abis Studio, 2013.
Sand Cliffs (*Faleze de nisip*), Dan Pița, Romania: Casa de filme 1, 1983.
Satantango (*Sátántangó*), Béla Tarr, Hungary/Germany/Switzerland: Mozgókép Innovációs Társulás és Alapítvány, Von Vietinghoff Filmproduktion (VVF), Vega Film, 1994.
#Selfie, Cristina Iacob, Romania: Media Pro Entertainment, 2014.
The Self Portrait of a Dutiful Daughter (*Autoportretul unei fete cuminți*), Ana Lungu, Romania: Mandragora, 2015.
Sequences (*Secvențe*), Alexandru Tatos, Romania: Casa de filme 4, 1982.
Seven Days (*Șapte zile*), Mircea Veroiu, Romania: Casa de filme 1, 1973.
Shadow of a Doubt, Alfred Hitchcock, USA: Skirball Productions, 1943.
Shoah, Claude Lanzmann. France/UK: Historia, Les Films Aleph, BBC, 1985.
The Shop around the Corner, Ernst Lubitsch, USA: Metro-Goldwyn-Mayer, 1940.
Skyfall, Sam Mendes, UK/USA: Eon Productions, 2012.
The Snails' Senator (*Senatorul melcilor*), Mircea Daneliuc, Romania: Alpha Films International, 1995.
A Soap (*En soap*), Pernille Fischer Christensen, Denmark/Sweden: Nimbus Film Productions, Garagefilm International, New Danish Screen, Zentropa Entertainments, 2006.
Sofia's Last Ambulance (*Poslednata lineika na Sofia*), Ilian Metev, Bulgaria/Croatia/Germany: Chaconna Films, Nukeus Film, Sutor Kolonko, 2012.
The South Pole (*Polul Sud*), Radu Nicoară, Romania: Studioul de Creație Profilm, 1992.
Spread Yourselves, Daisies aka *Spin a Yarn* (*Înșir'te mărgărite*), Grigore Brezeanu, Aristide Demetriade, Romania: Societatea actorilor Teatrului Național din București, 1911.
Stalker, Andrei Tarkovsky, Soviet Union : Mosfilm, Vtoroe Tvorcheskoe Obedinenie, 1979.
State of Things (*Stare de fapt*), Stere Gulea, Romania: Filmex, Studioul de Creație Cinematografică al Ministerului Culturii, Studioul de Creație 4 Cinerom, 1995.
Stone Wedding (*Nunta de piatră*), Dan Pița, Romania: Studioul cinematografic București, 1972.
Storm of Love (*Sturmflut der Liebe* aka *Venea o moară pe Siret*), Martin Berger, Germany/Romania: Mondo-Film-Vertrieb GmbH, 1929.
A Stormy Night (*O noapte furtunoasă*), Jean Georgescu, Romania: Oficiul Național al Cinematografiei, 1943.
Stranger Than Paradise, Jim Jarmusch, USA/West Germany: Cinesthesia Productions Inc., 1984.
Sunday at Six (*Duminică la ora șase*), Lucian Pintilie, Romania: Filmstudio București, 1965.
The Sun Rises (*Răsare soarele*), Dinu Negreanu, Romania: Studioul cinematografic București, 1954.
Sunshine, István Szabó, Hungary/Germany/Austria/Canada/France/UK/USA: Alliance Atlantis, Bavaria Film and TV Fund, Channel Four Films, InterCom, Kinowelt Filmproduktion, 1999.
Sweet Little Lies (*Minte-mă frumos*), Iura Luncașu, Romania: MediaPro Pictures, 2012.
Symphony of Love (*Simfonia dragostei*), Ion Șahighian, Romania: Soremar Film, 1928.
Taxidermia, György Pálfy, Hungary/Austria/France: Amour Fou Filmproduktion, Eurofilm Stúdió, Katapult Film, La Cinéfacture, Memento Films Production, 2006.

The Temptation (*Pokuszenie*), Barbara Sass, Poland: Agencja Produkcji Filmowej, Prostar Holding, Telewizja Polska, 1995.
Thank You for Each New Morning (*Díky za kazdé nové ráno*), Martin Šteindler, Czech Republic: Ceská Televize, Czech Film Corporation, 1994.
The Thief of Bagdad, Raoul Walsh, USA: United Artists, 1924.
Three Days before Christmas (*Trei zile până la Crăciun*), Radu Gabrea, Romania: Total TV, 2011.
Three Stories about Sleeplessness (*Tri price o nespavanju*), Tomislav Radic, Croatia: Hrvatska Radiotelevizija, Korugva film, 2008.
Time of the Gypsies (*Dom za vesanje*), Emir Kusturica, Yugoslavia/UK/Italy: Forum Sarajevo, Ljubavny Film, Lowndes Productions Limited, 1988.
Tirana Year Zero (*Tirana viti 0*), Fatmir Koçi, Albania and France: Alexis Films, Ciné-Sud Promotion, Kkoci Production, 2001.
Too Late (*Prea târziu*), Lucian Pintilie, Romania/France: Filmex, 1996.
Touch Me Not (*Nu mă atinge-mă*), Adina Pintilie, Romania/Germany/Czech Republic/Bulgaria/France: Manekino Films, Rohfilm, Pink Production, Agitprop, Les Films de l'Étranger, HBO Romania, 2018.
Train of Life (*Train de vie*), Radu Mihăileanu, France/Belgium/Netherlands/Israel/Romania: Belfilms, Canal+, Hungry Eye Lowland Pictures, Noé Productions, Sofinergie 4, Raphaël Films, 1998.
Traitor (*Trahir*), Radu Mihăileanu, France/Switzerland/Spain/Romania: Cactus Film, Filmex, Parnasse Production, Xaloc, 1993.
Traps (*Pasti, pasti, pasticky*), Věra Chytilová, Czech Republic: CNTS, Cinemart TV, Krátký Film Praha, TV Nova, 1998.
Tudor, Lucian Bratu, Romania: Studioul cinematografic București, 1963.
Un chien andalou, Luis Buñuel, Pierre Braunberge, France, 1929.
Uncle Marin, the Billionaire (*Nea Mărin miliardar*), Sergiu Nicolaescu, Romania: Casa de filme 4, 1979.
University Square: Romania (*Piața Universității-România*), Stere Gulea, Vivi Drăgan Vasile, Sorin Ilieșiu, Romania: Studio of Cinematographic Creation of the Romanian Ministry of Culture, 1991.
The Unknown Soldier's Patent Leather Shoes (*Lachenite obuvki na neznayniya voin*), Rangel Vulchanov, Bulgaria: Boyana Film, Sredets Grupa, 1979.
Vacation on the Black Sea (*Vacanță la mare*), Andrei Călărașu, Romania: Studioul cinematografic București, 1963.
The Valley Resounds (*Răsună valea*), Paul Călinescu, Romania: Studioul cinematografic București, 1949.
Videograms of a Revolution (*Videogramme einer Revolution*), Harun Farocki, Andrei Ujica, Germany: Harun Farocki Filmproduktion, 1992.
Vlad the Impaler: The True Life of Dracula (*Vlad Țepeș*), Doru Năstase, Romania: Casa de filme 5, 1978.
The War of the Worlds: Next Century (*Wojna swiatów – nastepne stulecie*), Piotr Szulkin, Poland: Zespol Filmowy Perspektywa, 1983.
Water Like a Black Buffalo (*Apa ca un bivol negru*), Andrei Cătălin Băleanu, Dan Pița, Micea Veroiu, Petre Bokor, Romania: Studioul cinematografic București, 1970.
The Way (*Yol*), Yilmaz Güney, Turkey/Switzerland/France: Güney Film, Cactus Film and Antenne-2, 1982.
The Wedding (*Wesele*), Andrzej Wajda, Poland: Film Polski, 1973.
White Gate (*Poarta Albă*), Nicolae Mărgineanu, Romania: Ager Film, 2014.
White Lace Dress (*Rochia albă de dantelă*), Dan Pița, Romania: Casa de filme 4, 1988.
Who Is Singing Over There? (*Ko to tamo peva?*), Slobodan Šijan, Yugoslavia: Centar Film, 1980.

Why Are the Bells Ringing, Miticǎ? aka *Scenes from a Carnival* (*De ce trag clopotele, Miticǎ?*), Lucian Pintilie, Romania: Casa de filme 1 and 5, 1982.
The Wife's Crusade (*Kreuzzug des Weibes*), Martin Berger, Germany: Arthur Ziehm, 1926.
William the Conqueror (*Wilhelm Cuceritorul*), Sergiu Nicolaescu, Gilles Grangier, Romania/France/Switzerland: Cine TV, Europa Films, Forum Films, 1982.
The Wolf of Wall Street, Martin Scorsese, USA: Red Granite Pictures, Paramaount Pictures, 2013.
A Woman of 33 (*Edna zhena na trideset i tri*), Christo Christov, Bulgaria: Boyana Film, 1982.
The World Is Mine (*Lumea e a mea*), Nicolae Constantin Tǎnase, Romania: Libra Film, deFilms, 2015.
Written on the Wind, Douglas Sirk, USA: Universal International Pictures, 1956.
You've Got Mail, Nora Ephron, USA: Warner Bros, 1998.
Zidane: A 21st Century Portrait (*Zidane, un portrait du 21e siècle*), Douglas Gordon, Philippe Parreno, France/Iceland: Anna Lena Films, Naflastrengir, 2006.

INDEX OF AUTHORS AND FILM TITLES

4 Months, 3 Weeks and 2 Days, 1, 5, 9, 20, 28, 30–3, 51, 54–5, 60–1, 78, 125–6, 144–5, 149, 159, 167, 171, 173, 178, 209, 218, 225–6
12:08 East of Bucharest, 1, 11, 20, 28–9, 33–4, 67, 70, 72, 76, 85, 100, 137, 140, 144–5, 149, 205, 208, 216, 221, 223, 233, 237

Achim, Gabriel, 11, 19, 86, 130, 133, 135, 266
Adalbert's Dream, 11, 20, 86–7, 135, 266
Aferim!, 11, 47, 104, 136, 221, 223
Agârbiceanu, Ion, 25, 260, 266
Akerman, Chantal, 40, 44
Apartment, The, 199–201
Apetri, Bogdan George, 18, 130, 199, 213
Aristotle, 10, 124–5
Asphalt Tango, 95, 105, 276
Aurora, 20, 28, 31–2, 34–5, 42–3, 106, 116–17, 119, 128, 202, 208–9, 220, 223, 276

Baudrillard, Jean, 60, 95, 98, 200
Best Intentions, 32, 272
Beyond the Hills, 10, 28–9, 31, 33, 35, 40, 51, 56, 127, 151, 154–8, 160–1, 178, 209, 218, 231

Bordwell, David, 5, 9, 31–2, 67–9, 96, 178, 181–2, 197, 254–5
Bradatan, Costica, 125, 213

C Block Story, 216, 222–3
Cage, The, 223
California Dreamin', 1, 212–14, 218, 220, 221, 223
Cantacuzino, Ion, 247–9, 278
Caragiale, Ion Luca, 27, 92, 248, 260, 278, 280
Caranfil, Nae, 1, 14, 19, 53, 86, 93–106, 218, 222, 228, 245, 266, 276, 282
Călinescu, Paul, 246, 249, 255–6, 279
Ceaușescu, 5, 15, 28, 35, 68, 76, 78, 85, 88, 92, 112, 138–40, 145, 169, 212, 222, 225, 254–5, 261–3, 269–70, 273, 279–80
Cernat, Manuela, 245, 249–52, 262–3, 266, 277–8, 280
Child's Pose, 16, 28, 32, 34–5, 208–9, 216, 218, 223, 232, 235, 237, 272
Chirilov, Mihai, 5–6, 111, 175, 217–18
Ciulei, Liviu, 25, 168, 247, 255, 257–60, 279
Closer to the Moon, 86, 100, 102–3, 228, 266

312

INDEX OF AUTHORS AND FILM TITLES

Coffee and Cigarettes, 20, 223
Contest, The, 267, 269
Crişan, Marian, 18–19, 130, 132, 215, 223
Cruise, The, 7, 26, 267, 269

Daneliuc, Mircea, 6–7, 16, 25–6, 52, 85, 105, 233, 255, 266–71, 276, 281
Deaca, Mircea, 15, 17, 197, 202
Death of Mr Lăzărescu, The, 1, 4, 10, 20, 24, 28, 32, 41, 54–5, 85, 109, 113, 115, 118–19, 124–6, 143–5, 149, 167, 173, 179, 201, 207, 209, 212, 219–20, 222–4, 229, 233
Dogs, 19, 130–1, 133–5
Dragin, Sinişa, 128, 275–6
Duma, Dana, 3–4, 15, 17, 104, 167, 179, 223, 252, 266, 272, 278

Earth's Most Beloved Son, The, 274–5
Ecaterina Teodoroiu, 249–50
Eliade, Mircea, 133, 229, 247, 275
Ellestrom, Lars, 110, 113–14
Elsaesser, Thomas, 8, 105, 179
Eruption, 257
Everyday God Kisses Us on the Mouth, 128–9, 275
Everybody in Our Family, 11, 20, 28, 32–3, 206, 208, 272

Firemen's Choir, The, 19
First of all, Felicia, 20, 44, 88, 136, 167, 173–4, 217
Forest of the Hanged, The, 25, 168, 247, 258–9, 280
Foucault, Michel, 186, 188, 193, 279
Francesca, 19, 127, 130, 167, 172–3
Fulger, Mihai, 3, 109, 212
Frye, Northrop, 9–11, 20, 125–7, 266, 281

Giurgiu, Tudor, 1, 8, 11, 18–19, 175, 223, 232, 271
Good Day for a Swim, A, 223
Gorzo, Andrei, 3, 20, 24, 42, 78, 85, 92–3, 109, 111, 179, 272
Graduation, 127
Gulea, Stere, 7, 94, 143, 168, 232, 271–2, 274, 281

Hames, Peter, 4–5, 20
Happiest Girl in the World, The, 20, 136, 167, 223, 266, 272

Heiddeger, Martin, 14, 28, 123–4, 136, 260
Hjort, Mette, 180–1, 236
Hooked aka *Angling*, 20, 136, 216, 218
Horizon, 19, 130, 132–3, 218, 281
How I Spent the End of the World, 1, 104, 199, 222–3

I Do Not Care If We Go Down in History as Barbarians, 16
Iacob, Raluca, 15, 18–19, 211
If I Want to Whistle, I Whistle, 10, 29, 176–7
I'm an Old Communist Hag, 232, 271
Independence of Romania, 245, 250
Iordanova, Dina, 2, 213
Istrati, Panait, 260
It Can Pass through the Wall, 20

Japanese Dog, The, 19, 223, 232
Jude, Radu, 1, 11, 16, 18–20, 25–6, 28, 32, 35, 47, 104, 167, 206, 223, 266, 272
Jung, Carl Gustav, 12, 128, 132–4, 136, 264, 267–8, 271–2, 281
Jurgiu, Tudor Cristian, 18–19, 223, 232

Konrad, George and Ivan Szelenyi, 244, 246, 276–7
Kovács, András Bálint, 13, 24, 26–7, 38, 44–5, 80–1, 99

Lacan, Jacques, 12, 14, 143, 148, 150
Land of Motzi, The, 249
Last Day, The, 130
Liehm, Mira, Antonin Liehm, 2, 4, 237, 250, 252–4, 257, 260–2, 264, 267, 278
Lord, 223
Love Sick, 175, 223
Loverboy, 126–7, 130, 177, 204

Marilena from P7, 207
Marinescu, Şerban, 274
Mazierska, Ewa, 236
Medal of Honor, 11, 88, 204, 212, 223, 233
Microphone Test, 26, 85, 168, 266–7, 269
Mirică, Bogdan, 18, 19, 130
Mitulescu, Cătălin, 1, 8, 18–20, 104, 177, 199, 204, 222–3

INDEX OF AUTHORS AND FILM TITLES

Morgen, 19, 127, 132, 136, 213, 217, 221, 223
Moromete Family, The, 7, 168, 271
Mungiu, Cristian, 1, 5, 7–10, 14, 17–20, 25, 28, 30–2, 35, 40–1, 51, 54, 61–2, 67, 78, 104, 108, 125, 144, 151, 157, 159, 167, 171, 174, 178, 199, 208–9, 212, 218, 222–3, 225, 229, 231–2, 276
Muntean, Radu, 1, 7, 9–10, 16, 18–20, 25, 28, 45, 47, 49, 54–5, 62, 104, 108, 125, 130, 137, 144, 147–9, 174, 175, 183–4, 188, 198, 212, 218, 223, 232–4, 237

Nasta, Dominique, 2, 3, 5–6, 12–13, 23, 25–6, 34, 47, 49–50, 55, 78, 81, 84, 104, 108–9, 114–15, 180, 200, 205–7, 210, 216–17, 220, 245, 248, 252–4, 260–2, 264–7, 271, 278, 280–2
Nemescu, Cristian, 1, 11, 18, 207, 216, 223, 276
Netzer, Peter Călin, 1, 11, 16, 18–19, 28, 32, 34–5, 88, 204, 208–10, 212, 223, 232, 235–7
Nicolaescu, Sergiu, 6, 18–19, 105, 227, 261–3
Nietzsche, Friedrich, 127, 136, 271, 274–5, 282
Niki and Flo, 6, 27–8, 31, 80–1, 87–1, 205, 276

Oak, The, 5, 27, 52, 91–2, 105, 126, 272–4
Occident, 9, 104, 212, 216–17, 221, 223, 276
Of Snails and Men, 11, 212, 221, 223, 232, 271
One Floor Below, 127, 130, 234
Other Irina, The, 127, 136, 167, 171–2
Outbound, 130, 176, 199, 213
Oxygen, 223

Paech, Joachim, 80, 83, 86, 89–90
Paper Will Be Blue, The, 1, 9–10, 28, 49, 54–5, 125–6, 136–7, 144–9, 173, 217, 223
Păunescu, Bobby, 8, 19, 130, 167
Pethő, Ágnes, 13, 65, 78, 91, 96–7, 103, 114
Philanthropy, 95, 98–100, 103, 218
Pintilie, Adina, 16

Pintilie, Lucian, 5–7, 14, 16, 19, 25–7, 31, 33, 52, 80–7, 91–2, 105, 126, 203, 205–6, 208, 255, 264–6, 272–4, 280
Piţa, Dan, 6–7, 16, 25, 92, 105, 227, 255, 260, 266–70, 280–1
Police, Adjective, 28, 32, 34, 43, 56–7, 62, 70–4, 76, 79, 127, 130, 134, 178, 184, 189–91, 193, 204–5, 218, 223
Pop, Doru, 2–8, 13, 16–20, 24, 50, 61, 78, 81, 84, 88, 92–3, 103–4, 107–11, 113–16, 118, 180, 197, 205, 209, 212, 217, 225–7, 247, 267, 281
Popescu, Constantin, 6, 16, 18, 199, 201, 272
Pororoca, 16
Porumboiu, Corneliu, 1, 8, 10–11, 13, 16, 18–19, 25, 28–9, 32–5, 43, 47, 49, 55–6, 58, 62, 65, 67–79, 85, 92, 100, 104, 106, 108, 130, 137, 140, 144, 178, 183–4, 189, 191–3, 204–5, 215–16, 222–3, 232–4, 237, 266
Preda, Marin, 168, 272, 274
Principles of Life, 20, 272
Puiu, Cristi, 1, 3–4, 6–12, 14, 18–20, 24–8, 31–2, 34–5, 41–2, 47, 50–1, 54, 62, 67, 79, 85, 87, 91, 99, 104, 106–11, 113, 115–16, 119, 125–6, 128–30, 136, 143–4, 167, 173, 179, 201–4, 209, 212, 214, 220, 222–3, 225, 229–30, 233, 275–6

Rage, 49, 218, 223
Rajewsky, Irina, 110, 115
Rădulescu, Răzvan, 6, 18–19, 27, 44–5, 87–8, 91, 108, 167, 173–5
Rebreanu, Liviu, 25, 168, 247–8, 258, 260, 278
Reconstruction, 7, 26, 80–6, 91–2, 100, 102, 265–7; see also Re-enactment
Re-enactment, The, 26, 33, 265; see also Reconstruction
Rest is Silence, The, 53, 100–4, 106, 245
Rocker, 223
Ryna, 1, 10, 15, 167, 169–71, 223

Sadoveanu, Mihail, 248–9, 260, 270, 278
Second Game, The, 73, 75–7
Sieranevada, 20
Silent River, 223
Sitaru, Adrian, 18, 25–6, 28, 32, 216–17, 223
Stojanova, Christina, 3–4, 10, 14, 16,

314

17, 94, 116, 119, 123, 128, 132, 136, 191, 192, 210, 222–3, 243–5, 249, 251–4, 262–4, 269, 273, 276, 278–80
Stuff and Dough, 3, 9, 19–20, 24, 79, 99, 108, 110–13, 115–17, 119, 126, 130, 173, 203, 208, 212, 214, 216–18, 229–30
Summer Holiday aka Boogie, 173, 175, 212
Sunday at Six, 264
Sundays on Leave, 19, 94–5, 97, 99, 103, 105, 222, 276
Şerban, Alex Leo, 3–4, 18, 20, 24, 37, 48, 108, 158, 212
Şerban, Florin, 18–19, 29, 176

Tales from the Golden Age, 55, 104, 199
Todorova, Maria, 2, 213
Traffic, 20, 223
Treasure, The, 11, 29, 43–4, 77, 136
Tube with a Hat, The, 20
Tuesday, After Christmas, 16, 45–6, 54–5, 175, 183, 186–7, 189, 198, 232–5, 237
Țuțui, Marian, 15, 250, 277

University Square, 19, 94–5, 143, 271
Uricaru, Ioana, 3, 6–8, 13–14, 18–19, 50–1, 108, 125, 137, 157, 192, 246, 277

Valley Resounds, The, 255–6, 261, 270
Virginás, Andrea, 15, 96, 180–1
Vlad Țepeș, 263
Von Franz, Marie-Louise, 132, 136, 267, 280

Waves, 217
Waves of the Danube, The, 258, 264, 280
Weissberg, Jay, 171, 223
When Evening Falls on Bucharest, or Metabolism, 16, 29, 73, 76–7, 79, 106, 178, 183, 204, 218, 223, 232, 266
White, Jerry, 243–4, 250, 276n
Wittgenstein, Ludwig, 10, 12, 14, 20, 123–4, 126–7
Wolf, Werner, 110–11, 115

Zenide, Ruxandra, 15, 18, 167, 169
Žižek, Slavoj, 33, 144, 147

INDEX OF TERMS AND CONCEPTS

aesthetics, vi, xi, 9–16, 20n, 35, 93, 96, 104, 121, 123–5, 127, 158, 212, 216, 222, 223n, 232, 278n, 283, 285–6, 291, 294
  impossible, 256, 269
  'maximalist', 104
  minimalist, 109, 119, 187
  modernist, 80, 84, 100
  new, 103, 105
  normative, 254, 257, 261, 264, 278n
  realist, 96
  self-reflexive, 96
analogue, 74–6, 181–2, 189–91, 193n, 206
animation, 190, 250, 260
anti-hero, 200–1, 204, 208–9, 259
anti-semitic, 275
apartment drama
archetype, 267, 281n
  puer aeternus, 264, 267–70
  see also shadow
art cinema, xi, 6, 210, 213, 277n
  modernist, 24, 100
  narration, 264
arthouse, 15, 25, 36, 157, 182
  films, 24, 36–8, 47
  small cinema and, 180, 182–3
astronomic time, 124, 133

austerity, vi, 7, 10, 14, 46, 51, 65, 151–7, 159, 161, 163
auteur, 5, 6, 7, 15, 16, 23, 24, 28, 33, 102, 143, 18, 182, 255, 266
  cinema, 216
  new Romanian, 29, 30, 33, 34
  tradition, 182
auteurist, 17, 35, 49n, 180
auteurship, 5, 7, 8
authenticity, vi, 9, 12, 37, 61, 76, 123, 126, 131, 144, 171, 190, 217, 234, 256, 258, 266
  aesthetics and, 124
  ethics and, 124
  existentialism and, 14

Balkans, xiii, 2, 213–14, 217, 220–1, 247, 250, 260, 277n, 282n
  Balkan cinema, 2, 17n, 222–3
Bazinian realism, 42–3, 93
blockbuster, 226, 229
  global, 190, 228
  Hollywood, 54
  international, 226
  nationalist, 245, 249–50
  Romanian, 229
Bulgarian Migration Cycle, 279n

INDEX OF TERMS AND CONCEPTS

Cannes (Film Festival), 1, 4, 7, 9, 211, 223n, 225, 247, 260, 280n
capitalism, 60, 112, 116
   transition to, 15, 169
   transnational, 238
capitalist, 113, 209
   consumerism, 88
   western, 5
cinema of process, 124, 128–9
cinéma vérité, 65, 87
cinematic realism, 12, 93, 96, 104, 106n, 212, 223n
   documentary and, 201
   New Romanian Cinema (or NRC) and, 12, 14, 20n, 50, 85, 109, 158, 176, 212
colonial, 143, 180
   auto-colonial, 213, 222
   self-colonising, 275–6
   self-exoticising, 220, 275
comedy, 20n, 24, 44, 95, 112, 114, 207, 208, 227, 230, 248, 253
   black, 55, 92n, 124, 136n
   comedy of manners, 250
   Hollywood, 280n
   musical, 192, 261
   national, 225
   period comedy, 266
   romantic comedy, 229
   satirical, 86
   tragic-comedy, 248
   see also ironic modes
communism, communist, xi, 2, 4–7, 16, 17n, 27, 60–1, 75, 92n, 94, 100, 103–4, 112–13, 115, 117, 125, 130–2, 141, 143, 149n, 169, 199, 201, 205, 212, 218, 220, 223n, 228, 231–2, 244, 247, 249, 256–9, 261–6, 268–9, 271, 275, 277n, 279–80n
   anti-, 271
   national, 225
   party, 86, 97, 138–9, 141, 148n, 232, 251–2
   propaganda, 26, 81–4, 86, 91, 97, 100, 102–3, 168–9, 269, 279n
communist cinema, 8, 15, 17, 251, 251–3
crime film, 111, 184–5, 191, 193n, 202–3, 234
crisis heterotopia, 186, 188
crystals of time, 27–9
culture, 6–7, 16, 17n, 59–60, 92n, 93–5, 104–5, 112–13, 117, 127, 134, 143, 157, 174, 181, 192–3n, 211, 220–1, 227–9, 231, 237–8, 243–4, 246–7, 264, 273, 280n
   model, 208–9
Czech velvet generation, 2, 20n, 23
Czechoslovak New Wave, 2, 4, 9, 26, 226, 254, 275

diegesis, 42, 52, 55–6, 58, 96–7, 159–60, 200, 202–3
   diegetic camera, 83, 89
   diegetic integrity, 52
direct cinema, 10, 87, 224n
dissident, 92n, 117, 265, 275
director, 5, 264
film, 81, 265
'decenteredness', 70
documentary, xi, xii, 5, 19n, 26, 28, 65, 78n, 86, 102, 143, 148, 222, 224n, 245, 249, 255, 266, 271, 276n, 280n
   fiction, 279n
   found-footage, 140
   investigative, 92n
   look, 85
   propagandistic, 83
   quasi-, 82, 87, 91, 265, 267
   reportage, 85, 245
   style, 201, 222
   tendency, 109
   see also cinematic realism

Eastern Europe/ Eastern European, 2, 8, 16, 17n, 23–5, 67, 76, 78n, 88, 94, 106n, 154, 168, 211, 213, 223, 246–8, 252–3, 260–1, 253, 264, 270, 270, 274–6, 276n, 279n, 281n, 282n
   cinema, xii, 2, 6, 8, 96, 180, 191, 244–5, 251–5, 257, 264, 267
   intelligentsia, 5, 244, 249, 246, 255
   modernism, 24
economy
   gross national income (GNI), 192n
   gross national product (GNP), 180–1, 192n
   market, 169, 212, 232
   of means, 37
   of time, 125
   Romanian, 161
   stylistic, 255
ethics, vi, 10–14, 20n, 81, 82, 86, 113, 121, 123–4, 136n, 149, 161, 267, 285, 294
   of representation, 81
   of time, 124

evil, 14, 58–61, 118, 124, 127–8, 130–6, 190, 204
  privatio boni, 128
existentialism, 9, 12, 14, 17, 136
existentialist, 8, 14, 111, 136, 124, 136, 259, 260, 264, 275
existentialist realism, 8–9, 12, 123–4, 136n, 259, 281n
expressionism, 3–4, 251

father figure, 198, 204–5, 209, 272
fascism, 244
  anti-, 279n
fascist, 249
  anti-, 258
feminist, 15, 128, 169, 174, 177, 179n
financing, 6–7, 53, 62n, 157, 226, 228, 254
French New Wave, 3, 4, 8, 19n, 93, 158, 182
  Nouvelle Vague, 23, 167
funding, 6–8, 18–19n, 53, 157, 163n, 226, 229, 244–6

genre, vi, 12, 15–16, 24, 27, 43, 58–9, 76, 78n, 106n, 110–11, 128, 131–2, 165, 171, 176–7, 180–91, 192n, 193n, 227, 229–31, 234, 238, 245, 250, 253–8, 261–2, 264–6, 273, 276, 279–81n; *see also* blockbuster, crime film, comedy, official genres, totalitarian genre paradigm, tragedy, western, women films
global, 161, 180, 183, 186–7, 191, 213, 232, 236–8
  consciousness, 138
  crisis, 153
  culture, 229
  space, 236–8
global cinema, xi, 8, 12, 15, 23, 228, 230, 237, 238, 243
  audience, 181–2, 185, 228, 230
  digital revolution, 193n
  film production, 181
  popularity, 184
globalisation, 223, 230
  of cinema, 227
  of media discourse, 231
globalised, 88–90, 228, 230
  Bucharest, 230
  generation, 231
  influence of Hollywood, 227
  mainstream, 181
  media imagery, 231
  world, 220

historical time, 124, 133, 136n
Hollywood, 6, 15, 28, 102, 157, 181, 185, 192n, 206, 228–9, 247, 251, 262, 278n, 280n
  classical, 254
  director, 183
  film, 86, 112
  star-studded, 266
  style, 209
  see also Hollywood blockbuster, Hollywood melodrama
Hollywoodisation, 227–31
Hungarian documentary fictions, 279n

identity, 16, 88, 90, 95, 142, 146, 152, 170–1, 209, 233, 238
  construction of, 89, 226
  cosmopolitan, 16, 227, 236
  crisis of, 95, 207
  gender and, 169, 256
  geography and, vii, 211
  memory and, 89
  parody and, 105n
  peripheral, 212
  Romanian, 213, 236–7
  transnational, 232, 238
  see also national identity
immediate realism, 108–9, 116, 118–19
impressionism, 30, 281
inauthenticity, 123
intelligentsia, 265, 269, 274
  early Romanian cinema and, 246–8
  Eastern European *see* Eastern European intelligentsia
  free-floating (*freischwiebende*), 17, 276
  Romanian, 18n, 249, 252, 265, 275
  Romanian state and, 16, 243, 251
  urban, 117
intermedial, 12, 89, 97, 104, 110
  imitation, 110, 115, 118
  references, 110–11, 113–15
  typologies, 110
intermediality, vi, x, xii, 11, 13, 14, 64–5, 96, 97, 100, 109, 110, 118, 274
  intertextuality and, vi, 13, 111
ironic, 28, 29, 31, 34, 70, 96–8, 100–6, 149, 207–9, 220
  ambiguity, 8
  artist, 10, 269
  commentary, 11, 97

language, 26–7, 32
self-ironic, 119
ironic narrative modes, 114, 266
   comedic, 9, 11, 124, 136n, 267, 271
   tragic, 9–10, 124, 136n, 267
irony, viii, 9–13, 20n, 52, 76–7, 97, 179, 199, 221, 281n
   black humor and, 222, 251
   framing/ de-framing and, 67–70
   minimalism and, 10, 12–13
   pathos and, 95, 281n
   reflexivity and, 12, 14, 69, 79n, 85, 87, 92n, 100, 103, 276
   satire and, 221
   subversive, 84

kitchen, vi, 15, 57, 67, 69, 172, 188, 197–209, 216, 218, 233
   eating, 69, 75, 116, 197, 201, 203–4, 217–18, 251
   food, 138, 152, 155–6, 197, 201, 217–18
   kitchen scenes, 198, 202, 204, 208
kitchen sink drama, 188, 216, 233

lesbian, 175
local and global, 88–90, 181, 191, 220, 228, 232, 236–7, 243

magic realism, 77, 158
marginality, 15, 213–14, 220–1
media, 1, 4, 14–15, 17–18n, 20n, 65, 69, 75–6, 78–79n, 75–81, 83, 85–7, 89–91, 95–6, 101, 105n, 107–8, 110–12, 114–16, 119, 125, 137–43, 149, 169, 172, 190–1, 193, 223n, 231
   representation, 14–15, 20n, 67, 73, 80–4, 91, 93, 96, 98, 107, 109–10, 112–13, 140, 191, 208, 212, 220, 231, 252, 274
melodrama, v, 13, 24, 50–2, 58–62, 128, 131, 176, 183–91, 192–3n, 229, 248, 250–1, 257, 269, 273, 277n
   global, 186
   Hollywood, 61, 183
   see also minimalism, music, myth, realism
metaphoric-allegorical, 6, 8, 16, 19n, 261, 269–71, 274
minimalism, v, vi, 11, 13, 24, 27, 36–8, 60, 62, 65, 108, 113, 116, 217
   cinematic, 38–9, 46
   excess and, 60
   melodrama and, 50–1, 60
   modernism and, v, 13, 21, 38, 40, 43, 93
   morality of, 46–7
   NRC and, 10–14, 40–1, 47, 48–9n, 50, 58, 62, 77, 107, 143, 192–3n, 198, 209, 217
   process of, 51
   realism and, 14, 42–3, 65, 96, 104–5
   reflexivity and, 12–13
   sound and, 13
   types of, 44–6
   see also cinematic realism, intermediality, irony, music, reflexivity, remediation, purposeful minimalism
mise-en-abyme, 35, 97, 99, 203
miserabilism, 6, 19n, 275–6, 282n
modernist
   aesthetics, 84, 100, 265, 271
   poetics, 84
   reflexivity, 91, 96; see also reflexivity, self-reflexivity
modernism, v, 12–13, 21, 24, 251
   abstract, 23
   cinematic, 38
   high, 96, 264, 270
   late, 26, 81
   reflexivity and, 43, 80–1; see also reflexivity, self-reflexivity
   Romanian, 25; see also minimalism and modernism
modernity, v, 23–4, 26, 87, 157, 246–7
mother figure, 204, 207–8
music, 13, 25, 33–5, 36, 46, 49n, 50, 52–61, 90, 112, 117, 187, 217, 218, 233, 235
   atonal, 25
   classical, 25, 61
   diegetic, 13, 14, 28, 50, 55, 58, 104, 109
   ethnic, 25
   extradiegetic, 109, 126
   melodrama and, 51
   message and, 200
   minimalism and, 46, 49n
   natural vs non-natural meaning of, 34–5
   non-diegetic, 52, 28, 54, 104
   original, 53
   score, 25–7, 33, 48n, 49, 51–5, 59
   source, 34, 50
   video, 82
   see also remediation, sound

INDEX OF TERMS AND CONCEPTS

myth, 10, 20n, 62, 77, 95, 98, 113–15, 118, 278n
  cinema and, 102–3
  communist, 263
  eschatological, 261
  melodrama and, 13, 51, 59, 193n
  Mioritza, 26
  official, 252
  revolution, 139
mythical, 10, 23, 125
  time, 125, 133
  see also remediation, mythopoetic
mythological, 24, 26, 114, 115, 118, 119, 134, 136, 209, 267, 271
mythopoetic, 16, 260, 266, 272, 275

narrative time, 52, 55, 267
nation, 14, 77, 102, 139, 142, 152, 154, 155, 159–61, 211
national, x, xi, xii, 15–16, 17n, 18n, 33, 77n, 83, 88, 91, 105, 132, 138, 157, 159, 181, 206, 211, 228–9, 230–1, 236–8, 247, 253, 261, 263, 266, 277n
  belonging, 243–4
  canon, 231, 238
  film culture, 231
  history, 101
  ideology, 148
  imaginary, 232
  literature, 250, 262
  narrative, 232
  place, vi, 15, 195
  psyche, 231
  space, 12, 214, 237
  trauma; *see also* trauma
national cinema, 1, 15, 30, 104, 180, 192n, 193n, 209, 225, 231, 233, 243–4
  concept of, 243
  history of, 252
  scholarship of, 244
  see also Eastern European cinema(s)
national film industry, 225–6, 227, 229, 246, 250, 254
  admissions, 226
  film production, 192n
  nationalisation of, 251–2
  restructuring of, 253
national identity, 213, 231, 233, 235–7, 244
  non-specific, 235–6
  post-national identity, 105n, 236

national integration, 244, 246, 251, 255, 262
national specificity, 226, 227, 230, 233, 260
  character, 274
  non-specific, 235–6
national to transnational, 12, 15–16, 227–31, 233, 236–8, 243–4
nationalism, 244, 251, 259, 261, 280n, 282n
nationalist, 255, 231, 245, 249, 275
  propaganda, 247
  ultra-, 275
naturalistic-nihilist, 17, 271, 273, 275
neocolonialism, 161
neoliberalism, 23, 65, 89, 93, 158, 159, 160, 176, 212
neorealism, 4, 23, 65, 87, 93, 157–60, 176, 212
New German Cinema, 19n
New Romanian Cinema, v–vii, 1–5, 7–17, 23–4, 26, 30, 33–7, 40, 43, 46–7, 50–1, 54, 58–62, 65, 77, 81, 87, 91, 92n, 93–4, 96, 103–5, 106n, 107–11, 114, 119, 123–5, 130–5, 136n, 137, 139, 143–4, 148–9, 157–8, 167–9, 171–2, 174–83, 191, 197–9, 205–9, 211–14, 216–18, 220, 222–3, 229, 232–3, 243, 259, 276, 281n
NRC, 3–11, 13–17, 18–20n, 47, 55, 116, 123–7, 130–1, 136n, 243, 266, 271–2, 276, 281n

off-space, 73–5
official, 72, 92, 104, 116, 139–40, 142, 245, 252, 257, 263–5, 265–8, 280n, 281n
  gender equality, 268
  ideology, 83, 168
  propaganda, 100, 117, 168
official film, 8, 199, 253, 279n
  critic, 263
  director, 262
  history, 245
  production, 279n
official genre (s), 245, 253, 255, 266, 279n
  communist musicals, 261
  construction of socialism, 255–8, 262, 279n, 281n
  delinquent youth, 265–6, 279n
  mafiosi thriller, 132, 273
  nationalist epic, 225, 231, 245, 258, 261–3, 273, 279n

resistance fighter film, 258, 262, 264, 279n
spies and saboteurs, 257–8, 263, 266, 279–80n

painterly effect, 188
painterly image, 74, 78n
patriarchal, 15, 168–70, 172–4, 207, 272
perceptual realism 198, 206
Polish 'black series', 20n
Polish Cinema of Moral Anxiety, 279n
Polish School, 279n
populism, 251, 280n
positive hero, 97, 256, 258, 264, 269
positive heroine, 258
postcolonialism, 95, 226
postcommunism, xi, 14, 16, 17n, 27, 67, 71, 79n, 80–1, 83–4, 91, 93–6, 98, 99, 125, 130, 151, 168, 180, 189, 205, 216, 236, 271–3, 275–6
 postcommunist cinema, 6, 17, 19–20n, 25, 103, 191, 216, 272, 276
postmodern, 128, 134, 144, 236, 276
 condition, 94, 105n
 reflexivity and, 93–4; see also post-reflexivity
postmodernism, 35, 94–6, 100
 mainstream, 96
 oppositional, 95
postmodernist, 103, 182, 199
postsocialism, 20n, 26, 76, 86, 102, 138, 160, 169, 253, 256–7, 277n
protochronism, 273, 280n
psychological functions (Jung)
 feeling, 134-5
 inferior, 134-6
 superior, 134
 thinking, 134
purposeful minimalism, 13, 50–2, 54, 58

real time, 40, 50–1, 52, 60, 71, 74, 76, 109, 125, 129, 189
realism, 9–10, 42, 50, 59, 62, 65, 76, 83, 109, 119, 125, 160, 171, 197, 207, 209, 212, 217, 234, 264, 266, 279n
 absorptive, 73
 artificiality and, 67
 hyper, 158
 melodrama and, 50
 psychological, 27
 subjective, 11
 testimonial, 276

see also existentialist realism, minimalism, socialist realism, neorealism, cinematic realism, magic realism, immediate realism, Bazinian realism, perceptual realism
realistic-descriptive, 17, 273–5
reenactment, vi, 40, 80–6, 88, 91, 102–3, 137, 266
reflexivity, vi, 12–13, 49n, 72–4, 80–1, 83, 86, 91, 94, 96–9, 103–4, 106n
 media and, 80–1, 96
 post-reflexivity, 96–7, 99
 self-reflexive, 14, 25, 30, 43, 69, 79n, 84, 86–7, 96, 99, 103–4, 111–12, 117, 119, 130, 135, 245
 self-reflexivity, 12, 26, 111, 116–18, 183
 see also aesthetics, irony, reflexivity and minimalism, modernist reflexivity, modernism, postmodernism, remediation, subjectivity
remediation, vi, 13, 14, 107–11, 113, 115, 119
 minimalism and, 107–9
 music and, 117
 myth and, 114
 reflexivity and, 116, 119
revolution, 5, 14, 18n, 24, 28, 30, 49n, 59, 62, 68–70, 74, 85, 95, 100, 124, 126, 137, 139–41, 143, 145–6, 179, 193n, 229, 237, 253–4, 261, 270, 279n
 December 1989, 5, 14, 28, 68, 85, 95, 100, 137, 139, 141, 143, 145, 199, 212
 televised, 68–9, 85, 95, 100, 139–41, 145–6
Romanian Film Center/ Centrul Naţional al Cinematografiei (CNC), 7, 53, 62n, 157, 277n
 National Office of Cinema (ONC), 246, 248–50, 253, 255, 278n
Romanian national cinema, 7, 16, 17, 20n, 93, 181, 227, 228, 231, 243, 245, 251; see also New Romanian Cinema, NRC, Romanian new wave
Romanian national television, 18n, 19n, 55, 138, 140, 142
Romanian national theatre, 106n, 277n
Romanian New Wave, 1–3, 7, 16, 17n, 30, 50, 93, 100, 104, 106, 108, 176, 180, 197, 229–31, 233–4

INDEX OF TERMS AND CONCEPTS

shadow
  collective 132
  personal, 133, 134–5, 268
shot, 29, 31–2, 51, 66, 68, 74–5, 87, 89, 126, 131, 162, 187–90, 199, 206, 209, 232, 261, 271, 277n
  counter-shot, 190, 200
  de-framing, 66–7, 70–1, 83
  establishing, 190–200
  framing, 28, 30–1, 51, 65, 67, 70–2, 80, 83, 90, 109, 115, 170, 187–8, 192n, 202–3, 205–6
  frontal, 66, 68, 77, 78n, 115, 135, 204, 216
  huis-clos, 15
  long, 25, 30, 32, 40–2, 46, 48n, 51, 57, 66, 69, 74, 109, 135, 187–8, 205, 209
  medium, 68, 74, 78n, 115, 187, 198, 201, 204–5, 209
  panning, 26, 30, 32, 188, 257
  POV, 32, 202–3
  static, 27, 30, 32–3, 66, 69, 72, 106n, 135, 187–9, 209
  tracking, 30, 32, 65, 71, 79n, 216
  travelling, 71
  wide-angle, 31, 191
  see also tableau shot
slow cinema, 33, 65, 72, 75, 180, 218
small national cinema, 180–2, 191, 209
social integration, 244, 246, 251, 263, 278n
socialism, 169, 251, 253, 261, 277n
socialist content, 256
socialist realism, 158, 168, 252, 256, 279n
  national form, 256
  see also Zhdanovism
sound, 26, 31, 33–5, 49, 58, 61, 83, 86, 108, 115–18, 143, 158, 188, 200, 217
  architecture of, 82
  aural, 33–4, 117, 216
  confined, 27, 35, 87, 218
  cosmopolitan, 236
  design, 13, 25–6, 33–5, 52, 54
  diegetic, 180, 186, 197
  direct, 26, 158, 217
  intimate, 87, 198–206
  national, 12, 214, 236–7
  noise, 116
  silence, viii, 33, 87, 132, 134, 201, 218
  soundscape, 13, 33–5n, 49n, 200, 216
  soundtrack, 23, 25, 52, 143, 217
  transnational, 15, 195, 236–8
  urban, 230–8
Southeastern Europe, 11, 131, 263, 278n
spectatorship, 13, 36, 38–41, 43, 46–8, 62, 66, 69, 78, 204, 251
stasis, 69, 76, 126
  movement and, 76, 126
subjectivity, 9, 82, 87, 149, 208, 264
  fragmented, 95
  reflexivity and, 80
system integration, 252–3, 255–6, 262, 278n, 270n

tableau, viii, 13, 25, 32, 41, 66–73, 76–7, 78n, 102, 106n, 109
  aesthetics, 69, 72, 106n
  figés, 209
  shot, viii, 13, 65, 67–8, 72, 74–5
  vivant, 30, 67, 256
temps morts, 40, 44, 46, 76
theatricality, vi, viii 27, 71–2, 86, 93, 96, 99, 101, 103, 187
time
  dependence of, 48n
  ethics of, 124
  fluidity of, 42
  handling of, 12–14
  physical, 51
  present, 103
  profane, 133
  representation of, 13
  space and, 42, 85, 94, 101, 236
  subjective, 124
  see also astronomic time, crystals of time, historical time, mythical time, narrative time, real time, time image, *temps morts*, world time
time image, 29
totalitarian genre paradigm, 16, 253–5, 258, 267, 275
tragedy, 26, 81, 124–5, 235, 237, 258
  tragic hero, 124, 271, 274
  tragic heroine, 25, 126, 178
transcultural, 226–7
transnational, 16, 227–8
transnational cinema, 223, 226–7, 229–31, 237–8, 243–4
  cosmopolitan and, 12
transnational film theory, 226
transnational imaginary, 236–7
transnational space, vi, 15, 195
transnational style 226–7, 238

322

INDEX OF TERMS AND CONCEPTS

transnational 'turn', 232–8
trauma, 4, 84, 88, 90–1, 114, 137–8, 143–4, 147–9, 170, 231, 237

West/ Western European, 5, 9, 17, 31, 34, 77, 88, 95, 105n, 117, 128, 174, 211–14, 220–1, 223n, 244, 246, 260, 266, 272–3, 275–6, 279n, 280n, 282n
  cinema, 150n, 243, 247, 263
  culture, 112, 127
  emigration to, 171
  gaze, 6, 273, 275
  modernism, 9, 24, 246–7

thought, 127
values, 95, 273
western, 24
  Balkan, 223
  spaghetti, 266
  Transylvanian, 227
witness, 9–10, 29, 68–9, 130, 150–1, 159–61, 163, 189, 204–5, 207, 217, 233–4, 269
women films, 167, 175–9, 183
world cinema, 9, 35, 243
world time, 136n

Zhdanovism, 252–3, 256

EU representative:
Easy Access System Europe
Mustamäe tee 50, 10621 Tallinn, Estonia
Gpsr.requests@easproject.com

www.ingramcontent.com/pod-product-compliance
Lightning Source LLC
Chambersburg PA
CBHW070013010526
44117CB00011B/1545